Licensing Entertainment

Licensing Entertainment
*The Elevation of Novel Reading in Britain,
1684–1750*

WILLIAM B. WARNER

University of California Press

BERKELEY   LOS ANGELES   LONDON

University of California Press
Berkeley and Los Angeles, California

University of California Press, Ltd.
London, England

©1998 by
The Regents of the University of California

Library of Congress Cataloging-in-Publication Data

Warner, William Beatty.
    Licensing Entertainment : the elevation of novel reading in Britain,
1684–1750 / William B. Warner.
        p.   cm.
    Includes bibliographic references and index.
    ISBN 0-520-20180-9 (alk. paper).—ISBN 0-520-21296-7 (pbk. : alk.
paper)
    1. English fiction—18th century—History and criticism. 2.
Popular literature—Great Britain—History and criticism. 3. English
fiction—Early modern, 1500–1700—History and criticism. 4. Books
and reading—Great Britain—History—17th century. 5. Books and
reading—Great Britain—18th century. 6. Literature publishing—
Social aspects—Great Britain. 7. Literature and Society—Great
Britain—History. 8. Authors and readers—Great Britain—history. 9.
Literary form. I. Title. PR858.P68W37 1998
    823'.409—DC2197-30171

Printed in the United States of America
9 8 7 6 5 4 3 2 1

The paper used in this publication meets the minimum requirements of
American National Standard for Information Sciences—Permanence of
Paper for Printed Library Materials, ANSI Z39.48-1984.

For Lizzie

Contents

Acknowledgments

For fellowship and sabbatical support in the early stages of research for this book, as well as in the later stages of writing it, I would like to thank the American Council of Learned Societies, the Clark Memorial Library in Los Angeles, and the State University of New York at Buffalo. The many friends and colleagues who have helped me with their critical advice over the years include Paula Backscheider, John Bender, Toni Bowers, Bob Erickson, Bill Graebner, Deidre Lynch, Paula MacDowell, John Richetti, and Everett Zimmerman. During the final stages of revision, I received invaluable advice from my teacher, Ronald Paulson. For expert help in manuscript preparation, I would like to thank Bob Devens. Lastly, my deepest debt goes to my most insightful and exacting critic, my wife, Elizabeth MacArthur. `

For permission to reprint those parts of this book that appeared as articles or chapters in books, I would like to thank Columbia University Press (chapter 1); Duke University Press (chapter 3); and Johns Hopkins University Press (chapter 5).

Preface
From a Literary to a Cultural History of the Early Novel

In *Licensing Entertainment* I rewrite the literary history of the novel so that it becomes a subset of the cultural history of print entertainments. I started this study by pursuing a familiar question from literary history: How did the novel rise to become the dominant modern literary form? But I located my answers by going outside the boundaries of literary studies, so as to study an other-than-literary scene of cultural production and consumption. Thus, before the rise of the novel (as a literary form), novel reading emerged as a mode of entertainment. The feedback loop between a type of print media—novels in small-book format—and a practice—avid reading for pleasure, as this reading was supported by the market in printed books—introduced into Britain an early instance of what I call "media culture."[1] Because of the unease this print entertainment produced among the practitioners of an earlier, more intensive humanistic practice of reading, the onset of media culture mobilized profound ambivalence and resistance. In Britain this resistance took the form of the antinovel discourse that proliferated alongside novels on the market.

1. In inscribing the history of the novel into the history of (print) media, I am writing against the modernist bias in contemporary cultural studies, which assumes that changes in twentieth-century media culture are fundamentally different from those that swept through culture in the seventeenth and eighteenth centuries. When it comes to the history of media entertainment, this book subscribes to "uniformitarianism," a doctrine developed by the eighteenth-century Scottish geologist and physician James Hutton. He "advanced the idea that those physical processes that operate to modify the Earth today, also were in operation in the past. The theory that geological secrets of the past are revealed in active processes of the present or 'the present is the key to the past' is known as *the doctrine of uniformitarianism*." (Buchholtz, *National Parkways Guide to Yosemite National Park*, 8.)

Behind the heroic, progressive, teleological "rise of the novel" narrative which has been told and retold in different variants since the 1750s, literary historians have had difficulty seeing the emergence of media culture. The rise of the novel narrative obscures the initial and ongoing relationship of the novel to media culture. I have attempted to overcome this primary misprision of literary history in several ways. In order to follow the exchanges between novels considered literary and those that resemble the formula fiction of our own day, I have sought to take account of the development of print-media culture as it informs the writing and circulation of novels, as well as of the antinovel discourse that develops along with the vogue for novel reading—and that offers an early instance of the modern anxiety about the effect of media on its consumers. I present the early novelists in their role as entertainers and media workers, rather than as the authors literary studies belatedly claims them to be. Throughout this study, I have used the term *novel* in an inclusive fashion to designate both the books early modern readers term novels and the elevated novels of Defoe, Richardson, and Fielding, which eschewed that label, but which tradition has considered formative instances of the novel as a literary type.[2] This catholic usage refuses to allow the term "novel" to have the gatekeeping function it usually has in literary studies, whereby it has filtered out noncanonical novels. In selecting novels for sustained interpretation, I have been guided primarily by their popularity with early modern readers: I have chosen *Love Letters*, *The New Atalantis*, and *Love in Excess* as they are the most notorious and widely read of the early novels; I offer a reading of *Roxana* instead of the more popular *Robinson Crusoe* because it rewrites, and implicitly critiques, those novels of amorous intrigue; *Pamela*, while setting out to reform the reader of the novel of amorous intrigue, became the most popular of all eighteenth-century British novels; and *Joseph Andrews*, Fielding's most powerful rejoinder to *Pamela*, is popular in its own right.

In order to unify a study of very different novels and writers, I describe

2. Recently Margaret Doody has also used the term "novel" in an inclusive fashion, though she broadens what she comprehends by the term to include ancient, medieval, and Renaissance romances within the category, which she regularly capitalizes as "Novel." My usage takes its point of departure from the effort of seventeenth-century critics to distinguish the short novella from the French heroic romance; whatever its conceptual inconsistencies, the distinction between romance and novel has played an important role in the history of novel writing (see chapters 1 and 2; for my differences from Doody, see chapter 2, note 4).

the mutations in a particular type of novel—what I call "the novel of amorous intrigue" (Beasley, *Novels of the 1740s*, 9). In my study, the novels of amorous intrigue serve as both the object of analysis and a common denominator, allowing me to compare novels written over different periods, for different purposes, within different itineraries of reading. This generic subtype is critically useful rather than descriptively necessary (Jameson, *Political Unconscious*, 145). It has enabled me to follow the exchange between types of writing that are usually separated by the conceptual categories of literary studies: prose fiction and "the" novel, or entertainment and literature. In order to investigate the relation between novels and the culture of their reception, close reading has proved as vital to this project as the study of the history of print media and reading practices.

I argue here not for an iconoclastic surpassing of the rise-of-the-novel thesis, but instead for its fundamental resituating. My study of the early novel is conservative in the ecological sense that it does not dispense with the old literary criticism and history, but instead recycles its texts and ideas, while adding new ones. Not a spontaneous event, the rise or elevation of the novel should be seen as a project directed not at instituting a new type of literature ("the" novel), but instead at a reform of reading practices. Thus I interpret the elevation of novels, undertaken in different ways by Defoe, Aubin, Richardson, and Fielding, as a creative early modern response by media workers and entertainers to the onset of market-driven media culture. My account offers a deliberate alternative to the story of heroic authorial innovation, given its definitive modern shape in Ian Watt's *Rise of the Novel*, as well as to the theoretically sophisticated revisions of that narrative offered in the recent studies of Nancy Armstrong, John Bender, and Michael McKeon. Within my alternative account, the elevation of the novel is a conscious cultural project that gives "the" novel an objective character; it offers an instance of an effective intervention in the directions of media culture through an expansion of the concept of literature. To those who read this study as an ingenious reassertion of the centrality of Richardson and Fielding, I would respond that I am in accord with traditional designations of their centrality, but I have changed the terms of that centrality. To those who complain that I have simply written another prequel to the rise of the novel narrative—by making Behn, Manley, and Haywood the first British novelists—I would respond that I do not assume the novel to be a type of literature, so I understand them as early and formative players in another story—that of the beginning of early modern print entertainment. Neither the canonical male writers nor the noncanonical women writers are valued and studied as radical origins of the modern novel; for example, neither group is inserted into an account of the origins of the modern subject.[3]

Three broad areas of modern scholarship have been indispensable to the development of my project. In seeking to understand the rise of the novel in other than literary terms, I have incurred a strong debt to recent books by Armstrong (*Desire and Domestic Fiction*), Bender (*Imagining the Penitentiary*), McKeon (*The Origins of the English Novel, 1600–1740*), Hunter (*Before Novels*), Gallagher (*Nobody's Story*), and H. Brown (*The Institutions of the English Novel*). I began this project by writing review essays of the first three ("Realist Literary History," "The Social Ethos of the Novel," "Taking Dialectic with a Grain of Salt," and "Social Power and the Novel"), and was privileged to have early access to manuscripts of the last three. My differences with the aforementioned studies are fundamental and I describe them in this study. But I share with their authors the desire to recast the question of the novel's rise in broad cultural and historical terms, without abandoning the values and methods of literary study. Because my understanding of the novel's rise took me toward a study of the exchange between novels written by women and those written by men, this study owes a strong debt to feminist literary histories of women's writing (Gardiner, Spencer, Todd), to theoretically informed studies of gender (Butler, Campbell, Gwilliam), and to two critics whose work falls into both categories (Backscheider, Ballaster). And because my account of the novel's rise gives centrality to the cultural problem of reading, I have also benefited

---

3. My study explores a part of the long history of subjectivity. However, throughout this study I have sustained a dogmatic skepticism about assimilating a version of "the invention of *the* modern subject" into my account of the elevation of novel reading. Narratives of this type have enormous allure; many see it as the central pay-off of the rise of the novel narrative. Part of the currency of Watt's *The Rise of the Novel* comes from the notion that novel reading mediates the formation of the modern subject. But historians of the novel should be given a check by the similar narratives developed in other contexts. The centrality argued for the study of the Renaissance and the Romantic period stems in part from claims that these epochs were the proper time for the appearance (or invention) of the modern subject. Thus, for example, Joel Fineman locates the first distinctly modern (Lacanian) subjectivity in Shakespeare's *Sonnets*, and Geoffrey Hartman attributes a crucially modern (Hegelian) subjectivity to the poetic corpus of William Wordsworth. Inevitably, each critical and historical narrative becomes qualified by the claims made by others. Rather than inventing the modern subject, novel reading contributes to the expansion of the range and types of subjectivity. Armstrong (*Desire and Domestic Fiction*) and Bender (*Imagining the Penitentiary*) have offered sophisticated accounts of historically specific forms of modern subjectivity in relation to eighteenth-century novels. This study will describe others.

from pioneering feminist studies of popular culture (Modleski, Radway), as well as from influential recent cultural studies of authorship (Rose, Stallybrass and White, Woodmansee), the book (Chartier, Martin), canon formation (Guillory), and the disciplines (Siskin).

The full alternative story of the novel offered in *Licensing Entertainment* can only be grasped if this study is read in its entirety. This is so because of the complex interplay between the emergence of novel reading for entertainment and the antinovel discourse, between that discourse and programs to elevate novel reading, and between elevated novels and the institution of the novel as a type of literature. I begin my study with a genealogy of the rise of the novel narrative from 1750 to the present. By exposing its diverse cultural uses and reflecting on its built-in biases, chapter 1 takes account of, yet also brackets the force of, some of the founding impulses of literary studies. I begin my alternative (cultural) history of the early novel in chapter 2 with Aphra Behn. Her pivotal role comes from introducing an already successful print form, the continental novel, to the British market. At a time when British culture was beginning to develop various kinds of rights and freedoms—of speech, of worship, to choose a monarch, and to choose for oneself in marriage—Behn's novels advance an enfranchisement of the reader as one entitled to choose what he or she will read for entertainment. Although Behn's *Love Letters* offers a probing critique of unlimited claims to freedom, chapter 3 shows how her novels, and the best-selling fiction of Manley and Haywood, develop the novels of amorous intrigue into the first formula fiction on the market. In chapter 4 I show how these novels incite the antinovel discourse, as well as the efforts of such novelists as Aubin and Defoe, who seek to rewrite novel reading so that it might be morally improving. The last two chapters of this study trace three phases of what I call the *"Pamela* media event": the first, described in chapter 5, is Richardson's provocative publication of his novel as an attempt to overwrite the novels of amorous intrigue; following this, and also detailed in chapter 5, is the torrent of critique, defense, sequels, and rip-offs unleashed by *Pamela* in the print culture of 1741–1742 and, in response, Richardson's recourse to the concept of novelistic authorship; finally, and outlined in chapter 6, is Fielding's development in *Joseph Andrews* of fundamentally different terms with which to license entertainment.

The conclusion suggests some of the long-term effects of the face-off between media culture and the elevated novel. The emergence since the middle of the eighteenth century of such genres as the gothic novel, detective fiction, science fiction, and the Harlequin romance suggests that while the institutionalization of "the" novel as a form of literature succeeds, it necessarily remains incomplete. Since the eighteenth century the system of media culture has underwritten the freedom of readers and spectators and has disturbed various projects to elevate and improve culture. The tension between media culture and literary culture structures the institution of literary studies down to the present day. My study of the novel suggests why the antagonism between art and entertainment may be interminable.

1 The Rise of the Novel in the Eye of Literary History

A GENEALOGY OF THE NOVEL'S RISE

Like every discursive practice that aspires to produce knowledge, literary studies uses narrative to map the terrain and explain the emergence of the objects it seeks to understand. One of the grand narratives of British literary studies might be entitled "The Progress of the Novel." It tells the story of the novel's "rise" in the eighteenth century (with Defoe, Richardson, and Fielding), of its achievement of classical solidity of form in the nineteenth century (with Austen, Dickens, Thackeray, Eliot, the early James, and Conrad), and of its culmination in a modernist experimentation and self-reflection (with the later James, Woolf, Joyce, and Beckett) that paradoxically fulfills and surpasses "the novel" in one blow. Or so one version of the story goes. Much of the labor of literary history—whether its task is considered additive or oppositional—has been directed toward discovering lines of influence, traditions and countertraditions, biases, lacunae, and hidden subplots to refine, challenge, and complicate this grand narrative of the novel's progress. The eighteenth-century segment of this narrative was consolidated in 1957 with the publication of Ian Watt's enormously influential book, *The Rise of the Novel: Studies in Defoe, Richardson, and Fielding*. Watt's study correlates the middle-class provenance of the eighteenth-century British novel with a realism said to be distinctively modern for the way it features a complex, "deep" reading subject.

Over the last forty years, "the rise of the novel" has been one of the most widely circulated narratives of English studies. Within the university curriculum, this narrative has functioned as a rationale and advertisement for our "pedagogical commodities"—guaranteeing the canonicity of certain texts by providing a literary history that frames their centrality. Far from having lost its fascination over time, the rise of the novel thesis has been updated and extended in recent books by Lennard Davis, Nancy Armstrong, John Bender, Michael McKeon, J. Paul Hunter, and Catherine Gallagher. More than a mere thesis about a genre, "the rise of the novel" has come to prestructure our approach to "the" novel, functioning like an optical apparatus for seeing the novel and its history. Alternative critical paradigms have been developed for interpreting both individual novels and the novel as a genre—I am thinking especially of the concepts of dialogism and heteroglossia (Bakhtin), mythic archetypes (Frye), the rhetoric of fiction (Booth), reader response (Iser), and textuality (Derrida), to name only a few of the most influential; however, all of these approaches, because they don't engage the distinct two-hundred-and-fifty-year history of the British novel's elevation into cultural centrality, fail to interpret our culture's investment in the novel. It is precisely because of the way in which history flows into and through Watt's book that it functions as a watershed in the consolidation of the novel's rise.

The limitations of Watt's account derive less from any misrepresentation of that earlier history than from the unreflective and unself-conscious way in which it repeats that history. Paradoxically, the early modern elevation of the novel speaks so clearly through Watt's enlightenment narrative of the novel's rise that his book obscures the historical and cultural strife that produced "the novel" as a coherent cultural object and then elevated its cultural address. In short, Watt's book speaks the modern institution of the novel so transparently that his reader is confronted with a certain opacity. This is not so much because of what he demonstrates or asserts; rather, it is because of what he can assume his reader will accept without demonstration, which has thus, over the long history of the novel's institutionalization, been half forgotten. From the first paragraphs of Watt's introduction to *The Rise of the Novel*, it is assumed that "the novel" is a legitimate aesthetic cultural object; that "the novel" is characterized by its realism; and that it begins with three English novel writers of the eighteenth century—Defoe, Richardson, and Fielding. How did it come about that Watt could assume the novel's aesthetic legitimacy, its realist calling, and its beginning with these three writers? These questions can only be answered by doing a genealogy of the literary history of the rise of the British novel, which is what I attempt to do in this chapter.

My strategy for breaking the spell of "the rise of the novel" and opening it to critical scrutiny is to ask where and when and why does that story begin to be told? This history of the British novel's beginnings turns out to have a history itself. In order to grasp the strangeness and difference, the complex diversity of earlier cultural inscriptions of novel reading and writing, one must defer the question that haunts and hurries too many literary histories of the early novel: What is the first real novel? This question is too determined by the bottom-line concern to maximize cultural value and minimize unwanted cultural expenditure. For several reasons, we should be skeptical of the efforts of those novelists and literary critics who hasten to designate the first real novel. First, the absence of an authoritative Greek or Latin precursor for the modern novel—the fact that there is no Homer or Sophocles for the modern novel—has encouraged the wishful performative of claiming that position for a range of different novels, within different national settings—among them, *Don Quixote, La Princesse de Clèves,* and the "new species" of writing of Richardson and Fielding. When one watches how literary critics have sought to adjudicate these claims, one inevitably finds a suspicious feedback loop: the general minimal criteria for being a "true" novel is elucidated through a first paradigmatic instance which then confirms the initial criteria (Davidson, *Revolution and the Word,* 84). The steady shift in the test criteria brought to bear over the last three centuries makes the definitive designation of the first real novel seem increasingly implausible.[1]

Any literary history focused around designating the first real novel—with its restless intention to promote and demote, and to designate winners and losers—cannot stand outside, but instead inhabits the terms of that culturally improving enlightenment narrative that tradition has dubbed "the rise of the novel." Before the emergence of the novel into literary studies and literary pedagogy, novels played a subsidiary role in several crucial cultural episodes: the debate, over the course of the eighteenth century, about the pleasures and moral dangers of novel reading; the adjudication of the novel's role in articulating distinct national cultures; and finally, the various efforts to claim that a certain representation of modern life is realistic. It is through these three articulations that the novel secures its place as a type of literature. By reconstructing these three episodes in the cultural institutionalization of the British novel, I hope to jump back to a time before Watt—to a time before the sedimentation and consolidation of criteria and cultural functions that institutionalize the idea of a "real," legitimate, valued, modern novel, which can then be given its lead role in "the rise of the novel." Fredric Jameson has suggested the analytical use-

---

1. See Cathy Davidson's witty and illuminating discussion of a bookseller's calculated promotion of the "first American novel" as at once patriotic and commercial (*Revolution and the Word,* 83–98).

fulness of genealogy for seeing a familiar object in a new way: "genealogy is not an historical narrative, but has the essential function of renewing our perception of the synchronic system as in an X-ray, its diachronic perspectives serving to make perceptible the articulation of functional elements of a given system in the present" (*Political Unconscious,* 139). It is only through compiling a genealogy of over two hundred years of literary history of the novel's rise in Britain that the latent elements of the novel's function in the generic system of modern literary studies can be exposed. I hope that such a genealogy will clear the ground for a cultural history of the early novel as a type of print-media entertainment.

THE SCANDAL OF NOVEL READING

Novels have been a respectable component of culture for so long that it is difficult for twentieth-century observers to grasp the unease produced by novel reading in the eighteenth century. In the later chapters of this study I will suggest why, during the decades following 1700, a quantum leap in the number, variety, and popularity of novels led many to see novels as a catastrophe to book-centered culture. Although the novel was not clearly defined or conceptualized, the object of the early antinovel discourse was quite precise—namely, seventeenth-century romances and novellas of continental origin, as well as the "novels" and "secret histories" written by Behn, Manley, and Haywood in the decades following the early 1680s. Any who would defend novels had to cope with the aura of sexual scandal which clings to the early novel, and respond to the accusation that they were corrupting to their enthusiastic readers. When Richardson and Fielding convinced many—both through their fiction and through its framing critical defense—that they had given modern fiction a more valuable range of purposes, the way was cleared for novels to become the object of literary criticism and literary history. Between Samuel Johnson's 1750 *Rambler* no. 4 essay on the new fiction of Richardson, Fielding, and Smollett and John Dunlop's three-volume *History of Fiction* (1814), a succession of essays, reviews, and literary histories mobilize criticism and alarm, praise and prescription in order to modulate the comparatively new vogue for novel reading. This body of criticism, the first sustained novel criticism in English, incorporates many of the themes developed in the previous fifty years to condemn or defend novel reading. Thus, in "An Essay on the New Species of Writing Founded by Mr. Fielding: With a Word or Two upon the Modern State of Criticism" (1751), Francis Coventry sounds a familiar thesis in mocking the "emulation" produced in readers by the French romances of an earlier day: "This [vogue] obtained a long Time. Every Beau was an *Oroondates*, and all the Belles were *Statiras*." Though Samuel Johnson could not account for the fashion for romance, his *Rambler* no. 4 essay describes the more powerful identification that recent "familiar histories" such as *Clarissa* and *Tom Jones* induce in their readers: "if the power of example is so great, as to take possession of the memory by a kind of violence, and produce effects almost without the intervention of the will, care ought to be taken that . . . the best examples only should be exhibited" (12). In other words, if novels put readers at risk of becoming automatons, the author must assume responsibility for the novel's moral effects.

The power and danger of novels, especially to young women not exposed to classical education, arise from the pleasures novels induce. But what, one might ask, is so pernicious about reading novels? Clara Reeve's *Progress of Romance* (1785) ends with a staged debate between the book's protagonist, the woman scholar Euphrasia, and a high cultural snob named Hortensius. Hortensius develops a wide-ranging indictment of novel reading, arguing, first, that novels turn the reader's taste against serious reading: "A person used to this kind of reading will be disgusted with every thing serious or solid, as a weakened and depraved stomach rejects plain and wholesome food" (II: 78). Second, Hortensius claims, novels incite the heart with false emotions: "The seeds of vice and folly are sown in the heart,—the passions are awakened,—false expectations are raised.—A young woman is taught to expect adventures and intrigues . . . If a plain man addresses her in rational terms and pays her the greatest of compliments,—that of desiring to spend his life with her,—that is not sufficient, her vanity is disappointed, she expects to meet a Hero in Romance" (II: 78). Finally, Hortensius argues, novels induce a dangerous autonomy from parents and guardians: "From this kind of reading, young people fancy themselves capable of judging of men and manners, and . . . believe themselves wiser than their parents and guardians, whom they treat with contempt and ridicule" (II: 79). Hortensius indicts novels for transforming the cultural function of reading from providing solid nourishment to encouraging exotic tastes; from preparing a woman for the ordinary rational address of a plain good man to conjuring romance fantasies of a "hero"; from instilling a reliance upon parents and guardians to inciting a belief in the reader's autonomy. Taken together, novels have disfigured their reader's body, vitiating the taste, passions, and judgment of stomach, heart, and mind. Here, as so often in the polemics around novels, the novel reader is characterized as a susceptible female whose moral life is at risk. By strong implication, she is most responsible for transmitting the media virus of novel reading.

From the vantage point of the late twentieth century, and after nearly nine decades of film and five of television, the alarm provoked by novel reading may seem hyperbolic, or even quaint. But a condescending modern "pro-pleasure" position renders the alarm with novel reading, and its effects on early modern culture, unintelligible.[2] Sometimes it is difficult to credit the specific object of the alarm of the eighteenth-century critics of novels: after all, we recommend to students some of the very novels these early modern critics inveighed against. However, given our current anxieties about the cultural effects of slasher films, rap music, MTV, or soaps, it is contradictory to dismiss those who worried about the effects of novels when they were new. Although it is difficult to know why early or late modern readers experience pleasure, we can trace specific effects of the eighteenth-century campaign against unlicensed entertainments. First, cultural critics sketched the first profile of the culture-destroying pleasure seeker that haunts the modern era: that of the obsessive, unrestrained consumer of fantasy (see chapters 3–4). Following this, such novelists as Richardson and Fielding, assuming the cogency of this critique, developed replacement fictions as a cure for the novel-addicted reader (see chapters 5–6). In doing so, they aimed to deflect and reform, improve and justify novelistic entertainment.

At least since Plato's attack on the poets, philosophers and cultural critics had worried about the effects of an audience's absorption in fictional entertainment. During the early eighteenth century the circulation of novels on the market gave this old cultural issue new urgency. Often published anonymously, by parvenu authors supported by no patron of rank, novels seemed irresponsible creations, conceived with only one guiding intention: to pander to any desire that would produce a sale. Like the slighter and cheaper chap books sold by peddlers (Spufford), novels were "disposable" books written in anticipation of their own obsolescence, and in acceptance of their own transient function as part of a culture of serial entertainments. Although they represented only a small part of print culture in the early decades of the eighteenth century, by the 1720s novels comprised one of the most high-profile, fashionable, and dynamic segments of the market.

2. For an example of an uncritical pro-pleasure position, see Ross, 1989; for my sense of the inevitable resistance to popular culture, see W. Warner, "The Resistance to Popular Culture."

Many of the vices attributed to the novel are also attributes of the market: both breed imitation, incite desire, are oblivious to their moral effects, and reach into every corner of the kingdom. As part of a culture of the market, novels appear as conduits of an uncanny automatism. In an introductory chapter to *Tom Jones*, Fielding relegates novel writers to the lowest rank of authors, because "to the composition of novels and romances, nothing is necessary but paper, pens and ink, with the manual capacity of using them" (IX: i). Once they had become the rage, nothing could stop novels on the market. Producers of novels appear as mere factors of the market. Using the by-now-clichéd terms for describing the Grub Street hacks, Clara Reeve emphasizes the accelerating multiplicity of novels, with rampant production allowing bad imitations to proliferate, and developing and using new institutions to deliver novels indiscriminately into the hands of every reader: "The press groaned under the weight of Novels, which sprung up like mushrooms every year . . . .[Novels] did but now begin to increase upon us, but ten years more multiplied them tenfold. Every work of merit produced a swarm of imitators, till they became a public evil, and the institution of Circulating libraries, conveyed them in the cheapest manner to every bodies hand" (II: 7). An uncontrolled multiplicity of novels threatens culture with metastasis. For the scholar surveying the production of many ages, the market has the effect of blurring the distinctness and expressive readability of culture. Thus, in his *History of Fiction* (1814), John Dunlop complains that while earlier epochs developed "only one species of fiction" which then could be read as "characteristic" of their age, more recently "different kinds have sprung up at once; and thus they were no longer expressive of the taste and feelings of the period of their composition" (III: 362). The critical histories written by Reeve and Dunlop aim to restore the character to culture.

If, according to a formula developed in the writings of Foucault, power operates less by repressing or censoring than by producing new realities and new objects and rituals of truth (*History of Sexuality*, 77–114), then the success of novels on the market changes culture by producing a need to read. Clara Reeve gives expression to this newly incited desire, writing: "People *must* read something, they cannot always be engaged by dry disquisitions, the mind *requires* some amusement" (97, emphasis mine). Between uncritical surrender to novel reading and a wholesale rejection of novels in favor of "serious" reading, Richardson and Fielding trace a third pathway for the novel. Reeve describes the strategy in terms of "writ[ing] an antidote to the bad effects" of novels "under the disguise" of being novels (85).[3] Coventry describes the manner in which Fielding, "who sees all the little movements by which human nature is actuated," intervenes in the market for novels: "The disease became epidemical, but there were no hopes of a cure, 'till Mr. Fielding endeavored to show the World, that pure Nature could furnish out as agreeable entertainment, as those airy nonentical forms they had long ador'd, and persuaded the ladies to leave this extravagance to their Abigails with their cast cloaths" (14–15). Here, according to Coventry, the addictive "disease" of romance, associated with the craze for new fashions, can only be "cured" by cutting new paths toward pleasure; then the old novels, with their corrupting pleasures, can be passed on, along with old dresses, to their lady's servant.

THE DEBATE ABOUT NOVELS

There is a striking difference between the British debate about novels conducted before 1750 and that conducted after. In the first half of the century, novel writers still felt obliged to respond to the old Puritan condemnation of stories as lies. Those who attacked novels attacked all novels, and comprehended a great deal in that category. The defenses offered for fiction by Manley, Defoe, and Haywood—that this "history has its foundation in fact"; that its representations of vice are cautionary; and so on—could seem "transparently insincere" to the skeptical (Williams, *Novel and Romance 1700–1800*, 7; see chapter 4 below). After the success of *Pamela* (1740), *Joseph Andrews* (1742), *Clarissa* (1747–1748), and *Tom Jones* (1749), however, the terms of the debate about novels shifted; those critics who stepped forward after the middle of the century to describe the salient features and communicable virtues of these two authors' works offered an unprecedented countersigning of the cultural value of their novels. Since the novels of Richardson and Fielding appeared to have merit, and since they developed solutions to the general threat presented by novels, banishing all novels from culture was now more than most critics were willing to wish for. After Richardson and Fielding, the issue for debate became much less whether to read than what kind of novel should be read, and what kind should be written. This gave new critical subtlety and specificity to the

3. This requires a cunning pharmacology. When Lady Echlin, Richardson's most morally exacting correspondent, warns that "the best instruction you can give, blended with love intrigue, will never answer your good intention," Richardson replies with a celebrated reformulation of the old demand that art should both amuse and instruct: "Instruction, Madam, is the Pill; Amusement is the Gilding. Writings that do not touch the Passions of the Light and Airy, will hardly ever reach the heart" (*Selected Letters*, 322 [Sept. 22, 1755]).

debate about novels. Attention became directed toward the psychology of response and toward the moral and pedagogical uses of novel reading. At the same time, as Ioan Williams has pointed out, there was a paradoxical countertendency, as the growth in number and influence of novels after mid-century makes novel reading a more pressing cultural issue and intensifies the conservative reaction against any novel reading for entertainment (Williams, *Novel and Romance*, 13–15).

A range of different critical strategies are used to situate, defend, and delimit this new segment of culture on the market. Particular acts of criticism rescued certain works from the general condemnation of novels. For Samuel Johnson, a critical intervention on behalf of the new novel meant arguing in favor of the "exemplary" characters of Richardson over the more true-to-life "mixed" characters of Fielding or Smollett (*Rambler* no. 4). William Warburton wrote a preface for the second edition of *Clarissa* in which he supports the improvement brought by entertaining fictional works and compares Richardson to Marivaux. Likewise, Diderot celebrates the wonderful moral efficacy of Richardson's fiction in his eloquent "Eulogy to Richardson" (1762). In a pamphlet published anonymously, "An Essay on the New Species of Writing Founded by Mr. Fielding" (1751), Francis Coventry, like Arthur Murphy in his biographical essay introducing Fielding's *Works* (1762), follows the basic procedure Fielding had devised in the many interpolated prefaces of *Joseph Andrews* and *Tom Jones*, transporting critical terms and ideas developed earlier for poetry, epic, and drama to the novel.

Since criticism presupposes a literary object for its discourse, the question arises as to how, within the context of the opprobrium directed at novels in the British context, one legitimizes criticism of novels. Coventry's pamphlet suggests the way his own performance of criticism develops in symbiotic relation to Fielding's original performance. Just as Aristotle extracted the "rules" of tragedy from Sophocles, so Coventry would make Fielding's performance the template for the "species" of writing he had "founded." As the "great Example" and "great original" for "future historians of this kind," Fielding's work provides the terms for a new inventory of neoclassical "laws": "As Mr. Fielding first introduc'd this new kind of Biography, he restrain'd it with Laws which should ever after be deem'd sacred by all that attempted his Manner; which I here propose to give a brief account of" (16). Coventry's manner of posturing as a critic—unctuous, defensive, and yet arrogant—is the very antithesis of the imperious law-giving practiced by Fielding's narrators. But both styles of address suggest that there is no preestablished discourse for the criticism of novels.

The critical defenses of individual novel writers did not convince all cultural critics who turned their attention to the new vogue for novels. The Reverend Vicesimus Knox, the master of Tonbridge School, puts the problem of the baleful influence of the new novels on boys at the forefront of his essay "On Novel Reading" (1778). He begins his meditation with a correlation that is unfriendly to all novels: "If it be true, that the present age is more corrupt than the preceding, the great multiplication of Novels has probably contributed to its degeneracy" (*Essays Moral and Literary*, 1778, in Williams, *Novel and Romance, 1700–1800*, 304–307). Knox then itemizes the problems with even the most favorably received of the modern novelists, declaring that, unlike the old romances, which exhibited "patterns of perfection" that "filled the heart with pure, manly, bold and liberal sentiments," or the "immortal work of Cervantes," whose "decent humour" could "excite a laugh, and leave the heart little affected," modern novelists all have features that render them not "perfectly adapted to the young mind." While Richardson's novels "are written with the purest intentions of promoting virtue," Knox complains that "scenes are laid open . . . and sentiments excited, which it would be more advantageous to early virtue not to admit." While the "cultivated genius" of Fielding entitles him "to a high rank among the classics," here too there are "scenes, which may corrupt a mind unseasoned by experience." He goes on to say that the writings of these better novelists often help to gain circulation of the novels of "our neighboring land of libertinism" [France], which "have seldom anything to recommend them to perusal but their profligacy." While the "licentious ideas" of the "coarse taste" of the "reign of Charles the Second" seem to have been supplanted most recently by the "sentimental manner" associated with Sterne, Knox worries that this still gives "a degree of gracefulness to moral deformity," and that it gives "the mind a degree of weakness," making it "unable to resist the slightest impulse of libidnous passion."

Before offering his own paranovelistic prescription for boys' reading—the *Telemachus, Robinson Crusoe*, Rollin's *History*, Plutarch's *Lives*, and the *Spectator*—Knox's critique of novels reaches the following climax:

> Such books, however pernicious their tendency, are the most easily attained. The prudence of their publishers suggests the expediency of making them conveniently portable. Every corner of the kingdom is abundantly supplied with them. In vain is youth secluded from the corruptions of the living world. Books are commonly allowed them with little restriction, as innocent amusements: yet these often pollute the

heart in the recesses of the closet, inflame the passions at a distance from temptation, and teach all the malignity of vice in solitude.

[Knox, from Williams, *Novel and Romance 1700–1800*, 306]

Among nonreligious critics, Knox defines the most extreme antinovel position. The essay also focuses one of the questions that shapes the eighteenth-century debate about novels—namely, what is to be done about the inordinate attraction that the young are showing to novel reading? Knox suggests the scope of the challenge the novel posed to earlier methods of controlling the amusements of a young boy or girl. When the novels' octavo and duodecimo format makes them "conveniently portable," and the post and the circulating libraries carry them to "every corner of the kingdom," novels become an ambient presence. This saturation of culture by novels defeats that most time-honored method for protecting the innocence of youth from "the corruptions of the living world"—namely, physically secluding them from the "temptations" and "vice" of that world. Still worse, when novels are transported into the "recesses of the closet" used for free private reading or writing, they insinuate themselves into the mental life of the young reader, where they can "pollute the heart," "inflame the passions," and "teach all the malignity of vice."

The new criticism of the novel often bolsters its authority through an appeal to history. While Knox's essay inserts the emergence of the modern novel into a conservative, devolutionary history, other commentators conceptualize novels as part of a progressive movement toward a valuably enlightened modernity. Thus Pope's editor, William Warburton, the Scottish divine and rhetorician Hugh Blair, and the professor of moral philosophy and logic James Beattie follow the tack of Samuel Johnson in *Rambler* no. 4 by offering brief histories of the development of the novel out of romance. While Warburton and Blair (in "On Fictitious History" [1762]) credit the French novelists (especially Marivaux) with inventing the modern moral novel, whereas Johnson and Beattie do not, all four of these early, anecdotal historians of the novel find a way to mark a sharp divide between the illusions of old romance and what the novel brings: "a faithful and chaste copy of real Lives and Manners" (Warburton, 123). The recent vogue for the *Thousand and One Nights* leads Beattie to develop a fanciful genealogy that traces its origins to the "fabulous narrative[s]" of the East: "the indolence peculiar to the genial climates of Asia, and the luxurious life which the kings and other great men, of those countries, lead in their seraglios, have made them seek for this sort of amusement" ("On Fable and Romance" [1783], Williams, *Novel and Romance 1700–1800*,

310). All four of these commentators represent the modern novel as an agent of an enlightened modern surmounting of old romance fictions. The novel breaks storytelling's self-imposed tutelage to outdated aristocratic notions of honor and love. The following is Beattie's account of the effect of Cervantes' *Don Quixote* on the martial romances previously in vogue:

> This work no sooner appeared, than chivalry vanished, as snow melts before the sun. Mankind awoke as from a dream. They laughed at themselves for having been so long imposed on by absurdity; and wondered they had not made the discovery sooner. It astonished them to find, that nature and good sense could yield a more exquisite entertainment, than they had ever derived from the most sublime phrenzies of chivalry.
>
> [Williams, *Novel and Romance 1700–1800*, 319–320]

Beattie places his own critical writing on the side of that solar power of reason to banish illusion and promote good sense in entertainment. While Warburton and Johnson evidence a scholarly range of knowledge, Beattie offers a slightly learned, gentlemanly blend of condescension and negligence about the earlier novel. The novel, after all, was still a cultural object it would not "do" to know too much about. Like Coventry and Blair, Beattie ends his text by extending his only unqualified enthusiasm for novels written in English to Fielding and Smollett. These three writers cast most other novels into the trash bin of culture.

Reeve's *Progress of Romance* (1785) is a carefully contrived strategic defense of the novel developed on two fronts: first, in response to conservative moralists such as Knox, who would interdict all novel reading for young people; and second, as a rejoinder to scholars and professors such as Beattie, who blend a patronizing and highly selective cryptohistorical support for a few novels with a sweeping condemnation of most novels and romances, whether old or new, foreign or domestic. Reeve promotes a tolerance for a broad spectrum of romances and novels in several ways. Her survey of the romance, from ancient times to the present, is more scholarly and patient than those of her precursors. Her use of the dialogue form allows her to avoid the pretensions to authority characteristic of a formal treatise, while incorporating into her text the debates about novels she is laboring to rearticulate. Within the term "romance" Reeve comprehends not only the Greek romance, the medieval romances (in both verse and prose), and the seventeenth-century heroic romance; she also includes the epics of Homer and the seventeenth-century novella, as well as the "modern novels" of France and England. Her inclusion of Homeric epic in "romance" is a classification dubious enough to be rejected by virtually every subsequent literary historian of the novel; but it gives Reeve's protagonist Euphrasia a way to refute the high cultural bias of her polemical antagonist Hortensius. In addition, by developing the term "romance" into a global category inclusive of narrative entertainments in print produced over a vast expanse of "times, countries, and manners," she uses the historical axis of her study to champion both unfashionable old romances and modern novels.

In the second half of the century, different positions upon what novels should be were often inflected through divergent critical valuations of Richardson and Fielding. In this way, the rivalry of Richardson and Fielding on the market in the 1740s is reproduced in the earliest literary criticism and history of the novel. Coventry proclaims Fielding's unheralded achievements and ignores Richardson, while Johnson's prescription for the novel's cultural role is rigged to favor Richardson's fictional practice. The pride of place that male critics such as Blair and Beattie give Fielding in the second half of the century is embedded in Reeve's *Progress of Romance*, in the arguments of Hortentius. Hortensius complains that Richardson's epistolary novels "have taught many young girls to wiredraw their language, and to spin always long letters out of nothing." Euphrasia responds by defending the cultural value of studying and imitating Richardson over the "studies" of an earlier generation: "Let the young girls . . . copy Richardson, as often as they please, and it will be owing to the defects of their understandings, or judgments, if they do not improve by him. We could not say as much of the reading Ladies of the last age. . . . No truly, for their studies were the French and Spanish Romances, and the writings of Mrs. Behn, Mrs. Manly, and Mrs. Heywood [*sic*]" (I: 138). For Reeve, Richardson reorients the spontaneous reader identification that worried the moral critics of the novel. In her view, none had demonstrated more clearly than Richardson how a morally improving emulation could be promoted. When the critic and dramatist Richard Cumberland writes of the dangers of allowing young women to read *Clarissa* and emulate its heroine, Anna Seward responds with an impassioned defense of Richardson's novel and its moral tendency (Williams, *Novel and Romance 1700–1800*, 332–335; 357–366). Letitia Barbauld edited Richardson's correspondence, and gives him the privileged beginning position in *The British Novelists* (1810), her fifty-volume selection of the most valuable novels of the previous century. By contrast, Scott devotes part of his introductory essay to defending Fielding against those who condemn his morality and indelicacy, especially when comparing him with Richardson. That the debate about the cultural value of novels often modulated into a debate about the comparative worth of Richardson and Fielding may explain the remarkable consensus transmitted into subsequent literary histories—which can seem very arbitrary to twentieth-century literary historians—that either Richardson or Fielding must be the true "father" of the British novel.[4]

THE CLOSURE OF THE DEBATE: SUBLIMATING NOVELISTIC ENTERTAINMENTS INTO LITERARY HISTORY

By the second decade of the nineteenth century there is evidence that the debate about novels had reached closure. Some would still oppose all novel reading, but it was an extreme position, usually held by members of the religious right (Williams, *Novel and Romance 1700–1800*, 17). Two ambitious editing projects give a new eminence to the novels of the previous century, and suggest the consolidation of the novel's cultural legitimacy. Each selection in *The British Novelists*, Barbauld's fifty-volume, twenty-eight-work collection, received an introductory essay, and every author except Francis Coventry received a biographical and critical essay rationalizing his or her inclusion. Between 1821 and 1824 the *Ballantyne's Novelist's Library* appeared, offering a selection of fourteen authors in ten volumes, edited and introduced by Walter Scott. Through these collections, the eighteenth-century canon of British novels begin to acquire palpable form (H. Brown, "Of the Title to Things Real"). A still more comprehensive rationale for novel reading is developed in the ambitious, scholarly

4. In the twentieth century, critics across a broad spectrum have tendered competing claims for Richardson (among them, Frank Kermode, Ian Watt, and Margaret Doody) and Fielding (including Wayne Booth, Ronald Paulson, and Martin Battestin). If one considers Richardson and Fielding as representing a synchronic opposition produced by literary history, then it may seem most reasonable to halve the matter amicably. In *Occasional Form*, J. Paul Hunter ends up agreeing with William Park that the only fair thing to do in this paternity suit concerning the true father of the British novel is "[to] divide almost equally the credit for creating what we call the novel"; in his formulation, their "polarities" "destined a rich dialectical future for the genre" (225). The implications of such a solution are worked out by Michael McKeon (*Origins of the English Novel*). However, making Richardson and Fielding appear as an exhaustive novelistic dyad, and locating that antagonism securely within the rise of the novel narrative, merely enhances the authority of that narrative. It is the writers of the novels of amorous intrigue, and (more generally) formula fiction as media culture, that get excluded. For a suggestive critique of the mythos of Richardson and Fielding as the double origin of a singular genre, as the gendered originators of the (British) novel, see Campbell, *Natural Masques*, 3–4.

three-volume history published in 1814 by John Dunlop and entitled *The History of Fiction: Being A Critical Account of the Most Celebrated Prose Works of Fiction, From the Earliest Greek Romances to the Novels of the Present Age.* In order to argue the cultural superiority of "fiction" to history, Dunlop quotes the following words from Francis Bacon:

> Fiction gives to mankind what history denies, and, in some measure, satisfies the mind with shadows when it cannot enjoy the substance: . . . Fiction strongly shows that a greater variety of things, a more perfect order, a more beautiful variety, than can any where be found in nature, is pleasing to the mind. And as real history gives us not the success of things according to the deserts of vice and virtue, Fiction corrects it, and presents us with the fates and fortunes of persons rewarded or punished according to merit. And as real history disgusts us with a familiar and constant similitude of things, Fiction relieves us by unexpected turns and changes, and thus not only delights, but inculcates morality and nobleness of soul. It raises the mind by accommodating the images of things to our desires, and not like history and reason, subjecting the mind to things.

By appealing to Bacon on the value of fiction, Dunlop not only invokes the authority of a major British thinker, he also leaps over one hundred years of wrangling about the moral effects of reading novels. In using the general term "fiction" for his history of romances and novels, Dunlop blurs the polemical stakes of the debate he would nonetheless recast. Eighteenth-century defenses of the novel (from Congreve and Richardson to Fielding and Reeve) usually engage a set of polar oppositions still familiar to us: the novel is to the romance as the "real" is to the "ideal," as fact is to fantasy, as the probable is to the amazing, as the ordinary everyday is to the high-flown exotic, and so on. Fiction was developed by Dunlop as a third term that can finesse yet reconcile these polar oppositions. Fiction does this by becoming art, delivering "a more perfect order, a more beautiful variety" than "nature."

Through Dunlop's use of Bacon, Renaissance and romantic aesthetics meet in a justification of fiction that is finally psychological. Through fiction, the reader is no longer "subject" to, or disgusted with, "a familiar and constant similitude of things." Instead, fiction "relieves" and "delights," and "raises the mind" "by accommodating the images of things to our desires." The cultural efficacy of fiction is argued to come from its successful gratification of the reader's pleasure. Dunlop's adaptation of Bacon to his argument assumes yet reverses the anxiety about the reader's pleasure that had motivated condemnations of the novel. In his glossing of Bacon's emphasis on "delight," it is apparent that the pleasure Dunlop was promoting is quite different from the pleasure which novel readers had been accused of indulging. Instead of obsessive, personal, deluded, erotic pleasures, we are called to soft, social ones: "how much are we indebted to [fiction] for pleasure and enjoyment! [I]t sweetens solitude and charms sorrow . . . " These pleasures are argued to improve and uplift the reader, by taking him or her into an elevated social and emotive space: "The rude are refined by an introduction, as it were, to the higher orders of mankind, and even the dissipated and selfish are, in some degree, corrected by those paintings of virtue and simple nature, which must ever be employed by the novelist if he wish to awaken emotion or delight" (xi–xii). Having affirmed its beneficent effects, Dunlop goes on to confirm the novel's rise from its earlier disreputable cultural position: "this powerful instrument of virtue and happiness, after having been long despised, on account of the purposes to which it had been made subservient, has gradually become more justly appreciated, and more highly valued. Works of Fiction have been produced, abounding at once with the most interesting details, and the most sagacious reflections, and which differ from treatises of abstract philosophy only by the greater justness of their views, and the higher interest which they excite" (xii–xiii).

This characterization of the novel helps us to apprehend the broader purpose of Dunlop's literary history—namely, to sublimate the novel so as to produce a new disposition, or arrangement, of novel reading. Neither exiling all novels from culture in favor of drama, epic, sermons, or conduct books nor favoring the simple uncritical acceptance of all novels into his narrative of the history of fiction, Dunlop's title tells us his history is to be "critical"—that is, it will judge works as to quality so as to focus only on "the most celebrated" prose fiction. What results in the works of both Reeve and Dunlop, as in every subsequent literary history, is a chronological panorama of culture in which selected cultural practices and productions are narrated as significant and valuable. By this means, literary history licenses (selected) entertainments by sublimating them.

The new dispensation for novel reading is developed by rearticulating the terms of the old debate. In introducing *The British Novelists*, Barbauld makes fun of the tendency of eighteenth-century apologists of the novel to downplay the centrality of entertainment as a motive for novel reading:

> If the end and object of this species of writing be asked, many no doubt will be ready to tell us that its object is to call in fancy to the aid of reason, to deceive the mind into embracing truth under the guise of fiction . . . with such-like reasons equally grave and dignified. For my own part, I scruple not to confess that, when I take up a novel, my end and object is entertainment; and as I suspect that to be the case with most readers, I

hesitate not to say that entertainment is their legitimate end and object. To read the productions of wit and genius is a very high pleasure to all persons of taste, and the avidity with which they are read by all such shows sufficiently that they are calculated to answer this end [I: 43–44]. . . . The unpardonable sin of a novel is dullness: however grave or wise it may be, if its author possesses no powers of amusing, he has no business to write novels; he should employ his pen in some more serious part of literature. [I: 45]

In turning away from "grave and dignified" justifications of the novel, Barbauld shifts to the first person ["I scruple not to confess"] to insist that the novel's "end and object is entertainment." But this is not the "mere" entertainment or empty pleasure-taking that had so worried the moralists of the previous century. Instead, Barbauld builds upon the idea of the novel as a sophisticated vehicle of performative entertainment, as Fielding's critical essays first conceptualize it to be (see chapter 6). Barbauld glosses what she means by the "legitimate" "end" of entertainment by applauding the "very high pleasure to all persons of taste" provided by "productions of wit and genius." As noted above, she culls twenty-eight works from a century of novel writing and frames the productions of each of fourteen authors with suitable introductions. In this way, novel reading is socialized and refined. Thus, while giving special privilege to Richardson's novels (*Clarissa* and *Sir Charles Grandison* occupy the first fifteen of the fifty volumes), Barbauld also censures some scenes in *Pamela* and *Clarissa* as too inflaming.

Although in introducing his history of fiction Dunlop writes as though the culturally elevating role for fiction were already achieved, in fact his own literary history is designed to further that end. To argue the centrality of fiction to culture, Dunlop begins his introduction with an elaborate analogy between gardening and fiction-making that quickly implicates his own literary history. Dunlop's development of the analogy between fiction, gardening, and literary history suggests that violence is a necessary element of cultivation. Just as the "savage" has gathered and placed around his dwelling plants that pleased him, so too has man lived events "which are peculiarly grateful, and of which the narrative at once pleases himself, and excites in the minds of his hearers a kindred emotion" (v). What are gathered are "unlooked-for-occurrences, successful enterprise, or great and unexpected deliverance from signal danger and distress" (vi). A gardener learns that one must not just collect, one must also weed the

useless or noxious, and [those] which weaken or impair the pure delight which he derives from others. . . . the rose should no longer be placed beside the thistle, as in the wild, but that it should flourish in a clear, and sheltered, and romantic situation, where its sweets may be undiminished, and where its form can be contemplated without any attending circumstances of uneasiness or disgust. The collector of agreeable facts finds, in like manner, that the sympathy which they excite can be heightened by removing from their detail every thing that is not interesting, or which tends to weaken the principal emotion, which it is his intention to raise. He renders, in this way, the occurrences more unexpected, the enterprises more successful, the deliverance from danger and distress more wonderful.

[Dunlop, *History of Fiction*, vii]

The same process that describes the "fine arts" of gardening and fiction-making—selecting, weeding, and intensifying, in view of pleasure—applies also to the literary history Dunlop composes. Dunlop's "critical" history of fiction becomes an improving and enlightening cultivation of fiction for culture. By using the fiction of widely different epochs to survey the variety of cultural achievements, literary history makes novels more than instruments of private (kinky, obsessive) gratification. Instead, they are drawn into the larger tableau of cultural accomplishment—what Dunlop calls "the advance of the human mind"—until disinterested moral and aesthetic pleasure appears to be the telos of all fiction-making.

To Dunlop, civilizing the novel requires a calculated violence. In a chapter entitled a "Sketch of the Origin and Progress of the English Novel," he offers a typology of the elevated novel whereby novels are divided into the "serious" (Richardson, Sheridan, and Godwin), the "comic" (Fielding and Smollett), and the "romantic" (Walpole, Reeve, and Radcliff). But before offering this schematic overview of what we would now call the "eighteenth-century novel," Dunlop weeds out others, giving cursory, negative treatment to the novels of Behn, Manley, and the early Haywood. Behn's novels, he informed his readers, "have not escaped the moral contagion which infected the literature of that age." Though Dunlop merely alludes to "the objections which may be charged against many" of Behn's novels, he ends by describing the "faults in points of morals" of Behn's "imitator," Eliza Haywood, as follows: "Her male characters are in the highest degree licentious, and her females are as impassioned as the Saracen princesses in the Spanish romances of chivalry" (III: 369–370). By "orientalizing" these early novels as inappropriately erotic—too feminine, too Latin, and too immoral—he writes into the margins of "The History of Fiction" some of the most popular novels published in England between 1684 and 1730.

While the writings of Reeve, Dunlop, Barbauld, and Scott suggest the closure of the debate about whether one should read novels, their novelistic criticism and literary history transmit two of that debate's central ideas: First, they accept the assumption implicit in the arguments of both the critics and the supporters of novels—that novels should be written in such a way that teenagers of both sexes can read them without harm; and second, they view novel reading as part of a reader's moral education. Like Mary Wollstonecraft in *A Vindication of the Rights of Woman* (1793), Clara Reeve understands the novel as a form for transmitting valuable social knowledge. Thus Reeve ends her literary history by describing a curriculum for the young reader. She quotes dire warnings, written by the moralist John Gregory and others, against the indiscriminate reading of novels by the young, and then extends these strictures to the blasphemous and indelicate classical texts put into the hands of young boys by their educators. Finally, she concludes that "selection is to be strongly recommended, and good books to be carefully chosen by all that are concerned in the education of youth" (II: 97). At the end of her history Reeve appends two lists for parents, guardians, and tutors, and "intended chiefly for the female sex"—"Books for Children," and "Books for Young Ladies." This two-stage course of reading includes fables, spellers, conduct books, periodical essays, and only one item on the second list that would be described today as novelistic: "Richardson's Works." Ironically, the final pedagogical turn of Reeve's literary history withholds from the young reader almost all of the romances and novels she has described in the foregoing work. Evidently, she expects that her two-stage curriculum will prepare young female minds for an informed and critical reading of the romances and novels described in *The Progress of Romance*. With Reeve, literary history acquires the pedagogical function it has continued to serve in literary studies: it becomes a reading list, with its entries contextualized by narrative, and the literary historian functions as the novel's culturally redeeming filter.

THE NATIONALIZATION OF THE NOVEL

How do eighteenth-century novels that happen to have been written in England come to be understood, by the late nineteenth century, as the first instances of that complex and valued cultural object known as "the English novel"? This change of the novel into a literary type is coextensive with the nationalization of culture and the rise of the discipline of English literary studies. The global shift by which European cultures moved from an older patriotism of competing characteristics to a modern idea of each nation's comprehensive and essential difference is beyond the scope of this study; nonetheless, given the central role that novel reading comes to have in the imagination of the nation as a community (Anderson), the emergence of literary histories of the novel is traversed by, but also helps to perform, what one might call the nationalization of culture (Brennan, "National Longing for Form," 49–56). By shifting the reference point backward in time, it is possible to understand how literary history contributes to the nationalization of the novel.

The consensus within contemporary British literary studies that the first "real" novels appeared in England is a post-Romantic idea. By contrast, eighteenth-century British cultural critics often gave France precedence over England in the invention of several different species of romances and novels. Above, it was noted that the anecdotal histories of the novel offered by Hugh Blair and William Warburton maintain that the general species of morally serious novels written by Richardson and Fielding gained its strongest initial expression in France. The British eighteenth-century "debate about the novel" assumes that the novels of different nations belong to the same cultural field: dire warnings against the pernicious effects of foreign novels imply their transnational mobility. Novels in the eighteenth century, like silent films early in this century, were considered a species of entertainment most likely to move easily across linguistic and national boundaries. Both the opponents and proponents of novel reading selected the novels of different nations from off the same shelves.[5]

As the producer of the greatest number and variety of fictions, France of the seventeenth and early eighteenth centuries is positioned as something of a "Hollywood" for romances and novels. Whether they favor or oppose novel reading, eighteenth-century critics assume that the novels of different nations, whatever their origin, become part of the same cultural terrain of readable entertainment. Literary historians such as Reeve and Dunlop discuss the novels of Cervantes, Marivaux, and Rousseau within the same conceptual coordinates as they discuss the novels of Richardson and Fielding. But during the nineteenth century, the novel was gradually nationalized. Influential critics such as Hazlitt and Scott came to understand novels as a type of writing particularly suited to representing the character, mores, landscape, and "spirit" of particular nations. In a different but no less complete way than poetry, the novel is reinterpreted as a distinct expression of the nation. However, this articulation of nation and novel has a rich pre-

---

5. My informal survey of advertisements for novels on the front and back pages of novels in the Clark Library, dating from the forty years after 1684, shows French novels—both in French and in English translation—commingled with novels in English written by British writers.

history. Over the course of the eighteenth-century debate about novels there develops a correlation that would inflect the whole institutionalization of the novel. Repeatedly it is claimed that England is to France as the (elevated) novel is to the romance, as fact is to fantasy, as morality is to sensuality, as men are to women. (Terms can be added to this series: genuine and counterfeit, simple and frothy, substantial and sophisticated.) Grounded in a caricature of France as effeminate and England as manly, this loaded set of oppositions is simultaneously nationalist and sexist. Proliferating inexhaustibly, these oppositions seem to touch every region of culture, and weave themselves like a gaudy thread through all the literary histories of the novel's rise. It is one of the goals of this study to unravel the gender politics of the institution of the (elevated) novel (see chapter 4).

We can grasp what is at stake in the nationalization of the novel by contrasting the early and later literary histories of the novel. In the literary histories of Reeve, Beattie, and Dunlop, the assessment of the value of different sorts of novels sometimes echoes clichéd tropes of national difference. However, the interpretations of particular writers unfold within the universalist horizon of a generous, catholic, enlightenment cosmopolitanism.[6] Such a broad, enlightened perspective on history, accessible to the leisured and cultured members of a certain class, is quite explicitly engaged in Dunlop's introduction to his *History of Fiction*:

> I have employed a few hours of relaxation in drawing up the following notices of [fiction's] gradual progress. . . . No works are perhaps more useful or agreeable, than those which delineate the advance of the human mind—the history of what different individuals have effected in the course of ages, for the instruction, or even the innocent amusement, of their species. . . . Such a delineation . . . retrieves from oblivion a number of individuals, whose now obsolete works are perhaps in detail unworthy of public attention, but which promoted and diffused in their own day, light and pleasure, and form as it were landmarks which testify the course and progress of genius. By contemplating also not only what has been done, but the mode in which it has been achieved, a method may perhaps be discovered of proceeding still farther, of avoiding the errors into which our predecessors have fallen, and of following the paths in which they have met success. Retrospective works of this nature, therefore, combine utility, justice, and pleasure . . . [xiv]

Dunlop's statement exudes a heady enlightenment confidence that he occupies a secure vantage point for the study of the "works" and "landmarks"

---

6. For an account of how cultural critique across boundaries of nation, race, and time is enabled by "cosmopolitanism," see the "Cosmopolitanism" entry in Yolton's *Blackwell Companion to the Enlightenment*.

of different epochs, languages, and individuals. It is from this analytical and reflective standpoint, presumed to rest outside the bias of a particular time or national place, that he allows fiction's variety to come into his view, and that allows him to "delineate" the progress of fiction. In short, Dunlop can write history because his knowledge makes him no longer a part of it. To unsettle this cosmopolitan perspective on fiction, one need only radicalize the difference among cultures and locate the historian of those differences within rather than outside a particular culture. This is a step we can begin to see taking place in Hazlitt and Scott.

Although Reeve, Beattie, and Dunlop recognize that novels afford a particularly vivid and exact representation of the manners of a time and people, it is not until Hazlitt, Scott, and Taine that the idea of the novel as a vehicle for expressing cultural difference becomes folded into an historicism that assumes a people and their culture are an organic totality, essentially different from other cultures in every aspect of their identity. Hazlitt gives Fielding first rank among English novelists for the way in which his realistic representation of character and manners helps express this difference. In his view, Fielding's novels come to embody English distinctness because his novels "are, in general, thoroughly his own; and they are thoroughly English . . . .What they are remarkable for is . . . profound knowledge of human nature, at least of English nature; and masterly pictures of the characters of men as he saw them existing" (112–113). Notice how these sentences detour general qualities of Fielding's novel, from being "thoroughly his own" to being "thoroughly English"; and from providing knowledge of "human nature" to providing knowledge of "English nature." Without defining the term "English," Hazlitt narrows the focus of Fielding's fiction to a rich, particular character and nature—namely, England. This nationalist interpretation of the final signified of Fielding's fiction is what, for Hazlitt, distinguishes Fielding from other novelists, and is also what gives him title to the greatest value.

The next conceptual step in the nationalization of the novel is readable in the first lines of Walter Scott's introductory essay on Fielding from a volume of the Ballentyne novels. Scott writes from within a related but distinct culture and nation—that of Scotland. For Scott, it is not so much Fielding who embodies England as it is England that embodies Fielding, not so much Fielding who writes England as it is "English Genius" that writes Fielding:

> Of all the works of imagination to which English genius has given origin the novels of the celebrated Henry Fielding are, perhaps, most decidedly and exclusively her own. They are not only altogether beyond the reach of

translation, in the proper sense of the word, but we even question whether they can be fully understood, or relished to the highest extent, by such natives of Scotland and Ireland as are not habitually acquainted with the character and manners of Old England. Parson Adam, Tow-wouse, Partridge, above all, Squire Western, are personages as peculiar to England as they are unknown to other countries. Nay, the actors whose character is of a more general cast, as Allworthy, Mrs. Miller, Tom Jones himself, and almost all the subordinate agents in the narrative, have the same cast of nationality, which adds not a little to the verisimilitude of the tale. The persons of the story live in England, travel in England, quarrel and fight in England; and scarce an incident occurs without its being marked by something which could not well have happened in any other country. This nationality may be ascribed to the author's own habits of life, which rendered him conversant, at different periods, with all the various classes of English society, specimens with inimitable spirit of choice and description, for the amusement of his readers.

[*Lives of the Novelists*, 46]

Here, as in Hazlitt, it is the novel's mimetic powers—especially its power to represent society as a complex assemblage of types—which makes the novel of the nation, and its author one of "her own" distinct genius. Under this interpretation, one framed by the historicist assumption that time works to transfigure manners, social reality becomes national reality, and the novel its proper medium. "English genius" realizes her own distinct identity through the novels of Fielding; authors become the avatars of this national spirit; and, by implication, the nation is a signified powerful enough to order and unify the history of literature. These assumptions take us close to the axioms of the national literary histories written in the nineteenth century.

How does romantic literary history resituate novels? In his study of literary history David Perkins itemizes the features of a romantic literary history as follows: "the importance attached to beginnings or origins, the assumption that development is the subject of literary history, the understanding of development as continual rather than disjunctive, and the creation of suprapersonal entities as the subjects of this development" (Perkins, 86). The literary histories developed out of these concerns have the formal shape of a *bildungsroman*. Within this very novelistic species of narrative, the central character (or subject) could be a genre (such as "the novel") or it could be the nation. In either case, literary history reads culture as a totality arranged around the subject, and depends upon the relay by which the mimetic claims of the novel allow literary history to represent the nation. The nation, people, or "race" can become, within a romantic literary history, the truth that particular genres, authors, and periods disclose. Within this global historical frame, bracing new questions about the historical causes of the ebb and flow of national genius can be posed. Thus, in his *Lectures on the Comic Writers*, Hazlitt speculates as to why the four great novelists of the mid-eighteenth century emerged at the same time. This enables him to develop the thesis that the novel's rise can be attributed to one of the bywords of English identity: the idea of liberty.

> It is remarkable that our four best novel-writers belong nearly to the same age [the reign of George II] . . . If I were called upon to account for this coincidence, I should waive the consideration of more general causes, and ascribe it at once to the establishment of the Protestant ascendancy, and the succession of the House of Hanover. These great events appear to have given a more popular turn to our literature and genius, as well as to our government. It was found high time that the people should be represented in books as well as in Parliament. They wished to see some account of themselves in what they read; and not to be confined always to the vices, the miseries, and frivolities of the great. . . . [In France] the *canaille* are objects rather of disgust than curiosity; and there are no middle classes. The works of Racine and Moliere are either imitations of the verbiage of the court, before which they were represented, or fanciful caricatures of the manners of the lowest people. But in the period of our history in question, a security of person and property, and a freedom of opinion had been established, which made every man feel of some consequence to himself, and appear an object of some curiosity to his neighbours: our manners became more domesticated; there was a general spirit of sturdiness and independence, which made the English character more truly English than perhaps at any other period—that is, more tenacious of its own opinions and purposes. The whole surface of society appeared cut out into square enclosures and sharp angles, which extended to the dresses of the time, their gravel-walks, and clipped hedges. Each individual had a certain ground-plot of his own to cultivate his particular humours in, and let them shoot out at pleasure; and a most plentiful crop they have produced accordingly. The reign of George II was, in a word, the age of *hobby-horses*: but, since that period, things have taken a different turn. [248–250]

After these words, Hazlitt goes on to regret the way in which the constant wars of the last fifty years have driven out this "domestic" interest and made what the king and nation do central, even to the point of restoring "the divine right of kings" (251).

There are several remarkable features to the way in which Hazlitt explains the comparatively sudden, and regrettably temporary, effulgence of English genius in the early (and by now canonical) novel writers—

Richardson, Fielding, Smollett, and Sterne—of the period of George II. First, he offers an early rendering of what is by now the classic explanation for the rise of the novel, correlating it with the rise of the middle class (with its protestantism, individualism, and domesticity—in other words, its subjectivity). But here, that thesis is not an abstract sociological correlation, applicable to all societies undergoing modern economic development. It is interwoven, at every point, with the central myths of English national identity—most crucially with the idea of what separates French "despotism" from English liberty. Thus, the political upheaval that brought the House of Hanover to the throne is said to have given "a more popular turn to our literature and genius." How did this "turn" come about? Although Hazlitt blurs the agency for this change through the use of a passive construction ("It was found high time"), he aligns the cultural with the political demands for representation as they express themselves "in books as well as Parliament." This brings into existence a new species of culturally enfranchised reader: one who demands a turn away from representations of the "vices, miseries, and frivolities of the great" and toward "an account of themselves." This break from cultural despotism (as expressed in the continental romance and novella) is grounded in the flowering of English liberty, which wins for each "a security of person and property, and freedom of opinion." Since this turn toward a more popular and "domestic" culture wins the English reader a certain "life" and "liberty," he (but perhaps not she) becomes propertied—"each individual had a certain groundplot of his own to cultivate his particular humours in." The novel—in the epoch of its flowering—thus allows every English citizen to realize a claim to the Lockean trinity of life, liberty, and property (Locke, *Second Treatise of Government*, VII: 87). English novels thus put English readers of a certain epoch in possession of a self.[7]

This Whiggish interpretation of the free golden age of the Whig mid-eighteenth century, written from the vantage point of Hazlitt's conception of English democratic identity, is embedded in every subsequent version of the rise of the novel thesis. I can suggest the suspiciously circular, self-confirming logic that gives this thesis its coherence by recasting its argument in the following way: If one begins by taking certain English novels of the mid-eighteenth century as the first real modern novels, then "the" novel's rise into popular and aesthetic centrality appears to be the result of the political, social, cultural rise of the middle class. Correlatively, if one

---

7. For an analogous argument, in slightly different terms, see Taine (*History of English Literature*, III: 268).

understands "the" (first real modern) novel as the expression of middle-class (democratic, Protestant) culture, then the novel is an English invention. How did the question of the novel's origin come to be posed within this reciprocally supporting circle of assumptions? Although Watt—and recently, more scrupulously detailed literary histories of the novel's rise, such as those of McKeon and Hunter—will correlate the novel's origin and rise with ideas and ideology and cultural formations of many different sorts, there are two common assumptions embedded in their development of the rise of the novel thesis. First, the French novels of the seventeenth century, as well as English novels before Defoe, are expelled from consideration as real modern novels, and exiled into a remote premodern twilight of aristocratic culture. This is done in spite of the fact that many of the claims made in eighteenth-century England regarding the greater verisimilitude of the novel over romance are anticipated in seventeenth-century French critiques of the heroic romance (Williams, *Idea of the Novel*). Second, the rise of the novel thesis affirms nationalist ideas—all too visible in the passage quoted from Hazlitt (above)—about the unprecedented freedom of the modern subject within the English national culture. To Watt and his heirs, the freedom of this modern subject may have required the political changes we associate with the democratic revolutions; but its fullest cultural expression comes from a middle-class reader's unprecedented freedom to consume reality in the form of novels.

How does the rise of "the" novel come to be an English story? The passages from Hazlitt and Scott discussed above suggest part of the answer. The nationalization of the novel prepares it for being interpreted as a privileged modern vehicle for subjectivity. Fielding is not just prized for representing the richly particular external social mores of England; he, along with those who follow him, also ratifies a new demand for middle-class self-representation; but paradoxically, these novel writers enable readers to become more themselves by becoming more English. In order to tell this enlightenment narrative of a people's movement toward freedom, there develops a new discourse—the national literary history—where the people, the race, and the national culture become subject and object, heroic agent and telos of their own autoproduction. This sort of narrative is anticipated by Scott and Hazlitt, but comes to fruition in Hippolyte Taine's *History of English Literature*. Taine's book tells the story of a distinct people, as it has felt the cumulative force of climate and history, through a reading of its literature. Within his narrative, authors are not isolated individuals; rather, they belong to and express different aspects of the "race."

Authors, together with what they write, become the purest expressions of the nation.

For Taine, the English novel not only expresses the English moral desire for virtue; it also expresses a practical impulse to map modes of good conduct. Several elements of Taine's description of the emergence of this "new kind" of novel are quite familiar—for example, his account of the contrast between, on the one hand, Spanish and French novels, which gratify the wish for "imagination" and "conversation," and, on the other, English ones, which depict "real life." For Taine, the novel expresses a middle-class reaction against the "obscenities" of Restoration high life. But these themes are spliced together with a much more sublime idea: that of a people's sudden birth into modern reality.

> Amidst these finished and perfect writings [that is, the English Classicism of Addison and Swift] a new kind makes its appearance, suited to the public tendencies and circumstances of the time, the anti-romantic novel, the work and reading of positive minds, observers and moralists, not intended to exalt and amuse the imagination, like the novels of Spain and the middle ages, not to reproduce or embellish conversation, like the novels of France and the seventeenth century, but to depict real life, to describe characters, to suggest plans of conduct, and judge motives of action. It was a strange apparition, and like the voice of a people buried underground, when, amidst the splendid corruption of high life, this severe emanation of the middle class welled up, and when the obscenities of Mrs. Aphra Behn, still the diversion of ladies of fashion, were found on the same table with De Foe's *Robinson Crusoe*. [456–457]

Within Taine's narrative of the novel's rise, England can only take the step beyond the aristocratic obscenities and the superficial feminine diversion afforded by "Mrs. Aphra Behn" by harkening to a "strange apparition," welling up "like the voice of the people," within culture. What does it mean that this "new kind" of writing is described by Taine in such conventionally romantic terms: as that which comes from within and below, and expresses its own irresistible desire to express itself? What are the characteristics of a writing described in this way? The general form of this movement toward utterance is more crucial than any particular content: its will to express, well up, and voice . . . what? Above all, its *self*. The novel becomes the privileged medium for the self's modern utterance.

If one looks at how Taine specifies the content of this "severe emanation of the middle class," one finds more evidence for the self as the final signified of the English novel. In summarizing the practical and moral impulses of the writings of Defoe, Addison, and Steele, Taine explains the inward and reflective turn that has given the English a more fully developed character than other peoples: "Two features are common and proper to [these books]. All these novels are character novels. Englishmen, more reflective than others, more inclined to the melancholy pleasure of concentrated attention and inner examination, find around them human medals more vigorously struck, less worn by friction with the world, whose uninjured face is more visible than that of others" (461). In his manipulation of a commonplace about coins and character, Taine aligns the reflective independence of the English with "human medals" more "vigorously struck" with character that is then conducted into their "character novels."[8] Within his survey of particular novelists, Taine attributes the special centrality of Richardson and Fielding to the novel's rise to the way in which their difference from one another expresses a primordial tension in English culture—that between "rule" and "nature." The passage introducing Richardson and Fielding has the heroic cast of grand cultural narrative. Here is one of the moments in which the essence of English race finds expression. If one attends to the way Taine renders this complex tension within the English people, one sees how the two cultural tendencies of this particular people could enact the conflict between law and desire that psychoanalysis makes constitutive of the self per se, and thus how the qualities of a particular race could dramatize the general conflict Freud finds endemic to culture and its discontents.

> Two principal ideas can rule, and have ruled, morality in England. Now it is conscience which is accepted as a sovereign; now it is instinct which is taken for guide. Now they have recourse to grace; now they rely on nature. Now they wholly enslave everything to rule; now they give everything up to liberty. The two opinions have successively reigned in England; and the human frame, at once too vigorous and too unyielding, successively justifies their ruin and their success.—Some, alarmed by the fire of an over-fed temperament, and by the energy of unsocial passions, have regarded nature as a dangerous beast, and placed conscience with all its auxiliaries, religion, law, education, proprieties, as so many armed sentinels to repress its least outbreaks. Others, repelled by the harshness of an incessant constraint, and by the minuteness of a morose discipline, have overturned guards and barriers, and let loose captive nature to enjoy the free air and sun, deprived of which it was being choked. Both by their

---

8. I am indebted to my colleague Deidre Lynch for understanding the importance of the conjunction of discussions of the "face value" of coins and character. See Lynch, *Economy of Character.*

excesses have deserved their defeats and raised up their adversaries. From Shakespeare to the Puritans, from Milton to Wycherley, from Congreve to De Foe, . . . irregularity has provoked constraint and tyranny revolt. This great contest of rule and nature is developed again in the writings of Fielding and Richardson. [462]

In this narrative Taine assumes the position of a worldly, knowledgeable cultural critic who can survey the impulses of many cultures and epochs, and narrate each episode in this history so it discloses something particular and fundamental about this national culture. Within this critical narrative, the Richardson/Fielding dyad indexes a global cultural opposition in a synecdochical fashion, so a primary polarity of human culture is formalized, then gathered into a collective national subject.

While Reeve's "progress of romance" and Dunlop's "history of fiction" are inclusively multinational and extend their histories backward to ancient and medieval times, as well as across the channel to include continental romances and novellas, national literary histories such as Taine's cut these temporal and spatial links. Traits of the British culture—empiricism, Protestant individualism, moral seriousness, and a fondness for eccentric character—are promoted from secondary characteristics of novels which happened to have been written in England to primary features of the novel's generic identity. While this process can be seen to begin in Taine's *History of English Literature*, several factors limit the nationalization of literature in Taine. First, his text actually elaborates itself through a sustained comparison of English and French culture and literature. In addition, his interest in the impulses of race and nation finally dissolves aesthetic issues and generic forms into cultural experiences broad enough to epitomize the entire human condition. By contrast, the earliest study that takes the English novel as its primary object—Sir Walter Raleigh's *The English Novel: A Short Sketch of its History from the Earliest Times to the Appearance of Waverley* (1894)—is written within the context of a discursive shift that Taine's book only anticipates—namely, the movement toward the institution of separate disciplines for the study and teaching of national literatures. As a professor at the University of Glasgow in Scotland, Raleigh, like Scott, has a distance from England that encourages him to correlate the novel written in English with his interpretation of English culture. With Raleigh's book of 1894, the nationalization of the novel in England reaches completion. In 1904, Raleigh becomes the first professor of English literature (exclusive of Anglo-Saxon literature) appointed at Oxford (Court, *Institutionalizing English Literature*, 156).

Far from the romantic expressionism of Taine, wherein novels bring to the surface impulses residing deep within the "race," Raleigh consolidates a concept of the nation through a more patient and rational inquiry into the origins of the English novel. What results is an early instance of what Lennard Davis, in *Factual Fictions,* calls a "convergent theory": the novel emerges from the sudden convergence of several different types of non-novelistic writing. While Hazlitt and Taine had assumed the inscription of the novel within a broad horizon of cultural impulses, Raleigh's genealogy is more narrowly focused. Directed less at large abstractions such as class, nation, and epoch, it attends to shifts in style, genre, and idea. Raleigh's study of the novel is familiar from most subsequent English literary history of the novel: it separates "the English novel" from anything not written in English or in England. The following passage shows how Raleigh describes the emergence of the English novel, after he concedes that there was an attempt in Congreve and Behn to bring the romance "into closer relation with contemporary life":

> The attempt failed for the time, and when at last achievement came, and the rise of the great schools of English novelists with Richardson and Fielding at their head was rendered possible, it was not wrought by the professed writers of romance, but by the essayists and party writers of the reign of Anne, by Addison and Steele, by Swift and Defoe, who formed their style under influences remote enough from the high flown impossibilities of the heroic romance. Thus, just as the sixteenth century saw the decline of the older romances of chivalry, so the seventeenth saw the rise, decline, and fall of this later and less robust romantic development; the heroic romance died and left no issue. . . . For the novel least of all forms of literature can boast a pure extraction; it is of mixed and often disreputable ancestry; and the novelist derives his inspiration, as well as his material, not chiefly from the pages of his predecessors in the art, but from the life of his time and the literature that springs directly from that life, whether it be a broadside or a blue-book.
>
> [Raleigh, *The English Novel,* 109]

Raleigh's literary history is predicated upon two separations: first, novels are separated from those earlier romance forms—whether the "romances of chivalry" or the "heroic romances"—which undergo their own "rise, decline, and fall." Raleigh delivers a decisive judgment: "the heroic romance died and left no issue." In discussing the fiction of Manley and the early Haywood, he dismisses them as weak and debased holdovers from romance. Second, Raleigh separates novels from the early novels of Behn and Congreve, whose effort to write in closer proximity to contemporary life "failed for the time." But then, from whence does the novel arise?

Raleigh links the rise of "the great school of English novelists" to a "mixed ancestry" of heterogeneous influences—character writing, Defoe's early realism, Bunyan, Spratt's goals for scientific prose, *Spectator* papers, *Robinson Crusoe*, and other writings—all said to be characterized by their proximity to "the life of [the] time."

Taine and Raleigh put forward a thesis about the novel that would never have occurred to Reeve or Dunlop: that the modern English novel has little or nothing to do with earlier novels and romances, and thus it did not develop out of Italian, Spanish, or French precursors. Instead, the modern English novel is said to derive from distinctly English discourses. This thesis not only narrows the field of cultural study, it also refocuses the question of the novel's origins through a national lens, so that it becomes: *what are the English origins of the English novel?* This question confirms the disciplinary coordinates of the English studies within which it is framed: the answers it finds are guaranteed in advance to emerge from within the study of British culture. By narrowing the vortex of the novel's formation, a nationalist British literary history produces a new object of cultural value now dubbed "the English novel." This then becomes the subject and eponymous protagonist in a series of literary histories, by Raleigh (1894), George Saintsbury (1913), and Walter Allen (1954), all entitled *The English Novel*. It also occurs within other titles, including William Lyons Phelphs' *Advance of the English Novel* (1916), Ernest Baker's ten-volume *History of the English Novel* (1924–1939), and Arnold Kettle's *Introduction to the English Novel* (1951). Within these literary histories, Richardson, Fielding, Smollett, and Sterne become the "dream team" of eighteenth-century fiction. After the revival of interest in Defoe at the beginning of this century, he is added as a fifth early master of the English novel. By the time Ernest Baker sets about writing his monumental work, the self-evident identity and value of the English novel justifies a "glance at pre-existing works," not only within English prose fiction, but also at those in foreign languages and literatures. Far from putting anything into question, the many foreign and domestic influences Baker traces for novels written in Britain merely lend support to what his volumes labor to secure—the distinctness of the "English novel."

With Ian Watt's *Rise of the Novel: Studies in Defoe, Richardson, and Fielding* (1957), the modifier "English" is implied but erased. Now the rise of the English novel, as read through the three authors whose names follow the colon in Watt's title, is said to accomplish the rise of "the" novel, that is, *all* novels. Just as the moralizing of the novel allows it to appear distinctively English, so the later nationalization of the novel written in

English allows "the English novel" to become a vehicle for more than a national subject. Within British literature, Watt's concept of "formal realism" becomes the general vehicle for modern subjectivity per se. In this way, a national literary history overcomes what had always worried the earliest promoters and elevators of the novel in Britain: the belatedness and indebtedness of English fiction. Watt's rise of the novel thesis, through its muted but implicit presumption of British priority in the development of "the" novel, underwrites the Anglocentrism of English literary studies while it seems to skirt it. In order to understand this presumption of the priority of the English novel, it is necessary to understand one more component of the novel's genealogy: its supposed realism.

THE NOVEL'S REALIST CLAIMS

Novels that are, at their simplest level, lively stories about people who never existed, have no necessary relation to moral life or national identity. The articulations between novels and morality and novels and nationhood are the contingent effect of the institutionalization of the novel this chapter has described. These articulations both lend support to and are grounded in a third, equally contingent connection—that between the "novel" and "real life." The idea that the novel effects a particularly compelling imitation of "real life" is as old as seventeenth-century critical claims on behalf of the novella against the romance. Similar claims were made on behalf of the anti-romance of Cervantes. But since the eighteenth century, the claim to represent "real" life and manners has never been merely descriptive; it has also been normative. To represent "real" life is to attain a more valuable species of writing. Making this claim on behalf of the novel and against romance was a way in which critics considered elsewhere in this chapter insert the surpassing of the old romance, with its fabulous elements and its extravagant codes of honor, into an enlightened movement toward a rational modern taste in entertainment.

Any systematic effort to deal with the many theoretical and historical horizons of realism is beyond the scope of this study. My concern is to understand how the realist claim so frequently made for novels operates as a third criterion for defining the novel and rationalizing its rise. Ever since critics and novelists have been making the "realist" claim for the novel, there have been compelling reasons for critical skepticism. First, any claim that the novel re-presents the real runs up against a systematic obstacle arising from its linguistic medium. No text, be it history, science, or fiction, once transported from the space or time of its production, and no matter how earnest its aspirations to facticity or truth, can bear a mark in its own language that verifies its relation to something outside itself. In short, there are no markers to distinguish a representation of the actual and its simulation (W. Warner, "Realist Literary History"). As a result, those who tender the novel's realist claims often augment unverifiable assertions with testimonials of belief and taunting mockeries of "unreal" writing—the early favorite for this treatment being romance. Typical in this regard is Francis Coventry on Fielding: "[*Joseph Andrews*] was not mere dry narrative, but a lively representative of real life. For crystal Palaces and winged Horses, we find homely cots and ambling nags; and instead of impossibility, what we experience every day" (16). In an oft-quoted celebration of the novel's mimetic powers, Hazlitt concedes poetry's affinity with "the divine," but claims novel's closer ties to "humanity":

> We find [in the novel] a close imitation of men and manners; we see the very web and texture of society as it really exists, and as we meet with it when we come into the world. If poetry has "something more divine in it," this savors more of humanity. We are acquainted with the motives and characters of mankind, imbibe our notions of vice and virtue from practical examples, and are taught knowledge of the world, through the airy medium of romance.
>
> ["English Comic Writers," 106]

In this passage the comforting repetition of the pronoun "we" and the use of intensifiers—novels offer a "close" imitation of men, society as it "really" exists comes through its "very" web and texture—suggests what Hazlitt's testimonial style only implies: the unverifiability of the novel's claim to teach "knowledge of the world."

The tenuousness of the novel's realist claim is evident from the wide historical vacillations in accepted critical wisdom as to what constitutes the most truthful representation of "real" life. When the novel's function as a guide to moral life is given greatest weight, as in the late-eighteenth-century debate about novel reading, then Richardson's oft-celebrated "writing to the moment" and his ability to take us into the "inmost reaches of the heart" led many critics to give him the surest claim to having represented "real life." By contrast, Fielding is valued by many critics not for his realism but for the wonderfully artful unity of his plot. But when Romantic critics such as Scott and Hazlitt bring to the fore the novel's powers to accomplish social description of the nation, the realist claim is tendered on Fielding's behalf. The nineteenth-century fascination with the idea of society as an organic totality made the novel seem uniquely appropriate for the study and analysis of society. This underlies the realist claims made for the novels of Dickens and George Eliot. While twentieth-century critics of Fielding often read his novels as highly artificial constructions of rhetoric, as late as the second decade of this century, George Saintsbury was insisting upon the essential "artificiality" of Richardson's *Pamela* and then describing Fielding's *Joseph Andrews* in these terms: "These are all real people who do real things in a real way now, as they did nearly two hundred years ago; . . . And we are told of their doings in a real way, too" (102–103). The context of these lines from Saintsbury does not elucidate what these four uses of the word "real" mean; instead its circular, tautological reiteration aims to give the word itself talismanic force; that the people and things in *Joseph Andrews* are as "real" "now" as they were two hundred years ago is a judgment the critic's reader must take on faith.

Why the insistence on the novel's realist claims? Derrida's writing suggests why it is that some concept of mimesis becomes inevitable within formulations of the cultural role of novels: a mimetic relation is implicit in the structure of the sign, in every effort at narrative, in the attempt to bring truth into the presence of consciousness through language. Modern media of representation—from the press to Hollywood cinema, from radio to contemporary television—lend support to a concept of representation as old as Western culture. I would describe that credo about realistic representation in this way: that it is possible to develop systems for representing what exists that have an autonomy, self-evidence, and presence to the spectator analogous to that ascribed to life itself; in other words, that it is possible to have representation that is free of rhetoric. How do readers and critics justify claims that a certain use of language refers to that which is not in language (the referent) in a fashion that is more compelling, precise, or "realistic" than other uses of language? As these claims begin to be made in the mid-eighteenth century, there are certain background axioms operating within such a claim. First, this claim does not establish a naively empirical relationship between word and thing, but unfolds within an understanding that the novel has a mediated aesthetic relation to what it represents (McKeon, *Origins of the English Novel*, 118–128). Thus, for example, a dialogue in a tavern is not, whatever its verisimilitude, the same as a transcript of an actual dialogue. Second, there is no criterion within language by which we can judge that one relation to a referent is more realistic than another. Finally, the realist claim is founded upon a judgment made at a particular time among a social network of readers who produce, consume, and criticize.

A pragmatic historical perspective upon the realist claim helps to explain the *lack* of consensus among readers, even within the same epoch, about the realism of the novels of Richardson and Fielding. First, the rhetoric used by each author for selecting language and speech genres for representing and entertaining is fundamentally different. Thus, for example, Richardson can draw from the low everyday forms of the personal journal and familiar letter, while Fielding writes "in the manner of Cervantes" and draws upon the formal codes of epic, mock epic, periodical, and criticism. At the same time, these writers select referents from different regions of the social world—for example, from the rich and the poor, from the upper and lower classes, producing effects of the "high" and the "low," the narrow and the expansive both within and between each author. However, the epistemological bias of theories of realism obscures the way in which shifts in the reader's experience of the realist effect can result from non-epistemological factors such as new topics, elements of fantasy, novel techniques of representation, and so on.

By now it should be apparent why claims to realism are so open to decay and revision. For the readers who experience the "realist effect" of a particular text's alignment of language and referent, the judgment that this or that novel is intrinsically realistic is a pleasing delusion. Because this delusion is often shared by a community of readers, it encourages the critical consolidation of a certain specific form of writing—for example, writing to the moment, formal realism, omniscient narrative, stream of consciousness writing—as a prescribed form for realistic writing. But the repeated use of a particular form for fiction wears away its realist effect, until it appears to be a mechanical formula fiction referring to nothing so much as to itself. In fact, because all the terms of the relation declared to be realistic (rhetorics of representation, selected referents, the realist effect experienced by readers) change over time, it is quite inevitable that novel writing and reading breeds new realisms. The decay of the realist effect of old realisms incites those practices and manifestos that promote a new species of realism. Of course, these shifts operate retroactively upon the existing archive of classic novels, producing changes in the critical judgment as to whether a single text—for example, *Tom Jones*—is realistic or unrealistic.

Because history undermines the naturalness and self-evidence of received modes of representing the real, it has proved difficult to sustain any "realist claim" made by or for a novel. Coventry, Hazlitt, and Saintsbury use the novel's realist claim the same way critics have used it ever since: to distinguish novels from non-novels, and to assess the critical value of different novels, and of their authors. In the nearly three hundred years of novel criticism in English since Congreve, one question—"Is it realistic?"—has served as the most generally accepted criterion of value. But while critics have often sought to regularize novelistic production around the goal of representing real life, readers, and the authors who write for them, have happily indulged periodic returns to romance, with its valuation of the "gothic," fantasy, and the naive pleasures of action and adventure. Thus Horace Walpole set out quite consciously to invent a new kind of "romance" by blending the "imagination and improbability" of old romance with the modern novel's imitation of natural manners and sentiment (see conclusion). Walpole's return to romance is only the first in a series. The early-nineteenth-century romantic novels of Godwin and Shelley develop the entertainment potential of the uncanny double; Scott's historical novels incorporate many elements of the early romances; and there is, in the late nineteenth century, a return by Stevenson and Kipling to stories of naive childhood adventure (Glazener, 369–398). In other words, though some critics and novelists have attempted to hegemonize novels through the concept of "realism," novel readers and writers have never accepted this leadership.

THE ART OF THE NOVEL

In the second half of the nineteenth century, the novel's realism is complicated and enriched by novelists such as Flaubert and James, who aestheticize the novel. While it may seem that such a movement would vitiate the novel's realist claims, in fact it aligns the novel with a critical tradition that goes back to Aristotle, whereby art's power to represent nature is dependent on its acceptance of inherited aesthetic forms and types such as tragedy, epic, and pastoral. While those novelists and critics who contend that the novel is a species of art seldom refer to eighteenth-century texts, their concept of the novel transforms literary histories of its rise. In Henry James' prefaces to the New York edition of his novels, later gathered by R. P. Blackmur into *The Art of the Novel*, and in Percy Lubbock's *Craft of Fiction* (1921), a new demand is made of novels that would accede to the condition of art: they must have "form." Of course, James never applies the concept of form as strictly as Aristotle and Boileau attempted to do for tragedy, or as precisely as literary critics routinely do in the interpretation of poetry. In other words, the novel's "form" is never supposed to disclose it essence. In his criticism of the novel, James uses analogies to drama, painting, and sculpture to make the case for its having a graspable contour, shape, or structure which gives it "form." For James, a novel has "form" if it achieves a unified and economic commingling of plot, character, and idea, although because he is so protective of the novelist's prerogatives, it is often difficult to be sure exactly what he means by the novel's "form." It is clear, however, which novels lack form: those "loose and baggy monsters" that James mocks and Victorian novel readers had been all too ready to indulge.

The successful articulation of the novel and art has several important effects upon the novel's cultural placement by the late nineteenth century. First, a new sophistication and irony attend critical considerations of the novel's realist claims. It is assumed that the novel's claim to realism depends upon its position as a kind of art, and its claim to represent the real unfolds not in opposition to the artificial, but through the illusion-engendering resources of art. The consensus among academic critics of this century that successful realism is grounded in a reciprocal interplay between literary form and mimetic function may be typified by the following sentence from the first page of F. W. J. Hemmings' *Age of Realism* (1971): "[I]n this volume we shall be concerned solely with the specific shape and content that the realist approach gave to the literary forms that seemed most naturally to embody it" (9).

The expectation that the best and most significant novels possess "form" helps transform the literary history of the novel, as well as the imagination of its rise. In the comprehensive literary histories of fiction such as those written by Reeve and Dunlop, the modern novel takes shape gradually, and never loses its affinities with a broad spectrum of earlier works. As long as the novel seemed free of the critical constraints that framed the cultural acceptance of epic, drama, and poetry, and its signal feature was the atavistic pleasures it afforded its readers, literary historians could trace the many interconnections between the modern novel and the romances of earlier epochs; and as long as the moral function or national telos of novelistic writing guided literary histories, the affinities of early English novels with Shakespeare's characters, Chaucer's stories, Cervantes' anti-romance, and the modern French novel seemed plausible and open to exploration. But once the novel's generic identity was understood to depend upon realist claims achieved through a particular form, the arrival of "the" modern novel appeared unheralded, contingent, and unexpected. Its first instance could now be sought. In the first decades of the twentieth century, a new drama comes into heroic enlightenment accounts of the novel's rise out of romance. The emergence of the modern novel comes to be represented as dependent upon an abrupt invention of new and more powerful techniques for representing reality.

In his book *The English Novel* (1916), Saintsbury develops a rather extravagant metaphor to describe the collective cultural labor entailed in perfecting the modern novel. He sees the four English novelists— Richardson, Fielding, Smollett, and Sterne—as constructing for the novel four wheels and a "wain," or undercarriage, indispensable to its forward movement through history: "Thus, in almost exactly the course of a technical generation—from the appearance of *Pamela* in 1740 to that of

Humphry Clinker in 1771—the wain of the novel was solidly built, furnished with four main wheels to move it, and set a-going to travel through the centuries" (132). But each of these novelists are then "found wanting for one reason or another." There is, it turns out, still something missing from novelistic form: "And what we are looking for now is something rather different from this—a masterpiece, or masterpieces, which may not only yield delight and excite admiration in itself or themselves, but may bring forth fruit in others . . . In other words, nobody's work yet—save in the special kinds—had been capable of yielding a novel-*formula;* nobody had hit upon the most capital and fruitful novel-ideas" (190–191). But "time" brings forth two remarkable novelists—Jane Austen and Walter Scott—to provide what is still lacking. These two "provided—for generations, probably for centuries, to come—patterns and principles for whoso would follow in prose fiction" (210). Their acts of formal invention complete the providential design of Saintsbury's literary history. In an analogous fashion, Ernest Baker's ten-volume *History of the English Novel* (1924–1939) attempts to "trace the process of natural selection by which a form evolved combining the two elements" essential to novels: "the interpretation of life" and "fictitious narrative in prose" (III: 5). This form becomes the "type," or prototype, for all the modern novels to follow.

By making "formal realism" the distinctive feature of the modern novel, and the invention necessary for its "rise," Watt's *Rise of the Novel* assumes and extends the arguments for formal invention developed more casually in the earlier literary histories of Saintsbury and Baker. While earlier literary historians had found various reasons to give Richardson and Fielding priority as the first real British novelists, the idea of the novel as a technical invention embedded in the literary histories of Saintsbury, Baker, and Watt gives a radical new sense, and ascent, to Richardson's programmatic claim to have written a "new species of writing," and to the proprietary authority Fielding would exercise over his "new province of writing." That literary historians of our century would have granted to Richardson and/or Fielding what few conceded them in the eighteenth century—patent rights to the invention of the novel—is one of the striking ironies of the novel's progress.[9]

9. In his *Idea of the Novel in Europe, 1600–1800,* Ioan Williams would revise Watt's thesis. By interweaving French and English developments, and showing how the critique of romance in the French seventeenth century anticipates later defenses of the novel over romance in the English eighteenth century, Williams argues not the "development of a new form but the evolution of an existing one."

The wide influence of *The Rise of the Novel* results in part from the way in which Watt adds an important new dimension to the story of the novel's rise, by updating its realist claim. By aligning Richardson's "writing to the moment" with the distinctly modern turn toward a rendering of private experience and subjectivity intensities, Watt redefines the object of novelistic mimesis from the social surface to the psychological interior. Watt's argument ends up redefining "the novel"—and the "formal realism" it is built upon—so as to revalue Richardson at Fielding's expense. How and why does the novel shift the terrain of its realist claims from the social surface to the ineluctable psychological interior? My speculation is that by the turn of the twentieth century, novelistic writing is but one of several kinds of representation within culture claiming to represent reality. Over the last decades of the nineteenth century and the first decades of this century, photography and cinema co-opt the sort of social description and precise verisimilitude of the visible surface central to nineteenth-century realism.[10] To sustain its realist claims, novel writers locate a more obscure object—one inaccessible to the camera lens—by turning inward. Now the most advanced novels—those, for example, of Joyce, Proust, Woolf, and Faulkner—are claimed by critics to effect a mimesis of the inner consciousness. The old aesthetic demand that art have a certain "form" receives a technological spin in the invention of what is supposed to be a narrative of "stream of consciousness." Just as the new media of photography and the phonograph and their merger into cinema enable a new set of realist claims to be tendered, so the novel is reinterpreted as the medium uniquely suited to representing the inner life. Within Watt's literary history, Richardson's "writing to the moment" can be revalued as the early modern precursor of the stream-of-consciousness writing attributed to some late modern novelists.

THE VORTEX MIS-SEEN AS AN ORIGIN

The three episodes I have traced in this chapter—the debate about the effects of novel reading, the nationalization of the novel, and the development of the novel's realist claims—suggest the way in which antagonistic historical strife becomes sedimented in one complex, ambivalent cultural object: "the novel." But discussing these episodes sequentially has

---

10. While nineteenth-century novels of the first quality are usually adorned with illustrations, twentieth-century novels usually are not. This suggests more evidence for a shift of twentieth-century novelistic representation away from attempts at visualization.

produced a distortion; in fact, all three are entangled and related. In order for the novel's moral effects to be taken seriously, it has to represent character truthfully; the idea that novels represent the social is a precondition for its nationalization; and both improving and nationalizing readers enhance the novel's realist claims. These three aspects of the novel's institution become the minimal criteria for identifying novels and for distinguishing them from "mere" fiction. Finally, this history—of improving novels, building nations, and articulating fiction with knowledge—becomes sedimented, and forgotten, as it functions within the novel as self-evident cultural object (Laclau, *New Reflections,* 34–35).

My genealogy of the novel's rise foregrounds the role of literary history in effacing differences active in the history of culture. By developing an elaborate analogy between fiction-making and gardening, Dunlop's literary history spatializes time, so the successive conflicts of the often-antagonistic types of fiction written in Britain over the course of a century are arranged to appear as one harmoniously balanced array of species which can be surveyed in the same way as, in one leisured stroll, one surveys a garden. However, it proves as implausible to have a literary history without an active literary historian as it is to have a garden without an energetic gardener. It is the evaluative role of the literary historian—in holding the scales over each text within a synchronic moment of judgment—that enables the narrative of the progress or history of romance, novel, and fiction to be told. Then the *way* that story is told has a feedback effect: which writers are included and excluded, brought into the foreground, cast into the shade, or weeded away determines what kinds of writing and authorship will come to count as a "tradition" that grounds subsequent value judgments. This is the ironic culmination of literary history. Literary history can easily become tautological and self-confirming, a garden wall to protect specimens collected against the very factors—history, change, difference—that a critical literary history might have interpreted.

Like a garden or museum collection, literary history turns the strife of history into a repertoire of forms. It does so by taking differences that may have motivated the writing or reading of novels within specific historical contexts—differences of religion, politics, class, gender, social propriety, race, or ethical design—and converting them into differences of a literary kind. Thus, for example, the polemic between Richardson and Fielding about the sorts of narrative and character that fiction should possess becomes deposited, within literary history, as two species of novel: the Richardson novel of psychology and sentiment, and the Fielding novel of social panorama and critique. The novels of amorous intrigue written by

Behn, Manley, and the early Haywood have an unclassifiable difference which puts them entirely outside the frame of literary history of the (elevated) novel.

Here is a way to describe the difference between a cultural and a literary history of the early novel. If we interpret the writings of Behn, Manley, and Haywood, and of Richardson and Fielding, as part of the cultural history of Britain, we would find complex patterns of antagonism and the later authors' conscious and unconscious efforts to distinguish their writing from that of their antecedents. This book charts these antagonisms, as they find expression, for example, in the differences between Behn's *Love Letters* and Richardson's *Pamela*. By contrast, literary history "finds," upon the archival table of its investigations, different novels which it then attempts to distinguish and classify. Differences among novels are no longer effects of history, but instead are the initial data for literary classification. Within its classificatory operation, the category "novel" acquires a paradoxical role: pre-given and yet belated in its arrival, "the novel" is made to appear ready at hand to the literary historian, but it is actually that which the literary history of the novel defines. Often presented as the humble, minimal, and preliminary axiom of a literary history, the idea of the novel as ethical, national, and realistic operates within the literary history of canonical texts as a kind of Law.

How is the eclipse of the influential strain of fiction written by Behn, Manley, and the early Haywood to be understood? Dunlop's dismissal of these three novelists from his history confirms a judgment that critics of the early amorous novel had been making since the 1730s. This negative judgment might be attributed to changes in sensibility, taste, or style, or to the idea that a certain formula has exhausted its appeal. But these words merely re-label rather than explain the cultural change we are trying to interpret. It is no doubt correct to argue that Behn's novels of amorous intrigue are an integral expression of the culture of the Restoration, characterized by the zeal for sexual license exhibited by the court of Charles II, its reaction against the dour asceticism of the Commonwealth, and its enthusiastic translation of French cultural forms. Such an historical placement of the early novel allows one to align its passing with the reaction, after 1688, against the excesses of the Restoration. Pleasures disowned become discomforting and, through embarrassment, a kind of unpleasure. But this fails to explain the popularity of the novels of amorous intrigue written after 1688 by Manley and Haywood. Some feminist literary historians have attributed the devaluation of Behn, Manley, and Haywood to their gender. However, the same critics who condemn this notorious trio applaud the moral improvement of the novel of amorous intrigue under-taken before Richardson by Jane Barker and Penelope Aubin. Explanations based on taste, political history, and gender fail to come to terms with the particular way in which the novels of Behn, Manley, and Haywood were devalued and overwritten in the 1740s.

The erasure or forgetting of earlier cultural formations is an obscure process. Unlike the latest clothing, cultural forms do not become entirely "used up." Cultural forms—from letters and love stories to national con-stitutions—can receive rejuvenating splices from sources as various as new technology, foreign transplants, and political strife. In other words, recy-cling seems to be the rule rather than the exception in culture. Thus, for example, the novel of amorous intrigue, developed in the late Restoration by Behn under the strong influence of the continental novella and the aris-tocratic literature of love, is exploited for politically motivated scandal and satire by Delariviere Manley in the *New Atalantis* (1709). Then, following the spectacular success of *Love in Excess* (1719–1720), this species of novel is turned into repeatable "formula fiction" on the market by Eliza Haywood in the 1720s. To remove elements from culture one needs to understand "forgetting" as, in Nietzsche's words, "an active and in the strictest sense positive faculty of repression" (*Genealogy of Morals*, II: 493). The incor-poration of the novel of amorous intrigue within the elevated novel of the 1740s—in, for example, *Pamela, Joseph Andrews, Clarissa,* and *Tom Jones*—is one of the means by which old pleasures are disowned and forgotten. In their novels of the 1740s, Richardson and Fielding promote this "forget-ting," first by defacing the novel of amorous intrigue, and then by provid-ing their own novels as replacements for novels they characterize as degraded and immoral. These new novels overwrite—by disavowing but appropriating, tossing out but recycling—the novels they spurn.

Reeve and Dunlop do not commit their literary histories to exercising a "good memory." Unlike certain late-twentieth-century counterhegemonic literary histories—whether feminist, African-American, or gay and les-bian—they do *not* set out to counteract a biased cultural memory. Reeve and Dunlop are, like most literary historians who follow them, constrained by the protocols of a culturally elevating literary history to be critical and selective, and thus forgetful. In the introduction to *The Progress of Romance*, Reeve tells her readers she seeks "to assist according to my best judgment, the readers choice, amidst the almost infinite variety it affords, in a selection of such as are most worthy of a place in the libraries of read-ers of every class, who seek either for information or entertainment" (iv). While Behn's novels are given cursory treatment in these two literary histories, the novels of Richardson and Fielding are given the positions of special priority they would retain in all subsequent accounts of the novel's rise. The success of the elevated novel in the 1740s—its appearance in culture as the only novel worthy of reading, of cultural attention, and of detailed literary history—pushes the early novels of Behn, Manley, and Haywood into the margins of literary histories, where they nonetheless never quite disappear, but serve instead as an abject trace or degraded "other" needed to secure the identity of the "real" (that is, legitimate) novel.

Starting with Reeve, a scholarly literary history develops a paradoxical relationship to the forgotten texts of the past. It retrieves from the archive and reads again what its contemporary culture has almost completely forgotten. This activity pushes Reeve toward a certain regret about the shifts in cultural value that can appear quite arbitrary to one who has looked long enough down the "stream of time":

> Romances have for many ages past been read and admired, lately it has been the fashion to decry and ridicule them; but to an unprejudiced person, this will prove nothing but the variations of times, manners, and opinions.—Writers of all denominations,—Princes and Priests,—Bishops and Heroes,—have their day, and then are out of date.—Sometimes indeed a work of intrinsic merit will revive, and renew its claim to immortality: but this happiness falls to the lot of few, in comparison of those who roll down the stream of time, and fall into the gulph of oblivion. [105]

Reeve finds two ways to naturalize the process of disappearance and forgetting she regrets. The first of these is through reference to the wheel of fortune that gives "princes and priests, bishops and heroes" "their day," then takes it away; the second is by using a metaphor, characterizing the movement of a "work of merit" down "the stream of time" into "the gulph of oblivion." While conveying the violence of cultural memory, these analogies, by producing a poetic sense of inevitability, also obscure the cultural strife at work within shifts in cultural memory. Thus for example, the differences of gender, politics, and class, which cast some down into "oblivion" while raising others up into prominence, are conducted through the literary histories that translate them for a later age. Though literary historians attempt to be "unprejudiced" (according to Reeve), embrace an ethos of "judgment, candor, and impartiality" (in Coventry's words), and invoke general moral or aesthetic grounds for critical judgment, they do not overcome the remorseless decisions of cultural history, but instead reflect them.

Since one of the meanings of "gulf" is a "whirlpool, or absorbing eddy" [*Oxford English Dictionary*], I can accommodate my thesis about the novel's rise to Reeve's metaphor: the elevation of the new novel of Richardson and Fielding over the old novel of amorous intrigue produces a vortex or whirlpool within the land(sea)scape of eighteenth-century British culture. Where one kind of reading is thrown up, another is thrown down; where one kind of pleasure is licensed, another is discredited. *This turbulent vortex of reciprocal appearance and disappearance is mis-seen as the origin of the novel.* But in order for the elevated novel to appear, the novel of amorous intrigue must be made to disappear into a gulf of oblivion. Thus birth requires a murder and burial.

While this vortex at the (apparent) origin of the (elevated) novel first appears in the cultural strife of the 1740s, it is also readable in subsequent histories of the novel's rise, in which Behn almost invariably becomes the abject trace of the effaced "other" novel. For George Saintsbury, Behn's best work, *Oroonoko*, is but "an experiment in the infancy of the novel." For Ernest Baker, although Behn "understood the need for verisimilitude, she never found out how to secure it, never evoked for an instant the illusion of real life" (*History of the English Novel*, III: 99–100).

Given the broad argument of this chapter as to the gradual sedimentation of a certain concept of the novel, it should not be surprising that Behn is disqualified as a real novelist by critics of this century. Her notorious sexual license makes her appear immoral; her indebtedness to the continental novella makes her appear un-English; and she is judged "unrealistic" for two contradictory reasons—while the artful intricacy of her novels of amorous intrigue appears improbable, her secret histories are all too factual. Thus, Baker dismisses *Love-Letters between a Nobleman and his Sister* (1683) as a "fraudulent attempt to exploit contemporary scandal" (III: 83). But Behn is still there: a successful and popular playwright, respected in her own day, buried in Westminster Abbey, and publishing novels nearly six decades before Richardson and Fielding, over three decades before Defoe. She also influences the most popular fiction writers of the next two generations, Delariviere Manley and Eliza Haywood. Consequently, Behn is recruited by later literary historians of the early novel as the exemplary instance of a prose fiction writer who stands on the brink of novel writing, but who fails to write novels. Within the classificatory operation of literary history, her writings are non-novels which help us to locate the first real novels. She provides the most celebrated miscarriages in the annals of pre-novelistic prose fiction. Behn serves—within the literary histories of Reeve, Dunlop, Saintsbury, and Baker—as one who helps us to see, through her negative example, the first real novels.

2 Licensed by the Market

Behn's Love Letters
as Serial Entertainment

BRINGING NOVELISTIC ENTERTAINMENT
TO THE BRITISH MARKET

Long before novels were claimed to be a type of literature, the first novel readers read to be entertained. By entertainment, I mean those recurrent social practices members of a culture use to divert and amuse themselves and one another. Entertainment, in this relatively modern sense, often entails representation. Thus, for example, oral storytelling and dramatic performance were two of the earliest forms of entertainment, and both have been described as precursors of novels. Anthropologists have argued that cultures use narrative to make sense of nature and history, and to articulate values. In literary studies, it is assumed that the representation of life and manners provided by novels tells us something crucial about the culture that consumes them. Why is this so? Because narrative entertainment that is "held among" participants (the word "entertainment" comes from the French verb *entretenir*, "to hold among") "takes hold" of those who entertain them. In the decisive but enigmatic exchange between the entertainment and the entertained, desire is engaged. Do entertainments gratify preexisting needs, or do they incite new desires? Do they support or challenge social order? Should they describe ordinary life, or offer access to enchanting alternative realities? These questions are taken up repeatedly by those who would reform, defend, or inflect entertainment. The discourse that results from these polemics invariably evidences the cultural unease with entertainment. Plato is one of the earliest of cultural critics to worry that entertaining stories, by their very power to absorb those they entertain, menace the rational and moral grounds of culture. Thus, in the *Republic*, he condemns the loss of self-control encouraged by many passages from Homer, and warns that the wise ruler must exercise "a censorship over our storymakers" (*Collected Dialogues*, 624).

The most basic forms of culture demand a massive instinctual renunciation. In order to avoid uncontrolled sexual rivalry, societies are formed around the taboo on incest (Freud, *Totem and Taboo*); in order to acquire the "right to make promises," humans must acquire the sense of guilt necessary to make themselves self-consistent (Nietzsche, *Genealogy of Morals*, II: 1–2); and finally, the greatest achievements in art and science may require the sublimation of desire (Freud, *Civilization and Its Discontents*). The repression that is the condition of the possibility of culture not only explains the allure of and resistance to entertainment; it also accounts for the effect of deflection that is most characteristic of entertainment. In order to please, entertainment *diverts* its consumers away from the ordinary. Through their free assent to the rule-bound space that produces what Huizinga calls the "magic circle of play," the entertained win, for the duration of the entertainment, a reprieve from the inhibitions of culture. But entertainment never constitutes an utterly different world; instead, it sustains an oblique relation to the culture it entertains.

Like all entertainers, Aphra Behn was obliged to compromise with her culture's ambivalence toward entertainment. In *Love Letters*, Behn promotes a liberation of the reader's desire by allowing her characters to transgress the law that binds subjects into culture. But far from offering purely escapist amusement, her first novel also reasserts the necessity of that law. Behn's crucial role in the history of the early novel does not derive from her being the first novelist, or even from her being the first woman novelist. However, more than any other writer, Behn was responsible for bringing the novel to the British market. Her ability to play this pivotal role has less to do with her literary talents than with her effective exploitation of three convergent factors, involving: (1) a shift in media, whereby the decline of the British theater made the print market the most promising venue for earning money; (2) the new currency of a genre, with the recent success of the short continental novel demonstrating its potential as a form of entertainment; and (3) the spectacle of sexual and political scandal, the elopement of Henrietta Berkeley, a member of a prominent Tory family, with her brother-in-law, Ford, Lord Grey of Werke, a leading supporter of the Duke of Monmouth, offering Behn a way to contribute, during the height of the succession crisis, to the propaganda campaign on behalf of Charles II.

Starting in 1682, several factors push Behn away from writing for the theater and toward the market in printed books. The decline of royal patronage and the decrease in new productions leads in that year to the union of the two officially sanctioned Restoration companies (those of the king's theater and those of the duke's theater). An intensification of the succession crisis means that, as a dedicated party writer, Behn finds the theater closed to her (Backscheider, *Spectacular Politics*, 106). Behn's movement from the theater to novel writing charts a path followed by later entertainers, such as Manley, Haywood, and Fielding. By moving from the concentrated spectacle of the theater to the diffuse spectacle of the printed book, Behn can elude the censure directed at her plays. Even before the lapse of the Licensing Act in 1695, many factors, from the stubborn non-compliance of the book trade to the unreliability of juries, limit Charles II's Licenser, Roger L'Estrange, from exercising the full control of the press he seeks (Feather, 52–55). The title page of the first installment of *Love Letters* obscures the identity of both its author and bookseller (Behn, *Love Letters*, x). Finally, by writing novels, Behn exploits the broad trends that make book reading an increasingly important form of entertainment. The expense of the earliest printed books means that only the most prestigious discourses of culture (for example, those of religion, law, and science) are printed. However, over the course of the sixteenth and seventeenth centuries, the decline in printing costs, together with the expansion of both literacy and the infrastructure supporting the circulation of printed books (the Post, the turnpike, magazines), encourages the emergence of printed books as a form of entertainment (see chapter 4).

In writing *Love Letters* as a novel, Behn turns to a form of writing whose flexibility and popularity had only recently become evident. Because of the novel's long history in European writing, its sheer plurality, and the amorphous ductility peculiar to novels, it is impossible to define the novel in any definitive way. However, I offer this minimal definition: the novel is short in length (compared with romance), it is written in prose rather than poetry, it usually takes sex and/or love as its topic, and it quite frequently tells a story of contemporary life, rather than of some earlier, ancient or legendary era. When compared with the epic, drama, and romance, the novel has, by the mid-seventeenth century, a rather modest cultural position, and is relatively untheorized by critical discourse.[1] By utilizing this

---

1. Two qualifications must be made to this definition: first, novels may be versified, and verse translations of Ovid were routinely considered novels; second, sometimes the stories in novels are as remote in time and space, and as idealized in manner and sentiment, as romances. For an account of the European novel in the seventeenth and eighteenth centuries, see Williams' *Idea of the Novel in Europe*; while referring backward to Boccaccio (the *Decameron*) as the most influential

minimalist definition of the continental novel, one can stay open to the different roles the novel assumes at different historical junctures.

During the seventeenth century, France functions for England as a kind of Hollywood for prose fiction. It sets the standards of taste, develops the new subgenres, advances the theoretical debates, and dominates novel publication with sheer numbers.[2] Three French novels published in the decade before Behn turned to novel-writing provide paradigms for her translation of notorious contemporary scandal—both amorous and political—into the novel. These novels are: Lafayette's *Princess of Monpensier* (French version, 1662; English version, 1666) and *Princess of Clèves* (French version, 1678; English version,1679), as well as the spectacularly successful anonymous *Les Lettres Portugaises* (French version, 1669; English version, 1678, as *Five Love-Letters from a Nun to a Cavalier* [translated by Roger L'Estrange]). While Lafayette carries the representation of refined manners and exalted love to new levels of verisimilitude, *Les Lettres Portugaises* helps produce a mode of representing the passions that seem concise, vivid, extreme, and "natural" by comparison with the heroic romances in vogue in the previous generation (Ballaster, *Seductive Forms*, 63). By giving an empirical inflection to the continental novel (Misch, *Restoration Prose Fiction*, vii–xiii; McKeon, *Origins of the English Novel*), British writers of the Restoration make novels still more effective vehicles for writing precisely targeted secret histories.

By beginning my cultural history of the early British novel with Behn, I am not claiming that she is "the first real English novelist." After demonstrating in the previous chapter how loaded and tendentious it becomes to ask what the first real novel is, I will not be attempting to enhance the authority of that cultural icon. Having cast suspicion upon the idea of an

---

modern practitioner of novel writing, Williams offers a survey of the Spanish novellas, such as those of Cervantes (*The Exemplary Novels*), and also covers the dizzyingly broad scope of French seventeenth-century practice, which includes the most influential novels of the period—those of Scarron and Lafayette, and *Letters from a Portuguese Nun to a Cavalier*. For a more fastidiously English account of the early novel, see Paul Salzman's *English Prose Fiction*. For a recent, much more expansive history of "the novel," comprising all romances and novels back to the ancient Greek and Latin romances, see Margaret Anne Doody's *True Story of the Novel*.

2. Thus Salzman notes that of 450 new works published in England during the seventeenth century, 213 were translations, and 164 of these were originally French. When one considers that some of the English nontranslations were patent rip-offs of French novels, the magnitude of the influence of French models becomes impressive, and after 1660 is only increasing.

inseminating paternal source for the novel's rise, I will refrain from designating a maternal matrix for the novel's birth. There are two problems with
such a casting of Behn. The first is a general one: By taking one enlightenment narrative—the rise of the novel as the literary and cultural vehicle for
mediating the middle-class subject's coming into its own—and translating
it into another—the novel as an instrument of woman's recognition of herself as subject free of tutelage under men—the rise of the novel narrative
persists in modified form within several recent feminist literary histories.
Thus, Jane Spencer's *Rise of the Woman Novelist: From Aphra Behn to
Jane Austen* assumes that a novelist such as Behn must be interpreted in
relation to a horizon of development that will properly arrive at "the
English novel," as characterized by moral seriousness, national identity,
and realist technology.[3] The second problem with casting Behn as the
mother of the English novel arises from her particular qualities. In her pioneering essay "Aphra Behn's *Love Letters*, The Canon, and Women's
Tastes," Judith Kegan Gardiner demonstrates why both progressive Whig
literary histories of the novel's rise and feminist histories of the rise of
women writers have problems accommodating their histories to the inces-
sant sex, the occasional sexism, and the consistent Toryism of Behn's writing. Rather than putting Behn forward as the first English novelist, or the
first woman novelist, Ros Ballaster demonstrates the thesis that Gardiner's
essay only suggests—that Behn's novels of the 1680s translate into an
English vernacular a well-developed tradition of French, Spanish, and
Italian novel-writing. The scholarship of Ballaster, Salzman, and Williams
puts to rest the thesis carefully cultivated within the rise of the novel tradition: that the continental novel had little importance or popularity in
England, and that it should therefore not be considered an influence upon
the canonical novels of Defoe, Richardson, and Fielding.[4]

3. For other critics making this claim for Behn, see Gardiner, "The First English
Novel," 217; Zimbardo, "Aphra Behn"; and Duffy's introduction to *Love Letters*,
viii.

4. For another critic's provocative approach to resisting the designation of "the
first real novel," see Doody, *True Story*. Doody demonstrates the indebtedness of
European romances and novels to the ancient Greek and Roman novel. By docu-
menting the scope and significance of ancient novels and the history of their publication and reception from the middle ages to the eighteenth century, she makes a
strong case for considering these novels as an integral part of the print-media culture of the eighteenth century. Like Doody, I am using the term "novel" in such a
way as to enlarge the textual field for the study of novels. The premises and procedures of my study, however, depart from Doody's in two ways. First, my reading
of the rise of the novel thesis develops its symptomatic significance within Western modernity in two ways—as part of the Enlightenment's own account of its

POLITICAL LOYALTY THROUGH LOVE?

In publishing *Love Letters* in three novella-length parts between 1684 and 1687, Behn rearticulates prose narratives of love so as to grapple with the political crisis that threatens her culture. Against those who would subject monarchical succession to the authority of Parliament, in the name of English liberty and the rights of citizens, Behn's novel develops a royalist defense of not just one king—Charles II, then James II—but of the institution of kingship. Yet, against the practice of arranged marriages which subordinates the desire of children to the interest of families, *Love Letters* argues on behalf of "marriage for love." But *Love Letters* does more than restrain political license or promote erotic freedom. At a time when reading print narratives became the prerogative of ever greater numbers of people, Behn's novels of the 1680s do what popular print culture on the market has done ever since: they legitimize the desires of readers, by gratifying them.

By attempting to reconcile erotic license with loyalty to the monarchy, Behn emerges as one of the central mythographers of Restoration monarchy. King Charles II's libertinage, which makes his personal pleasure a very visible part of his reign, means that it is increasingly difficult over the course of his reign to represent him as an exemplary king or father, even in the most restricted and practical sense of his having provided an heir to secure a stable Stuart succession. The succession crisis refers to the struggle between Parliament and Charles II to determine whether the succession should be by strict descent through the Stuart line or by parliamentary des-

---

surpassing of an earlier benighted belief in myth and superstition, and as a component of the institution of literary studies, with "the" novel as one of its privileged objects of study. For this reason, I am as interested in the origins and utility of the rise of the novel thesis as I am in the fact that its erasures have produced blindnesses (for example, about the early centrality of novels written by women). In short, Doody is too quick to dismiss the rise of the novel thesis as a simple error resulting from an Occidental bias against a genre with an Oriental pedigree, the ancient novel. Second, because I am more interested than Doody is in the phenomenon of cultural change—evident, for instance, in the onset of media culture or the institution of "the" novel as a form of literature—my method seeks to highlight the differences as well as the continuities between, for example, Behn's first novel *Love Letters* and Richardson's *Clarissa*. By contrast, the final section of Doody's study, entitled "Tropes of the Novel," describes those tropes or archetypes (such as "Breaking and Entering," "Tomb, Cave, and Labyrinth," and "The Goddess") common to ancient and modern novels. In this way, Doody's readings help to give "the Novel" a quasi-religious, transhistorical, mythopoetic agency in culture.

ignation to assure a Protestant, as the only guarantee of "English liberty." The rhythms of this decade-long crisis put the authority of the monarchy in play. During this period, the nation finds itself between monarchy and democracy, no longer secure in the first and not yet arrived at the second. This chronically divided country betrays a fundamental ambivalence about the proper locus of political power and engages a version of the "fort/da" game Freud describes in *Beyond the Pleasure Principle*: it says to its kings, first, "go away" (1649), then, "no, come back" (1660), then, "no, go away" (1688). Such a vacillation makes it increasingly difficult to assert the naturalness of a single political arrangement and exposes the way any alignment of power is historically contingent and arbitrary. Because these political antagonists use mere words, images, and ceremonies to uphold or challenge monarchy (Backscheider, *Spectacular Politics*), this cultural struggle has the effect of exposing the spacey groundlessness of political authority.

In the dedication to part II of *Love Letters* (1684), Behn is most explicit about her design: Thomas Condon, the young member of a prominent royalist family, can only realize his full loyalty to the king by becoming an impassioned lover, and he can best do this by reading the novel she dedicates to him. Given the way Behn's story of Silvia and Philander will demonstrate the political danger of a transgressive love, why does she tell her young dedicatee to achieve political loyalty through erotic love? After the manifold proscriptions and interdictions of the Commonwealth, the Stuart monarchy seeks a certain liberation of desire. The Tory cultural mythographers, Behn prominent among them, seek to sustain a politically correct and personally satisfying synthesis of desire and loyalty, pleasure and royalism. This synthesis may be seen working in the public persona of the first earl of Rochester and in Behn's most successful play, *The Rover; or, the Banished Cavaliers* (1677). Yet the central action of the *Love Letters*—the seduction of the royalist Silvia by the rebel Philander—suggests the problem with this celebration of license. If desire follows the pathway of transgression of the law, it becomes difficult to imagine how to reconcile desire and loyalty. Behn's dedication seeks to solve this problem by teaching Thomas Condon, a politically exemplary but not very amorous adherent of the Tory cause, that the story of the love affair of a "French Whig" and his Tory sister-in-law can make him a better subject, by making him a more ardent lover.

In the dedication of *Love Letters*, Behn deepens love by developing a contrast: between that love that works only by gazing on dumb pictures, or on the silent charms of the body, and the love that comes from the "intrinsick value" of "wit and good humor"; the latter is "always new" like a

"Book where one turns over a new leaf every minute, and finds something diverting, in eternal new discoveries" (6). Through this comparison, Behn reroutes a superficial momentary desire for beauty—organized around superficial seeing—into a set of amorous exchanges modeled upon reading books and writing letters. Only in this way can love win variety, duration, and interiority.

By expanding the ethical claims for love, Behn articulates love with the highest political virtue: loyalty to the monarch. She closes her dedication with a personal testimonial to the value of love:

> who can be happy without Love? for me, I never numbered those dull days amongst those of my Life, in which I had not my Soul fill'd with that soft passion; to Love! why 'tis the only secret in nature that restores Life, to all the felicities and charms of living; and to me there seems no thing so strange, as to see people walk about, laugh, do the acts of Life, and impertinently trouble the world without knowing anything of that soft, that noble passion. . . . [7]

Behn's dedication suggests that her novel should function as an aphrodisiac. She offers a testimonial for this drug, and prescribes it for Lord Condon, who, she claims, has resisted its attractions too long. Although the text that follows suggests the liabilities of love and why it must inevitably frustrate its pursuers, Behn here represents herself as a confirmed addict, and hopes to "turn on" Condon. In Behn's dedication, the seduction of Thomas Condon as reader becomes co-implicated with a seduction of him into love. This double seduction is supposed to tie all readers into the Tory cause she and Condon champion. However, Behn's text reproduces rather than overcomes the contradiction between libertinism and the institution of political order. The arbitrary voluntarism of her articulation of loyalty and love in this dedication helps to predict, against Behn's intentions, the failure of Silvia's love and England's loyalty in 1688.

The double provenance of *Love Letters*—as a polemical intervention within a political crisis, and as a translation onto the English market of a well-developed species of continental novel—indicates why we should read *Love Letters* in a fundamentally different way from the way we read novels of a literary type. Nothing is more crucial and symptomatic of this text's remoteness from later conceptions of literariness than its serial publication as three separate novels between 1684 and 1687. Behn responds to the popularity of the first part of *Love Letters* by producing two successive sequels to the novel—part II in 1685, with a modified title, *Love Letters from a Nobleman to His Sister: Mixt With the History of their Adventures;* and part III, in 1687, with a new title, *The Amours of Philander and Silvia.*

Because *Love Letters* stays open to the unfolding of an historical crisis and a scandalous affair, each sequel offers the next chapter in an ongoing real-life drama. This publication history helps account for a remarkable fact: conceived as a three-episode series, the three distinct novels that comprise *Love Letters* were read separately by most readers during Behn's lifetime.[5] My reading demonstrates how the seriality of *Love Letters* enables it to function as a prototype for later media culture. So as to grasp the patent differences among the three parts of the novel, I will refer to each part by the key word in its original title that most aptly describes the general tendency of each; thus, for part I (1684), I refer to *Letters*, for part II (1685), *Adventures*, and for part III (1687), *Amours*. I reserve the title *Love Letters* for the assemblage of three parts into one novel.

LOVING TO THE VANISHING POINT OF DESIRE; OR, A RENDEZVOUS WITH THE FATHER

Behn's exaltation of erotic love has scandalized her readers ever since the seventeenth century. Because Philander and Silvia are related by marriage but still choose to act out their love, their story develops extraordinary claims to personal freedom. How can "love" motivate such absolute claims to freedom? If one reads through a good deal of the more or less conventional language with which Philander and Silvia justify an incestuous love, this is what one finds: Philander, and then Silvia, takes the other as being the thing which, if the self could possess it, would bring an incomparable bliss and the greatest freedom from the social law. Silvia and Philander shape this idea of each other into a certain enunciation: there is something about the beloved that is radically singular, and only its possession can fulfill the uniqueness of their own love. Since each lover appears as a necessity to the other, it is hardly surprising that shamelessly little persuasion is needed for Philander to win Silvia to the course of action she already desires. The difficulty of achieving the lovers' imagined bliss within any realized social exchange is evidenced by the novel's most unqualified statement of happiness. After the couple has encountered and overcome all the obstacles presented by Myrtilla, rivals such as Cesario and Foscario, and the

5. No collection of the three novels into one volume is listed in the standard O'Donnel bibliography of Behn until 1694; this 1694 collection is labelled the "second edition" of *Love Letters*. Paula Backscheider has found an advertisement for a collected 1687 *Love Letters*, and one copy in a library at Cambridge. Starting in 1694, each edition of *Love Letters* is a collection of three novels into one volume (with continuous pagination), so each of the three original epistolary dedications is followed by one part of the novel.

crisis posed by Philander's first-night impotence, and after Silvia has arranged a night with Philander that promises unqualified erotic surrender, but before that night actually takes place, Philander writes a letter full of ecstatic expressions of the happiness he imagines. "*Mahomet* never fansied such a heaven, not all his Paradise promis'd such lasting felicity . . . as Silvia . . . Oh, I am wrap't (with bare imagination) with much a vaster pleasure than any other dull appointment can dispence . . . [T]hou sacred dear delight of my fond doating heart, oh, whither wilt thou lead me . . . ?" (86) Philander has only grasped unqualified happiness, prospectively, in the form of an Oriental fantasy, entailing an absolutist possession of the very thing he wants. Philander's way of enunciating his anticipated bliss suggests the impossible temporality of this happiness. He imagines it in the future anterior: not yet come in the present, but imagined as already grasped as experience and thus already in the past.

Silvia and Philander's project is an arduous and radical one: to locate a means to pursue the thing they desire, irrespective of the law against it. Philander's tree markings align his efforts with the pastoral idea of a space and time set apart for clandestine love. In Behn's *Miscellany*, published in 1684, the year after the writing of the *Letters*, there are two poems, "A Voyage to the Island of Love" and "The Golden Age," which echo Philander's idea that some time long ago, there was a "golden age," or far away a place, where erotic freedom appeared natural and innocent. Thus, while awaiting another meeting with Silvia, Philander watches the birds at play, and envies their erotic freedom: "[H]ere's no troublesome Honour, . . . but uncontroul'd they play and sing, and Love; no Parents checking their dear delights, . . . every little Nest is free and open to receive the young fletch't Lover; . . . nor do the generous pair languish in tedious Ceremony, but meeting look, and like, and Love, imbrace with their wingy Arms, and salute with their little opening Bills . . ." (35). Warm, mobile, moist, and open, this is a place of continuous possession, where the lover lies forever on the breast of the beloved and there is no pathos of distance. This "golden age" or place for love is a phantasmatic non-place or u-topia constructed through a removal of fathers, mothers, and the law, an Edenic garden without the tree of the knowledge of good and evil or any divine interdictions. But when Philander strides toward Silvia's garden, to act upon his desire, it turns out he is going toward rather than away from the father he would elude. Like the numberless desiring protagonists in later popular fiction, Philander has a rendezvous with the Law.

As long as the love of Silvia and Philander does not move beyond the stream of love letters that passes between them, their letters seem to serve to license that love, in spite of its violation of the law against incest. However, early in the *Letters*, Philander wins a rendezvous with Silvia, but proves impotent. Here, sex is not sublimated into a union of two souls, nor is it interpreted as a sign of love or merely reduced to comic bawdry. This scene allows the text to evidence the limit that is internal to their love. The external obstacles to Philander and Silvia's sexual pleasure have been overcome, but at the very brink of possession the indispensable support of their pleasure droops. Why is Philander impotent? In her introduction to the Virago edition of *Love Letters*, Maureen Duffy suggests that Philander's unexpected impotence is a signifier of license—Philander is "clapped out" and his impotence is "a tell-tale signal that he is not the true lover" he claims to be. There are, however, several problems with this medico-historical explanation of Philander's impotence. Nowhere in part I of *Love Letters* does Philander say or do anything to indicate that he is anything but extravagantly in love with Silvia. Nor does this impotence recur. In part II, the *Adventures*, Silvia does not get the pox her sister has warned her against, but instead gets pregnant. If we read the impotence scene with care, we can understand Philander's impotence as an index of the complex resistance—at once cultural and psychological—that menaces what we might describe as love's attempt as self-licensing.

In the letter describing the impotence scene, Philander announces that "my Silvia" is "yet" a "Maid," and wonders what "snatcht my (till then) never failing power" (57). Philander's long, anxious, vexed, and breathless letter poses and reposes this question. He wonders if he is "enchanted by some Magick Spell," if "Silvia's beauty" is "too Divine to mix with Mortal Joys." He confesses that he had "some apprehensions of fear of being surpriz'd" during his stay with her, because of the near encounter with her father in the garden, on the way to her apartment. Philander even tries to blame Silvia, who by "every tender touch still added fuel to [his] vigorous Fire," until by her "delay" it "consum'd it self in burning" (59). But all of these explanations are in turn rejected. His analytical faculty in this letter is as powerless as his physical faculties had been in bed: he writes, "I want Philosophy to make this out,"(59) and then simply describes what happened.

The scenes immediately adjacent to the impotence scene help explain the source of Philander's impotence. There are three parts to the letter narrative; the first and third describe Philander's approach to and withdrawal from Silvia's apartment, while the second, central part describes the lovers together, when Philander's impotence interrupts a sequence that seems headed for sexual gratification. Because of its literal description of sex—

with roving hands, avid gazes, arousing moans, and ambiguous resistance—
this is the type of scene that scandalizes later readers, rendering Behn's
novel "unreadable" for two centuries. The scene is written in a rapturous
style that is a prototype of the "purple prose" with which erotic transport
will be described in popular fiction from Haywood to the Harlequin
romances. Philander describes himself as drinking in the sight of Silvia as
she is ready for sex: "I beheld thee extended on a Bed of Roses, in Garments
which, if possible, by their wanton loose negligence and gaiety augmented
thy natural Charms" (58). As their kisses intensify, Silvia enunciates the
"no" to his desires which he construes as a "yes": "Oh, my Philander do
not injure me,—Be sure you press me not to the last joys of Love;—Oh
have a care or I am undone for ever; restrain your roving hands,—Oh
whither would they wander,—My Soul, my joy, my everlasting Charmer,
Oh whither would you go" (58). Silvia's words offer a seventeenth-century
model for those scenes of Hollywood film melodrama in which the heroine
at first resists but then returns the hero's embraces. Not only does Silvia
permit his freedoms, her desire is reciprocal, a fact which brings him to the
height of passion when he recognizes it: "I saw (Yes Silvia not all your Art
and Modesty could hide it) I saw the Ravishing Maid as much inflam'd as
I; she burnt with equal fire, with equal Languishment . . ." (58–59). The
restraint of "Art and Modesty," like Silvia's diaphanous garments, only augments the desirabililty of that which they would veil. But when Philander
tries to possess the thing he desires, he finds "on a sudden all my power was
fled . . . nor all my Love, my vast, my mighty passion, could call my fugitive vigor back again" (59). Philander's libertine ambition has received an
internal check. Then the solitude of the lovers is interrupted by a "noise"
at Silvia's "Chamber door" that "alarmed us."

Philander cannot explain his own impotence because he looks for reasons in the wrong place—in himself, in Silvia, in the scene of their encounter, but not in the garden outside Silvia's apartment. Philander's impotence is provoked by the figure who haunts their love tryst, Silvia's father
and his own father-in-law, whom he encounters first furtively, then more
insistently, on his approach to and withdrawal from Silvia's apartment.
From the description of their first encounter, it is clear that the count has a
competing scenario for the evening. There is a fear-inducing gothic cast to
Philander's account: "coming through the Garden, I saw at the farther end
a man, at least I fancy'd by that light it was a man, who perceiving the
glimps of something approach from the Grove made softly towards me, but
with such caution as if he fear'd to be mistaken in the person, as much as I
was to approach him: and reminding what Melinda told me of an assigna-

tion she had made to Monsieur the Count—Imagin'd it him; nor was I mistaken when I heard his voice calling in low tone—Melinda—At which I mended my pace, and e're he got half way the Garden recover'd the Door, and softly unlocking it, got in unperceiv'd . . ." (58). In its description of the figure as indistinct in both gender and identity, this passage reproduces the anxiety Philander felt at the approaching man, for he only gradually pieces together the fact that it is Silvia's father. That approaching figure is described as Philander's double—just as surely on the prowl in the garden for sex, and as fearful of detection, as he.

On his escape from Silvia's apartment, Philander, disguised as Melinda, is importuned still more aggressively by the count to gratify his desires. In contrast to Philander's distressed narrative, which has circled with obsessive prolixity around the symptom of his impotence, the count hails Philander with the concise address of one who knows how to command: "Now Melinda I see you are a Maid of Honour,—Come retire with me into the Grove where I have a present of a heart and something else to make you, that will be of more advantage to you than that of Alexis . . . [D]o you design I shall take your silence for consent? If so, come my pretty Creature, let us not lose the hour Love has given us . . ." (60). When Philander would resist by declaring, "'I am no whore, sir,'" the count rejoins, "'No, . . . but I can quickly make thee one, I have my Tools about me, Sweet-heart, therefore let's lose no time but fall to work'" (61). Who is this person? He is not simply an oversexed father-in-law, nor a nobleman exercising his prerogatives upon the servants of the house. This father is described in such a way as to give him a phantasmatic force and mythical resonance, as one who should be read as a kin to the primal father Freud describes in *Totem and Taboo*, who controls sexual access to all the women and enjoys a pleasure that is obscene because it is utterly devoid of guilt (Žižek, *Enjoy Your Symptom!* 124–129).

The appearance of this archaic figure has the power to push Philander into a threefold feminization: he is unmanned by his impotence with Silvia; he protectively assumes the disguise of "Melinda's Night Gown and Head Dress" (60); and, finally, he becomes the object of the father's desire. Being disguised as Melinda returns Philander to the garden in precisely the correct garments to play the role of a resisting Melinda within his father[-in-law]'s plans for an evening of pleasure. The words with which he describes his predicament suggest how this figure of the father doubles his own position: "[T]o go had disappointed him worse than I was with thee before; not to go, betray'd me" (61). But it also reverses it, for while, at the crucial instant, "Philander the Young the Brisk and Gay" (57) had all his power vanish, the "brisk old Gentleman" presents Philander/Melinda with all-too-material evidence of his vigor: "with that he clapt fifty Guinnies in a Purse into one hand, and something else that shall be nameless into the other, presents that had both been worth Melinda's acceptance" (61). Philander, the narrative suggests, will have his hands full if he tries to compete with this man.

When Philander crosses into Silvia's garden, he discovers that ambivalently charged obstacle to his bliss, the obscene father, who would control the women for himself. This father is much more than the blocking figure that complicates the career of so many lovers in New Comedy. The father in the garden is a fear-inducing residue of the prehistoric order of pleasure—a potent, manipulative, garden-stalking, money- and penis-wielding figure who has the power to interrupt their bliss. This figure is less a real prehistoric figure than he is a phantasm of culture, circulating in this scene, enunciating the implicit "no" of the Father. Philander's very presence there—as a son-in-law who already has legal access to *one* of his daughters—is a transgression of the law of incest, instituted, Freud hypothesizes in *Totem and Taboo*, by the sons after the murder of the Father. As in the Oedipus story, the aim of desire transgresses the accustomed social limits for legitimate sexuality. The "no" of the Father haunts Philander at the moment of potential erotic success. That Philander can't forget what he'd prefer for the moment to keep outside his affair—the exteriority inside the love chamber, the "extimate" Father-in-and-of-the-Law—means that a certain negativity cannot be unbound or disentangled from the thing desired. For Philander, Silvia suddenly is the site of certain "discontents of culture" (Lacan, *Seminar* VII: 150) resulting from the repression of polymorphous pleasure after the killing of the Father.[6] But Silvia and Philander, as venturesome lovers feeling their own internal law of desire, find themselves at war with the discontents culture would enforce. How is this paternal monster able to enter into Silvia's chamber at the moment of the lovers' bliss, to render Philander impotent? He is partly able to do this because he is more than an empowered sexual rival who has prior claims to control the social-sexual exchanges in his household: he is also an object of identification for Philander. Philander aspires to accede to the sort of erotic mastery and freedom this father displays. Because this father is more than an external social agent, because he also makes demands from *within* Philander and Silvia, he can induce Philander's impotence.

6. See Lacan, *Seminar VII*, on the discontents of culture focused into the "thing" desired in courtly love.

Because the obscene father that balks the lovers' desire in this scene is a phantasmatic object, his character wavers. As Silvia's feelings oscillate between a primordial fear and a more moderate social guilt, her father the count changes his demeanor. Before the impotence scene, Silvia presents her father as a dangerous discoverer of their incestuous love: "being rash, and extreamely jealous," "nothing would inrage him like the discovery of an interview like this . . . when you come by stealth; when he shall find his Son and Virgin Daughter, the Brother and the Sister so retir'd, so entertain'd.—What but death can insue, or what's worse, eternal shame?" (49) But after the father actually discovers their affair, he appears as the benign and good oedipal father, one whose moderate love produces not fear but guilt: "my Father enter'd my Cabinet, but t'was with such a look—as soon inform'd me all was betray'd to him; a while he gaz'd on me with fierceness in his eyes, which so surpriz'd and frighted me, that I, all pale and trembling, threw my self at his feet . . ." (90). What follows is a pathetic scene in which her father, instead of storming, "turn'd into a shower so soft and piercing, I almost died to see it; at last delivering me a paper—'here,' (cried he, with a sigh and trembling interrupted voice) 'read what I cannot tell thee. Oh, Silvia,' cried he, '—thou joy and hope of all my aged years, thou object of my Dotage, how hast thou brought me to the Grave with sorrow?'" (90–91)

In their approach to their rendezvous, Silvia and Philander had seemed to want nothing more than to find a utopian time warp within the historical world for the safe conduct of their love. The conventions of pastoral poetry and courtly love help to justify side-stepping the conventional moral law. These lovers feel sublimely confident of the inner good of what they desire, self-blessed and righteous in moving toward one another. Why? The eruptions of the father's "no"—most weakly in Silvia's last defense of her "honor," then in Philander's disabling impotence as the mark of an archaic paternal curse—suggest how their approach to what they desire has been prestructured as transgression. A secret movement toward the negative has been at work in their incestuous object choice: it is no accident that they are "brother" and "sister," nor that within the garden that was supposed to offer a refuge from paternal authority their father appears. Since the language of interdiction directs pleasure, it is only by going back along the trail of these interdictions that the most complete freedom is realized, and it is only there that the most exquisite pleasure is sited. The utopian place apart is an imaginary idea of unity and bliss secretly founded upon the thing—here figured as the primal father and his "no!"—it only apparently avoids. Through the transgression of the law, the subject turns toward the thing desired as that object acquires a certain thing-like negativity.

MARRIAGES MADE IN HEAVEN

On the way to the thing each desires, Silvia and Philander have "bad dreams": the inopportune appearance of the father, the eruption of rivals, and, after Silvia's flight and Philander's implication in a plot against the king, the menace of the Law, all intercede to separate the lovers. To balk these obstacles, Silvia abandons all for her beloved: "Parents and honour, interest and fame, farewell—I leave you all to follow my Philander" (100). To win their freedom, Silvia flees from home, hides in disguise, and escapes from paternal authority through marriage to Philander's "property," his retainer Briljard; Philander escapes from imprisonment; and they both flee the country. Near the end of the *Letters*, Silvia articulates a remarkably comprehensive claim to freedom in what she herself calls an "invective against Marriage" (112). Silvia's turn toward general social critique is consistent with themes developed in Behn's dramas, in which the young and beautiful brides are "bought" by wasted old city merchants, and powerful families use alliance through marriage to advance declining fortunes. With a bitter irony, Silvia's letter tags these all-too-worldly practices as marriages "made in heaven." But, after discrediting these practices, she ends her letter in a lyrically affirmative key, by conceptualizing the terms with which to legitimize her flight with Philander as a "marriage" heaven truly "designs and means." The subtle rhetorical maneuvers Silvia deploys in this defense of her flight from her family and toward Philander suggest what haunts the radical claim to personal freedom:

> [T]hat's a heavenly match when two Souls toucht with equal passion meet
> (which is but rarely seen)—when willing vows, with serious consideration,
> are weigh'd and made; when a true view is taken of the Soul, when no base
> interest makes the hasty bargain, when no conveniency or design of
> drudge, or slave, shall find it necessary, when equal judgements meet that
> can esteem the blessings they possess, and distinguish the good of eithers
> love, and set a value on each others merits, and where both understand to
> take and pay; who find the beauty of each others minds, and rate 'em as
> they ought, whom not a formal ceremony binds (with which I've nought
> to do; but dully give a cold consenting affirmative) but well considered
> vows from soft inclining hearts, utter'd with love, with joy, with dear
> delight when Heaven is call'd to witness; She is thy Wife, Philander, He
> is my Husband, this is the match, this Heaven designs and means . . .
> [111–112]

If Silvia's critique of the cynical uses of marriage has focused upon the mercenary manipulation of the young by the old, then this passage reconfigures the economy of the marital exchange so that the lovers themselves appear as the only parties to the exchange. Rather than being traded by others, they are at once consumers and products, united by a reciprocal purchase of one another that reconciles rational assessments of intrinsic value with spontaneous feeling. The passage begins by describing the rare condition that makes such a "heavenly match" possible: "when two Souls toucht with equal passion meet." There follow five more "when" clauses describing the thoughtful activities of cognition and assessment that ground a match "when" lovers consider, weigh, take a "true view," esteem and distinguish the "good" in one another. This prepares us for the siting of the action, "where" both "understand to take and pay." This reciprocal purchase has been made by lovers who are bound not by a "formal ceremony" but by "well considered vows from soft inclining hearts, utter'd with love, with joy, with dear delight" within a final modifying condition—"when Heaven is call'd to witness." The whole passage seeks to free the performatives of the marriage ceremony—the reciprocal "I do's" of the participants—from the enabling conditions that give them legal force: a license secured; a legally ordained performer of the ceremony; no "reasons" to prevent marriage; and so on.

We may detect what menaces Silvia's staging of her marriage by taking note of the wording that culminates her general description of "a heavenly match": "She is thy Wife, Philander, He is my Husband." This double enunciation is spoken from a mixed vantage point, one that is both inside ("my") and outside ("she") the reciprocal purchase the passage had seemed to make the necessary and sufficient ground for their marriage. The first part of this clause finesses this absence of a third vantage point by simulating the words of a legally constituted authority for marriages—the words of the minister at the end of the Protestant marriage ceremony: "I pronounce that you are man and wife" (*Book of Common Prayer*, 304). But ending the second clause by describing the "husband" as "my" instead of "your" makes Silvia the enunciator of this crucial sentence. After this declaration of their marriage, the "this" in "this is the match, this heaven designs and means" seems to slide between the general match the passage has described and the more particular match between Silvia and Philander this letter seeks to legitimize. The sudden shift from the general to the particular enables Silvia to elide the particular difficulties that embarrass this marriage: the fact that Silvia and Philander are "brother" and "sister," which makes the arrival of a third standpoint of enunciation, especially of a legally authorized one that is empowered to make the lovers husband and wife, impossible.

Silvia's carefully developed metaphor for their "marriage"—as a simultaneous, reciprocal purchase of each by the other—seems to free the lovers by shifting them from objects to subjects of the transaction. But the surreptitious insertion of the third authorizing position suggests the lack at the heart of this formulation. The rhetorical development by Silvia of the concept of a heavenly, because freely contracted, love is itself an implausible idealization which overwrites the logic of the negative and transgressive that has motivated their desire. The postscript appended to this very letter suggests the continued insistence of the law, breaking into an affair they would sequester and protect: "*since I writ this, I say the House where I am is broken open* with Warrants and Officers for me, . . . it seems they saw me when I went from my lodgings and pursued me; haste to me, for I shall need your Counsel" (112). Neither is Philander free of the problem of the father-in-and-of-the-Law. He writes to Silvia from the Bastille, telling her that "I am arrested at the suit of Monsieur the Count, your Father, for a Rape on my lovely Maid" (107). After solving the problem of the father's suit to repossess his daughter through Silvia's marriage to Briljard, Philander is arrested for his part in the novel's version of the Rye House plot of 1683, and writes that he "may fall a sacrifice to the anger of an incens'd Monarch" (114). Within the political allegory the *Letters* elaborates, the love of Silvia and Philander, in spite of all its pastorale excess, is proffered as a regulative model for a people's loyalty to a monarch: love and loyalty are conferred not with a "cold consenting affirmative" but with "well considered vows . . . uttered . . . with dear delight." It is not until the sequels to the *Letters* that the reader is confronted with the corrosive effects, for both Silvia's love and Behn's propaganda, of Silvia's defiant object choice.

SERIAL ENTERTAINMENT

Throughout the early modern period, scandalous trials have often seeded the most avid consumption of print media.[7] On November 23, 1682, Ford, Lord Grey of Werke was brought to trial at the King's Bench by George Earl of Berkeley, the father of Henrietta Berkeley, for her abduction. The charge read against Lord Grey and his five co-conspirators suggests, with delicious

7. See *Private Lives and Public Affairs,* Sara Maza's study of the trials in pre-Revolutionary France, for an account of the power of trials to produce a media event through which cultural critics can read the obsessions of a culture.

hyperbole, the extent of Grey's transgression, claiming that they acted "falsely, unlawfully, and devilishly, to fulfil, perfect, and bring to effect, their most wicked, impious, and devilish intentions . . . to commit whoredom, fornication, and adultery, . . . [and] against all laws, as well divine as human, impiously, wickedly, impurely, and [in order] scandalously, to live and cohabit, did tempt, invite, and solicit . . ." (Behn, *Love Letters*, 444). In a private letter to Henrietta, Dr. John Tillotson, later Archbishop of Canterbury, urges her to do what she steadfastly refused to do in the trial—return to her father's side. Tillotson describes her sin as "of that heinous nature as to be for ought I know without example in this or any other Christian nation" (ibid., 465). The trial became the source of newspaper commentary and political satire and resulted in the publication of the transcript as *The Trial of Ford Lord Grey* (1682). In publishing the *Letters*, Behn gave the curious readers of the *Trial* more of what they wanted. Behn draws many elements of the intrigue of Silvia and Philander from the *Trial*, and uses the elopement to write "political propaganda" for the royalist side (Backscheider, *Spectacular Politics*, 110–117). For Behn, the entertainment potential of Henrietta's story arises from all that Silvia's model Henrietta does to win freedom from the father and his legal surrogates: she elopes with her brother-in-law (Lord Grey/Philander), marries his instrument (William Turner/Briljard), and, when Grey is implicated in the Rye House Plot, flees the country. Behn's central inflection of the trial comes from imagining the extent of the amorous passion necessary to do what Silvia/Henrietta does in defying "all laws, as well divine as human" (444).

As a fictionalized rendering of the action behind a scandalous trial, part I of *Love Letters*, the *Letters* (1684), is already inscribed in the logic of seriality. However, Behn wrote the *Letters* so it could stand alone. Paradoxically, the historical incompleteness of the love story—the elopement of Lord Grey/Philander and Henrietta/Silvia—and the political action—the succession crisis—recounted in the first part of *Love Letters* prompts Behn to give the novel a provisional sense of narrative closure, through the deus ex machina of Philander's surprise escape from prison, and his arrangement for Silvia to flee with him into exile. In this way, the end of the novel reaches the end of the action as summarized in the "Argument" that precedes the novel. The continuation of the narrative in the *Adventures* (1685) is neither required nor prefigured by any words or actions in the *Letters*. What intervenes to "incomplete" the *Letters* and call forth a sequel is its popularity.

In writing a sequel to the *Letters* Behn is, once again, giving her readers more of what they want. She composes the *Adventures* (1685) so it faces both backward toward the *Letters* and forward toward its continuation in the *Amours* (1687). The *Adventures* gathers the earlier action into its own forward movement by encrypting retellings of the *Letters* in at least two points in the action, and by reinterpreting the action of the *Letters* so that Philander appears as a calculating libertine who only feigned true love for Silvia. In addition, the *Adventures* ends using the classic "to-be-continued" techniques for serial fiction on the market, leaving many threads of the action untied and making an explicit promise to "Faithfully relate" in a sequel what is labeled Silvia's "Fate" as an "unhappy Wanderer" (252). Although the publication of the *Adventures* seems the direct result of Behn's need for money and her support for the Stuart cause, her continuation of a novel that had seemed to reach closure has important implications for the future of print entertainments on the market. By developing the formal techniques for writing sequels, Behn helps to chart a path toward a market-based print-media culture that others, such as Manley, Haywood, and Richardson, would follow. By reading the sequels of the *Letters*, we can analyze the pleasure-seeking ethos that may be endemic to serial entertainments.

A sequential reading of these three novels allows us to grasp the heterogeneity of texts only retroactively given a limited interpretive coherence. Though the three novels never achieve a simple unity, they are not an inchoate collection. As royalist propaganda, they are like letters addressed to the shifting moods of a public, in the brace of the shifting political rhythms of the succession crisis. One cannot get these three-novels-in-one to close around the single formal structure or authorial intention that some literary critics have sought to discern in *Love Letters*.[8] If *Love Letters* does not meet the usual expectations for novels, what kind of coherence *does* it have? That question can only be developed by taking account of its seriality. In order to capitalize upon the success of *Letters*, Behn shaped each of

---

8. Janet Todd's 1993 edition has performed an invaluable service to scholars by restoring the original seriality of *Love Letters*. By contrast, in the first modern edition of the novel, that published in 1987 by Penguin Virago, Maureen Duffy seeks to make *Love Letters* conform as much as possible to what the novel came to be after its institution within literary studies: a work that subordinates its invocation of history to its fictionality, that gives priority to private and domestic concerns over any political and public ones, and that provides consistent characters moving through a unified plot disclosing a focused set of themes, all of which allows readers to divine the coherent design of the author. In order to shift *Love Letters* toward this modern understanding of the novel, Duffy excises the most direct expressions of Behn's participation in a male political culture—the three dedications published with each installment of the novel.

its two sequels in such a way that they obeyed the logic of serial fiction on the market: each sequel meets the reader's demand for comforting continuity and enticing variation. This has enormous consequences for the way in which the novel progresses over the course of its three-year publication. Between installments, characters such as Philander and Silvia do not so much develop as undergo mutation; the plot does not unfold according to a single linear logic, but instead proliferates as a repetitive but variant ensemble of plots, often with a self-parodying resemblance; and, finally, such themes as love and loyalty undergo surprising reversal. Paradoxically, it may be most historically precise to look in *Love Letters* for the properties of a series that are familiar from a medium such as television.

Although the three parts of *Love Letters* do not develop according to principles and forms that later become mandatory for "the novel," an alternative coherence arises from the way the parts contain common events and scenes. This produces the odd resemblance to each other of three novels in a series which yet remain quite different. Each sequel repeats with a difference the general situation of the first installment: lovers seek to overcome that which blocks their desire. But in each novel, characters take different positions within this scenario. Thus, for example, Silvia is the "naive" beloved become pure lover in the *Letters*, but Octavio occupies this position through most of the *Adventures* and *Amours*, as Calista does in Philander's narrative (in Cologne). Philander is the conspiring seducer in the *Letters* and in his Cologne narrative, while Octavio and Briljard assume that role in the *Adventures*, and Silvia does so in the *Amours*. The count and Myrtilla are blocking figures in the *Letters*, but Philander acquires some of that role in the *Adventures*, the Count de Clarinau takes the role in Philander's Cologne narrative, and Sebastian assumes it in the *Amours*. Finally, each novel begins with a similar opening situation: at the beginning of the *Letters*, Silvia and Philander have just discovered their passion, and now must confront its complications; at the beginning of the *Adventures*, Silvia and Philander have escaped as lovers on a honeymoon and are befriended by Octavio, only to have Philander forced from her side; at the beginning of the *Amours*, Silvia and Octavio have escaped to a village to be married, but are immediately arrested by an agent of the Dutch parliament. When Sebastian rescues Silvia from arrest, takes her to his house, and bars his nephew Octavio from easy access to her, there is a return to the initial situation of Silvia and Philander in the *Letters*. Each novel contains one big, lush sex scene—a late-night assignation that is interrupted; an "honest" lover forced out of character to lie; scenes in which a lascivious father-figure is tricked by young lovers; an abduction; a harsh political verdict that separates lovers;

a duel or threatened duel; and the discovery of an illicit act of infidelity. These repetitions have the cumulative effect of putting in question claims to love made by particular characters at particular moments in the action. Further, since characters assume different positions within variable narrative sequences as they expand and transform over the course of the three novels, narrative does not support the stable identity of character. This has been a recurrent critical complaint against the novel.[9] In the *Amours*, the only way Behn's narrator can secure the moral coherence of Octavio's character is to remove him from the compromising flux and reflux of the serial narratives.

THE FALL INTO DIPLOMATIC SUBJECTIVITY

The shift in the narrative form and plot situation from the *Letters* to the *Adventures* suggests that Behn engages in something of a thought experiment. She seems to be asking herself, What would happen if my outlaw lovers were given what they have sought throughout the *Letters*—almost complete freedom from the restraint of fathers and the Law? Will they find that utopian place apart that they have envisioned in their letters? And what sort of novelistic narrative will such a relaxation of cultural restraint entail? The modification of the title—to the old title *Love Letters from a Nobleman to his Sister* is added *Mixt with the History of their Adventures*—only hints at the sea change that has overtaken the novel. The *Letters* makes the love letters between Philander and Silvia its central axis. Although the ideal communication circuit of "love letters between"— with its shared project, utopian goal, and assumed transparency of meaning—is periodically interrupted by others, the first-person letter narratives of the *Letters* indulges the desire-laden claims to reciprocal understanding made by the young lovers. By contrast, as a mixture of "letters" and "history," the *Adventures* gives the love letters of Philander and Silvia a sub-

9. The problem with reading *Love Letters* through modern concepts of novelistic character may be demonstrated by a sentence from Maximillian Novak's essay, "Some Notes Toward a History of Fictional Forms: From Aphra Behn to Daniel Defoe." After alluding with approval to Barbara Hardy's Jamesian proposition that "an author's moral vision . . . must ultimately be considered part of the form," Novak diagnoses the "problem" with Behn: "Aphra Behn's problem with *Love-Letters* (1684–1687) arises precisely from her incapacity to sustain any consistent attitude toward her characters and their action" (127). While she views Behn much more favorably than Novak does, Duffy's efforts to legitimize *Love Letters* by demonstrating the consistency of character and authorial intention seems to me as misguided as Novak's condescension. Critical attempts to read *Love Letters* as a novel *avant la lettre* only end up making it appear as a novel *manqué*.

sidiary place to new correspondences as well as to the story of their "adventures," a word that suggests the extraordinary doings of these entangled agents.

In this new communication situation, the lovers' claim to singularity becomes increasingly difficult to sustain. The nearly omniscient third-person narrative shifts easily from one character perspective to another and frames a much more complex and varied set of communications. Now correspondence from the same site of writing becomes fractured and multiform; thus, after his flight to Cologne, Philander writes three very different letters to three different characters. In addition, reception by a single reader becomes disjunct: Silvia writes to Octavio, telling him, "We French Ladies are not so nicely ty'd up to the formalities of vertue, but we can hear Love at both ears" (142). This fundamental change in the novel's communication network entails a concomitant shift from the radical honesty of self-disclosure in secret to a rhetoric of writing that observes diplomatic protocols of self-interest and disguised intention. As correspondences bleed into one another, who shows which letter to whom and what is known to have been shown to whom become the pivots of power and influence. Within this tangle of communication, the third-person narrative of the *Adventures* frames letter narratives so as to qualify their truth and casts a harshly ironic light on the amorous pretensions of its "love letters." Letters are so emptied of their declared meanings that characters and the reader are encouraged to read through them, as well as the hollow pretensions of the speaker, to reach some withheld meaning.

What in the novel's situation helps explain this mutation in the circuits of communication? Many of the immediate plot complications of the *Adventures* result from problems carried over from the *Letters*: because Silvia first appears in Holland not as the openly avowed mistress of Philander, but as a fugitive disguised as a boy, she becomes the object of Octavio's fascination; because Silvia and Philander are impecunious strangers in Holland, they accept Octavio's help; and, finally, because Philander is discovered to be an enemy of the French monarch, the Dutch parliament drives him away from Silvia's sickbed into a second exile in Cologne. But these tribulations are symptomatic of a more global change in the lovers' situation. While *Letters* tells the story of an extravagant love seeking to overcome the authority of the father and the Law, the *Adventures* unfolds in a space of relative equality and horizontal affiliation in which love problems develop out of the rivalry of equals for the thing each desires. If the *Letters* traces the transgressive turn that afflicts absolute claims to freedom made in the father's house, the *Adventures*, by following the diplomatic maneuvers of equal subjects, apparently free of fathers or the Law, takes characters through perverse deflections of desire.

To make up for the absence of binding laws between states and avoid the dangers of perpetual warfare, early modern states developed diplomacy. Essentially agonistic in structure, and guided by the wish to advance the interests of one's own state, diplomacy developed the ethos and protocols for a relatively lawful pursuit of self-interest. The first treatise on diplomacy, by François de Callières, is entitled *On the Manner of Negotiating with Princes* (1716). Cognate with a broad vein of Renaissance thought about the centrality of self-interest in all human behavior, developed originally by Machiavelli, Hobbes, and La Rochefoucauld, the discourse of diplomacy developed a more restrained, formalized, and rule-bound fashion to advance ends which remain essentially self-interested. The word "diplomacy" is derived from the Greek, diploma, "folded letter," in reference to the letters diplomats sent back and forth to their princes. Important early practitioners of a correspondence, diplomats disguised their communications in several ways: they folded their letters to hide their contents, which were often kept secret by being written in a ciphered code, and they discussed the most effective way to conceal their true intentions behind apparent ones. The movement between the *Letters* and the *Adventures* involves the eclipse of the idealized, honor-bound, vow-strewn correspondence Philander and Silvia had exchanged as lovers, and their development of a discourse, subjectivity, and modus vivendi appropriate to diplomacy. While this shift can be traced through Philander's change from lover to libertine, it is most decisive in Silvia's gradual change from a relatively simple amorous subjectivity to a divided diplomatic subjectivity. This metamorphosis of character is the central event in the *Adventures*.

SILVIA AS THE EROTIC BODY OF THE LICENSE OF OTHERS

How and why does Silvia change? During the short time during which Silvia and Philander live together in Holland, Silvia falls sick and Philander is forced into exile in Germany, and political imperatives explode the love dyad into a fantastic geometry of proliferating triangles: Octavio becomes the friend of Philander and the (secret) lover of Silvia; Briljard, the tame instrument of Philander and clandestine husband of Silvia, emerges as a secretly aspiring lover; Briljard seduces Silvia's lady-in-waiting, Antonett, who harbors an infatuation with Octavio; Philander seduces Calista, sister to Orlando, away from the Count of Clarinau, while continuing to profess his love for Silvia in letters to her. To complicate these heterosexual love triangles, there is a strong homoerotic current between women as well as between men, which is quite explicitly addressed by the text. Arranged in a complex multiple entanglement, and thrown into potentially antagonistic relations, these characters must depend on one another, but their interests and desires diverge.[10]

It is only through practicing a new kind of reading, writing, and acting that Silvia wakes from the plenitude she has imagined her love with Philander to be and accepts the imperatives of her new situation. Her change begins with the lack she feels upon reading the first letter Philander writes after he takes up residence in Cologne. In her reply, Silvia complains that Philander's letter is "cold—Short—Short and cold as a dead Winters day. It chill'd my blood" (144). She feels its difference from those "soft" letters he used to write her: "Loading the Paper with fond Vows and Wishes, which e're I had read o'er another wou'd arrive, to keep Eternal warmth about my Soul . . ." (147). With continuity and softness, surplus and warmth, Philander's remembered letters delivered maternal sustenance. Cut off from that warm presence, Silvia finds herself thrown into a dim half-awareness of a sign she dare not interpret: that of Philander's infidelity. The rest of the *Adventures* unfolds around Silvia's approach to and withdrawal from this sign, which is familiar yet strange, impossible and

---

10. I have benefited from Ellen Pollak's essay "Beyond Incest: Gender and the Politics of Transgression in Aphra Behn's *Love Letters Between a Nobleman and His Sister*." In a reading of *Love Letters* indebted to Eve Sedgwick's *Between Men: English Literature and Male Homosocial Desire*, Pollak interprets Silvia's desiring relations with men as a subordinate term in a phallic and homoerotic rivalry between men—explicitly, between Philander and Silvia's father, between Philander and Cesario, and between Philander and Octavio. Silvia's "semiotic education" is said to consist in learning this (feminist) truth. Pollak confers a valuable political valence on Silvia's career as a cross-dressing libertine at the end of the *Amours* in two ways: by seeing it both as Silvia's savvy rejoinder to her previous inscription within a homoerotic commerce between men and as a way to expose the arbitrariness of this patriarchal sexual economy. In this way, Silvia's play with her gender acquires the sort of self-conscious performativity that Judith Butler makes the only pathway to an equivocal liberation from the constraints of heterosexual normativity. In spite of the rigor of Pollak's reading of *Love Letters*, I find two problems with it. First, because she makes sexuality an effect of power (not something related to power, but a mere ruse of power), Pollak cannot make any sense of the positive valence Behn gives to love in all her writings, nor can she give any credit to Behn's probing critique of Silvia's decline. Second, Pollak's understanding of gender is anachronistic in the way it assumes the centrality of sexuality as a primary radical of human identity. Foucault's writings have argued the modernity of this assumption. For me, part of the interest of Restoration texts such as *Love Letters* comes from the way in which their polymorphous play with gender and sex suggests an alternative to modern concepts of social identity.

necessary—in other words, uncanny. But Silvia is not yet willing to become an active interpreter. When she consults Briljard about the meaning of this letter, his own motives lead him to push her toward the knowledge she fears. Simply trying to enunciate the possibility of Philander's falsehood makes her faint: "'Oh, Briljard, if he be false—If the dear Man be perjur'd, take, take kind Heaven! the life you have preserv'd, but for a greater proof of your revenge'—And at that word she sunk into his Arms . . ." (148).

The aggressive and unseemly assault Briljard makes on Silvia's body begins a sequence of scenes in which the pursuit of self-interest transmogrifies the amorous transactions of the novel and gradually divides Silvia from an earlier, relatively naive and unreflected subjectivity. There are several stages in this progress: Briljard, suddenly in physical possession of Silvia in the privacy of her bedroom, feels a surge of desire for her. His kinky "rape upon her Bosom" (149) while Silvia is unconscious takes him to the point of actual rape, when Octavio and Antonett suddenly interrupt them. Briljard quiets Antonett's suspicions by starting an affair with her. Octavio's suspicions, both in Briljard's presence and after his withdrawal, so alarm Silvia that she initiates her own investigation. Alone again with Briljard, she uses a tour de force of stage acting to draw him into a confession of his physical assault upon her. Over the arch of this sequence of scenes, Silvia goes from being the pathetic victim of the plots of others— Philander, Briljard, and Octavio—to being a diplomatic player with a scheme of her own: to uncover the proof of Philander's infidelity.

As Silvia's role in the action becomes more active, her body goes from being the passive thing that attracts the designs of others to being the surface for her own artful inscriptions. When Silvia faints at the thought of Philander's infidelity, Briljard seeks to open her body to his desiring arms, hands, lips, and eyes. The argumentative structure of this passage from the third-person narrative gives a justifying turn to Briljard's attempt on Silvia by allowing the reader to relax his or her own censor and consume, with a certain shocked pleasure, an action which is at once tawdry and improbable.

> . . . she sunk into his Arms, which he hastily extended as she was falling, both to save her from harm and to give himself the pleasure of grasping the lovely'st body in the World to his Bosome, on which her fair face declin'd cold, dead and pale, but so transporting was the pleasure of that dear burden, that he forgot to call for, or to use any aid to bring her back to life, but trembling with his love and eager passion he took a thousand joys, he kist a thousand times her Luke-warm lips, suckt her short sighs, and ravisht all the sweets her bosome (which but guarded with a loose

Night Gown) yielded his impatient touches. Oh, Heaven who can express the pleasures he receiv'd, because no other way he ever cou'd arrive to so much dareing . . . urg'd by a Cupid altogether malicious and wicked, he resolves his cowardly Conquest, when some kinder God awaken'd Silvia, and brought Octavio to the Chamber door. [148]

This passage is rife with casuistical excuses. It begins by recounting the "lucky" circumstances that suddenly bring Briljard the very thing he desires, with a pleasure so great he "forgot" to call for help. Then the narrative deploys the trope of an apostrophe to the absent rhetorical powers necessary to express a pleasure so extreme—"Oh, Heaven who can express . . ." This apostrophe prepares for the long, momentum-gathering period which describes how Briljard develops the transgressive impulse to carry his "rape upon [Silvia's] Bosom" to the point of actual rape, before Octavio's interruption. First Briljard feels the magnetism of this accessible body, despairs "by fair means to win her," recalls the happy circumstance of her having secured the door herself, uses the nearness of the bed to move her body there, remembers witnessing the "killing joys" she had given Philander, and then "resolves his cowardly Conquest." Several factors alibi the moral baseness of this attempted rape. The syntax of this long period, built out of a chain of hurried paratactic clauses, indexes the automatism of that passion that takes control of the subject's action. A fortuitous chain of circumstances naturalizes the taking of this "luckey opportunity." The invocation of mythic agents ["love," "Cupid"] and the use of euphemism ["killing joys," "conquest"] allows the narrative to soften Briljard's brutal transgression of the most basic codes of civilized love.

Why does the narrator alibi and naturalize an action she clearly abhors?[11] Such a narrative allows this unseemly action to initiate an expansion of the novel's libidinal economy around Silvia's vulnerable body. Thus the bare imagination of what has transpired between Briljard and Silvia in her locked bedroom eroticizes the gaze of the jealous Octavio as he scans Silvia's bedroom for signs of a sexual transgression. His pointed interrogation of her forces her to look at herself in the mirror, in which the disarray of her dress serves as evidence that she's been the object of an erotic attack she cannot remember.

Briljard's "rape" upon Silvia's bosom, Octavio's investigatory accusations, and Silvia's response precipitate a change in Silvia. She is no longer

---

11. Though for much of the *Adventures* this gender is downplayed, her gender is suggested here, and later, during Octavio's investment, the narrator's identification with female witnesses makes her gender explicit.

willing to play the forlorn and jilted lover. Her situation requires that she employ the sort of conscious manipulation that has most characterized Briljard, the "low" character from whom she would differentiate herself. Silvia's investigation is advanced in a scene containing the quick wit and ingenious reversals familiar from Restoration stage comedy. To win an amusing tit-for-tat revenge for Briljard's assault on her body, Silvia not only must act what she does not feel, she must also make cynical use of her body as a lure to a desire in which she has no share:

> . . . meeting [Briljard] with a smile, which she forc'd she cry'd, "How now Briljard, are you so faint hearted a soldier, you cannot see a Lady dye without being terrifi'd." "Rather Madam," (replied he blushing a new) "so soft hearted I cannot see the loveliest person in the World fainting in my Arms, without being disorder'd with grief and fear, beyond the power of many days to resettle again." At which she approacht him, who stood near the door, and shutting it, she took him by the hand and smiling cry'd, "And had you no other business for your heart but grief and fear, when a fair Lady throws her self into your Arms, it ought to have had some kinder effect on a person of Briljards youth and complexion." And while she spoke this she held him by the wrist, and found on the suddain his pulse to beat more high, . . . "Oh Madam do not urge me to a confession that must undo me, . . ."—"You that know your sentiments may best instruct me by what Name to call em, and you Briljard may do it without fear.—You saw I did not struggle in your Arms, nor strove I to defend the kisses which you gave."—"Oh Heavens" cry'd he transported with what she said, "is it possible that you cou'd know of my presumption and favour it too? . . . ; my hands, my eyes, my Lips were tir'd with pleasure, but yet they were not satisfied, oh there was joys beyond those ravishments of which one kind Minute more had made me absolute Lord:" "Yes and the next" said she, "had sent this to your heart"—Snatching a Penknife that lay on her Toylite, where she had been writing, which she offered so near to his bosome that he believ'd himself already pierc'd, so sensibly killing were her words, her motion, and her look, he started from her and she threw away the Knife, and walking a turn or two about the Chamber, while he stood immovable with his eyes fixt to earth, and his thoughts on nothing but a wild confusion . . ." [158–159]

Silvia uses her language and touch to move Briljard toward the disclosure of what he had done to her. First, she playfully asks him about his faint-hearted response to her fainting; then she stokes his desire by talking dirty with innuendo and double meaning; she uses her touch to turn him into the sensitive and responsive body whose pulse races and breast heaves with sighs. Finally, Silvia draws a full disclosure by pretending a consciousness of his assault. When, in his unsuspecting effusions, Briljard describes the pleasures he has stolen from her, and the still greater pleasures he barely missed, Silvia responds with her "killing" "words." Part of the pleasure of this scene comes from the way Silvia pulls off a full reversal of power positions: here the ravisher is ravished, the rape upon her bosom is repaid with a theft of his secret desire.

This scene offers its reader the pleasure of the battle of transparent egos. By the end of Silvia's successful investigation, nothing remains hidden. Thus she turns feminine "weakness" and vulnerability to advantage, and emerges as the masterful actress with a resolute heart. But behind her witty manipulation of appearances, Silvia prototypes the central figure of the formula fiction of the first decades of the next century: the self-interested ego pursuing personal advantage at the expense of others. Her exposure of Briljard is not an isolated set piece. Coming at the end of a sequence which begins with Briljard's attack on her bosom, this scene inaugurates Silvia's full participation in the self-interested manipulation and disguise characteristic of a diplomatic subjectivity. As if she understood that Silvia's use of trickery and disguise requires a fundamental shift in her character, the narrator shows a certain awkwardness in introducing Silvia's stratagem: "she call'd up all the Arts of Women . . . [and] assumed an Artifice, which indeed was almost a stranger to her heart, that of Gilting [Briljard] out of a secret which she knew he wanted generosity to give handsomely . . ." (157–158). But with the success of this "artifice," Silvia cannot return to the sort of naiveté and innocence that had been ascribed to her prior to this sequence in the novel. The reduction of love to a subordinate term in the struggle of egos contending for power becomes the underlying assumption of the libertine narrative Philander sends Octavio, describing his sexual intrigue with Calista. At the same point in the narrative, Antonett delivers her lecture to Silvia on the delicate art of reconciling love and interest. She urges Silvia to view love as a species of gambling, whereby even if you lose, you must keep on playing. By analogizing love and gaming, Antonett assumes the fungibility of desire, as well as the substitutability of erotic objects. The resultant acceleration of the circulation of the subject as an object of desire offers a strategy for maximizing Silvia's value. But by emphasizing the compulsive cast to gambling and loving—whether one wins or loses, one must "continue the game"—Antonett's words of advice suggest the more sinister turn of the subsequent action. While her advice has a limited aim—to nudge Silvia toward taking advantage of the opportunities provided by Philander's absence and Octavio's passion—its ludic characterization of love suggests the pathway that the novel's action takes as it moves from "love" to "adventures" to "amours." Once Silvia begins diplomatic negotiations, in order to protect her interests among a field of contending egos, she cannot stop. Life becomes a continuous negotiation.

EXTREME MASQUERADE

Two-thirds of the way through the *Adventures*, there is a scene that climaxes the unbridled rivalry of desiring subjects. Placed near the center of *Love Letters*, it marks a crucial shift from the "love" that dominates the *Letters* and the erotic intrigue that will predominate in the *Amours*. In a scene of extreme masquerade no one appears as himself or herself to others; instead, four major characters arrive to receive, but none finds the thing he or she desires. This scene is produced at the intersection of two designs shaped around disguise and substitution (Silvia's and Briljard's) and an accident: Octavio is called away by his prince, and then returns unexpectedly, at the very moment when he will see Silvia's (apparent) betrayal of him. But this extreme masquerade is the culmination of a much broader set of incidents precipitated by Philander's letter narrative to Octavio. As a proof of his declared love, Silvia demands that Octavio hand over the letter narrative from Philander ("Come, come, produce your credentials . . ." [195]). She hints with gay eyes that if Philander has proven false she will reward Octavio with what he wants. Octavio wavers between love and honor. Silvia's fit of rage with Octavio means she does not notice the moment at which he relents and would have handed her the letter. Letters passing between Silvia and Octavio negotiating the exchange of Philander's letter for sex with Silvia are intercepted by Briljard. For Octavio's delicate and indirect proposals, Briljard substitutes forged responses that are crassly direct. In anger at this indelicacy, Silvia makes a perverse object choice. Instead of enjoying the lover to whom she is becoming increasingly attracted, Silvia plots the maid-substitution trick with Antonett so as to dupe Octavio out of his letter. Octavio freely volunteers Philander's letter to Silvia in advance of any assignation, but Briljard intercepts it and takes it to the rendezvous he has planned under Octavio's signature. Briljard prepares for his night with Silvia by taking a philter to enhance his potency. When the scene unfolds, it is narrated from the vantage point of Octavio, the only character who does not play someone else, but who instead watches as a voyeur off stage. Briljard (thought to be Octavio) delivers the letter to Silvia (thought to be Antonett), and is led up to her (Antonett's) mistress's bed chamber to have his reward with Antonett (thought to be Silvia). Octavio seems to receive ocular proof of Silvia's infidelity. Because he's taken an overdose of "love philtre," Briljard (as Octavio) is impotent, leaving both himself and Antonett frustrated in the (imagined) gratification of their desires. Downstairs, Silvia weeps over the letter that proves Philander's infidelity, while Octavio waits outside to confront the unknown rival for Silvia's favors, who never appears.

Because this scene is controlled and comprehended by no one agent within the novel, because none even knows what is happening in the scene as it unfolds, and because it overthrows the design of all of its participants, this scene produces disturbances in the narrative that are only cleared up by the end of the *Adventures*. What is happening is only known, at the time of its happening, to the narrator and reader: we see Briljard's forgery substitutions (but no one else does); we see Silvia's substitutions (as only Antonett does); and so, in following the assignation from Octavio's vantage point, we see him mis-seeing. It is only after a protracted exchange of letters, which at first merely compound their misunderstandings, that Silvia and Octavio at last discover the truth.

What is the meaning of this scene? At the moment when the characters would possess the thing they desire, it vanishes before their eyes. Hoping against reason for a sign that would vindicate Philander's love, Silvia reads the letter that proves his infidelity; Briljard gains Silvia (actually Antonett) but is impotent; Antonett receives Octavio (actually Briljard) but is left dissatisfied; Octavio comes to Silvia's apartment for love and sees another take his place. Through this action, each experiences the collapse of the sublime object of their desire. In a space where there is no law to prohibit access to the object one desires, in the space of mobile desire—the masque—the negative appears in a particular form: desire is not reciprocal but chiasmic. Everyone gets double-crossed. Thus the perverse detouring of desire: Antonett (together with the narrator) desires Octavio, who, with Briljard, desires Silvia, who desires Philander, who desires Calista . . . This series is open-ended. Although Silvia and Octavio use mutual disclosures to recover from the collapse of value this scene in the *Adventures* effects, the scene rehearses the pure erotic agon that becomes central in the *Amours*. Then each character either enters the contest to take over the phallic function of shaping the direction of a seedy common action, or simply withdraws.

THE RETURN OF THE FATHER

By imagining potentially utopian spaces of relative equals, like the masquerade and the communal living arrangement, the central narrative of *Adventures* allows its characters to pursue the thing they desire with remarkable freedom. Obstacles to gratification erupt from among the rivals. By contrast, the *Amours* is marked by the return of the central obstacle to erotic bliss that is present in the *Letters*—the specter of paternal authority, in both its public political form and its private familial guise. At the same time, the narrative of the *Amours* gradually draws back from the close identification with the subject positions and emotional investments of particular lovers. Readers are given the effect of a reverse zoom. In other words, what gradually asserts itself is the viability of alternative vantage points from which to view and evaluate the actions of the many different lovers of *Love Letters*. This is most literally the case in the passage near the beginning of the *Amours* in which the narrator describes Silvia's disguised rendezvous with Octavio in a small Dutch village. The whole account is told from the vantage point of the spy sent by the Dutch parliament. Because of Briljard's calculated accusations, the Dutch spy suspects Octavio of consorting with French spies against the House of Orange. While the messenger is at first skeptical of the charge against someone of Octavio's character, his doubts fade as he hears that Octavio is waiting in the inn for two French gentlemen:

> He waits at some distance from the House unseen, tho' he could take a View of all; he saw Octavio come often out into the Balcony and look with longing Eyes towards the Road that leads to the Town; he saw him all rich and gay as a young Bridegroom, lovely and young as the Morning that flattered him with so fair and happy a Day; at last he saw two Gentlemen alight at the Door, and giving their Horses to a Page to walk a while, they ran up into the Chamber where Octavio was waiting, who had already sent his Page to prepare the Priest in the Village Church to marry them. [263]

When the arresting officer serves his warrant "to secure him as a Traytor to the State, and a Spy for *France*," the spy's address to the disguised Silvia is comically inappropriate. But although the spy misconstrues the action, the arresting officer still functions as the blocking figure in the romance of Silvia and Octavio. The lovers' "amour" is always already entangled with competing social interests. By representing Dutch political authority, this episode folds the love story back into the active political horizon that had been latent since Philander's exile from Holland in the *Adventures*. At the same time, Briljard's attempt to use political intrigue to separate the lovers reactivates the oedipal tensions of the text. When Silvia and Octavio are in the power of the Dutch parliament, their love becomes subject to the moral judgments and strictures of Octavio's prudish old uncle Sebastian. Although Sebastian rescues them from Briljard's false charges, he warns Octavio to break off this affair, because its "wild extravagances" have ruined his reputation in the provinces. When, through a reversal that comedy so often inflicts on those who are skeptical about love, Sebastian himself falls in love with Silvia, the lovers are returned to the coordinates of oedipal rivalry, interdiction, and the obscenely desiring father whom Philander and Silvia had confronted in the *Letters*. In pursuing Silvia, Sebastian begins as a comically inept elderly novice, but quickly turns on Octavio, suspects him of having sex with Silvia, and becomes arbitrary, vengeful, and angry, to the point of driving Octavio from Silvia's company. As the zeal of blocking "fathers" such as Sebastian and the Count of Clarinau becomes blatant, the rebellion of the younger generation becomes aggressive. When Octavio watches in hiding as Sebastian and Silvia go toward their planned marriage, his feelings of envy, desire, and murderous intent express primal fantasies of oedipal victory over the father. When, in the midst of dangerously transgressive sex with Silvia in Sebastian's house, Sebastian is accidently killed by Octavio's pistol, which discharges during a struggle, Octavio's oedipal wish is realized, but in such a way as to keep his "virtue" intact.

The reactivation of the analogy between love and politics in the *Amours*, and the return of accounts of the rebellion led by Cesario that lay behind the action in the *Letters*, does not mean that we get much by way of official history; quite the contrary, in fact. A secret history of events leading up to the Monmouth Rebellion entails oedipally fraught love stories which comport quite easily with the "amours" of the central narrative. Thus, when Tomaso tells the story of Cesario, and Briljard continues the narrative later on, we get an account of the progress of a rebellion, involving Cesario's temporary reconciliation with his father the king, the progress of Cesario's fatal passion for the older Hermione, his perverse failure to break with the rebellion, and the machinations surrounding leadership of the rebellion, whereby Hermione and Fergusano compete for control of Cesario's will. Because Cesario's love object, Hermione, is an aging busy-body, and because of the way in which Cesario persists in an attempt to kill his own father, Cesario appears as one whose mother fixation evidences a failure to surmount his oedipal desires. In vacillating between the council of Fergusano and that of Hermione before his invasion, Cesario seems to be a child lost without his father. Like Silvia, he is drawn into a series of unsavory compromises that gradually engulf him in a defeat which appears tragically unnecessary. Just as Silvia's developing libertinage causes her to lose touch with the restraints of a loyal love, so Cesario loses touch with the natural attachments to father, custom, and law. In both, the result is the same: a riot of self-interest and delusion. These "amours" are

seen from the outside, so less weight is given to any personal subject position. When Tomaso recounts the way he hides from the king's men who try
to capture him during a visit to his lover—he conceals himself on the top
of a huge four-poster bed (339)—love escapades acquire anecdotal value as
entertainment. Stories of amorous political intrigues take on the same fictional cast as Philander's embedded narrative of the seduction of Calista.
Because the number of stories of intrigue and amours keeps increasing, and
because we are viewing them from a greater distance, the *Amours* develops
a pervasive sense of irony.

MAGICAL SEX

As the *Amours* becomes an anthology of amours, as each becomes more
ingeniously fictional than the last, and as the echoes between the different
intrigues become evident, repetition corrodes the novelty, uniqueness, and
value Behn and her narrator have tried to ascribe to love throughout the
first two novels of *Love Letters*. In order to develop a counterforce to the
comic neutralization of love's power, the narrator uses the mastery of her
own language to offer the reader the magic of sex. Thus, after Silvia and
Octavio's arrest, but before Uncle Sebastian becomes a troublesome rival,
the narrator moves the lovers toward another big scene of sexual bliss.
Because of similar yet distinct external conditions, this scene at once
resembles and differs from the erotic scenes between Silvia and Philander
in the *Letters* and between Philander and Calista in the *Adventures*. The
narrator's asymmetrical treatment of Silvia and Octavio indexes the central dilemma of the *Amours*—that of how to narrate the individual's
(relentless) pursuit of pleasure at the same time that the narrator affirms
the higher ethical potential of loyal love. While the *Letters* allow Silvia and
Philander to argue the higher spiritual value of love and the *Adventures*
stages a cynical tongue-in-cheek affirmation of sexual pleasure through
Philander's seduction of Calista, the narrator of the *Amours* describes a
scene of magical sex in order to defend her new pair of lovers—Silvia and
Octavio—from the criticism that her own narrative breeds.

The narrator sketches the conditions for the climactic erotic union of
Silvia and Octavio. First, Octavio has been warned by his uncle of the political dangers of dalliance with the married Silvia, and Silvia is still true to
the vows of fidelity she swore to Philander in imagining "marriages made
in heaven." The narrator describes the qualities in Silvia that make her
receptive to Octavio's love yet also a love object who will eventually torment and jilt him. This account of Silvia's character swerves away from

familiar ethically neutral clichés about "woman," and toward a much more tendentious remarking of Silvia's use of sex to gain power:

> . . . and we must conclude Silvia a maid wholly insensible, if she had not been touch'd with Tenderness, and even Love it self, at all these extravagant marks of Passion in Octavio; and it must be confess'd, she was of a Nature soft and apt for Impression; she was, in a word, a Woman. She had her Vanities, and her little Fevibleses, and lov'd to see Adorers at her Feet, especially those in whom all things, all Graces, Charms of Youth, Wit and Fortune agreed to form for Love and Conquest: She naturally lov'd Power and Dominion; and it was her Maxim, That never any Woman was displeased to find she could beget Desire. [278]

While the narrator is unqualified in her praise of Octavio, the characterization of Silvia is much more equivocal. The narrator does not appear to see any contradiction in declaring Silvia to be one "touch'd" with "Tenderness" and "even Love" at the same time that she "naturally" "lov'd Power," and spouts a maxim to justify this manipulative use of others' desire. Yet even here, early in the *Amours,* as Silvia is falling into love and sex with Octavio, the narrator remarks the tendencies that will explain her development, over the course of the *Amours,* into an unprincipled, power-hungry woman of intrigue.

The narrator describes the punctual contingent moment when the lovers spontaneously lose themselves in sex. Here, the narrator marshals all her own rhetorical powers to defend the erotic necessity of this moment against the skepticism about the spiritual union of two souls that earlier moments in this series inevitably provoke. This casuistical defense of the lovers' transgression, through the elaborate ebb and flow of syntax and idea, allows the narrator to practice her own seduction of the reader:

> [Octavio] longs and languishes for the blessed Moment that shall give him to the Arms of the ravishing Silvia, and she finds but too much yielding on her part, in some of those silent lone Hours, when Love was most prevailing, and feeble Mortals most apt to be overcome by that insinuating God; so that tho' Octavio could not ask what he sigh'd and dy'd for; tho' for the Safety of his Life, for any Favours; and tho', on the other side, Silvia resolv'd she would not grant, no, tho' mutual Vows had passed, tho' Love within pleaded, and almost unresistible Beauties and Inducements without, tho' all the Powers of Love, of Silence, Night, and Opportunity, tho' on the very Point a thousand times of yielding, she had resisted all: But oh! one Night; let it not rise up in Judgement against her, you bashful modest Maids, who never yet try'd any powerful Minute; nor you chast Wives, who give no Opportunities: One night—they lost themselves in

Dalliance, forgot how very near they were to yielding, and with imperfect Transports found themselves half dead with Love, clasp'd in each others Arms, betray'd by soft Degrees of Joy to all they wished. 'Twould be too Amorous to tell you more; to tell you all that Night, that happy Night produc'd; let it suffice that Silvia yielded all, and made Octavio happier than a God. At first he found her weeping in his Arms, raving on what she had unconsidering done; and with her soft Reproaches chiding her ravished Lover, who lay sighing by, unable to reply any other way, he held her fast in those Arms that trembled, yet with Love and new-past Joy; he found a Pleasure even in her Railing, with a Tenderness that spoke more Love than any other Language Love could speak. Betwixt his Sighs he pleads his Rights of Love, and the Authority of his solemn Vows; he tells her that the Marriage Ceremony was but contrived to satisfy the Ignorant, and to proclaim his Title to the Crowd, but Vows and Contracts were the same to Heaven: He speaks—and she believes; and well she might, for all he spoke was honourable Truth. He knew no Guile, but uttered all his Soul, and all that Soul was Honest, Just, and Brave; thus by degrees he brought her to a Calm. [279–280]

In order for Silvia to yield "all," and for Octavio to utter "all his Soul," each of the characters within the scene, and the narrator in the way she narrates the scene, must break through manifold reticences and interdictions. Before sex, Octavio cannot "ask what he sigh'd and dy'd for"; though dismayed to find herself yielding "too much," "Silvia resolv'd she would not grant [Favours], . . . she had resisted all." Within the ellipsis of this period, which describes Silvia's successful resistance of her own desire, we get a series of four embedded "tho'" clauses that build up a counterpressure to her abstinence by describing all that pushes her toward yielding: "tho' mutual Vows had passed," "tho' Love within pleaded, and almost unresistible Beauties and Inducements without," "tho' all the Powers of Love, of Silence, Night, and Opportunity," and "tho' on the very Point a thousand times of yielding." Here the old metaphor of the lady's heart as a besieged fortress has been psychologized so as to make her mind the site of an affective ambivalence.

In a sudden reversal, the erotic knot is cut with the sharp punctuality of one interjection: "But oh! one Night." This "one Night" locates the occasion of the lovers' lapse, while the "oh!" is the ejaculation of the narrator, spoken in sympathy for the distress supposed to be felt by the heroine and her lover. Before describing what happened one night, the narrator offers a casuistical defense of her characters, addressed to the two types of women supposed to be most severe in assessing this moment in the heroine's lapse—"you bashful modest Maids, who never yet try'd any powerful Minute; nor you chast Wives, who give no Opportunities." Here, differences in perspective and circumstance are used to alibi in advance the transgressive moment the narrator then describes. In the way Behn describes not what "he" or "she" did, but what "they" did "one Night," two agents become one, and there is a shift from active to passive voice: "they lost . . . forgot . . . they found themselves . . . clasped in each others arms, betrayed . . . to all they wished." Who or what betrayed them to all they wished? The syntax and rhythm of this sentence are carefully shaped by the narrator to shift the lovers, without any intervening conscious intention, from collective agents to passive recipients of a consummated passion. Paradoxically, they are brought to "all they wished," by something other than themselves, which is at once everything (in the situation) and nothing (in their conscious intention). This is the alibi and riddle of their passion.

The erotic rhythm of this passage comes from the incessantly renewed tension between law and desire, the "no" and "yes" spoken not just in the lovers' hearts, but in the narrator's language as well. Thus the narrator does not simply yield "all" of the scene she claims to know. Instead, she withholds a part of it by introducing her own excisions into her representation of the "all" that Silvia yields as sex and that Octavio returns as vows. The narrator resorts to oblique suggestion, euphemism, and ellipsis to censor the description of sex in the name of propriety: "'Twould be too Amorous to tell you more; to tell you all that Night, that happy [i.e., lucky] Night produc'd; let it suffice that Silvia yielded all, and made Octavio happier than a God." The hyperbole and euphemism of "happier than a God" and the repetition of "Night, that happy Night" are flourishes that denote the excessive gratifications of the moment at the same time that they observe the propriety of a narrator who won't tell the "all" she insists was "yielded."

With the words "At first he found her weeping," the narrator returns the characters and reader to the ordinary present from that utopian time-outside-time of sex. In this moment, each lover articulates the contradiction between gratification and guilt. Silvia weeps and raves, and utters "soft reproaches" to Octavio, whose body expresses his passion, while Octavio holds her "fast," his "Arms" "trembled, yet with Love and new-past Joy . . ." (279). The "railings" of Silvia, who is swept up within ambiguous countercurrents of speech and body, please Octavio with a "Tenderness that spoke more Love than any other Language Love could speak" (280). First speechless before these reproaches, Octavio then delivers a high-minded moral defense of what they have done. This vindication of the extreme marriage of two hearts should have a familiar ring to the careful reader of *Love Letters*. It recapitulates the critique and defense of "marriages made in heaven" that Silvia had developed in her letter to Philander after her elopement (see above). At the center of this defense is the idea of the separate legitimacy of the exchange of lovers' vows: "he tells her that the Marriage Ceremony was but contrived to satisfy the Ignorant . . . but Vows and Contracts were the same to Heaven: He speaks—and she believes" (280).

The simple and vivid reciprocity of "He speaks—and she believes" should bring the conceptual development of the passage and scene to a close. But because this defense of illicit love repeats an earlier defense of the illicit love of Silvia and Philander, and because, in receiving Octavio's vows here, Silvia is violating the vows she made in her earlier letter to Philander, Octavio's defense has a corrosive effect on the uniqueness he is claiming for his own love and fidelity. The singularity of vows is imperiled by the machinery of textual repetition. Perhaps sensing that she cannot control this dramatic irony at her hero's expense, the narrator makes an extraordinary gesture. She draws upon her privileged relationship to the temporality of the narrative diagesis—she knows where the story she is telling is going to end—and deploys her powers as a quasi-omniscient narrator to enter the mind of her protagonist and offer a guarantee of the truthfulness of Octavio's vows. Silvia is right to believe Octavio's vows because, the narrator assures us, "all he spoke was honourable Truth. He knew no Guile, but uttered all his Soul, and all that soul was Honest, Just, and Brave; thus by degrees he brought her to a Calm" (280). These words of the narrator propel Octavio into a sphere beyond social compromises; his vows, and the narrator's confirmation of them, are not only a warranty against infidelity; they also assure the reader that if things should go wrong the fault must be found elsewhere—most obviously in the receiver of these vows, Silvia. Further, this passage suggests the gendered desire at work in the narrator's idealization of Octavio. The only way that there can be a man's love that is not a hostage to fortune, the only way that there can be a man immune to the love-destroying philandering of a Philander, is for there to exist someone like Octavio: someone whose truth, soul, honesty, justice, and bravery can be fully articulated; one, in short, whose "all" can be focused into a vow spoken in one moment, but that is good for all time. Octavio is the character who, because he has the "right to make promises," affirms the speculative possibility of a "marriage made in heaven." Throughout the rest of the *Amours*, Octavio becomes a vehicle for that wish and idea.

DISAVOWING SILVIA IN THE NAME OF LOVE

Behn's narrator seems to recognize that the ethical coherence of *Love Letters* can only be sustained by splitting the characters of the novel between those who can honor vows (Octavio and Calista) and those to whom vows are merely a way to dupe others (Philander and Silvia). How much is one to weight this final enunciation of the value of vows? Aphra Behn seems to try, in the series of novels called *Love Letters Between a Nobleman and His Sister*, to post love, and the ecstatic pleasures of sex, as a counterweight to the egotism and me-firstism implicit in the desire for freedom. Love seems, at points in this text, to offer a magical reconciliation of freedom and necessity, bodily impulse and circulation within a social symbolic. However, the action of *Love Letters*—in which singularity is overtaken by repetition and love objects prove all too open to substitution—suggests the difficulty of this reconciliation. Even Octavio's valedictory claims for his vows have something implausible about them: they are, as he and the narrator seem to realize but not be able to fully accept, hopelessly out of tune with the ruling ethos of the *Amours*. If Behn's *Love Letters* gives considerable reign to an ethos of personal freedom from instituted authorities, it also explores the question—given special urgency by the succession crisis—of what could ground human relations freed from instituted ethical authority by a desire open to endless substitution of erotic objects. The final assertion of the value of vows is entirely consistent with the royalist argument that too many subjects of the Stuart monarch were finding ways to disavow their vows of loyalty to their king. But, within the central love story of *Love Letters*, this solution is practiced in the mode of paradox: Octavio can only affirm the value of his love by disavowing the woman he loves.

The plot of the *Amours* attempts to resolve the discrepancy between a cynical social practice and the values Behn is determined to assert. At the same time that Octavio is withdrawn from the amorous action of the *Amours*, Behn makes him the vehicle for affirming the possibility of loyal love. This solution is orchestrated in the lavish stagecraft of Octavio's admission into the monastic Order of Saint Bernard. There, the narrator as subject comes to the fore as an eye-witness who speaks in the mode of personal testimony: "I my self went among the rest to this Ceremony" (379). Aligning herself throughout the ceremony with the pathetic responses of female observers, the narrator writes, "For my part, I swear I was never so affected in my Life, with any thing, as I was at this Ceremony" (383). What affects the narrator is a gorgeous baroque ceremony, offered as a set piece to the reader, that takes Octavio heroically beyond Silvia and all she has come to represent. For the narrator, this elevation of Octavio into "heaven" confirms his special grace and his spiritual movement beyond the compromises of amorous intrigue. By enfolding Octavio within a pious religious spectacle, the narrator consoles herself for the loss of the happy union between Silvia and Octavio that the narrative had seemed to promise: "for my part, I confess, I thought my self no longer on Earth; and sure there is nothing gives us an Idea of real Heaven, like a Church all adorn'd with rare Pictures, and the other Ornaments of it . . ." (381). After the religious service but before his investiture, Octavio is described as kneeling to submit his "delicate Hair" to the scissors of a "Father": "at which a soft Murmur of Pity and Grief, fill'd the Place: Those fine Locks, with which Silvia had a thousand times play'd, and wound the Curles about her snowy Finger, she now had the dying Grief, for her Sake, for her Infidelity, to behold sacrificed to her Cruelty, and distributed amongst the Ladies, who at any Price would purchase a Curl" (382–383). Parts of Octavio's body circulate as relics of a profane hagiography. This pathetic climax of the sacrifice of youth and beauty not only fixes blame squarely on Silvia; by cutting and distributing Octavio's locks for a price, the erotic pleasure of the couple is lost, yet at the same time recuperated, in the mode of entertainment.

While the generous, sympathetic language of the narrator elevates Octavio to sublime heights, Silvia receives all the rigors of the narrator's skeptical critique. This results in a drastic downward revision in Silvia's value. In the passage that describes her response to Octavio's investiture, the narrator not only displays Silvia's vanity and selfishness, she also goes from a fairly straightforward description of Silvia's suffering to ironic qualifications of Silvia's grief, to generalizations about Silvia's "wretched" qualities, and to a rather surprising reinterpretation of Silvia's first love for Philander:

> It was a great while before [Silvia] could recover from the Indisposition which this fatal and unexpected Accident had reduced her: But as I have said, she was not of a Nature to dy for Love; and charming and brave as Octavio was, it was perhaps her Interest, and the loss of his considerable Fortune, that gave her the greatest Cause of Grief. Sometimes she vainly fancied that yet her Power was such, that with the Expence of one Visit, and some of her usual Arts, which rarely fail, she had power to withdraw his Thoughts from Heaven, . . . : But again she wisely considered, tho' he might be retriev'd, his Fortune was disposed of to Holy Uses, and could never be so. This last Thought more prevailed upon her, and had more convincing Reason in it, than all that could besides oppose her Flame; for she had this wretched Prudence, even in the highest Flights and Passions of her Love, to have a wise Regard to Interest; insomuch that it is most certain, she refused to give herself up intirely even to Philander; him, whom one would have thought nothing but perfect Love, soft irresistable Love could have compell'd her to have transgress'd withal, when so many Reasons contradicted her Passion: How much more then ought we to

believe that Interest was the greatest Motive of all her after Passions? [383–384]

At this point of the narrative, the narrator arrogates a new freedom of interpretation. She not only speculates that it is "perhaps" Silvia's interest which leads her "wisely" to consider that she could not retrieve her fortune, she also deflates the "power" that Silvia "vainly fancied" she has to seduce Octavio from his new vocation, power that the narrator herself has described as magically efficacious over the course of the *Adventures* and the *Amours*. In addition, the narrator also condemns what she calls Silvia's "wretched Prudence, even in the highest Flights and Passions of her Love." She extends this charge with a surprising interpretation: that even in Silvia's first passion for Philander, where one would think that only the purest love would counter all the reasons for not fleeing with Philander, interest has been crucial. Since this interest vitiates her first love, it is no surprise that it has operated in all her "after Passions." Here the narrator's claim is rather strange. What is the interest or prudence working in Silvia's flight with Philander? While she asserts that one interest has been decisive, the narrator does not specify what it is. Here, the narrator seems to refuse the sequential, transformational, après-coup interpretation that has shifted the terms of the narrative, characters, and action in each installment. In other words, the narrator resists the central logic of serial form so evident over the course of the three parts of the novel, and implicit in the anti-ethics of her libertine protagonists. The narrator's retroactive interpretation of Silvia's initial love for Philander composes her history into one incriminating whole. This interpretation seeks to foreclose any sympathy the reader may have had for Silvia as one who has been thrown into love, and into a vortex of action and suitors she cannot really control, in both the *Adventures* and the *Amours*. What does this accomplish? The narrator seems to be taking a personal interest in degrading Silvia, the erotic object of the narrator's object of erotic fascination, Octavio. It gratifies the narrator's wish to debase the value of the former heroine at the same time that Octavio is sublimated, raised up, and preserved (in the mode of nostalgia) as too perfect for this world. In the *Amours*, the lens through which we see the heroine has shifted: the narrator's attack upon her female protagonist contributes to Silvia's loss of any consistency of character. The narrator has become as biased as her characters.

After the investment of Octavio and his removal from the erotic triangle that has dominated the novel since the beginning of the *Adventures*, Silvia becomes an adventuress. Undergoing a devolution in character, she is emptied of any nuanced subjectivity and removed from any of the constraints of the social law. Silvia is a prototype of the protagonist who has figured prominently in formula fiction ever since, and who is a simple, self-promoting ego who pursues a complex career of intrigue and action in hopes of advancing his or her interest and pleasure. Now love is no more than a series of ways to advance one's power, within a continuous zero-sum struggle for advantage. When Silvia pursues her amorous schemes deep into her own pregnancy, the narrator is most explicit and harsh in describing her decline: "only her Shape was a little more inclining to be Fat, which did not at all however yet impare her fineness; and she was indeed too Charming without, for the deformity of her indiscretion within; but she had broke the bounds of Honour, and now stuck at nothing that might carry on an Interest, which she resolved should be the business of her future life" (375). Silvia is here anathematized as a spiritual monster, whose outward beauty has an ironic relationship to her inward "deformity." By the end of the *Amours*, Silvia is precisely the opposite of what Richardson will make Pamela and Clarissa, who, as ideal realizations of the modern author function, are responsible, consistent, self-conscious, and exemplary. However, the narrator's efforts to interpret Silvia retroactively never quite work. Moralistic condemnations of Silvia fall short of the complex and shifting character positions projected earlier in the series. The human faults of the embattled heroine of the *Letters* must be sacrificed to the exigencies of the series into which Behn has plotted her.

Ready to leave behind any of the parameters of consistency of character, Silvia launches a career of pure adventurism. Here, the sort of masquerade that appeared as an inadvertent collaborative moment at the climax of the *Adventures* is exploited in a cynical and instrumental fashion in Silvia's seduction of Don Alonzo. This threefold seduction—in which she first disguises herself as the male "Bellumere," then as the nameless but dazzling court beauty, and finally appears as herself—anticipates the vertiginous disguises of Haywood's *Fantomina* (1725). Silvia's escapade provides a paradigm for the sort of formula fiction that Manley and Haywood would popularize in the first decades of the eighteenth century. As a projector who is passionate, vacillating, self-interested, deceitful, and fascinatingly various, Silvia appears less as a single character than as a sort of personification of the novel on the market. By assuming the role of author of her own amours, Silvia engages yet manipulates the exchanges endemic to fiction on the market and expresses the most dubious aspects of Behn's female authorship (Gallagher, *Nobody's Story*, 14–34). Through the lead character's devolution from something better—the Silvia of the *Letters*—the novelistic series entitled *Love Letters* already encodes an ethical critique of the sort of novel it helps to bring to the British print market. Thus the overdetermined legacy of *Love Letters* for eighteenth-century novelists: it displays the novel of amorous intrigue in formation at the same time as it develops a probing ethical critique of its agonistic ethos. It interrupts the same narrative pleasures it promotes.

3   Formulating Fiction for the General Reader

Manley's New Atalantis
and Haywood's Love in Excess

THE GENERAL READER

Behn's novels of the 1680s trace a new pathway for published entertainment. Through the adventitious development of the novel of amorous intrigue, *Love Letters* and the other novels published in the 1680s and 1690s transmit a form of fiction which Manley and Haywood will use to write the best-sellers of 1709 and 1719. The novels of amorous intrigue published by Behn, Manley, and Haywood in the decades after *Love Letters* distinguish themselves from the tide of other printed matter by their enormous popular success and the scandal they provoke. For reasons noted in the previous two chapters, these novels have been, by and large, excluded from modern narratives of the novel's rise. The institution of the novel after 1750 defines the novel as moral, English, and realist; by contrast, the novels of amorous intrigue appear sexually immoral, French, and fundamentally unrealistic, either because they are scandalously factual or because they are pure fantasy. These oppositions are fortified and extended when literary histories code the true novel in English as masculine and the novel of amorous intrigue as feminine. It has been the project of a revisionist feminist literary history to challenge this masculinizing of the novel—consolidated by Watt's *Rise of the Novel* but still found to be working, in updated theoretical garb, in the more recent histories of the novel by Davis, McKeon, and Hunter (Gardiner, "The First English Novel," 204–207; Ballaster, *Seductive Forms*, 16; Straub, "Francis Burney," 216–218). One feminist response—to align the genre of the novel with the female gender—simply reverses a tendentious mapping of culture. In this chapter, I suggest reasons why the novel cannot in fact be gendered.

The new formula fiction of Delariviere Manley and Eliza Haywood

achieves its distinctive popularity and scandal by appealing not to any particular type of reader but to what I will call the general reader. What is
meant by "general reader"? Their reader is "general" in the negative sense
of not being limited in scope or narrowly restricted. Having only their
engagement with the novel in common, a diverse plurality of readers can
enjoy the same novel, so its reading can become "general" in the second
sense of "widespread," "common," or "prevailing." It is clarifying also to
specify what the general reader is not. The general reader does not have a
clearly delimited ideological position within the cultural field; the general
reader is not a subject with a defining difference of class, race, gender, or
sexual preference; and the general reader does not have a specifiable identity, such that a novelist would know in advance how to move her or him.
Instead, the sort of formula fiction that I will be investigating in this chapter requires thinking of the reader—whether as a group or as a single individual—as being plural in terms of interests, with a perversely polymorphous liability to be hooked by many zones of readerly enjoyment. The
general reader is not a vague or capacious universal, but is, instead, a specific concept. Thus, Joan Copjec has argued that the concept of the "general
subject" does not "poorly or wrongly describe a subject whose structure is
actually determinate but precisely indicates a subject that is in some sense
objectively indeterminate" (Copjec, *Read My Desire*, 147). For the writer
and bookseller working the early modern print market, this indeterminate
but alluring "general reader" becomes the target audience the successful
appeal to which assures monetary advantage. It has been so for publishers
ever since. The popularity of Manley's *New Atalantis* and Haywood's *Love
in Excess*, and the notoriety of the many novels the latter published in the
1720s, seem to depend upon these writers' formulation of fiction with traits
appealing to this "general reader."

To read the early novel through its appeal to the general reader will help
overcome some of the difficulties that have arisen in recent feminist literary histories. Since the 1970s, the feminist study of early writing by
women has had the important role of bringing the novels of Behn, Manley,
and Haywood back into print, critical discourse, and literary histories. But
this project of feminist reappropriation has sometimes been guided by
political values and conceptual terms that have obscured the actual significance of Behn, Manley, and Haywood in early modern culture. One strand
of feminist criticism has considered these three novelists as early instances
of "women's writing," in which a female author writes as a woman for
other women, reflecting upon, and sometimes contesting, life within patriarchy. Even when the feminism of these early women writers is open to

sustained questioning, as it is in the studies of Jane Spencer and Judith Kegan Gardiner, the goal of feminist literary history remains one of isolating a more or less autonomous current of women's writing for inclusion in the canon of valued literary works (Todd, *Sign of Angelica;* Schofield, *Masquerade Novels of Eliza Haywood*). It is when the canon is understood, through an analogy with electoral representation, as a site for an "imaginary politics of respresentation" (Guillory, *Cultural Capital,* 3), that critics feel called upon to dub Behn the "first English novelist" (see chapter 2). A second way of reading the novels of amorous intrigue reads backward from the contemporary Harlequin romance, so as to situate them as an early instance of women's popular culture. Developed out of Marxist understanding of the various ways in which narrative can express the legitimate utopian longings of subordinate groups, and following modern cultural studies of women's romance (Modleski, *Loving with a Vengeance;* Radway, *Reading the Romance*), this mode of reading enables critics to put aside questions of literary genre or aesthetic value, and focus upon the fantasy life of early modern women. Toni O'Shaughnessy Bowers suggests we see novels of amorous intrigue as "the direct ancestors of modern supermarket romances" with "their sexually demanding men and innocent, desirable, passive women, and their insistence that sexual violence, correctly interpreted, reveals or engenders love" (Bowers, "Sex, Lies and Invisibility," 59). The editors and contributors of *Fetter'd or Free?* (Schofield and Macheski) seek to negotiate the contradictory impulses Radway discovers in the readers of modern romances, who seek to protest and yet to escape temporarily the roles prescribed by patriarchal culture, roles that romance makes appear both limiting and desirable (Radway, *Reading the Romance,* 16–18).

In the first sustained study of the genre, *Seductive Forms: Women's Amatory Fiction from 1684 to 1740,* Ros Ballaster offers critiques of both of these feminist ways of reading the novel of amorous intrigue. Ballaster faults critics who are too ready to interpret the eighteenth-century woman novelist by reading backward from the account of the struggles of nineteenth-century women writers offered in Gilbert and Gubar's influential *Mad Woman in the Attic.* Ballaster notes that these feminist critics always find the same message behind women's narrative manipulations: "Rage at patriarchal oppression is the 'truth' behind every woman's fiction and the feminist critic's job is to discover and uncover its strategies of concealment" (21). Seeking to develop a more nuanced concept of the way in which fantasy operates in amatory fiction, Ballaster also faults the modern students of romance for assuming "that women readers identify solely with the dominant female subject position represented in the text, that is, that of the embattled heroine" (ibid., 28). Ballaster finds another way to chart the compositional strategies of Behn, Manley, and Haywood in writing "woman's amatory fiction." Lacking British models for this fiction, these authors looked to seventeenth-century France, where they found a broad band of "feminocentric" narratives which they could popularize (ibid., 66). Unable to account for the precise way in which these novels were read by consumers of the early novel, Ballaster undertakes an "analysis of the specific address that Behn, Manley, and Haywood make to female readers and the interpretive conflict between the genders that is the structuring feature of their amatory plots" (ibid., 29).

However it is Ballaster, not Behn, Manley, or Haywood who assumes the centrality of writing texts that "address" women readers; it is she, not any of them, who puts the apostrophe "s" behind the first word in her generic designation, "women's amatory fiction." The term "feminocentric" allows Ballaster to obscure the fact that the French romances, secret histories, scandalous chronicles, and novels which offered models for Behn, Manley, and Haywood were written and read by both men and women.[1] If one looks more closely at the French texts Ballaster invokes, the term "feminocentric" becomes problematic. First, in those novels and romances that render the woman the object of desire, narrative often focuses upon the affect and adventure of male characters who aspire to relatively remote women. Are these texts centered on the women they monumentalize or on the men who love them? Second, it is difficult to know what Ballaster means by the "feminocentric" novels. Behn's dedications are usually to men; her novels, like those of Manley, are intended to intervene in political culture and, in order to do so, must "address" men; Behn, Manley, and Haywood all feature men as well as women as central characters; in the beginning of the second part of *Love in Excess*, a poem by Richard Savage celebrates Haywood as a mistress of the passions of both sexes. Only much later in Haywood's career, with the *Female Spectator* (1744), could a significant portion of her writing be said to be directed at female as opposed to male readers. Scholars have not yet demonstrated for the early eighteenth century the sort of market segmentation reviewers describe later in the century.

---

1. For the heroic romance, Madeleine de Scudéry is central, but so are Honoré d'Urfé and Gautier de la Calprenède. While Marie d'Aulnoy and Lafayette are influences for Manley and Behn, so too are novels written by men, such as the *Lettres Portugaises*. On the practices of collaboration that blur the gender boundaries of authorship in seventeenth-century French salon writing, see DeJean, *Tender Geographies*, 1–16.

By seeking to gender the origin, content, and destination of these novels (as being from women, about women, and to women), feminist critics align their readings with the project that motivates virtually all post-enlightenment feminist and Marxist interpretations of popular culture: how does the subject who would be free (here, woman) resist or negotiate some compromise with the power of an oppressive system (here, patriarchy) in order to win authority in view of (some possible future) liberation? The use of this leading question to guide reading underestimates something we will find repeatedly in the novels of amorous intrigue: the fact that their inventive complications of the ordinary courtship plot, through the use of masquerade, incite a desire which is polymorphous, and which exploits the pleasures of cross-gender identification. Precisely because they blur the identity of subject positions, these fictions can interpellate a general reader.

I would suggest another, albeit more circuitous, way in which to articulate the novels of amorous intrigue with feminism. Although they cannot be assimilated into a consistent feminist politics, Behn, Manley, and Haywood develop forms of entertainment that are crucial to modern forms of subjectivity, including post-enlightenment feminism. Like their precursors on the continent, Behn, Manley, and Haywood mix new comedy situations with a cynical, modern libertine ethos so as to intensify the erotic tension, gender strife, and sexual explicitness of the conventional love story. The discourse of liberation propounded in their novels is woven out of particular Restoration and eighteenth-century contexts—the realist political discourse developed out of Hobbes, Machiavelli, and Mandeville; the Tory individualism and libertinism epitomized by such Restoration rakes as the first earl of Rochester; and a baroque aesthetics of excess. Behn, Manley, and Haywood weave these elements into tightly wrought narratives which present sexualized bodies and amoral egos plotting to secure their own pleasures at the expense of others. The formal traits of these novels (their brevity, their subordination of all narrative interest to intricate plotting, and the shell-like emptiness of their protagonists) support their ideological content: a licentious ethical nihilism and a sustained preoccuption with sex, explicitly rendered. The popularity of these novels seems to depend upon turning the empty ego of the central protagonist into a reader's seat from which readers can follow a blatantly self-interested quest for victory on the field of amorous conquest.[2] Even after they lose their explicit relation to

2. J. Paul Hunter argues that novel reading was uniquely fitted to those readers who were learning how to live in such anonymous urban spaces as London (*Before Novels*, chapters 3 and 5).

politics, the novels of amorous intrigue retain the agonistic assumptions and cruel realism of political discourse.

By developing the first formula fiction on the market, Behn, Manley, and Haywood invent a form of private entertainment that incites desire and promotes the liberation of the reader as a subject of pleasure. It is the novels of amorous intrigue that Richardson and Fielding set out to reform and replace in the 1740s. All these early novels—from Behn to Fielding— play a crucial role in the formation of the bourgeois public sphere (Habermas, *Structural Transformation*, 48–56), the enlightenment critique of the self's self-imposed tutelage, the late-century revolutions, and modern feminism, which begins in England with Mary Wollstonecraft. This, I will argue, is the actual if circuitous sense in which Behn, Manley, and Haywood contribute to the formation of modern feminism. Rather than anticipating modern feminism, as do the French "querrelles de femmes" or Mary Astell's *Serious Call*, the novels of amorous intrigue do something more general and global: as a form of media culture they teach readers— men as well as women—to articulate their desire and put the self first, through reading novels in which characters do so (Lacan, *Seminar* VII).

In order to account for the development of formula fiction, I will briefly describe the changes that overtake the novels of amorous intrigue between 1684 and 1740. In texts such as Behn's *Love Letters* and Manley's *New Atalantis*, the novel of amorous intrigue develops a coded system of reference to "great men and women" so as to use fiction to ensnare political opponents in the contagion of scandal. By separating these novels from the context of early political-party writing, and by shaping stories of thin fictional characters into complexly plotted action, Haywood develops formula fiction addressed to a market of general readers. As a streamlined and autonomous vehicle of fictional entertainment, the novel of amorous intrigue eludes the post-enlightenment conception of coherent political identity and precedes the narrative of liberation and enslavement, subversion or co-optation which provides the ur-plot of Marxist and feminist accounts of popular culture. The novels of amorous intrigue are an early instance of what I will call "media culture," provisionally defined within the eighteenth-century context as the practices of production and consumption associated with print media. This culture of, by, and for a print market is more polyvalent and promiscuous in its address and effects than feminist and Marxist readings have allowed. Media culture does not exclude ideology of different sorts; instead, it offers an infrastructure for the diverse ideologies and class positionalities contending in culture in the early modern period. Its only consistent ideology is that of pleasure itself. The novels of amorous intrigue—through the plotting of their pleasure-seeking protagonists—support the pleasure-seeking reader sequestered in a more or less private act of reading. These novels trigger a public-sphere debate about reading around this question: how is culture to license—that is, sanction but also control—the powerful new reading pleasures these novels produce? As both novelists and their critics align and conflate the dangerous pleasures of reading novels with those associated with the sexualized body, the debate that swirls around the novel of amorous intrigue becomes lodged within the novels of Manley and Haywood. But before tracing the terms of this debate, we must sharpen our understanding of the early novels, by asking what a novel of amorous intrigue is. It is a question best answered by going back to Behn.

POLITICAL INTRIGUE, NOVELISTIC INTRIGUE

Near the end of Behn's *Love Letters*, Silvia carries on an intrigue with a young nobleman named Don Alonzo. This affair not only offers an extension and simplification of earlier intrigues in the novel; within the context of the novel's account of Silvia's movement from impassioned lover to jaded libertine, it also suggests her gradual moral debasement. Silvia's character becomes flattened and simplified, as character is subordinated to the artifice of intrigue, coolly and cunningly performed. This episode offers a relatively self-contained example of the sort of narrative formula that Behn uses in her short novels (such as *The Fair Jilt* and *The Unlucky Chance*), that Manley would modify and incorporate in the anthology of adventures that comprise the *New Atalantis*, and that Haywood would perfect into the numerous novels published after the success of her best-seller and first novel, *Love in Excess*. By describing Silvia's affair with Don Alonzo as if it were an autonomous novel, and by going on to suggest what makes it typical of many novels published by Behn, Manley, and Haywood through the 1730s, I can develop a general profile of the novels of amorous intrigue and clarify the moral scandal of their popularity.

The following is a brief sketch of the Don Alonzo adventure. Silvia, "going upon a Frolick to divert herself a day or two" (385–386), dresses as a young man and, attended by a page, she sets out on the road. At a small tavern she is struck by the appearance of a young Don Alonzo, whom the master of the hotel reports is of quality but is now "*Incognito*, being on an Intrigue" (386). At supper, Don Alonzo and Silvia, the latter disguised as Bellumere, drink wine and share stories of erotic conquest. Don Alonzo tells Bellumere/Silvia of the wager he entered into at court with one Philander to seduce a countess, of whose favors Philander had been bragging. Don

Alonzo describes his successful intrigue—which involves deflowering the maid of the countess and then receiving, on three successive nights, the favors of the lady herself. Silvia, fired with passion, meditates exposing her true sex, but conceals herself for fear of his proven "inconstancy." She then asks, "Were you never in Love?" (393) Don Alonzo denies ever having been subject to love, but reports his passion at the sight of someone he had seen passing in the street in Brussels, the "whore" of a man who had recently taken orders; the latter being Octavio, the "whore" turns out, of course, to be Silvia herself. Silvia blushes. Forced to share a bed with Don Alonzo in the crowded inn, Silvia delays going to bed, stays dressed and awake to avoid discovery, and looks at Don Alonzo asleep, while reading "a little Novel, she had brought" (395). After exchanging rings as a token of friendship, they take separate roads to Brussels. The second part of the episode begins with Silvia's diversion of money Octavio had given her to enable her to retire respectably from the world; she uses it instead so that she may appear in lavish equipage and apparel on the "Toure" (416). Don Alonzo and Philander fall in love with this anonymous beauty. Silvia then assumes a masquer's garb to follow Don Alonzo into the park. She contrives that he sees upon her ungloved hand the ring that he has given Bellumere (418). After an artful duel of wits, Silvia refers the aroused and ardent Don Alonzo to Bellumere's apartment. To Silvia, "her Conquest was certain: He having seen her three times, and all those times for a several Person, and yet was still in Love with her: And she doubted not when all three were joyn'd in one, he would be much more in Love than yet he had been" (420). At her apartment, Silvia, disguised as Bellumere, greets Don Alonzo, leaving him ravished and confused to hear the same voice coming from this man that he has just heard coming from the fair incognito in the park. Silvia/Bellumere offers to introduce her/his "sister" to Don Alonzo, retires to get her, and returns in "a rich nightgown" as "the sister," to be also recognized by Don Alonzo as the anonymous court beauty and the incognito from the park—and also as Silvia herself (421). Now Don Alonzo renarrates the desire he felt on their night in the tavern as a homoerotic temptation he had resisted (422), and there follow eight days and nights of erotic pleasure. Thereafter, Silvia contrives a temporary return to her affair with Philander, and, in addition, pays off Philander's useful retainer, Briljard, with sex. The novel's last page offers a final postscript on the affair, with Silvia and Briljard taking such good advantage of Don Alonzo that "they ruin'd the Fortune of that young Nobleman" (439).

In the Don Alonzo episode of *Love Letters*, one can detect the distinctive traits of the novels of amorous intrigue, whereby narrative action comes under the sway of the intriguer's intrigue. The adventure begins with a disguised encounter that produces a strong and immediate erotic charge. Alonzo's arousing narrative (the story of his wager with Philander) embeds a brag (concerning his absolute erotic mastery) and issues in a claim (that he has never been in love). Finding her ambition piqued, the protagonist is called on to seduce Don Alonzo. Although contingencies of setting and situation are fraught with erotic potential (with, for example, the two forced to share the same tavern bed), and with hints of a promiscuous and polymorphous sexuality where anything might go, sexual resolution is blocked. The libertine's aim is not a merely physical possession, but a psychic mastery won through the other's confused erotic surrender. This requires an organized imbroglio or entanglement of the action, achieved through an intrigue, allowing the intriguer to prevail over the dupe/adversary, and to turn that victory into a communication to a third position—the ear of the social who can register and applaud the intriguer's skill. This social is sometimes a general public, sometimes a select intimate. To develop such an action, part II of the Don Alonzo episode shows the intriguing protagonist developing a scheme—pivoting on a succession of cross-gendered masquerades—that takes control of the action. The intriguer develops probabilistic calculations of his or her opponent's behavior out of a Machiavellian anthropology which assumes "the uniformity of human nature, the power of the animal instinct and emotions, especially emotions of love and fear . . ." (Benjamin quoting Dilthey, *Origin of German Tragic Drama*, 95–96). The mastery of the schemer depends on a general knowledge of psychology and physiology; the intrigue becomes a test of this mastery (Weber, "Genealogy of Modernity," 16–17). The reader watches the social exchange over the shoulder of the intriguer, illuminated by the harsh irony of the scheme.

The intriguer's machinations, consolidated into a scheme, become the plot's engine. The scheme entails a sadistic flattening of the social field and its agents which, in turn, assures the cynical superiority of the intriguer. While embedded in intrigue, the protagonist cannot have the luxury of a "deep" identity; a shifting set of social masks allows him or her to manipulate the social, as if from the outside, as a fixed and limited set of codes, conventions, and types. The intriguer is essentially alone and self-interested in his/her intriguing; alliances of purposes are provisional and open to disruption; the scheme is shaped to divide all others into solitary agents. By becoming an artist of manipulation, the intriguer turns plot into plotting, the theater of history into a spectacle of theatricality. Issues of point of view, epistemology, or narrative framing that are so important in other types of novels are here subordinated to a direct narrative of the headlong rush of the action. The very simplicity of character and motive—characters come freighted with almost no history, each agent automatically seeks to expand his/her power vis-à-vis others—gives these novels a strong sense of ludic immediacy. At the same time, the plotting of rivalrous egos produces an accelerating complication of the action, which none can fully control. For the duration of the intrigue, the plot produces variety, interest, and absorption, offering a kind of performance by both intriguer and author for the reader. The plot hooks the reader. Whether the scheme succeeds (as here) or misfires, whether it brings sex (as here) or death (as in other novels), an unveiling of identities closes the action. The fiction often ends with a movement out of the magic circle of intrigue and into the banality of the ordinary, here marked by Don Alonzo's financial ruin.

To adapt Clauswitz's famous adage, the novel of amorous intrigue suggests that sex is politics pursued by other means. Behn composed the first novels of amorous intrigue in Britain by braiding together several distinct elements: the stingingly abusive satiric discourse of early English party politics; the secret histories of Lafayette and Gabriel de Bremond (for example, the latter's *L' Hattigé: or the Amours of the King of Tamaran. A Novel*), with their disguised reference to public figures; and the Spanish dramas and novellas of court intrigue, with their scheming protagonists. In their crossing of love and politics, the machinations of the schemer are at first articulated with the ground rules of political strife, but end up transforming the love plot into a kind of political discourse. Critics have suggested how Behn's *Love Letters*, as well as her most famous novel, *Oroonoko* (1688), lend themselves to being read as political allegories of the betrayal of a monarch by his people (L. Brown, *Ends of Empire*, 56). But even Behn's novels of amorous intrigue which have no overt political reference (*The Fair Jilt*, *Agnes de Castro*, and *The History of the Nun: or, the Fair Vow-Breaker*) involve an ethos of power, rivalry, and cunning consonant with the diplomatic and military maneuvering of the early modern state.

NOVEL-READING BODIES

When, in the first decade of the eighteenth century, Delariviere Manley undertakes her comprehensive assault upon the Whigs then dominating the court of Queen Anne, she uses the novel of amorous intrigue to forge her own heady combination of sex and politics. Manley's best-seller of 1709 is titled *Secret Memoirs and Manners of several Persons of Quality of both Sexes. From the New Atalantis, an Island in the Mediterranean*. Imitating the scandalous chronicles published in France (Ballaster, *Seductive Forms*,

56–60), this text's popularity with readers makes it a most effective instrument for producing political scandal. But why does this text achieve such popularity? Readers have perhaps never failed to show an avid interest in the sex lives of the rich and famous. In *Nobody's Story*, Catherine Gallagher suggests that the effectiveness of Manley's political intervention, which depends on the scandal it produces for public characters, depends not on an authoritative factual, and reliably masculine, account of the sexual excesses of the Whig leaders, but rather on Manley's crossing politics with femininity and fiction. By giving her stories a greater fictional autonomy and absorptive erotic power, and by imbuing her narratives with the greater sexual scandal associated with women, Manley's novel-writing becomes successful political-party writing. Gallagher's reading suggests that Manley's crossings of politics and femininity, politics and fictionality are at once intended and symptomatic, rhetorical and effects of a particular historical occasion. Manley's feminine fictive power depends upon her ability to adapt to the political moment, through the framework of the scandalous chronicle, the form that Behn had made popular on the English print market in the 1680s—the novel of amorous intrigue. When Manley takes us, through the eyes of Lady Intelligence and the other narrators in the *New Atalantis*, behind the public facades of political legitimacy into the private sex lives of the great, we always find the same thing—lives conforming to the roles and positionalities found in novels of amorous intrigue. Manley's central Tory political allegory is woven by aligning Whig leaders with the schemer of the novel of amorous intrigue, and the English people with the innocent victims these voracious men and women seduce and destroy.

In the *New Atalantis* there is a fundamental tension between its framing allegory and the succession of unrelated narratives it frames. Its stories of vice are supposed to be contained by the moral commentary in dialogue offered by Astrea and Virtue at the close of each narrative, but Manley's use of the novel disrupts the pretension to epistemological and moral stability her political satire is supposed to restore, and opens her to the charge of libel directed at her by Steele in the *Tatler*. Although Steele and Manley are both successful denizens of that early print market, they use very different means to mobilize private reading subjects. The *Tatler* is part of the movement, associated with the growth of "sensibility," that foregrounds a garrulous, reflective, moralizing witty "tattler" or talker who can persuade readers to virtue by establishing a current of reasoned discourse about it. Through the dialogical strategies of this journalism, which involves quoting the letters of his correspondents, Steele produces a text that is critical and serial, and that consists of a miscellany of many elements. Because of the brevity of each number, swift changes of topic, and a carefully calculated tone of urbane nonchalance, the *Tatler* and the *Spectator* are designed to be anti-absorptive. Manley's *New Atalantis*, however, has a different tendency. By detouring the representation of social vices into the form of novels, and by making those novels sexy and absorptive, two kinds of bodies are engaged—the explicitly sexualized bodies of the novel's protagonists, and the bodies of the novel readers. The representation of the social is not mediated through a garrulous tongue that tattles, or through the less insinuating eye of a spectator; in other words, the reader's body is not sublimated into an instrument of conversation and cognition; instead, Manley intrigues her reader with a narrative which is structured to seduce the reading body into pleasure. It is this tendency of the novels of amorous intrigue that makes them a scandal in early-eighteenth-century British culture.

The way in which novelists incorporate novel reading within their novels is one symptom of the increased urgency of the debate about the scandal of the body absorbed in reading novels. While Behn barely represents novel reading in her fiction, Manley finds nuanced ways in which to do so, thereby engaging the larger issue of how or whether to license reading pleasure.[3] In the second part of the *New Atalantis*, Manley offers her own conduct-book warning against the dangers of romance reading. In her fictional casuistical defense, in the character of Delia, of her bigamous marriage to her cousin John Manley, the misbehavior of Manley/Delia is attributed to the romances which are read to her and her sister by "an old out-of-fashion aunt, full of the heroic stiffness of her own times, [who] would read books of chivalry and romances with her spectacles. This sort of conversation infected me and made me fancy every stranger that I saw, in what habit soever, some disguised prince or lover" (223–224). After a declaration of love by her cousin John Manley/Don Marcus, Manley/Delia narrates: "I was no otherwise pleased with it than as he answered something to the character I had found in those books that had poisoned and deluded my dawning reason. However, I had the honour and cruelty of a true heroine and would not permit my adorer so much as a kiss from my hand without ten thousand times more entreaty than any thing of that nature could be worth" (224). By aligning the delusions of novel reading

3. I have already noted one exception to Behn's neglect of this topos: when Silvia needs to keep herself awake while Don Alonzo sleeps, she reads a novel.

with the proverbial madness of love, Manley shifts Cervantes' satire on reading into a feminine register. For many of Manley's readers, the moral efficacy of this warning is vitiated by the fact that it appears in an anthology of novels less refined and more licentious than the heroic romances Manley mocks.

How does Manley come to confer on novel reading the power conventionally ascribed to love—that of infecting and poisoning reason? If we can answer this question, we will better understand why the *Tatler*'s Bickerstaff had lampooned Manley for the "artificial poisons" the *New Atalantis* communicated to its victims (Steele, *Tatler*, 63). In one of the most nuanced and compelling of her novels in the *New Atalantis*—the story of Charlot and the duke—Manley offers a sustained account of the pleasures and dangers of novel reading. The plot has two basic movements. In the first phase of the novel, the duke uses a prudential discourse to educate his ward Charlot to be a pattern of virtue, but then, in an unexpected reversal, ignores his own discourse and falls in love with her. In the second part, the duke prescribes a course of novel reading in order to seduce Charlot, while she, heedless of the second prudential discourse the countess offers her at court—"withhold sex until you get marriage"—plunges into illicit love, betrayal, and final ruin. Within this, the first full-scale novel in the *New Atalantis*, novel reading becomes the vehicle of a perverse (anti-)education which, by articulating reading with transgression of the Law, makes novel reading constitutive of a new erotic modern subjectivity.

Manley's narrative of the story of the duke and Charlot varies the old theme of the corruption of innocence by experience by figuring innocence as one who is unread, and experience as one who has read too much. Because Charlot is left to the care of the duke by her father upon his death, and because her own mother and the duke's first wife have died long before, Charlot is under the absolute control of the duke. She becomes a blank slate ready to receive her new "father's" cultural inscriptions. Since Charlot comes from a good family with a dowry of £40,000, the duke, who raises her with his own younger daughters, plans on marrying her to his son. Manley begins her narrative by offering a portrait of the duke which suggests why he is ideally suited to be the cynical manipulator of others. His meteoric rise in the court of William III results from the cunning and dissimulation exercised according to the "wise maxims of Machiavel who aimed to make his Prince great, let what could be the price" (28). The narrative moves from an account of the politic discrepancy between the duke's virtuous words and his self-interested actions to a description of Charlot's first education. In a version of the Pygmalion myth, the duke casts Charlot as a living expression of his specious attachment to virtue, thereby making her a repository of the patriarchal superego:

> The Duke had a seeming admiration for virtue wherever he found it, but he was a statesman, and held it incompatible (in an age like this) with a mans making his fortune. Ambition, desire of gain, dissimulation, cunning, all these were notoriously serviceable to him. 'Twas enough he always applauded virtue, and in his Discourse decried vice. As long as he stuck close in his practice, no matter what became of his words; these are not times when the heart and the tongue do agree! However, young Charlot was to be educated in the high road to applause and virtue. He banished far from her conversation whatever would not edify, airy romances, plays, dangerous novels, loose and insinuating poetry, artificial introductions of love, well-painted landscapes of that danger-ous poison. Her diversions were always among the sort that were most innocent and simple, such as walking, but not in public assemblies. Music, in airs all divine; reading and improving books of education and piety; as well knowing, that if a lady be too early used to violent pleasures, it debauches their tastes for ever to any others. [30][4]

The duke's successful politics is founded upon a rigorous separation of moral theory and political practice: a discourse of virtue disguises a secret pursuit of power and gain. The phrase "However, young Charlot was to be . . ." marks the shift to a description of the different road he charts for Charlot. In order for her to achieve a perfect virtue, Charlot is to shun "airy romances," "dangerous novels," and "loose and insinuating poetry" which produce "artificial introductions" of the "dangerous poison" of love. At the same time, for her "diversions," along with walking and divine music, she can read "improving books of education and piety."

In the admonitory lecture which this passage introduces, the duke repeats all of the injunctions contained in the conduct books for ladies, but then augments and rationalizes them through appeals to the late-seventeenth-century psychology founded upon the essential egotism of all humans. The duke's discourse differs from that of conventional conduct books through his emphasis on the strategic rewards of feminine virtue. For example, according to him, at the center of Charlot's practice must be a self-negation that fights back the dangerous impulses of her native intel-ligence: "She had a brightness of genius, that would often break out in

---

4. It seems to me that Ballaster misedits the last two clauses in the cited passage by putting a period after "piety"; this has the effect of detaching from the last sen-tence I have quoted (listing proper entertainments) the two clauses beginning "as well knowing" and ending "to any others." I have modified the passage to conform to the punctuation of the second edition of 1709.

dangerous sparkles." The display of her wit, though "she spoke never so well," must often "disgust" others, who will prefer their own words to hers. The practice of "modesty" and "silence" not only protects her [as the moral conduct books would say] against "self-love, vanity and coquetry," it will allow her to gratify the desire of others to be heard, and to hear the faults of others while she conceals her own (30–31). But in order to protect Charlot against the greatest danger to her virtue, the duke introduces the very thing he would protect her against: "But his strongest battery was united against love, that invader of the heart; he showed her how shameful it was for a young lady ever so much as to think of any tenderness from a lover, till he was become her husband . . ." (31). Having devised an apparently foolproof educational defense of Charlot's virtue—by cutting off access to this dangerous passion through reading, and imposing conduct that would discourage its spontaneous appearance in her heart—the duke takes the further precaution of insisting that she should, if desire still appeared, suppress it before it takes possession of her. Quoting Pythagoras, he tells her: "'[T]he assaults of love were to be beaten back at the first sight, lest they undermine at the second'"; and, should it take root, quoting Plato, he advocates a wise policy of concealment: "'[T]hat the first step to wisdom was not to love; the second so to love, as not to be perceived'" (31). The last advice gives Charlot a tincture of the duke's own policy in diplomacy and disguise.

Charlot's education is an apparent success: "the young Charlot *seemed* to intend herself a pattern for the ladies of this degenerate age" (31; italics mine) But in the surprising denouement to the sequence describing Charlot's first "education," corruption comes from outside the zone of conscious cultivation. Her fall also pushes the reader to speculate upon the desires which have motivated the duke in his formation of Charlot. The duke supplements his charge's education with diversions at his country estate that are designed "to confirm the young Charlot in that early love of virtue" and "to unbend her mind from the more serious studies." But what evades his censorship of romances, novels, and "lascivious" poetry are scenes from Ovid that represent virtuous goddesses provoking desire in others: "They sung and acted the history of the gods, the rape of Proserpine, the descent of Ceres, the chastity of Diana, and such pieces that tended to the instruction of the mind." The next sentence, beginning "One evening . . . ," shifts from a tense which assumes repeated action in the past into the diagetic present. Here, in a scene which stages a spectacular unity for Charlot as Diana, the virgin huntress, the duke's educational program for her culminates and her own desires are successfully sublimated. Charlot's virtuous performance as the virgin Diana produces a sublime image dangerous to others. Positioned as the Acteon-like reader/spectator in this scene, the duke is stunned to find that, behind this emblem of female integrity, there comes a voice which divides him from himself.

> One evening at a representation where Charlot personated the goddess, and the Duke's son Acteon, she acted with so animated a spirit, cast such rays of divinity about her, gave every word so twanging, yet so sweet an accent, that awakened the Duke's attention; and so admirably she varied the passions, that gave birth in his breast, to what he had never felt before. He applauded, embraced, and even kissed the charming Diana. 'Twas poison to his peace, the cleaving sweetness thrilled swiftly to his heart, thence tingled in his blood, and cast fire throughout his whole person. [32]

What gives Charlot playing Diana the power to send a sweet poison of desire through his blood? The duke's education had succeeded in producing a virtue in Charlot fittingly expressed in her assuming the role of Diana opposite Acteon. As a goddess of chastity and wild animals, protected by her nymphs, as well as by her own skill at archery, Diana comes to her secret grotto, "to bathe her limbs in the cool crystal" (Ovid, *Metamorphoses*, 62). It is this cool apartness, the oneness and self-completeness of virtue, which fascinates the transgressive gaze of the wandering Acteon (in the myth), as well as the cynical duke (in the novel). But the unity of Charlot is only speculative. The duke's educational program produces the paradoxes of any effort to teach innocence: to teach the innocent to protect themselves against vice, this program must inform; by offering an admonitory version of the desire it would shun, this discourse risks inciting the passion it would ward off. More problematically, the duke, to assure at least the appearance and reputation of honesty, counsels deceit. Carrying a desire hidden even from herself, the virgin Charlot returns in the form of the goddess Diana to confront the duke; as Diana, her voice carries an uncanny cadence which, like the water Diana tosses in the face of Acteon in punishment for his transgressive gazing, has the power to produce a metamorphosis in the duke. In going from the self-possession of a statesman to the castrated self-division of a tormented lover, the duke must confront a representation—that of Charlot as Diana—in which the desire of two subjects meets.

Between Charlot's first and second education, the duke goes from the position of the consumer of desire-inducing fiction (watching Charlot's performance as Diana) to being the devisor of a fictional program to induce desire in Charlot. The steps the duke takes also make clear the difference between a conventionally idealized love story and a novel of amorous intrigue. After her success as Diana, Charlot is distressed at the duke's visible alteration, and misinterprets his withdrawal as evidencing disapproval for her having excelled too visibly in acting her part (58). But her appeals to him for reassurance that she has done no wrong merely intensify his suffering: "By this time the Duke was fallen upon a chair that stood next him, he was fully in her reach, and without any opposition she had leisure to diffuse the irremediable poison through his veins" (32). Lost in love for Charlot, the duke temporarily falls away from his own diplomatic discourse: he has sleepless nights of torment during which his sense of duty (not to corrupt his own ward) and interest (not to disrupt with marriage his suit to the dowager princess) wage war with his lustful desire. He flees to the court to work and tries other lovers, but feels no peace. Jealous of his son, to whom Charlot was to be betrothed, the duke sends him on the Grand Tour. The moral conflict between love and honor is resolved when the duke "opened a Machiavel, and read there a maxim, 'that none but great souls could be completely wicked.' He took it for an Oracle to himself. He would be loath to tell himself, his *soul was not great enough for any attempt. . . .* Charlot was necessary to his very being! All his Pleasures faded without her! . . . Therefore Charlot he would have" (34). With moral scruples at an end and seduction his only goal, the duke schemes to change the desires of his ward.

Charlot's second education must undo the virtue produced by her first education. The duke's scheme is based on Charlot's previous forced abstention from what we might term the natural reading predilection of adolescents: "He had observed that Charlot had been but with disgust denied the gay part of reading. 'Tis natural for young people to choose the diverting before the instructive" (35). Therefore, the Duke calls her to "a noble library in all languages, a collection of the most valuable authors, with a mixture of the most amorous" (35). He frees her from her governess, and gives her the key to the library, ostensibly "to improve her mind and seek her diversion" (35). She is delighted with this double freedom, and promises, in language upon which the context bestows a dramatic irony, "that no action of hers should make him repent the distinction" (35). The duke immediately "[took] down an Ovid, and open[ed] it just at the love of Myrra for her father." The Duke is not too jaded to blush at the transparency of his designs: "conscious red overspread his face." The scene of Charlot's first novel reading provides a spectacle of auto arousal which is itself arousing.

> She took the book and placed herself by the Duke; his eyes feasted themselves upon her face, thence wandered over her snowy bosom and saw the young swelling breasts just beginning to distinguish themselves and which were gently heaved at the impression Myrra's sufferings

made upon her heart. By this dangerous reading he pretended to show her that there were pleasures her sex were born for, and which she might consequently long to taste! Curiosity is an early and dangerous enemy to virtue. The young Charlot, who had by a noble inclination of gratitude, a strong propension of affection for the Duke, whom she called and esteemed her papa, being a girl of wonderful reflection and consequently application, wrought her imagination up to such a lively height at the father's anger after the possession of his daughter, which she judged highly unkind and unnatural that she dropped her book, tears filled her eyes, sobs rose to oppress her and she pulled out her handkerchief to cover the disorder. [35]

If the duke's first education of Charlot constructs her as desirable because of her virtue, novel reading deforms and reforms her as a desiring subject. Here novel reading is represented as having the power to induce a spontaneous change in its reader.

The duke's selection of Charlot's reading assignment is crucial. In the *Metamorphosis*, Ovid tells of a young princess named Myrrha who cannot accept any of her many suitors because of her incestuous love for her father. In despair she attempts to commit suicide, and is saved by an old nurse who, discovering her secret passion, arranges to deliver her to her father's bed during the Ceres festival, when his wife is away. After numerous midnight rendezvous, he uses a lamp to discover his unknown lover, finds with horror it is his own daughter, and seeks to kill her with a sword. Myrrha flees. Reading Ovid produces an automatic response in Charlot: she drops her book, weeps, sobs, and seeks to cover the "disorder" of her body with her handkerchief. The transformative power of this text is attributed by the narrator to the way it takes Charlot's own virtuous qualities—her "noble inclination" of "gratitude" and "affection" for the duke; her wonderful powers of diligence (or "application"), concentrated thought (or "reflection"), and "imagination"—and channels these qualities into a dangerous act of identification with Myrra. Because of the way this particular Ovid story resonates with desires that Charlot has never felt, but to which she is susceptible, this reading can do two apparently contradictory things: it engages Charlot's conscious sense of justice while it indirectly suggests corrupting "pleasures her sex was born for." By inducing Charlot's sympathetic identification for the fate of Myrra—who receives her father's "unkind and unnatural" "anger" after his "possession" of her—reading this novel prepares her for the different scenario the duke is casting her in. His scheme will allow Charlot to repeat the action she has enjoyed as a reader—Myrra's seduction of the father—at the same time that his own kindness toward her will offer a happy revision of the "unkind and unnatural" "anger" of

Myrra's father. In this scene novel reading produces a metamorphosis hardly less complete than Ovid's. Charlot goes from a chaste maid to a desiring woman. Any unease Manley's reader might feel at looking over the duke's shoulder at "her face . . . her snowy bosom . . . her swelling breasts" is warded off by the framing of this scene with conduct-book warnings about the dangers of such reading: "By this dangerous reading . . . Curiosity is an early and dangerous enemy to virtue" (35).

Having softened her body and mind with novel reading, the Duke then delivers his final injection of poison: ". . . He drew her gently to him, drank her tears with his kisses, sucked her sighs, and gave her by that dangerous commerce (her soul before prepared to softness) new and unfelt desires" (36). A body disordered by reading can now be put in conjunction with a body disordered by watching her read: "He pressed her lips with his; the nimble beatings of his heart, apparently seen and felt through his open breast! the glowings! the tremblings of his limbs! . . . and eminent disorder—were things all new to her that had never seen, heard, or read before of those powerful operations struck from the fire of the two meeting sex" (36). Using a euphemistic language to suggest the autonomous movement of bodily parts Manley won't name, this passage implies that it is but one short step from the automatic reading of texts to the automatic response of bodies aroused. This "first" sexual exchange takes both Charlot and the duke beyond the operations of the will to bodies subject to an erotic "poison" first introduced by novel reading: "But the Duke's pursuing kisses overcame the very thoughts of any thing but the new and lazy poison stealing to her heart and spreading swiftly and imperceptibly through all her veins; she closed her eyes with languishing delight! delivered up the possession of her lips and breath to the amorous invader, returned his eager grasps and, in a word, gave her whole person into his arms in meltings full of delight!" (36) Although Charlot and the duke modestly stop short of the full sexual possession so clearly in reach, neither they nor the narrator can evade the pharmacological change wrought in Charlot's blood. "He saw and favoured her modesty, secure of that fatal sting he had fixed within her breast, that taste of delight which powerful love and nature would call upon her to repeat" (36). Now addicted to the sweet poison suffused in her blood, Charlot has been programmed to repeat the pleasures taught her in this scene.

The banal familiarity of this seduction should not distract us from the way it situates reading amorous fiction as uniquely powerful. This representation of the poisoning effect of reading and sex—as each produces a hunger that can only be gratified with more sex and reading—aligns a virgin reader's reading of amorous novels with an all-powerful "father's" seduction of an innocent virgin. In the two parts of this narrative the metaphor of poison is systematically applied to reading and spectatorship. The duke feels the poison of desire induced by watching Charlot play a scene from Ovid and the kisses she gives him; this same poison gains entrance to Charlot when she reads the Ovid story, and is then kissed by the duke. In both cases the poison is ambiguously distributed between reading and touching: the two are metonymically connected and their effects complementary. Rather than distinguishing between reading and touching, spectatorship and acting, this passage elides the distance and difference between the two. Novel reading achieves the effects of touching at a distance; it becomes touching by other means. Both reading and touching have the power to poison and drug the subject with an addictive need for sex. This way of figuring novel reading also precludes considering Charlot as a passive victim. Since her seduction requires her own imaginative sympathy with what she reads, Charlot is represented as being complicit with her seduction. Thus Manley's narrator analyzes the pleasure that Charlot feels at the duke's climactic avowals of love—she is pleased with the new importance she has in the eyes of one she had looked up to; she enjoys this new distinction. The catalytic effects of novel reading disclose desires that a virtuous education has concealed but cannot eradicate.

In the final stage of Charlot's second education, there is a displacement from the sexualized body, aroused by novel reading, to the novel-reading body. After his departure for court, the duke leaves Charlot with his library. This extraordinary scene—coming between seduction and literal sex— effects a displacement from sex to an orgy of reading. This orgy sublimates her longing in his absence into an uninhibited reading of "the speculative joys of love." The passage contrasts dangerous books with her earlier reading, so the latter begin to appear "airy and unreal."

[The Duke] was obliged to return to court and had recommended to her reading the most dangerous books of love—Ovid, Petrarch, Tibullus— those moving tragedies that so powerfully expose the force of love and corrupt the mind. He went even farther, and left her such as explained the nature, manner and raptures of enjoyment. Thus he infused poison into the ears of the lovely virgin. She easily (from those emotions she had found in her self) believed as highly of those delights as was imaginable. Her waking thoughts, her golden slumber, ran all of a bliss only imagined, but never proved. She even forgot, as one that wakes from sleep and the visions of the night, all those precepts of airy virtue, which she found had nothing to do with nature. She longed again to renew those dangerous delights. The Duke was an age absent from her; she could only in imagination possess what she believed so pleasing. Her memory was prodigious. She was indefatigable in reading. The Duke had left orders she should not be controlled in any thing. Whole nights were wasted by her in that gallery. She had too well informed her self of the speculative joys of love. There are books dangerous to the community of mankind, abominable for virgins, and destructive to youth; such as explain the mysteries of nature, the congregated pleasures of Venus, the full delight of mutual lovers and which rather ought to pass the fire than the press. The Duke had laid in her way such as made no mention of virtue or honour but only advanced native, generous and undissembled love. She was become so great a proficient that nothing of the theory was a stranger to her. [37]

This passage is fascinating in the way it replaces with a scene of reading the scene of erotic climax the narrative seemed to be preparing us for. The curriculum that the duke and Manley shape to defer, sublimate, and prepare for passion—reading about sex—is here represented *as* sex. In this way the foreplay of reading becomes the true erotic climax of Manley's novel. Its position in the narrative clues us to this shift: the scene comes in the position in the narrative diagesis where the duke would take full sexual possession of Charlot; it is carried forward with all the precautions appropriate to such a moment—no interruptions are to be permitted; Charlot is not to be "controlled" in anything; time offers no constraint to her complete indulgence of her new passion. But instead of consummating sex, she reads about sex. The automaton-like responses of the novel reader make this sex appear like masturbation. In this belated secondary education, or anti-education, books deliver all the secrets of natural sexual delights ("mysteries of nature . . . congregated pleasures . . . full delight of mutual lovers"). With this excess of the "speculative joys of love," it is appropriate that her own reading practice takes on an excessiveness of energy and quantity associated with great sexual feats: "Her memory was prodigious. She was indefatigable in reading." Little wonder that her earlier education and practice of virtue would appear utterly unreal.

Manley knows that the "dangerous books" which "ought to pass the fire" include her own books. Thus, when her narrator addresses the question of reading books which arouse, she implicitly marks her own text off as that which may be preoccupied with sex but is finally oriented toward virtue. By stopping short of a literalism ascribed to the books Charlot reads, Manley's own text can inscribe in its purview the sort of reading it warns its reader against. However, it is this dubious claim—that Manley's own book offers a warning against the worst kind of erotic reading—which becomes an issue in subsequent debates about the effects of novel reading.

After Charlot's seduction is complete and the duke has departed with the king, Charlot makes a confidant of a young countess, who gives her worldly cautions about her position. Within the story of passion Charlot and the duke are composing, the countess reads an entirely different meaning— namely, Charlot's willful abandonment of her own interest:

> . . . the Countess who was bred up in the fashionable way of making love, wherein the heart has little or no part—quite another turn of amour. She would often tell Charlot that no lady ever suffered herself to be truly touched but from that moment she was blinded and undone: the first thing a woman ought to consult was her interest and establishment in the world: that love should only be a handle towards it: when she left the pursuit of that to give up herself to her pleasures, contempt and sorrow were sure to be her companions. No lover was yet ever known so ardent, but time abated of his transport . . . [40]

The countess's advice constitutes a second prudential discourse, the very opposite of that of virtue. She promotes a diplomatic and disguised pursuit of one's own interest and warns that if Charlot does not learn to comport herself like a savvy player in an amorous intrigue, she will play the role of the dupe. Manley's narrative is carefully balanced so that Charlot appears as the sympathetic victim of her own idealism and virtue; she lives the love she expresses. Charlot's indecision in responding to the countess's advice is vividly rationalized: "Charlot knew not how to digest this system of amour; she was sure the Countess knew the world but thought that she knew not the Duke, who had not a soul like other men" (41). The countess is skeptical as to Charlot's claim that the duke is different from other men; she warns her that he "had took exactly the same methods to make his fortune" (41). Finally, the countess urges her to withhold her favors until he arranges marriage with her, and to read "the History of Roxelana who, by her wise address brought an imperious sultan, contrary to the established rules of the seraglio, to divide with her the royal throne" (41). This final reading suggestion has a fascinating resonance with the future direction of the British novelistic entertainment: Defoe rewrites the novels of amorous intrigue with *Roxana*, and Richardson's *Pamela* tells the story of a servant girl who pulls off the material victory here ascribed to the protagonist of the "History of Roxelana."

How are we to assess Manley's incorporation of the antinovel discourse into her own novels? The duke/Charlot "novel" is a conduct discourse against novel reading followed by a seduction scene catalyzed by reading novels. Why do we get this kind of scene in Manley, and later in *Love in Excess,* the first novel of amorous intrigue written by Haywood? Since by then the novel is being written in relation to a public-sphere discourse about the pleasures and dangers of novel reading, these early novels incorporate the antinovel discourse into their own plots defensively—that is, in order to fend it off, they co-opt a discourse that challenges the novel's right to circulate. Manley recuperates the antinovel discourse for a distinctly novelistic pleasure. The perceived danger of novel reading, expressed, for example, in the duke's first lecture, erects the interdictions of the social superego against the naive ego's quest for reading pleasure. Then, when the subject is seduced into transgressing the law against novel reading, and the obscenely desiring father lifts the ban upon novel reading, there is a narcissistic turning around of the ego upon itself (Freud, "On Narcissism"). Then the subject, here Charlot, metamorphoses into a novel-reading body destined to live a desire that is essentially transgressive.

The moral opposition to novels like those of Behn and Manley, which had been building over the first two decades of the eighteenth century, provokes other defenses from Manley: she borrows a refined critical apology for the moral value of fiction from a French conduct book to introduce her first prose fiction, *Queen Zarah* (1705); in the preface to the *Memoirs of Europe,* the sequel to the *New Atalantis,* Manley defends the *New Atalantis* as satire; and finally, in her autobiographical self-defense, *Revella* (1714), she celebrates the novel's power to move—we might say "turn on"—its readers.[5] This final rhetoric of reading pleasure—what has been described in this reading of one novel of the *New Atalantis* as the automatism provoked by novel reading—becomes articulated in the Frenchman D'Aumont's celebration of Manley in the introduction to *Revella.* D'Aumont uses a psycho-physiology of baroque excess to explain why Manley's texts have made her an object of curiosity and celebrity:

> I have not known any of the moderns in that point come up to your famous author of the Atalantis. She has carried the passion farther than could be readily conceiv'd: Her Germanicus on the embroider'd bugle bed, naked out of the bath:—her young and innocent Charlot, transported with the powerful emotion of a just kindling flame, sinking with delight and shame upon the bosom of her lover in the gallery of books . . . are such

5. For a discussion of the French sources of Manley's purloined preface, see Bartolomeo, *A New Species of Criticism,* 23. The preface to *Queen Zarah* derives from the attack on the heroic romances by the defenders of the new fiction in the manner of *La Princesse de Clèves.*

representatives of nature, that must warm the coldest reader; it raises high
ideas of the dignity of human kind, and informs us we have in our
composition, wherewith to taste sublime and transporting joys: after
perusing her enchanting descriptions, which of us have not gone in search
of raptures which she every where tells us, as happy mortals, we are
capable of tasting. [4]

In this passage D'Aumont reduces "the *Atalantis*" to a series of narrative
highpoints in which a succession of aroused bodies are naked and available
for "possessing" both by the seducers within the narratives and, through a
projective identification, by the readers' bodies, warmed and absorbed by
Manley's "enchanting descriptions." By 1714 Manley is leaving behind the
context of party politics, and defends her writing for its power to "move"
readers to "transporting joys." As she announces in *Revella*, "hence-
forward . . . [I will] write for pleasure and entertainment only, wherein
party should no longer mingle . . ." (117). By representing herself as a
celebrity author rather than a morally vigilant satirist, Manley finally
accepts the separation of novel reading and politics explicitly advocated by
the male friend and narrator of *Revella*, Sir Charles Lovemore, a separation
that is implicitly endorsed by Steele, Addison, and many others. This not
only means that she is retracing the movement that Behn had followed
incompletely in the 1680s, leading from political discourse intended to
influence affairs of state to novels intended as entertainment; it also suggests that readers and authors of the early eighteenth century are accepting a more settled separation of politics and fiction, and a location of novel
reading in a private sphere of reading entertainment. This changed location
of novel reading is reflected in Manley's own collection of novels, the *Power
of Love* (1720), but is most fully achieved in the novels published by Eliza
Haywood in the 1720s.

FORMULATING FICTION

Every so often a runaway success changes the form of media on the market. For example, the use of special effects, stunts, and quick-cut editing in
Star Wars changed a broad spectrum of Hollywood production after 1977
(W. Warner, "Spectacular Action"). Eliza Haywood's three-part best-seller,
Love in Excess (1719–1720), builds on the potential already evident in the
novels of amorous intrigue written by Behn and Manley. Haywood
expands the number and popularity of novels on the market through a set
of compositional changes. First, she writes her novels outside the context of
party politics and patronage, and therefore drops the political rationale and

address of the earlier novelists.[6] Haywood's novels eschew the disguised secret history that allows Behn's *Love Letters* to be about the succession crisis, and dispenses with the elaborate allegorical machinery of Astrea's tour through Atalantis used in Manley's *New Atalantis*. At the same time, Haywood drops the use of the Theophrastan "character" which Behn uses to deepen and complicate her presentation of Silvia at the beginning of the *Amours*, and which Manley uses to introduce a complex figure such as the duke in *New Atalantis*. What results is character simplified into a function of position in the narrative. Settings—like the lush nocturnal garden—are abstracted into generality. While love and lust figure prominently in the novels of Behn and Manley, Haywood gives a special privilege to love over every other social value, and subordinates traditional claims to improve the reader to the relatively new one of offering diversion and entertainment. All these changes slim down the novel of amorous intrigue into a repeatable formula on the market, grounded in a private reading practice of a general reader. Haywood's repositioning of the novel of amorous intrigue is both the cause and the effect of her remarkable novel production during the twenties and thirties, which enabled her to become the most prolific novel writer of the century (C. Turner, *Living by the Pen*). It is the sheer quantity of Haywood's production in this period, and the unprecedented popularity it enjoys, which helps give the bad name to novels throughout the century.

In order to entice the general reader to buy and read novels for entertainment, Haywood develops a new kind of formula fiction for the market. Her novels of amorous intrigue have the signal traits of formula fiction on the market recognizable from the eighteenth century to the present day, from gothic novels to detective fiction, from science fiction to contemporary romance. I will describe this interlocking set of eight traits through reference to Haywood's first and most popular novel, *Love in Excess* (1719–1720). This novel establishes Haywood's fame and sets the type which she varied in her novels of the following decades. The eight traits are as follows.

(1) The main characters in formula fiction are parsed into heroes and villains, the good and the evil. The protagonist of *Love in Excess* is Count

6. Richetti notes the shift by which even her explicit imitations of Manley's *New Atalantis* turn political satire into a general social criticism of the great (Richetti, *Popular Fiction*, 159–167); Ballaster notes that of all Haywood's novelistic productions, only *The Adventures of Eovaai* (1736) attempts a pointed attack upon the (Walpole-led) Whig ministery (Ballaster, *Seductive Forms*, 151–158).

D'Elmont, the gay and noble but oddly susceptible hero who gradually changes from a superficial sexual opportunist to a high-souled lover. Around this figure are arranged a set of contrasting characters: the virtuous victims of love (Amena in part I and Melliora in parts II and III) and the voracious rivals for D'Elmont's love—the restless, domineering, over-passionate Alousia (in parts I and II) and the extravagant Italian Ciamara (in part III). In the second part of the novel, Alousia and the baron are evil plotters, dangerously extreme in their passions, and intent on manipulating others for their pleasure. D'Elmont and Melliora are the noble but balked lovers: they inhabit situations not of their own making, love in pained silence, and exercise restraint in their plotting.

(2) In formula fiction, action, incident, and plotting take precedence over ideas or character. The nature of its action is not what is most crucial to formula fiction. In the late nineteenth century, Henry James and Robert Louis Stevenson debated whether it was more interesting to center novels on inward thought or on pirate adventure. For formula fiction, the most decisive element is the way in which action is organized and paced according to a rhetoric of expectation that keeps the reader wondering, "What will happen next? I must know." Radway, in describing the element common to commercial fiction, sums up "plot" as being that which can "catch a reader up in a story that seems to propel itself forward with force" (Radway, "The Book of the Month Club," 276). In *Love in Excess* the elaboration of sexually motivated intrigues is the engine of action and interest; complication is produced by multiple plots and their misfirings. To facilitate the foregrounding of plot, characters must be simple or "flat," as opposed to complex and "round." Characters are defined less by anything they bring to the narrative before their appearance in it than by their position in the plot. Haywood does not usually even provide the quick summary histories of characters that are found in Manley and Behn.

(3) In formula fiction the big payoff in reader pleasure comes from the surprising and wonderful reversal that answers the question, "How will things turn out?" I have already pointed out how the schemes central to novels of amorous intrigue give a rigorous mechanism to the action. Whether plots are known in advance or are only disclosed as they unfold, the reader's suspense derives from wanting to know if the scheme will succeed. This entails a contradictory division of sympathy between plotters and dupes: the former are favored for their mastery and wit, the latter for their vulnerability and innocence. In *Love in Excess* Haywood does not bestow upon any one character the predominant authority and power that Manley often confers upon her intriguers, so plot takes on a ludic chanciness,

feelings appear more spontaneous, and the action is less predestined than it is in Manley's novels. This comparative openness of Haywood's plot allows for surprising turns to the action: plots sometimes misfire, bringing bad fortune to the plotter and good fortune to the dupe; and often the dupe becomes aware of the intriguer's scheme, and reverses the action through a counterplot. The use of surprising reversals makes Haywood's novels especially well-adapted to the early modern print market. Central motifs of her fiction—misdirected communication, interruption just before the moment of sexual climax, accidental detours of the action—have the effect of deferring narrative closure so as to require more novel writing. In this way, it is what links these novels to the market—repetition and seriality—that gets woven into the workings of the plot.

(4) Formula fiction is rife with didactic messages. It is by the way in which Haywood's *Love in Excess* counterposes virtuous love to intriguing lust, the "fable of persecuted innocence" (Richetti, *Popular Fiction*) to the rapacious ego, that characters come to personify values readied for action. This iconography of character interpellates general readers into a morally charged amorous ideology. Didactic messages may be explicitly stated or they may merely be underlying, but they are clear. Thus, D'Elmont is punished in the second part of the novel for his central crime in the first installment, in which he marries Alousia, a woman he does not love. The automatism of the action at the climax of part II is the effect of schemes and machinations contending in a space which, from the position of agents, may appear aimlessly mechanical. But from the vantage point of readers, this action achieves a pleasing moral design: the villains are hoisted on their own petard, while the good characters are eventually rewarded with each other.

(5) Formula fiction, as its name implies, follows pre-established formulas which require no justification on grounds outside the fiction. To say "it's just a romance/detective fiction/thriller" rationalizes a novel's elements through a tautological invocation of the already known. Formula fiction does not depend upon the authority of literary genre as established by criticism (for example, tragedy or epic), or appeal to criteria (whether mimetic, ethical, or aesthetic) outside of reading for entertainment. Formula fiction's imitation of previous formulas helps account for its coherence for readers as well as for its reticence about aspiring to any higher cultural calling. Rather than claiming originality or singularity, or evolving a distinct authorial style, the writers of formula fiction rely upon the continuity of received formulas as the matrix for pleasing variation. Variety is achieved by using widely accepted formulas, but shifting or mixing them, or doing

one better. The obvious indebtedness of Haywood's first novel to the novels of amorous intrigue only enhanced the potential market for *Love in Excess*. In his defense of comedy and romance against the critical conceptions developed from the higher forms of tragedy and epic, Northrop Frye argues that the pleasure of the former, like that involved in reading detective fiction, comes from a sense of removal from actual experience, or from realistic high mimetic expectations, so that the reader can inhabit a conventionalized narrative with "exceptionally vigorous pacing." Then aesthetic pleasure comes from watching how the author's rhetorical skill works within conventions (Frye, *Natural Perspective*).

(6) Formula fiction accommodates incompleteness, fragmentariness, or last-minute revision. Rather than justifying the narrative as a unified whole, it makes use of sequels and outrageous delaying tactics to draw out the action and prolong suspense. Imitating the successful serial publication of *Love Letters* and the *New Atalantis*, *Love in Excess* is published in two parts, and then, after its runaway success, receives a third and final installment. While all-at-once publication of a work complete in itself confirms the coherent design of the author, the use of serial publication allows for a more nuanced playing of the market. Thus, the three parts of *Love in Excess* do not have the symmetry, equal length, and thematic echoes found in the three parts of *Tom Jones*. Rather, Haywood's divisions are as opportunistic as a Hollywood movie ending that has been reshot after prescreening. As the element that provides variety in repetition of the already proven, seriality is the form-disrupting form of media culture.

(7) With formula fiction, the basic exchange is entertainment for money. Formula fiction sometimes makes claims to improve readers, but these are usually quite dubious, tendered only in order to evade censure or censorship. *Love in Excess* does not even pretend—in either its dedication or its poems in praise of Haywood—to bring its reader anything but pleasure. But even though these novels do not make higher claims to moral truth or beauty, ideological work is being done in even the most formulaic entertainment. In *Love in Excess*, for example, the licentious sexuality of the upper class is glorified, the subordination of women to men is condemned but reinscribed, heterosexual love is made a touchstone of social value, and so on.

(8) Formula fiction does not encourage the self-reflection familiar from high-brow culture. While lacking a systematic critical reflection, however, formula fiction does incorporate a certain defense of itself. Thus, for example, *Love in Excess* carries a rather complex account of the pleasures of

novel reading. Perhaps Haywood anticipated the resistance her novels would produce in the culture of their reception.[7]

This brief description of formula fiction shows how Haywood, by abstracting and simplifying the novel of amorous intrigue, opens it to a potentially endless repetition on the market. With this reformulation of fiction, she reaches beyond the implied audiences of earlier novels—the courtly coteries addressed by the *précieux* with the French *grands romans* and *La Princesse de Clèves*, or the party-political audience of Behn's secret histories and Manley's scandalous chronicles. Haywood's schematic treatment of character and intricate development of involving action make the novel an entertainment machine. The very elements of these novels that drew the scorn of cultural critics—their shallowness, their opportunistic seriality and shameless repetition, and their absence of compelling ethical justification—all fitted this new commodity so as to thrive on an urban print market of diverse buyers ready to pay cash for entertainment. Haywood's novels anticipate the products of what Adorno and Horkheimer (*Dialectic of Enlightenment*) pejoratively dub "the culture industry," but which I shall describe in less tendentious terms as "media culture."

FIGURING THE GENERAL READER

Although Haywood does not attempt a political or moral justification of her fiction, she does defend the reading and writing of novels. Over the course of three linked debates about novel reading, and one big sex scene in part II of *Love in Excess*, she defends novel reading as an autonomous pleasure of the private reader engaged in erotic fantasy. Within this defense of novel reading, Haywood figures the general reader of her novels as one free of particular ideological and moral investments, and open to the diverse play of fantasy. D'Elmont initiates the first discussion about reading after he notices Melliora reading in a garden. With her unaware that he is watching, he gradually approaches her to interrupt her reading, and she appears to him at that moment to be possessed of the charming self-

7. Frye discusses formula fiction while seeking to distinguish Shakespeare's more fantastic comedy and romance from Ben Jonson's more referential and descriptive social comedies. Frye argues that literature is just as formulaic and convention-bound as formula fiction (Frye, *Natural Perspective*, 4–5). In both literature and formula fiction, one's toleration for repetition depends upon whether one enjoys, and therefore will extend one's reading energies to, the form in question.

completeness Freud (in "On Narcissism") ascribes to narcissism and its attractions to others: "he perceived Melliora lying on a green Bank, in a Melancholy but a charming Posture, . . . her Beauties appear'd if possible more to advantage than ever he had seen them, or at least he had more opportunity thus unseen by her, to gaze upon 'em . . . he stood for some moments fix'd in silent Admiration . . . Melliora was so intent on a Book she had in her Hand, that she saw not the Count 'till he was close enough to her to discern what was the Subject of her Entertainment" (II: 24). The circular relay of gazes in this scene eroticizes reading: the gaze of the reader of Haywood's novel is borne, through the "silent" and "fixed" gaze of the central character, to the body of the heroine, herself absorbed in reading. In the autoerotic movement Freud associates with the ego's turning around upon itself in narcissism, the act of reading (that is, reading of a book by Melliora, reading of Melliora by D'Elmont, and reading of the whole scene by Haywood's reader) enfolds and completes the reading subject. Finding that Melliora is reading the philosophy of Fontenelle, D'Elmont frames an elegant conceit: if that gentleman had known her, he would have written of love and Melliora. When she refuses the compliment by "blush[ing] Extremely" and affirming the value of serious reading, D'Elmont adds that she is lucky to be born in an age that has these treatises from the previous age, "since (I am very Confident) this, and a long space of future Time will have no other Theme, but that which at present you seem so much adverse to [that is, love]" (II: 25). With the words of her lead character, Haywood reflects upon the vogue for novels of love like her own, which menace the reading of serious authors such as Fontenelle. This debate produces a silent "disorder" in the heroine which D'Elmont reads as the first sure sign of her love for him. He holds her in his arms but ventures no further.

The second debate about reading casts Melliora as the strict censor of "softening" and amorous reading. When the Baron D'Espernay's sister Mellantha seeks "to divert the Company with some Verses on Love," Melliora uses the occasion to condemn the "passion," and also, the narrator tells us, "to Conceal it in her self" and "check what ever hopes the Count might have." But her austerely moral condemnation of the verses the others have enjoyed allows her to become the witty and intellectual woman whose condemnation of love merely incites desire for herself:

> [Melliora] Now Discovered the force of her Reason, the Delicacy of her Wit, and the penetration of her Judgment, in a manner so sweetly surprising to all that were Strangers to her, that they presently found, that it was not want of Noble, and truly agreeable Thoughts or Words to

express 'em, that had so long depriv'd them of the Pleasure of hearing her; she urg'd the Arguments she brought against the giving way to Love, and the Danger of all softening Amusements, with such a becoming fierceness, as made every Body of the Opinion that she was born only to Create Desire, not be susceptible of it her self. [II: 34]

By exposing the fierce force of penetrating reason behind the modest reticence of the beautiful woman roused to speech, this scene gives Melliora a phallic power. Because Melliora's chaste arguments against love and softening amusements invoke the Law, those amusements seem all the more delicious. "Not a little alarmed" to see her "appear so much in earnest," D'Elmont seeks a private interview to explore what might lie behind the severe expressions of this superego. There, he finds a novel reader in undress (II: 34).

Behind Melliora's virtuous condemnation of "softening Amusements" there is another kind of reading practice and another kind of desire. As a novel reader, Melliora is represented neither as virginally apart nor as a formidable polemicist; rather, she is portrayed as an erotic object, just come from her bath, "lying on a Couch in a most Charming Dissabillee" with her hair flowing down her shoulders. Her gown is white and her body, as open as a book, "discover'd a Thousand Beauties." But D'Elmont is not just enchanted by finding her in "undress"—he is also interested in her mind and reading, and anxious to make discoveries. Thus, "casting his Eyes on the Book which lay there, [and finding . . .]it to be Ovid's *Epistles*, How Madam (Cry'd he, not a little pleas'd with the Discovery) dare you, who the other day so warmly inveigh'd against Writings of this Nature, trust your self with so Dangerous an Amusement? How happens it, that you are so suddenly come over to our Party?" (II: 35) To deflect this criticism, Melliora deploys arguments which have the contradictory logic of the three reasons Freud describes as being offered to the reproach of having chipped a borrowed kettle: each reason contradicts the other two, but all three pursue the logic of the alibi. First, Melliora insists that it is only by chance that she reads Ovid: "Indeed my Lord (answer'd she, growing more Disorder'd) it was Chance rather than Choice, that Directed this Book to my Hands, I am yet far from approving Subjects of this kind, and Believe I shall be ever so." Then she bolsters her excuse by exempting herself from the dangers this reading might pose for other readers: "Not that I can perceive any Danger in it, as to my self, the Retirement I have always liv'd in, and the little propensity I find to entertain a Thought of that uneasie Passion, has hitherto secur'd me from any Prepossession, without which, *Ovid*'s Art is Vain." Then D'Elmont refutes this argument in such a way as to use the topic of reading to take her from representations to the reality of love: "[N]ow you Contradict your former Argument, which was, that these sort of Books were, as it were, Preparatives to Love, and by their softning Influence melted the Soul, and made it fit for Amorous Impressions . . ." (II: 35–36). D'Elmont's rejoinder pushes Melliora to her third defense of reading novels. To deflect the central reason for condemning novels—that they prepare the fancy to move from fiction to reality—Melliora invokes the powers of the critical reader like herself who is more intent upon noting the "Misfortunes that attended the Passion of *Sappho*, than the Tender, tho' never so Elegant Expressions it Produc'd: And if all Readers of Romances took this Method, the Votaries of *Cupid* would be fewer, and the Dominion of Reason more Extensive" (II: 36). Melliora's opposition between love and reason is taken up and contested by D'Elmont, and allows them to have a disguised discussion of their own forbidden love. D'Elmont finally makes an explicit avowal of love, while Melliora feels more sympathy for him than she should.

Haywood's staging of these interlocked debates does not merely follow the familiar if perverse economy by which warnings about the dangers of novel reading lead to an enactment of those dangers. By incorporating the critique of novel reading that has anathematized her own writing, Haywood exploits the erotic potential of what we might call the scandal of the reading body. These scenes unfold three positions in the debate around novel reading: first, Melliora adheres to the improving reading of the previous generation against the encroachment of new forms of reading; then, she offers a moral rant against the baleful effect of those "softening amusements"; finally, she is "discovered" to be a novel reader after all, offering inconsistent casuistical arguments to exempt herself from her general proscription of novel reading. By mapping D'Elmont's seduction of the virtuous Melliora onto Haywood's seduction of the reader who would abstain from novels, Haywood allows her heroine to become a figure for the general reader she intends to seduce. This rehearsal of the debate around novels prepares for the fictional climax Haywood uses to implicate her reader in the general desire she ascribes to her characters. For when D'Elmont, with the help of his "friend," the scheming baron, inserts himself in a plot from one of the novels whose reading he promotes—secretly entering Melliora's room when she is sleeping, and for a moment resisting waking and seducing her—he plumbs her desire. D'Elmont (together with the reader) finds that Melliora, although she champions philosophy, condemns the danger of "softening amusements" in company, and claims the critical powers to resist emulating the amorous behavior of novels, nonetheless has desires indistinguishable from those who succumb to the allure of novels. While she dreams, Melliora is implicated in the delusion she has mocked in both novel readers and lovers: "in a Lovers Mind Illusions seem Realities" (II: 37).

Haywood's narrator defines, in the terms of a general psychology of human desire, that which makes all men and women susceptible while dreaming: "[W]hatever Dominion, Honour, and Virtue may have over our waking Thoughts, 'tis certain that they fly from the clos'd Eyes, our Passions then exert their forceful Power, and that which is most Predominant in the Soul, Agitates the fancy, and brings even Things Impossible to pass. Desire, with watchful Diligence repell'd, returns with greater violence in unguarded sleep, and overthows the vain Efforts of Day" (II: 47). Freud never said it better. In terms remarkably close to the psychoanalytic understanding of fantasy, and the role of dreams in evading the moral censor, Haywood describes how desire works through fantasy to allow Melliora to effect through sleep what others do through novel reading: "Melliora in spite of her self, was often happy in Idea, and possessed a Blessing, which shame and Guilt, deter'd her from in reality" (II: 47). This prepares Melliora, at the moment when the desiring hero lingers by her bedside, to act out her desire. Building toward the first erotic climax of the novel, Haywood's narrator tells us that when Melliora dreams,

> Imagination at this time was Active, and brought the Charming Count much nearer than indeed he was, and he, stooping to the Bed, and gently laying his Face close to her's (Possibly Designing no more than to steal a Kiss from her unperceive'd) that Action, Concurring at that Instant, with her Dream, made her throw her Arm (still Slumbering) about his Neck, and in a Soft and Languishing Voice, Cry out, O! D'Elmont Cease, cease to Charm, to such a height—Life cannot bear these Raptures! . . . [II: 47–48]

By offering a parenthetical speculation about D'Elmont's intentions— "(Possibly Designing no more than to steal a Kiss . . .)"—the narrator assumes an uncharacteristic tentativeness about her hero. After Melliora's rapturous gesture, the narrator alibis his failure to leave his unconscious lover's side:

> Where was now the Resolution he was forming some Moments before? If he had now left her, some might have applauded an Honour so uncommon; but more wou'd have condemn'd his Stupidity, for I believe there are very few Men, how Stoical soever they pretend to be, that in such a Tempting Circumstance wou'd not have lost all Thoughts, but those, which the present opportunity inspir'd. That he did, is most certain,

for he tore open his Wastcoat, and joyn'd his panting Breast to hers . . ."
[II: 48]

There follow the virtuous protestations Melliora makes in waking, countered by D'Elmont's resolve not to leave her at the moment when her desire has become so transparent to him. Like the climactic sex scenes in the novels of Behn and Manley, this scene incites an eroticized roving gaze, a lawful-conduct discourse, and a euphemistic language for body parts which condenses the drive and the law in a baroque excess of purple prose (II: 49). The interruption of Melantha, which "saves" Melliora, merely teases the reader (II: 50).

The plot device upon which this scene turns—the coincidence of Melliora's dream about her lover and his bedside presence during that dream—constructs an alibi for both lovers and readers. Because Melliora speaks her desire in a dream, she is spared the charge of immodesty; her grasping D'Elmont at the very moment he is about to depart excuses him for acting on his passion. But these two excuses for the characters also operate within the reading debate about novels as an alibi for the reader. The reader who gratifies her/his fantasy desire through reading novels does what the privately dreaming Melliora and the lucky D'Elmont do: she or he responds to a desire represented as fateful and natural. By relieving the characters of the charge of blatant sensuality, the narrator releases the reader to consume the purple prose and eroticized situations of this fiction. But further than this, by dissolving particularized subjectivity into automatized bodies, this sort of scene of intense sexual arousal helps to generalize subject positions by blurring identity. The two characters and the reader flow into one scene of polymorphous sexual arousal, where the drive exceeds the subject position through which it operates (Lacan, *Seminar* VII, 43–56).

THE NOVEL OF AMOROUS INTRIGUE AS MEDIA CULTURE

How are we to define the cultural location of the novels of amorous intrigue? I have noted several fundamental problems with interpreting Behn, Manley, and Haywood as instances of women's popular culture: first, their novels are not cast in the form of an address to a woman reader; second, although the author is sometimes figured as a woman, she is not consistently feminist; and third, there is no evidence that the early modern print market was segmented by gender. On the other hand, I have shown that the plot-centered rhythms of the novel of amorous intrigue facilitate its address to a general reader. Such a general reader does not belong to the lower orders of society. John Richetti, in a retrospective qualification of his own use of the term "popular" in *Popular Fiction Before Richardson*, has pointed out that the novels of Manley and Haywood assume a more literate reader and affluent book buyer than the ballad collections and chap books surveyed in Margaret Spufford's *Small Books and Pleasant Histories* (Richetti, *Popular Fiction*, xviii). Nor do the novels of amorous intrigue have the broad reach across classes that Ronald Paulson argues for signboards, *Joe Miller's Jests*, or Hoyle's book on whist (Paulson, *Popular and Polite Art*). There may be very compelling historical reasons why it is difficult to articulate the concept of the popular with culture before the late eighteenth century. In *Discourse on Popular Culture*, Shiach demonstrates the gradual relocation of the term "popular" from the political to the cultural sphere. Only after that shift can the social sphere be presumed to support cultural collectivities given coherent identity through their expression as popular culture. Marxist and feminist conceptions of cultural identity and popular culture, widely associated with democratization, seem to depend upon a late-enlightenment conceptualization of peoples by class, gender, nationality, or "race" (in the special nineteenth-century sense) not yet available in the early eighteenth century. Only after those changes have occurred can novels be said to articulate, in Taine's words, "the voice of a people."

My readings of Manley and Haywood also suggest the liabilities of the literary paradigm for interpreting the novels of amorous intrigue. Any effort to place these novels under the rubric of literature ends by judging them as lacking and falling short, by coming too soon. Thus, in the first two chapters of this study, I noted the way in which the literary histories of the novel, such as those of Saintsbury and Baker, feature Behn and Haywood as the false starts and miscarriages on the way to the legitimate novels that follow them. But even when the high literary agendas of literary histories have been displaced by a more analytical study of culture, the novel of amorous intrigue continues to be discredited. Thus important studies of Richetti, Hunter, and McKeon position Behn, Manley, and Haywood as on the way to, but always falling short of, the truly novelistic, because they lack the self-conscious posture of literary realism. Such a positioning of Manley and Haywood is explicit in the title and text of Richetti's pioneering *Popular Fiction Before Richardson* (1969), but it persists in Hunter's treatment of all three novelists as writers "before novels" in his 1990 book of that title. McKeon allows Behn, Manley, and Haywood to figure in the "origins" of novels, but not the actual writing of them; instead, their narrative matter contributes to the ideological matrix out of which, through the dialectical machinery of McKeon's plotting, novels by Cervantes, Swift,

Bunyan, Defoe, Richardson, and Fielding may arise (W. Warner, "Realist Literary History").

Instead of being popular or literary, the novels of Behn, Manley, and Haywood should be understood as instigators of a new contagion of reading deemed a threat in early modern Britain. Such a third possibility can be broached by exploring the latent meaning of the topos of novel reading as poison or infection. In chapter 1, I noted that from the eighteenth-century literary histories of Reeve and Dunlop to those of Saintsbury and Baker, there is an extension, upon critical-ethical grounds, of the earliest condemnations of novel reading as threatening the body of culture with poison or infection. Such a tendentious characterization of the dangers of novel reading unfolds within a larger struggle about the directions of culture. In the next chapter I seek to interpret the reasons for such a volatile response to reading for entertainment. In the *Gutenberg Galaxy*, Marshall McLuhan characterized the Augustan satirists as prescient if panicked critics of the global threat that print media presents to classical literary culture. Swift and Pope's defense of classical culture pivots upon locating themselves upon one side, and the grub-street writers on the other, of the loaded set of oppositions which proliferate around true genius and mechanical writing: ancient is to modern, as high is to low, as genius is to mechanism, as literature is to hack writing, as brain is to fingers, as literature-as-learning is to literature-as-writing, as literary author is to hack.[8] On the favored side of this divide, there is the promise of a neoclassical reconciliation of culture and nature; on the other side, there is the uncontrolled reproduction of print as a menace to culture. In *The Dunciad*, the bookseller, as unprincipled media worker on the print market, emerges as a comic villain who pollutes a prior body of literary culture supposed to be pure. Grub-street writers sometimes found an ingenious way to counter yet accommodate such attacks, by endorsing and repeating the mythological framework developed by the satirists, within an inverted celebration of their own popular writing (MacDermott, "Literature and the Grub Street Myth," 27).

Manley and Haywood's opportunistic recuperation of the antinovel discourse within their novels shows how to turn the critique of modern reading to advantage. In Charlot's seduction through reading, the dart of love/ reading enters the body with sudden violence and infects the blood with the

---

8. For this schematization of oppositions as the "grub-street myth," see MacDermott, "Literature and the Grub Street Myth," 17–18; representing the Augustan satirists as anxious and gloomy critics of modernity is a commonplace of eighteenth-century studies. For commentary, see Hunter, *Before Novels*, 106–109.

poison or potion to which romances like *Tristan* gave a magical efficacy. While Manley keeps a hold, albeit a tenuous one, upon the didactic warning against novel reading, the pyrotechnics of her erotic prose strive for the automatic arousal attributed by the old romances to the pharmacology of love. In Haywood's *Love in Excess* the perils of novel reading only subsist as a resistance in the heroine which the ardent hero must overcome. By administering love "in excess"—that is, as an overdose—the resistance of Melliora and of Haywood's novel reader can be overcome. Through their inscription of the reading debate, Manley and Haywood attempt to transpose the figure of the automaton-like novel reader from an object of cultural scandal to one that produces fascinated identification. But by vanquishing the cultural superego that would control reading pleasure within her text, and by acceding to the role of arbitress of passion, gifted with the art of arousing her readers, Haywood opens the way for a vengeful return of the superego. In this way, she exposes herself to the misogynist critique of reading that Pope launches in *The Dunciad* (see chapter 4, below).

In *Popular and Polite Art*, Paulson adopts a qualified version of E. P. Thompson's Marxist mapping of culture to develop one of the favored tropes for describing high culture's economic use of subcultures. Now the artist goes to the raw but vital regions of culture, for a transfusion of sustaining fluids. "It is a reciprocal action: the subculture tries to make its raw experience—its vulnerability—bearable; and the culture tries to make the subculture's gestures safe and unthreatening. . . . And occasionally an artist tries to incorporate something of the subculture as a transfusion to revise English literature and art" (xiv). In this way, Hogarth, Richardson, and Fielding can be figured as the ingenious recyclers of culture who draw upon writers such as Behn, Manley, and Haywood for use in great works. In such an account, the subculture offers itself as a current of popular art that can revitalize what is Paulson's proper critical concern—the art of Hogarth and Fielding. In critics less favorable than Paulson to high culture, the voracious high-cultural artist takes on the more sinister aspect of a vampire.

The negative valence of these two metaphorical definitions of culture—the literary cultural one of infection, and the popular cultural one of the vampire—suggests the tendentious uses to which these metaphors have been put. The novels of amorous intrigue are different from and other than popular or aesthetic culture. The very set of oppositions produced by the Marxist and literary historical paradigms—high/low, culture/subculture, legitimate/marginal, official/popular, colonial/subaltern—cannot accurately describe the cultural struggle that has produced it as an explanatory paradigm. They are, as Laclau and Mouffe have suggested in *Hegemony and Socialist Strategy*, a set of antagonistic equivalents by which one side or the other seeks to map and hegemonize all of culture from one specific vantage point—that of high literary culture, or that of the people. But if the novels of amorous intrigue are neither the source of poisonous infection nor a proper victim of the high-cultural vampire, if they are neither an early form of popular culture nor a precursor of the legitimate aesthetic object called "the novel," then what are they? I am seeking a third way in which to describe this terrain. My reading of Manley and Haywood's two best-selling novels suggests that they become powerful and disturbing precisely because they do not interpellate any particular reader—whether female or male, whether aristocratic, bourgeois, or popular. Appealing neither to a literary reader nor to any particular type of reader, Haywood formulates her fiction to appeal to a general reader, that is, to any member of the open set of readers who would purchase a book for entertainment. Its address to a general reader, and the atavistic consumption practices it was said to produce in them, depends in turn upon the plot-centered rhythms, and ludic repeatability, of the novel of amorous intrigue.

The specter of the novel reader as automaton anticipates many later representations of media-addicted consumers (of film, television, rock music, and so on), and suggests that these novels can be seen as one starting point for the powerful exchange between what are today referred to as "the media" and "culture," in the anthropological sense of an ensemble of social practices developed around consuming media. Thus, the spectacular popularity and scandal of the early novel of amorous intrigue may be one of the first instances of what I suggest calling "media culture." This term avoids the normative pull of the term "high literary culture," the nostalgic romantic imprecision of "popular culture," and the tendentious opprobrium of "mass culture."[9] The term media culture fuses together two elements. In the early modern period, the medium in question is print. Print

9. In a book entitled *Media Culture*, Douglas Kellner offers a brief history of the Frankfurt use of the term "mass culture," and of the Birmingham school's recourse to the term "popular culture," as well as of the terminological problem with both: by emphasizing the "culture industry's" powers of mass deception, the activity of consumers is devalued; however, within some celebrations of the popular, the critical functions of cultural studies are suspended; so he, too, advocates the term "media culture." Although I find Kellner rather too confident that one can stand outside and above media culture and both plumb its ideologies and correct its politics, we agree upon the strategic usefulness of the term "media culture." It offers a way to take account of the "circuit of production, distribution, and reception through which media culture is produced, distributed and consumed . . . and calls attention to the

media had always been characterized by (1) continuity of form (each printed text is the same) and (2) portability; in this period, too, new developments bring (3) important changes in the character and distribution of print media over the quickly developing eighteenth-century information highway: now, circulation is regulated by a uniform postal code and facilitated by the new turnpikes (Laugero, "Infrastuctures of Enlightenment") and commercial lending libraries; further, uniformity in text production and the efficiency of the new distribution network promotes (4) a commodification that subordinates the particular ideological content of novels to variations of proven formulas intended to win new purchases; and finally, (5) the ductility and mobility of print media increase the speed of cultural exchange.

The novels of amorous intrigue expand cultural and social practices of reception and production in several ways. Because larger geographical and population units can be touched by the same media, printed texts enhance communication at a distance. The profitability of the new media commodities accelerates imitation and a contradictory double demand—to produce the effect of the latest hit, yet appear enticingly new; to be, paradoxically, recurrently new. Seduction of the reader depends upon the appearance rather than the fact of novelty. The compositional strategies that issue from this marketing imperative are familiar from Hollywood film production: a recourse to adaptations, translations, sequels, prequels, and so forth. While the profit potential of print media frees the author from the patron, it makes him or her dependent upon the bookseller, as an agent of the market. The dissemination of new styles, fads, fashions, and modes of living is accelerated, and can become the focal point of collective identification. The circulation of the image or name of the author allows him or her to become a secondary commodity as a "celebrity." In the scramble to become visible in the increased flows of print culture, the book comes to encode its own self-advertisement. Finally, the popularity of novels produces a new specter within the discourses of cultural criticism: that of the reader as pleasure-seeking automaton, liable to an imitative acting-out of novelistic plots—through rash elopements, erotic intrigue—or the displacement of these passions into a debilitating masturbation.

It should be evident by now that the separation implied in my parallel lists of the features of print media and those of print culture cannot be sus-

---

interconnection of culture and communications studies" (Kellner, *Media Culture,* 33–35).

tained. By coupling two terms—"media" as a reference to the print medium, and "culture" as a reference to the cultural forms and practices associated with the vogue for novels—into one term, "media culture," I am seeking to suggest the synergistic feedback set going around the currency of the novels of amorous intrigue. Thus the term "media culture" suggests both a repertoire of objects in circulation—novels on the market in the early modern period—and an interrelated set of cultural practices, readers, authors, printers, and so on, as each supports and expands the other. It is the very difficulty in distinguishing cultural objects and cultural practices in the media culture of the early novel that suggests that they are in fact two sides of a common phenomenon. Understood in this way, media culture can be neither simply the vilified other of legitimate literary culture nor the object of celebration as the culture of the people; nor can it be viewed as a neutral set of objects and practices. Instead, media culture opens a plural and ambiguous ground for morally contested pleasures. Those who would reform media culture invariably discover the need to compromise with it. Thus, although Pope constructs *The Dunciad* as the very antithesis of the waste products of print culture, many a critic has noted his dependency on the media culture he condemns. In chapter 5 I argue that Richardson's programmatic effort to replace the novel of amorous intrigue with a new species of writing can only succeed by becoming a new, morally enlightening species of . . . media culture. Before turning to the programmatic efforts to elevate novel reading that begin with Defoe, I turn to the ambiguous figure that sits at the center of the eighteenth-century struggle to license entertainment: the novel reader.

4 The Antinovel Discourse and Rewriting Reading in *Roxana*

"They became what they beheld."
—Blake, *Jerusalem*

"My consumers, are they not also my producers?"
—Joyce, *Finnegans Wake*

By the 1720s the success of novels on the British print market, and the peculiar powers attributed to absorptive novel reading, made reaching, knowing, and influencing the reader a central preoccupation of print-media workers and cultural critics. But what is a reader? Within their mobile and transient co-articulation, reader and text dissolve into the act of reading, leaving no trace of what they have been to and for each other. Most reading simply disappears. Only through the belated secondary elaboration of writing—commentary, criticism, letters to the editor, or autobiography, for example—does a reader translate reading into graspable form. But even when this translation is ventured, there is no one to vouch for its success. The discrepancy between reading and writing persists, and in fact may be irreducible. Little wonder that there is a fundamental difficulty in knowing the reader and shaping his or her reading practices. Whether for the opportunistic projector on the eighteenth-century print market or for the historian of reading practices, a purchase upon novel reading comes only indirectly, through a study of the remnants of writings left in the wake of reading. By first mapping the cultural struggle around novel reading that opened in the 1710s and 1720s—from the antinovel positions of Shaftesbury and Pope to the pronovel positions of Manley and Haywood—I will then be in a position to interpret the tactics Defoe used to rewrite novel reading in response to the success of the novels of amorous intrigue. In *Roxana*, Defoe assembles a series of novels in which the machinations of the scheming ego reach such extremes that they short-circuit the pleasures of absorptive novel reading.

Over the course of the long eighteenth century, between the Restoration and the early nineteenth century, novel reading came to rival play-going as a principal form of entertainment. In order to pursue their careers as entertainers, Haywood and Fielding follow Behn in migrating from the theater to novel writing. Because the unease with the novel reader extends an earlier unease with the spectator of drama, it is instructive to compare them. In both, it is supposed that pleasure puts moral conscience to sleep. Both antitheatrical discourse and antinovel discourse warned that beguiling but morally irresponsible representations could seduce the spectator or reader into an unconscious emulation—into, in Blake's succinct formulation, "becoming what they beheld." But the novel's dependence upon print media gave a specific new turn to the antirepresentational discourse directed against it. If plays could cause riots, novels could act at a distance. If plays put too much control in the hands of the playwrights, actors, and directors of the theater, novels put too much power in the hands of the reader, and of those who wrote and sold what they read. If plays offer an unseemly spectacle of vice, novels invite readers to produce this spectacle within their own head. While the play's concentration of spectacle increased its danger, it opened it to state control. The very diffuseness of novelistic spectacle made its effects uncertain, and its control nearly impossible.[1]

Novels do not achieve their distinctness as a species of entertainment because of their plots or their subject matter. Like the novels of Behn, Manley, and Haywood, plays of the seventeenth and eighteenth centuries often used plots rife with intrigue and sex. What sets novels apart from plays is their particularly opportunistic use of the print medium. While publication of dramatic texts could enhance the popularity and influence of a live play, novels inhabit print as their primary medium (Benjamin, *Illuminations*, 87). So in order to deepen our understanding of how novel reading became an early instance of media culture, and in order to map the coordinates of the reformation of novelistic narrative attempted by Defoe, it is necessary to inscribe the struggle to shape novel reading within a more general interpretation of print media.

1. Another study would be required to determine the many interconnections between the antinovel discourse of the early modern period and the antitheatricalism that precedes it, and that continues to develop throughout the eighteenth century. Thus, for example, the worry about emulation enunciated by Shaftesbury concerning the theater is also a commonplace of the antinovel discourse; Shaftesbury described "the English stage . . . from whence in all probability our youth will continue to draw their notion of manners and their taste of life . . ." (II: 314). On the difference between concentrated and diffuse spectacle, within a very different context, see Debord, *The Society of the Spectacle*.

NOVELS AS PRINT MEDIA, ONLY MORE SO

Since ancient times, writing has had a decisive role in enabling trade, constituting civil and religious authority, and accumulating knowledge (Inglis, *Media Theory*, 6–10; Martin, *History and Power of Writing*). Writing may be the sine qua non of complex social organization, but from Luther's translation of the Vulgate to the penning of the Declaration of Independence, it has also served as a means of contesting instituted authority. The French historian of reading, Roger Chartier, suggests that there is an "internal contradiction" at work between, on the one hand, the controlling efforts of author, bookseller-publisher, commentator, and censor, and on the other, the practice of reading, which, he claims, "by definition is rebellious and vagabond":

> The book always aims at installing an order, whether it is the order in which it is deciphered, the order in which it is to be understood, or the order intended by the authority who commanded or permitted the work. This multi-faceted order is not all-powerful, however, when it comes to annulling the reader's liberty. Even when it is hemmed in by differences in competence and by conventions, liberty knows how to distort and reformulate the significations that were supposed to defeat it. The dialectic between imposition and appropriation, between constraints transgressed and freedoms bridled, is not the same in all places or all times or for all people.
>
> [Chartier, *Order of Books*, viii]

While this passage risks situating reading within too stark and too romantic a polarization of constraint and liberty, it reflects the larger stakes of the market's emancipation of reading, and the resulting struggle around the licensing of novel reading in eighteenth-century Britain.

Too often, literary histories of the novel make a foray into the history of reading so as to provide a context and backdrop for the main event—the rise of the novel as a literary type. Reading practices are seen as one of many global changes sweeping across late-seventeenth- and early-eighteenth-century culture, and converging to produce "the" novel. These changes include: new ideologies characterized as progressive, empiricist, secular, and modernist; more and cheaper print commodities facilitated by the end of licensing and the eclipse of patronage; and changes in the location and nature of reading as it becomes increasingly prevalent and acquires its distinct modern character as silent and private (Watt, *Rise of the Novel*, chapter 2; Hunter, *Before Novels*, chapter 3; Chartier, *Order of Books*, 21–22). While few would dispute the importance of these changes, my study suggests that a struggle around reading practices is not a subsidiary circumstance but, instead, is the central event in the novel's eighteenth-century history. Chartier's three-part program for "a history of reading" allows one to grasp the several components of novel reading in their complex and often conflictual imbrication. He calls for three areas of study which "academic tradition usually keeps separate: first the analysis of texts, be they canonical or ordinary, to discern their structures, their themes, and their aims; second, the history of books and, beyond that, the history of all objects and forms that bear texts; third, the study of practices that seize on these objects and these forms in a variety of ways and produce differentiated uses and meanings" (2–3). If we consider novel reading under these three rubrics, we can see how the cultural struggle around licensing novel reading carries its effects into the form and content of novelistic texts, the material shape of novels as books to be read, and the reading practices which proliferate around novels.

The spread of print produces general shifts in the content of books, enabling books to become the favored form for novels. Kaufer and Carley offer a synthesis of the effects of print on a previously scribal culture in which, with writing both "scarce" and expensive, the watchword of culture was "make sure [writing] does not become dated," "mundane," or compromised by ideas of tenuous authority (Kaufer and Carley, *Communication at a Distance*, 29). This helps explain why, within scribal culture, writing became the vassal of the timeless, the lofty, and the generally accepted. According to Kaufer and Carley, the spread of print subverted these assumptions about textual content, and developed previously concealed possibilities. Now texts could render content that had three new traits: timeliness, practicality, and originality. By the seventeenth century, this stress on the quotidian is made explicit by the very names of many of the new print genres: "war journals, newsbooks, dailies, newspapers, periodicals, and novels" (ibid., 32). In addition, a whole category of writings derived their value not from being about an extra-mundane spiritual world, but by being practical guides to living; among these were the new periodicals (such as the *Spectator*), conduct books (such as *A Lady's Calling*), cook books, books designed to aid the occupations (such as Defoe's *Complete English Tradesman*), and so on. Finally, rather than accumulate authoritative, already assimilated cultural knowledge like that found in almanacs or Bibles, classical texts or legal commentaries, the new books could devote themselves to writing—whether scientific or fictional—that claimed to be original or new. Chartier's account of the development, during the sixteenth and seventeenth centuries, of the cheap chapbook sold by pedlars offers an inventory of these new uses of print and the shift in read-ing tastes they imply. In his wide-ranging study of the cultural contexts of English fiction, Hunter confirms that the young, mobile, ambitious urban reader most ready for the novel was developing a strong inclination for texts that were timely, practical, and new (Hunter, *Before Novels*, 75–81).

This mutually imbricated threefold shift in the content of printed texts is reflected in the novelistic writing of Behn, Manley, and Haywood. The French heroic romances (of D'Urfé, La Calprenède, and de Scudéry) that were in vogue before their eclipse by the seventeenth-century novella emulated the complex structure of classical epic, promoted a sublime ideal-ization of romantic love, and purveyed a courtly version of assimilated social wisdom. By contrast, *Love Letters*, the *New Atalantis*, and *Love in Excess* were timely (the first two with a vengeance), claimed to offer a cyn-ically practical view of sex and love in the *beau monde*, and promised an entertainment that pleased through its novelty. The oppositions Kaufer and Carley use to schematize those changes are relational, and the shift from one to the other should not be viewed as secure or unidirectional. Thus, Defoe's *Roxana* will later claim to trump the novelistic secret histories of Behn and Haywood by being still more timely, practical, and original than theirs. When claims to timeliness and novelty put the novel in danger of being trivial, Richardson and Fielding will have recourse to Christian tragedy and classical epic form in order to invest *Clarissa* and *Tom Jones* with the timelessness, exalted status, and assimilated knowledge associated with high art (see conclusion).

Modern media theory has put special emphasis on the way in which changes in the precise form of media modify the cultural practices impro-vised in their wake. In the twentieth century, for example, after its devel-opment in the 1920s, radio shifted from being a large furniture console for the parlor (in the thirties) to being lodged in the dashboard of the automo-bile (by the forties); from there it shifted to being portable (in the fifties), and to being the boombox and Walkman of the seventies and eighties. Each new mutation of the radio set provided a matrix of possibility for new cul-tural uses of radio, and these new uses supported the expansion of radio programming. Thus the enhanced portability of the radio seems to have been the condition of the possibility of radio's widely recognized role in sponsoring a popular music targeted at teenage consumers, and for the birth of what we have come to call "youth culture."

Scholars of the history of reading have been at pains to remind literary critics that when it comes to the book, one can discern the same crucial inter-dependence of form, content, and cultural practice sketched above with radio. Texts—the immaterial idealities that are the objects of both scholarly editions and critical analysis—only reach the hands and minds of readers through the physical medium of the book (Chartier, *Order of Books*, 10). The eighteenth-century spread of novels was contingent upon their format. The recent study by Edward Jacobs of a 1757 circulating-library catalogue of the bookseller William Bathoe—claimed to be "the first of its kind in London"—suggests the way in which three distinct format levels—descending from folio to quarto to octavo and duodecimo—were used as broad organizational categories to divide books according to the cultural prestige they embodied, the durability of the knowledge they claimed, and the expense they entailed.[2] By the late seventeenth century, novels settled into the duodecimo or octavo format, a niche between the grander bound-book formats and the modest chapbook. These two formats, which novels held for most of the eighteenth century, had several advantages: they produced small, portable volumes that were much less expensive than the quarto or folio volumes, yet flexible in accommodating novels of vastly different length. Thus, for example, leaving aside front matter, Haywood's *Fantomina* (1725) was 35 pages in length in duodecimo, while the seven volumes of the first edition of *Clarissa*, which varied in length from 309 to 405 pages per volume, totaling 2,474 pages (Sale, *Samuel Richardson*, 45–48), was also in duodecimo. The relative cheapness of small formats opened books to broader readership, while their small size made them easy to carry in one's pocket into private-reading spaces, such as bed, the garden, or on a journey.[3]

2. Jacobs' analysis was developed in a paper presented at the 1994 ASECS annual meeting entitled, "Buying into Classes: the Construction of Genre and Tradition by Circulating Libraries, Catalogues, and the Provincial Book Trade in Eighteenth-Century England."

3. The short novels published by Haywood in the 1720s could be as cheap as one shilling (1s.), while in the same decade, five of the six novels published by Penelope Aubin in duodecimo cost one shilling and sixpence (1s. 6d.) each. When Richardson published *Pamela* and *Clarissa* in the 1740s, his standard price in the duodecimo format was 3s. per volume. Accepting Roy Porter's estimate that three loaves of bread would cost 1s. and a dinner 1s. 6d., and given that one of Richardson's volumes in duodecimo would cost slightly more than a pair of women's shoes or a pig (Porter, *English Society*, xxv; C. Turner, *Living by the Pen*, 145), then one must conclude with Watt that eighteenth-century novels remained costly by modern standards (Watt, *Rise of the Novel*, 42). But even before the circulating library brought novel reading within the reach of most people with some discretionary income by the middle of the century, if a novel was popular, less costly means of publishing were available: it could be published in its entirety or as an excerpt in magazines, or it could be published in parts, as weekly or monthly "numbers," wrapped in blue covers and priced at between a few pence and 1s. each (C. Turner, *Living by the Pen*, 146). In addition, then as today, books were often available as "remaindered" items

Just as booksellers published personal devotional works in the small-book format, so they also facilitated the privatizing of novel reading by offering novels in the octavo/duodecimo format.

From the beginning, the popularity of novels gave them special currency on the print market. By limiting copyright to two renewable fourteen-year terms, the Queen Anne Law of 1710 circumscribed the perpetual copyright traditionally claimed by the London booksellers and undercut the legal grounds of the royal monopoly traditionally enjoyed by the Stationers' Company. Although booksellers battled throughout the century to regain the perpetual copyright once protected by royal authority, and only lost the decisive legal battle with *Donaldson* v. *Becket* in 1774, the new legal order meant that as old copyrights lapsed, booksellers had economic incentives for finding copyrights to shore up their lists with new works. It was this same thirst for the new that had once pushed printing from Latin to the vernacular (Inglis, *Media Theory*, 15). Novels had several advantages in meeting the press's thirst for new material. First, as Haywood's publication of thirty-six novels in the 1720s demonstrates, the use of variations on proven formulas could provide a steady stream of new print commodities (C. Turner, *Living by the Pen*, 177–182; see also above, chapter 3). Second, the novel's ability to assemble a diverse group of readers—women and men, the learned and the barely literate, the young and the old—enabled the successful novel to build a large general audience. Finally, the sheer speed with which readers could read novels and with which authors could write them enabled novels to best serious writing as a means of meeting the accelerating demand for print. All three factors allowed novels to flourish on a print market in which "more is better" because quantity provides economies of scale that augment the bottom line. The importance and profitability of novel publishing is suggested by the fact that most booksellers, from the most prestigious ones (Dodsley, Millar, and Cadell) to the most disreputable (Curll), published novels (ibid., 89–90). In both Britain and America, over the course of the century, novels constituted an increasingly large proportion of printed matter.

Throughout the early modern period, commentators worried that changes in printing and reading practices threatened the serious writer who

---

or through second hand sale (ibid.). The duodecimo and octavo formats varied in size from about 4 × 7 inches to about 5½ × 8 inches. Authors and booksellers moved novels freely between the two formats. Thus Haywood published in both, doing a more expensive collection of her novels and poetry in octavo format in 1742. While most of his novels were published in duodecimo format, Richardson published more lavish editions in octavo of both *Pamela* (the sixth edition, with engravings) and *Clarissa* (the fourth edition).

cleaved to the higher callings of print culture. Thus, in "A Modest Plea for the Property of Copyright" (1774), Catherine Macaulay worried that the *Donaldson* decision would encourage the print market's tendency to produce "trifling wretched compositions as please the vulgar; compositions which disgrace the press, yet are best calculated for general sale" (ibid., 41). The market's exploitation of timely, novel, and practical subject matter, and its development of the potential offered by the small-book format, seemed to Leibniz, as early as 1680, to presage a "barbarous" disorder in culture. Leibniz saw "that horrible mass of books which keeps on growing" as putting in question values at the center of humanistic culture:

> the hope of glory animating many people at work in studies will suddenly cease; it will be perhaps as disgraceful to be an author as it was formerly honorable. At best, one may amuse himself with little books of the hour which will run their course in a few years and will serve to divert a reader from boredom for a few moments, but which will have been written without any design to promote our knowledge or to deserve the appreciation of posterity. I shall be told that since so many people write it is impossible for all their words to be preserved. I admit that, and I do not entirely disapprove those little books in fashion which are like the flowers of a springtime or like the fruits of an autumn, scarcely surviving a year. If they are well made, they have the effect of a useful conversation, not simply pleasing and keeping the idle out of mischief but helping to shape the mind and language. Often the aim is to induce something good in men of our time, which is also the end I seek by publishing this little work . . .
> [McLuhan, *Gutenberg Galaxy*, 302–303]

Hovering between tolerance and condemnation, acceptance and dread, this passage gives expression to Leibnitz's two incompatible thoughts about the "mass" of these "little books of fashion" which have suddenly flooded his culture: he worries that by turning readers and writers from serious study, they menace an order of print organized to privilege the arduous ideals of lasting knowledge and "honorable" authorship; and yet, he finds that these books have the transient charm of flowers, and that they might be turned, like conversation, to improving use. Anticipating the ambivalence felt by many later cultural critics toward seductive new market-based entertainment, this passage moves from high-minded condemnation ("horrible mass") to an equivocal reconsideration ("At best one may amuse . . .") or resigned acceptance ("I do not entirely disapprove"), and then to a final complicity. Leibniz himself is writing the preface to his own "small book." It is precisely because of their diminutive size, their charming power to "amuse," and their insidious way of changing reading practices one book at a time that these little books have an irresistible power to unsettle an old print media order of knowledge. By sanctioning a host of new pleasures, they erode the earlier discipline of books.

Once novels establish themselves on the market, many readers view novel reading with the same double feeling Leibnitz evinces for little books. When cultural critics attack the dangerous effects of novel reading, it could shock the devotees of fiction. Thus, in Shaftesbury's *Moralists: a Philosophical Rapsody* (1709), Philocles is bewildered that his interlocutor, Palemon, "damned even our favorite novels: those dear, sweet, natural pieces, writ most of them by the fair sex themselves" (*Characteristics*, II: 11). Because they appear "dear," "sweet," and feminine, these novels are especially liable to insinuate themselves as personal favorites of the private reader. Thus, when the *Spectator* warns women against the dangers to their chastity posed by the month of May, it adjures its "fair readers to be in particular manner careful how they meddle with romances, chocolate, novels, and like inflamers, which I look upon as very dangerous to be made use of during this great carnival of nature." This way of warning against novels makes them appear as seductive as May's "gay prospects of fields and meadows [which] naturally unbend the mind, and soften it to pleasure" (no. 365, April 29, 1712). In the first decades of the century, few justified novels as transmitters of knowledge, but many were finding their pleasures as irresistible as chocolate.

Critics of the new reading practices develop a characteristically modern alarm at changes which appear both global and inevitable. In his *Advice to an Author* (1710), Shaftesbury's use of the first-person plural implies that he cannot himself stand outside the general effects of the commercialization of print media that he laments: "We go to plays or to other shows, and frequent the theater as the [fair] booth. We read epics and dramatics as we do satires and lampoons; for we *must of necessity know* what wit as well as what scandal is stirring. Read we *must;* let writers be ever so indifferent" [italics mine]. As a high cultural critic, Shaftesbury is dismayed at the threefold lack—of a discerning public, of authors who aspire to greatness, and of a critical "standard" all might accept by "mutual consent." Shaftesbury attributes this decline in culture to the author's position as supplier of the print market's assembly line of entertainments. The reader's lax compulsion to consume—"read we must"—may, Shaftesbury speculates, "be some occasion of the laziness and negligence of our authors, who observing this need which our curiosity brings on us, and making an exact calculation in the way of trade, to know justly the quality and quantity of the public demand, feed us thus from hand to mouth; resolving not to over-stock the

market, or be at pains of more correctness or wit than is absolutely necessary to carry on the traffic" (*Characteristics*, I: 173). By offering criticism
and advice to authors, Shaftesbury summons them to a new kind of vigilance about the effects of written entertainments, and anticipates the mid-
century efforts by a broad spectrum of novelists and critics to institutionalize authorship as a system for controlling the effects of reading (see
chapters 5 and 6, and Conclusion). To counteract the worry about market-
based novels, a broad spectrum of readers justifies novels as a necessary self-
indulgence. As a young woman, Lady Mary Wortley Montagu yearns to
get her hands on the second part of the *New Atalantis* in spite of its ques-
tionable value (Manley, *New Atalantis*, v); as a mother, she asks her daughter to send a list of novels, for though most are "trash" or "lumber," "they
will serve to pass away the idle time" (Watt, *Rise of the Novel*, 44). Whether
viewed as "trash" or as "dear sweet natural pieces," novels had come to
appear to many as an inevitable enjoyment. In the preface to *The Noble
Slaves* (1722), Penelope Aubin, though a lay preacher, rationalizes the publication of her novels as a way to allow the reader "to pass away that time
that must hang heavy on our hands: and books of devotion being tedious,
and out of fashion, novels and stories will be welcome" (C. Turner, *Living
by the Pen*, 50). Once the prohibition of novel reading has lost its efficacy,
the reform of novel reading becomes an urgent cultural strategy.

In the early eighteenth century, novels are associated with a shift in the
technique and location of reading. Because of their explicitly erotic character, the novels of Behn, Manley, and Haywood seem to require silent, private, individualized reading. Hunter has suggested that it was Protestant
respect for the individual, combined with developments in eighteenth-
century domestic architecture, that supported a "culture of the closet" as a
space apart for "secret contemplation and private reading" (Hunter, *Before
Novels*, 157). But once institutionalized, this shift in the location of reading could facilitate novel reading as well as prayer. Solitary reading also
enabled what one might call compulsive reading—like that undertaken by
Manley's Charlot alone in the library (see chapter 3), and like the mesmer-
izing effects of reading *Clarissa* or *Sir Charles Grandison* described in testimonials sent by Lady Bradshaigh and Colley Cibber to Richardson (Eaves
and Kimpel, *Samuel Richardson*, 182). Rousseau dates his emergence into
continuous self-consciousness from the time of his atavistic late-night
novel reading with his father (Rousseau, *Confessions*, 7–8). In the eighteenth century, readers began reporting, "I couldn't stop reading until I
turned the last page." The idea of other people reading novels in a place of
sanctioned solitude produced worries about, in Hunter's words, "idleness

or, worse, stimulation of the mind and imagination toward improper longings" (Hunter, *Before Novels*, 158). In other words, solitary readers might
do what Rousseau claims he resisted doing during his apprenticeship—
namely, withdraw from a circulating library any of those "dangerous books
that a beautiful woman of the world finds awkward, because one can only,
she says, read them with one hand" (Rousseau, *Confessions*, 40).[4]

It is but one short step from the need to read to the right to read. Behind
the diverse positions on reading epitomized here in the apprehensions of
Leibniz and Shaftesbury, the admonitions of the *Spectator*, the apologies of
Lady Mary Wortley Montagu and Aubin, and the testimonials of addicted
novel readers, there lies an assumption crucial to the early-modern emancipation of reading: that every mature literate adult has the right to choose
his or her own reading. The effort of Charles II to implement licensing practices on the French model after the Restoration—by appointing Roger L'E-
trange as royal licenser and by cutting the number of booksellers from
between thirty-nine and fifty during the Commonwealth to twenty (Martin, *History and Power of Writing*, 276)—was the last British effort to control reading from above. With the political transformations of 1688 and the
lapse of the licensing act in 1695, there was a decisive victory for "unlicensed
printing" (Milton, *Areopagitica*, 486) and for an arduously Protestant testing of the individual reader through an unfiltered and robust exposure to
the diversity of books. Every author, printer, and bookseller who set out to
incite and gratify the new need to read would, at the same time, be advancing this right to read.

It is tempting to see absorbed, addictive novel reading as simply resulting from a new market-sustained system of print entertainment. Then the
subject matter of love and sex plotted into intrigue provides the novel's
alluring content; the medium-priced book, in duodecimo or octavo format,
and transmitted by the postal system and the turnpike, provides the physical means by which the novel reaches an enlarged group of readers; and
silent, solitary reading practices provide the preferred mode for consuming
the novel. Taken together, these changes compose the novel as a distinct
form of enthralling entertainment and promote the "right to read." But
cultural critics are right to be wary of a techno-determinist print-media

4. I have been aided by Elizabeth MacArthur in my translation of the Pléiade
edition. Chartier warns that the distinctly modern shift toward silent solitary reading was far from complete or unidirectional (Chartier, *Order of Books*, 20). In the
nineteenth century, making novels collectively readable was part of a strategy
undertaken by authors such as Dickens to make novels socially accountable.

explanation of historical changes in reading practices (Hunter, *Before Novels*, 156 n.30; M. Warner, *Letters of the Republic*, 4–19; Czitrom, *Media and the American Mind*). The size or price of a book does not predetermine what books will get written and published, or how readers will read those books. The previous two chapters describe the inventive tactics devised by Behn and Manley to intervene in their political culture, as well as the compositional changes that enabled Haywood's new formulation of the novels of amorous intrigue. In other words, the market for printed books does not have the character of a self-regulating totality such that, in Laclau's words, "the transformation of the system, as in any self-regulating totality, can only take place as a result of the development of the internal logic of the system itself" (Laclau, *New Reflections*, 52). The print market is not the insidious and pervasive agent, whether benign or demonic, of our modernity. The print market is no one thing. Instead, it is a cultural as well as an economic space, allowing for plural, antagonistic, nondialectical forms of articulation. By what they write and read, and by what they demur at reading and writing, authors and readers are constantly displacing print culture. In the spaces of the market all the elements of novel reading that have been examined in this study—the form and content of novelistic texts, the shape and character of the book, and the diverse effects of novel reading—become focal points of manifold efforts to reshape or redirect reading practices. And each of these factors inflects the writing of novels. In a circuit that none fully comprehends, readers and writers reshape a culture they can never control.

THE SCANDAL OF THE NOVEL-READING BODY

A specter haunted early-modern Europe: that of the novel reader reading. This specter—cast as characters ranging from Don Quixote to Madame Bovary—is understood to be mindlessly absorbed by the text he or she reads, and compulsively addicted to its pleasures. Whence comes this abject figure of the novel-reading automaton? The new order of print culture that has been sketched in this chapter—including the form and content of texts, the small-book format, and the shift in reading practices—subverts the efforts by church and state to control print in the Renaissance and the seventeenth century. In order to critique an earlier humanistic tradition, as well as transmit ancient and modern knowledge, eighteenth-century writers, booksellers, and readers harness print media to pursue their ambitious educational project. However, the new print medium also threatens this Enlightenment project. Thus, as the passage from Leibniz quoted above suggests, a suspicion develops among a broad range of cultural critics that reading small books for pleasure may menace the Enlightenment educational project from within. As a symptom of the shift of reading practices examined in this chapter, the phantasm of the errant novel reader appears along the fault line between good and bad reading.

We can begin to probe the meaning of this figure by noting that from the beginning of the antinovel discourse, the novel-addicted reader in Britain is usually gendered female. The contingent fact that most of the popular novelists were women may have contributed to gendering the reader feminine. But the currency of this topos should not lull one into accepting it as an historically accurate account of reading. In two recent feminist studies of women's writing and reading in the eighteenth and nineteenth centuries, Cheryl Turner and Kate Flint find compelling reasons for separating the cultural icon of the (dangerously susceptible) woman reader from the diverse practices of actual women. Flint's study of autobiographies of women writing about their reading, and of novels aimed at women shows how a broad range of texts—from studies of physiology and psychology and advice manuals to pedagogical writing and the periodical press—produce a discursive construction of the "woman reader" in view of her reformation. But "although many commentators chose to believe or desire that women read in certain ways," Flint suggests a variety of reading practices which cannot be simply described as absorptive and escapist; they can be improving, self-conscious, critical, and community-building. As such, they offer "resistance" to the figure of the woman reader (Flint, *Woman Reader*, vii–viii).

In her study, Cheryl Turner complicates the eighteenth-century stereotype of the woman reader by offering evidence that women read texts other than novels, and often chose to read critically (C. Turner, *Living By the Pen*, 137–139). Such a critical rearticulation of women's reading is an explicit theme in such novels as Charlotte Lennox's *Female Quixote* (1752) and Jane Austen's *Sense and Sensibility* (1811). Turner also cites a range of evidence suggesting that from the beginning of the century to its end, from Haywood's eroticism to More's didacticism, and in spite of the larger role women assume in authorship as the century proceeds, novels were written to appeal to both sexes. Thus, she shows that men as well as women confessed to, or were accused of, reading novels in a voracious, absorptive manner: Boswell has Noble send him "a fresh supply of novels from his circulating library, so that [he is] . . . well supplied with entertainment"; Leigh Hunt describes himself as a "glutton of novels"; and the *Gentleman's Magazine* of 1767 frets that "It must be a matter of real concern to all considerate minds, to see the youth of both sexes passing so large a part of their time in reading that deluge of familiar romances" (ibid., 131). Finally, in spite of the cliché of the woman novel reader haunting the circulating library, Turner finds a discrepancy between this stereotype and the records of John Marshall, a leading bookseller of Bath, who kept records of subscribers between 1793 and 1799 that show 35, 30, 29, 30, 32, 22, and 29 percent of his members to have been women during those years. Turner concludes that, since "men were the main subscribers at an establishment in a fashionable spa town where one might expect to find an unusually high proportion of women with the leisure and education to read, the contemporary preoccupation with female readers should not be interpreted literally as describing a numerical dominance" (ibid., 136). Instead, she argues that this preoccupation expresses cultural tensions around two issues. The first of these is that women's leisure reading, as evidenced by circulating library use, upset those who wanted women doing useful domestic or commercial work. Second, circulating-library use might not just transmit romance delusions—it could also give women access to reading that could put in question traditional cultural authority (ibid., 137).

Given the novel's address to and success with a broad spectrum of general readers, the question arises as to why, in eighteenth-century Britain, writers so often circulate this stereotype of the novel reader as female. No doubt, like contemporaneous critiques of vanity and luxury, writers mobilize a powerful vein of misogyny to locate the responsibility for the commodification of reading in women (L. Brown, *Ends of Empire*, 103–134). Recruiting certain themes of eighteenth-century misogyny can help consolidate the figure of the woman reader. If, following Turner, Flint, and others, we understand the eighteenth-century topos of the woman novel reader not as a representation of what was, but as a discursive formation, what function does this figure serve? First, it allows for a simplification of reading. Through the assumption that woman are easy to understand, or, as Pope writes, that "women have no character at all," it is supposed that the female reader will easily receive the impressions to which she is exposed, and will therefore imitate novels most automatically. But second, by attributing novel reading to the female sex, reading is mystified: the woman reader becomes a fascinating enigma. Finally, the figure of the woman reader eroticizes reading through the presumption of an automatic relay: if a reader reads erotic novels, then she will act out by having sex. This figure of the woman reader can function as an admonitory figure for men as well as for women: because novels render readers sensitive and erotic, they menace men with feminization.

Of course, the assumptions about reading encoded in the "woman reader" are partly contradictory—how, for example, can reading be both simple and productive of mystery? But the different aspects of the woman reader are made plausible by the commonsensical notions of gender difference, and help promote a containment of novel reading. The abject figure of the woman reader allows those who circulate such a figure to sort reading into the good and the bad, that which is to be encouraged and that which is to be suppressed. In other words, the cultural struggle around novel reading is the secondary effect of a more global effort to institutionalize book reading. The specter of the novel-reading automaton is an inverse afterimage of the Enlightenment project of a rationally motivated reading; the latter produces the former as its own particular nightmarish phantasm. Ironically, in order to promote their own improvement of reading, some twentieth-century feminist historians of reading have repeated the same eighteenth-century patriarchal bifurcation of reading which they critique.[5]

5. The issue of how to take account of the activity of the reader/audience/spectator has become one of the Gordian knots of cultural studies. Because Flint's *Woman Reader* offers a fundamentally different account of reading from my own, it will be useful to offer a brief critique of her study. Through a sequential account of reading models, reading practices, and novelistic reflections upon women readers, Flint's study stages a dialectical exchange that carries the woman reader beyond a constricted pedagogy toward a feminist self-enlightenment. Flint's female reader eludes the clichés about the woman reader by reading in a different way: "Reading, in other words, provided the means not only . . . for the Victorian woman to abnegate the self, to withdraw into the passivity induced by the opiate of fiction. Far more excitingly, it allowed her to assert her sense of selfhood, and to know that she was not alone in doing so" (330). What's wrong with this picture of reading? First, Flint assumes what is never demonstrated: that men and women read in fundamentally different ways. By bifurcating and gendering the reader who is the focus of her feminist study, Flint follows the same trajectory she traces in the ideological construction of the woman reader by those who would rein in her freedom to read (for example, the writers of patriarchal conduct books); in other words, she turns the reader into a writer. Speaking in the name of subjectivity as self-production through writing, Flint reforms the woman reader. Although this exchange between reading and writing valuably suggests the complex interconnections of the two, the antisocializing, eccentric, individualistic, perverse, aleatory side of reading gets lost along the way. In the last pages of Flint's book, the bonding among women becomes the *telos* of women's reading, allowing its recuperation for a feminist politics. By producing too stark a polarity between reading that is enslaving because it submits to the itinerary of a patriarchal conduct discourse, and reading that is liberating for the way in which it helps rewrite women's identity as feminist, Flint's study evolves into a guide on how women should read. But by turning "the woman reader" into a potential woman writer, Flint's study suppresses the question of the individual or group (of whatever gender) reading for pleasures which will not be subordinated to

De Certeau suggests that a particular concept of the book lies at the heart of the enlightenment educational project: "The ideology of the Enlightenment claimed that the book was capable of reforming society, that educational popularization could transform manners and customs, that an elite's products could, if they were sufficiently widespread, remodel a whole nation. This myth of Education inscribed a theory of consumption in the structures of cultural politics" (De Certeau, *Practice of Everyday Life*, 166).

This Enlightenment project is structured around a certain concept of education as mimicry, with a "scriptural system" that assumes, in De Certeau's words, "[that] although the public is more or less resistant, it is molded by (verbal or iconic) writing, that it becomes similar to what it receives, and that it is imprinted by and like the text which is imposed on it" (ibid., 167). By De Certeau's account, the expansion since the eighteenth century of the powers that inform (from standardized teaching to the media) has reinforced the presumption that only producers (educators, artists, revolutionaries, and media workers) initiate and invent. Correlatively, this model assumes the idea of the consumer as a passive receptacle (ibid.). In developing his techno-determinist account of the influence of media on culture, McLuhan cites Blake's formula that forms one of this chapter's epigraphs, "They became what they beheld" (McLuhan, *Gutenberg Galaxy*, 265). In McLuhan's formulation, each new technology could hypnotize its consumer, producing an "identification of viewer and object," a "somnambulist conforming of beholder to the new form or structure" (ibid., 272). The early-eighteenth-century antinovel discourse promotes the fear that the novel reader will become absorbed in an unconscious mimicry. But both the danger of novel reading and its teaching opportunity, both its currency as media culture and its potential for elevation, arise from the same idea: that a reader/consumer can be made to conform to the object.

De Certeau develops a counterimage of reading so as to overcome the stark polarities—production/consumption, active/passive, empowered/disempowered—that have conducted cultural hierarchies from the eighteenth century to the present (De Certeau, *Practice of Everyday Life*, 166–167). He does so by using the opposition writing/reading as the "general equivalent and indicator" of the opposition production/consumption. This has the effect of putting in question the controlling authority of writing as active production. Thus De Certeau offers reasons as to why reading resists

---

another's scribal project. (For a feminist critique of eighteenth-century "gendered strategies" compatible with Flint's study, see Runge, "Gendered Strategies.")

being policed: it cannot be known in advance, determined in its effects through writing, or studied with certainty. Though reading is taught, made the object of certification, and given various instrumental functions, it has that about it which confounds and exceeds these efforts. De Certeau advances an account of reading which is nomadic, eccentric, and active. In the introduction to his book, he describes reading as a kind of self-loss rather than a self-consolidation:

> In reality, the activity of reading has on the contrary all the characteristics of a silent production: the drift across the page, the metamorphosis of the text effected by the wandering eyes of the reader, the improvisation and expectation of meanings inferred from a few words, leaps over written spaces in an ephemeral dance. But since he is incapable of stockpiling (unless he writes or records), the reader cannot protect himself against the erosion of time (while reading, he forgets himself and he forgets what he has read) unless he buys the object (book, image) which is no more than a substitute (the spoor or promise) of moments "lost" in reading. He insinuates into another person's text the ruses of pleasure and appropriation: he poaches on it, is transported into it, pluralizes himself in it like the internal rumblings of one's body. Ruse, metaphor, arrangement, this production is also an "invention" of the memory. . . . The thin film of writing becomes a movement of strata, a play of spaces. A different world (the reader's) slips into the author's place. [xxi]

Indebted to Barthes' account of the perverse itineraries of reading in *Pleasure of the Text* (1973), this passage, by insisting on the way reading practices can also be irregular, singular, and improvisational, puts in question the educational idea(l) of reading as an activity which can be instituted as normative. De Certeau's image of the reader helps explain the resistance to reading for entertainment which appears in the culture of the novel's first circulation. Novels cannot be comprehended as communications of information complicated by fantasy or by unconscious desire that is understood as a kind of "noise." Instead, they seem to be written in order to incite a pleasure in excess of any possible closure around a signified communication. For this reason, novel reading provoked the worry as to how pleasure infects the knowledge-centered, improving potential for reading. Novels are particularly problematic vehicles of cultural reform.

If reading can be wasteful rather than accumulative, transitory rather than enduring, casually appropriative rather than responsibly disciplined, then it is entirely appropriate that Leibniz would find the new reading of small books to be a menace to the higher calling of Renaissance book culture, that Shaftesbury would reproach authors as pimps gratifying the reader's lazy compulsion to read, and that many critics characterize the act of novel reading as feminine. But if reading "pluralizes" the reader rather than consolidating his or her social or psychic identity, then the admonitory figure of the woman reader as a pleasure-seeking automaton will not in fact account for the practice of early-modern readers. Readers drift across the gender divide that is drawn by eighteenth-century misogyny and assumed by twentieth-century feminist studies of that misogyny. De Certeau's account of the anarchic potential of reading offers an alternative to that instrumental educational itinerary that requires that we read in order to do something else. By contrast, in De Certeau's account, when one picks up a written text and exercises one's autonomy through reading, one achieves a local inversion of the hierarchy that had been presumed to operate through reading. The line from the end of Joyce's *Finnegans Wake* that forms the second of this chapter's two epigraphs—"my consumers, are they not also my producers?"—might be transformed into—"my readers, are they not also my writers?" Because of the larger field of market exchanges that bear up and sustain them in reciprocal embodiments that may be transgressive, irresponsible, or merely whimsical, consumers reach back along the loop of products to influence producers. It is not merely through what they buy, it is also through how they read that readers, through a certain deferred action, write their writers, retroactively. In doing so, readers confound any simple opposition or hierarchy of writing and reading.

De Certeau's concept of reading means there may be something in the very nature of reading which eludes analysis. The sheer range of eighteenth-century efforts to shape reading practices offers indirect evidence of reading's uncontrolled plurality. Thus, for example, doubts about the nature of readers provoke the *Spectator*'s market analysis in a familiar passage from *Spectator* No. 10. There, Addison ends an articulation of his periodical's aims by describing the three types of readers he seeks to address: the fraternity of fellow Spectators, the "blanks of society," and the female world. Such attempts to produce a typology of readers, in order to anticipate their responses, in fact imply their errancy and unpredictability. Different typologies of audience are attempted later in the century by Fielding and Hogarth. In our own period, reading has proven resistant to becoming an ordinary object of pedagogy or historical study. While modern media and communications make earlier ideals of literacy appear increasingly elusive or wishful, many contemporary readers practice a species of "aliteracy" that would have been unthinkable in the eighteenth century: they know how to read but choose not to (Siskin, "Eighteenth Century Periodicals"). In a rejoinder to Robert Darnton, Roger Chartier offers skeptical reservations about any positivistic program for a history of reading (Chartier, *Order of Books,* 18 n.24). Chartier notes that even literary critics—those who have a large disciplinary stake in understanding reading as interpretation—have theorized the existence of limits, internal to the process of reading, to any convergence of reading around semantic content.

REWRITING READING

If reading is the empty center of early-modern print culture, like a particle with a short half-life it can be known indirectly, through its traces as writing. The critics I have cited suggest the existence of a broad public censure of novel reading before 1720. On the competitive print market of the early eighteenth century, texts contend to shape what reading is and should be. In the unruly critical exchange that ensues, texts modify each other so that, for example, novels develop a symbiotic relationship with the antinovel discourse. Thus, when the antinovel discourse produces the figure of the absorbed novel-reading automaton, Manley and Haywood introduce that figure into the narrative as an object of seduction and erotic interest (see chapter 3). Then this eroticized recuperation and the antinovel critique fuse to become the stereotype of the absorbed novel reader.

Writers of the 1720s pursue very different strategies for shaping those inchoate reading practices licensed by the print market. Some writers appear to stand apart from the scandal of novel reading; Pope's corpus, for example, seems to be as different from the novels of amorous intrigue as writing can get. However, the whole neoclassical project—its concept of the decorum of writing according to the clear separation of generic types, its dependence upon classical models for writing, and its suspicion of the new—seems conceived to offer a stay against the accelerating market production of books to pander to the transient and vulgar tastes of the reader. Pope's vastly successful subscription publication of his translation of Homer's *Iliad* gives him independence from the print market. Through the publication of Homer, the classic text par excellence, Pope articulates his poetry with a text of timeless aesthetic value, grounded in several millennia of critical acclaim, and offered to his subscribers as "grade A" cultural capital. In the 1717 preface to *The Works of Mr. Alexander Pope,* Pope reflects upon the "unreasonable" expectations of the writers and readers of books: "The first seem to fancy that the world must approve whatever they produce, and the latter to imagine that authors are obliged to please them at any rate" (147). He then proceeds to sketch a contract for a civil exchange between an independent author and a disinterested, critically informed reader. By offering his poetry as an exemplar of literary culture, Pope seeks to write from a strategic cultural position far above the field of novel writing and other vulgar, abject effusions of the print market.

But Pope's poetry also capitalizes on some of the same reading tastes that were incited and gratified by the early novels. Thus, two of the poems first published in the 1717 *Works*—*Eloisa and Abelard* and *Elegy to the Memory of an Unfortunate Lady*—take up the theme of unrequited love in a tone of impassioned extremity similar to that found in the *Love Letters from a Portuguese Nun to a Cavalier* and Behn's *Love Letters*. While the line in *Rape of the Lock*—"As Long as Atalantis Shall Be Read"— intends to deflate the pretensions of the baron's cutting of Belinda's lock, this work (written between 1712 and 1714) offers a mock-heroic exploitation of the gender strife, disguised intentions, and amorous battle found in the novels of amorous intrigue.

By elevating and sublimating some of the themes of earlier amorous fiction, Pope's poetry purifies writing, while disdaining to take note of its vulgar practitioners. But when Eliza Haywood attacks Pope's dear friend Martha Blount with insinuating scandal, Pope makes Haywood the prize in a pissing contest between booksellers in the 1728 *Dunciad* (Mack, *Alexander Pope*, 411). In *The Dunciad*, Pope does not assume a strategic position outside the terrain of debased grub-street writing. Instead, he accepts vulgar print culture as his habitat. De Certeau has elaborated the difference between strategic and tactical intervention in terms that help explain the stealth and cunning of Pope's writing: "The space of a tactic is the space of the other. Thus it must play on and with a terrain imposed on it and organized by the law of a foreign power. It does not have the means to keep to itself, at a distance, in a position of withdrawal . . ." (De Certeau, *Practice of Everyday Life*, 37). Here, Pope's foreign powers are the grub-street booksellers, Haywood, as one of their most successful authors, and the debased reading both encourage. By making Haywood the erotic prize in the pissing contest, Pope condenses female authorship, easy virtue, and cultural filth. Haywood's fecund posture and her position as a prize in a phallic display of profit-hungry booksellers allow Pope to offer an ironic celebration of her prolific production and spectacular popularity in the 1720s. As Ros Ballaster has shown, it is Haywood's textual promiscuity, rather than her personal life, that makes her a type of Dullness, the poem's explicitly feminine goddess of cultural disorder (Ballaster, *Seductive Forms*, 160–162). Although Pope would seem to wish to expunge novels from culture, attacks such as these make novels come to appear as impure cultural objects tinged with a stain of evil which enhances their cultural power. Novel reading acquires a magical impurity, thereby giving the figure of the novel reader an aura of transgressive importance.

By the 1720s, novel reading had become a scandal, but also an opportunity. The public-sphere debate about the dangers of novel reading meant that anyone who had the temerity to write a narrative that could be accused of being a novel felt obliged to offer in its preface a defense of the text being introduced. In his preface to *A Select Collection of Novels* in 1720, for example, Samuel Croxall notes that "the great Abuse of Novels (as no good thing in the world escapes being perverted) require[s] a few words to be premised, for the removing of such prejudices as that abuse has occasioned against all performances of this kind" (Williams, *Novel and Romance*, 71). In his broad study of the prefaces to eighteenth-century novels, Joseph Bartolomeo suggests several reasons to be skeptical about the claims made in these prefaces: they can offer thin alibis in order that sexy scandal can pass the censor; their rhetoric often appears as contradictory, occasional, and opportunistic as the novels they introduce; and they rarely offer a conceptually systematic groundwork for their own writing practices (Bartolomeo, *New Species of Criticism*, 19–20). But incoherence has its uses. Bartolomeo suggests that the various, obliquely incompatible ways in which the preface to *Robinson Crusoe* defends reading should be understood as a way to expand readership: "An exotic, moral, and true story told in modest language would presumably appeal to a variety of readers in a variety of ways" (ibid., 36).

If one reads the prefaces of the most popular and prolific British novelists of the 1720s (Haywood, Defoe, and Aubin) as developing a defense of fiction against the charges of untruthfulness and the introduction of indecent examples, one can trace the emergence of an apology for novels. In order to counter the accusation that novels are dangerously delusive lies, the novelists rejoined that their narrative actually happened just as it is told (Defoe, Haywood, Aubin); or that, although it may be fictional in incidental particulars, "the foundation of this is laid in truth of fact" (preface to *Roxana*); or (most cunningly) that even though it may be untrue, it has eschewed romance improbabilities and will have an improving effect on the reader (Williams, *Novel and Romance*, 74). To the accusation that novels would induce the reader's dangerous imitation of the wicked actions of the hero or heroine the novelists rejoined, first, that the providential design of the plot, wherein the good triumph and the evil are punished, produces a warning against wrongdoing and an incentive to emulate virtue (Defoe and Aubin [Bartolomeo, *New Species of Criticism*, 32]); and second, that representations of vice (such as the wiles of a thief or a libertine) offer a practical warning to the unwary (Haywood and Defoe). To the accusation that certain representations and language must have a pernicious effect on their reader, novelists offer a defense of hot and alluring subjects. Haywood defends her "warm" scenes by insisting that "without the expression being invigorated in some measure proportionate to the subject, it would be impossible for a reader to be sensible how far it touches him, or how probable it is that he is falling into those inadvertencies which the examples I relate would caution him to avoid" (Dedication of *Lasselia*, 1723, quoted in Williams, *Novel and Romance*, 79). Conversely, Defoe's editor cleans up the language of one of his most disreputable memoir writers, Moll Flanders, by providing her with a new linguistic "dress."

REWRITING THE NOVELS OF AMOROUS INTRIGUE

By 1720, the success of the novels of amorous intrigue was salient enough to provoke many of the epoch's leading cultural players to respond to them. In the rest of this chapter I will consider how Daniel Defoe sets out to reform novel reading. He accepts the premise that the most powerful way to reform novel reading is to write novels differently. Late in a long career of writing for the print market Defoe writes, in a brief five years, the texts that make him a central figure in the history of the British novel: *Robinson Crusoe* (1719), *Memoirs of a Cavalier* and *Captain Singleton* (1720), *Moll Flanders, Journal of the Plague Year* and *Colonel Jack* (1722), and *Roxana* (1724). At least since Clara Reeve's *Progress of Romance*, the critical reception of these novelistic narratives has been determined by the effort to situate Defoe within the narrative of the novel's rise and development. The spectacular and enduring success of *Robinson Crusoe* seems to require a prominent place for Defoe, but Defoe's narratives do not make the ambitious, self-conscious claims to be practicing a "new species" of writing made by Richardson, Fielding, and their critical defenders after 1750. The solution developed in the literary histories has been to give Defoe an honored place apart, as a storyteller who is able to carry "the air of authenticity to the highest pitch of perfection" (Walter Scott, quoted in Peterson, *Daniel Defoe*, 61–62), but whose fictional illusion of "reality" and "life-likeness," "vividness or distinctness" results from a documentary attention to "details and minutiae" (William Caldwell Roscoes, quoted in Peterson, *Daniel Defoe*, 61–62).

The central labor of criticism of Defoe since the mid-twentieth century has been to contest the idea of him as an isolated and eccentric original, by disengaging readings of Defoe from the anachronistic aesthetic teleology of an earlier literary history. As with Behn, Manley, and Haywood, the question of what this narrative contributes to the formation of "the novel" makes much of what is found in Defoe appear primitive and naive, odd or useless. The sustained effort to read Defoe in relation to his avowed purposes and the discursive contexts of his own epoch has enabled scholars to find alternative grounds from which to value the compelling coherence of his early novels. In the rigorously historical studies of Defoe (from those of Watt and Novak to those of Backscheider, Bender, and Faller), as well as in more recent studies of gender (Pollak) and colonialism (Hulme, L. Brown), the very coarseness of Defoe's narrative filter allows his writings to conduct a more ample and complex documentation of eighteenth-century realities. But these historicizing studies do not address the role his novelistic narratives play in the history of eighteenth-century reading.

The cultural struggle around novel reading in the 1720s offers a context for grasping why the narrative form of Defoe's novels offered an effective vehicle for shaping reading practices. If Haywood's *Love in Excess* was a best-seller of the year 1719, so was *Robinson Crusoe*. While Haywood follows up her success by publishing another novel of amorous intrigue nearly every three months throughout the 1720s, Penelope Aubin publishes seven novels designed to uplift the virtue of their readers, starting with *The Life of Madam de Beaumount* (1721).[6] Within this competitive setting Defoe's novels, like Aubin's, are shaped to produce an ethical alternative to prevailing patterns of reading for entertainment. Defoe's ability to produce such novels depends upon the particular form of memoir he develops in *Robinson Crusoe* and uses in all his subsequent novels. The evidentiary authority of the narrative is grounded in one axiom: since the memoir writer lived this experience, he or she is close to it. The primary narrative voice actualizes this presence to the facts by telling his or her personal history as a sequence of events, with a maximum of transparency, and in the present tense (Bender, *Imagining the Penitentiary*, 47–50). This primary narrative voice embodies the young, libidinous, venturesome protagonist of the action, presenting past life in broad summary or in detailed scenes of action and dialogue, strung together from the beginning to the end in the order in which it was lived. The relative simplicity and apparent naturalness of this narrative technique produce an illusion of immediacy for which Defoe's novels have been admired since their publication. Schol-

---

6. Paula Backscheider has noted certain parallels between Haywood's *Love in Excess* and Defoe's *Robinson Crusoe*, as well as the relation of both to Aubin (Backscheider, *Daniel Defoe*, 225–228).

ars (for example, Raleigh, Davis, and Paul Hunter) have derived its traits from the protocols of early modern science, journalism, and spiritual autobiography.

But in order to prevent his narrative memoirs from spinning off into a disconnected episodic series of scenes and adventures, and in order to prevent the reader from becoming absorbed in mere entertainment, Defoe develops a second retrospective voice within the narrative, which enters the text periodically to reflect upon the larger direction and meaning of the protagonist's life. This voice is critical, synthetic, and judgmental, and often invokes fate or Providence to suggest the larger patterns into which the individual's life has flowed, in spite of its conscious intentions. The interplay between these two "voices" of Defoe's narrative has been a central critical problem in his reception (Zimmerman, *Defoe and the Novel*). Because of the ironic tension that subsists between the two voices of Defoe's narrative, each can seem to be a contrived performance. Though the two voices or strata of Defoe's narrative cannot be made to "add up," they are nonetheless indispensable to the effects of Defoe's text (Watt, *Rise of the Novel*; Marshall, *Figure of Theater*; Faller, *Crime and Defoe*; Paulson, *Beautiful, Novel, and Strange*). Most crucially for this study, Defoe's development of the double-voiced memoir narrative enables him to make a particularly cogent intervention on the print market of his day. His narratives indulge what they censure, repeat what they proscribe. His double-voiced narrative allows him to write other print genres, like criminal biography and the erotic secret history, to which he has moral objections. At the same time, he can offer his own moral texts as a corrective and substitute for the pleasures of the narratives he would replace. Most crucially, the second admonitory voice in the text allows the reader to resist being absorbed by the fictional lures of a particular genre: the enticement to adventure and new beginnings of travel writing, the liberating effect of criminal transgression, and the devious and furtive lubricity of sexual intrigue.

How does Defoe's *Roxana* rewrite the reading experience provided by the novels of amorous intrigue? Critics have noted the affiliations between Defoe's text of 1724 and the secret histories made popular by Behn, Manley, and Haywood. The third-person narratives of Behn, Manley, and Haywood take the reader into an affect-laden, supercharged sympathy with the thoughts and sensibilities of the characters. Their narratives reach an extreme of sympathetic identification in the big scenes of sex, in which purple-prose passages encourage absorption in the erotic rhythms of the action. Although both Manley and Haywood develop a critical counterpoint within their narratives—through the staged discussions of the "moral" of each biography in the *New Atalantis,* and the sudden disasters at the end of *Love in Excess* II and *Fantomina*—neither attempts the sustained ethical critique of Defoe's novels. Defoe's double-voiced narrative allows him to make Roxana one who not only lives, but after living, recollects and interprets. This double-voiced narrative projects Roxana as a character absorbed by her experience as an absorbed reader, as well as a narrator who subjects that character to analytical control through an act of writing. By editing Roxana's narrative, Defoe subjects the naive absorbed reader to critique and reformation. The violence of this cultural project is evidenced by the problematic sudden ending of *Roxana,* which offers less a conclusion than a collapse of the narrative. For this reason, it has posed the most serious critical problem for those arguing the text's relatively advanced status as "a novel" in the modern evaluative sense of a self-consciously conceived unity.[7]

If one considers *Roxana* as a single novel, it offers a somewhat haphazard sequence of episodes, with cross references and a progress of sorts, woven together by the secondary retrospective narrative. But as with *Love Letters,* the *New Atalantis,* and *Love in Excess,* there are fundamental problems with treating *Roxana* as a single novel: the questions arise as to whether the novel is consistent with itself and whether the central character is self-identical. Instead of writing *Roxana* as a unity, Defoe fashions a "serial" named "Roxana" that effects a parodic repetition of the novels of amorous intrigue. In *Roxana,* Defoe performs an experiment: he applies the modus vivendi of the novels of amorous intrigue (the ego at play for advantage, disguise, erotic intrigue, and so forth) in a world ordered upon different principles. What results at its most prosaic level is a practical critique of these novels as actual models for social behavior: through them, we learn that beauty cannot last for ever; men throw off their mistresses when they lose their charms; sex leads to pregnancy; and so on. None of these mundane realities prevents Roxana, the leading character of the "series," from achieving spectacular successes; nor do any of them precipitate the

7. For an essay arguing the greater aesthetic control of Defoe's *Roxana* in comparison to Behn's *Love Letters,* see Novak, "Some Notes Toward a History of Fictional Forms." Paradoxically, many critics have characterized *Roxana* as the most psychologically, ethically, and aesthetically coherent all of Defoe's novelistic narratives (see, for example, Faller, *Crime and Defoe,* 202). Zimmerman shows how it expresses the ethical quandaries the earlier novels had pretended to resolve through the "sleight of hand" of repentance (Zimmerman, *Defoe and the Novel,* 155). I would argue that at least some of the coherence of *Roxana* results from precursor texts: compared with travel narratives and criminal biographies, the novels that *Roxana* imitates (those of Behn, Manley, and Haywood) are long, artful, and psychologically complex.

sudden disaster which befalls her. While the discrete novels comprising the series acquire a certain continuity and resemblance, it is its rewriting of the novels of amorous intrigue that gives this series of novels its deeper unity.

A sequential inventory of the several parts of *Roxana* reveals, first, a (failed) novel of courtship, followed by the five novels of amorous intrigue, and, finally, a novel of pursuit. This sequence of more or less discrete novels can be plotted in terms of the issue of power. As a background to the central action, Roxana marries a fool and comes to realize that the patriarchal systems of property transmission leave a woman like herself essentially powerless (5–25). To this extent, she assimilates her husband's dominant trait: she declares herself a fool for having married a fool and having put her fortune in his hands. The rest of the series will describe her effort to retrieve her fortune in the double sense of wealth and luck. After Roxana and Amy solve the problem of dispensing with Roxana's children, the action proper can begin. In the first novel, which I'm calling "The Landlord Husband," Roxana, with Amy's help and urging, puts her body "in play" in order to realize her income potential (25–58). In the second novel, "The French Prince," Roxana, disguised as "La Belle veuve de Poictou," wins a limited mastery by accepting the servitude of being a kept mistress (58–111). In the third novel, "The Dutch Merchant," Roxana wins and holds equal power with the male by refusing to enter the scenario of courtship and rejecting the Dutch merchant's proposal of marriage (111–162). In the fourth novel, "High Life as Roxana," Roxana realizes an apogee of social mastery by fashioning herself into a spectacle that is irresistible to the king (162–208). In the fifth novel, "Roxana's Reformation," Roxana effaces her dubious reputation (as the notorious "Roxana") by becoming, or dressing as (the two are nearly the same in this text), a Quaker, beginning to ameliorate the situation of her abandoned children, and finally marrying the Dutch merchant, returned from his departure in "The Dutch Merchant" (208–265). In "Susan's Supplement" to the fifth novel, at last, and unexpectedly, the series reaches its limit. Here, the narrative collapses into a retroactive sequence of flashbacks offering an account of Roxana's oldest daughter Susan's demonic quest for the recognition of her mother (265–330).

While the segments of this series recount strikingly different adventures, each of the novels can function as part of a series because they share certain recurrent features: a commercial stocktaking by which Roxana translates her adventure into cash; a new beginning in a new geographical and social setting, where the secrets of the past (pertaining to marriage, jewels, or affairs) pose a danger to the present; and the use of masquerade as both a necessity and a source of pleasure. In each novel the action reaches a climax around a moment of seduction, involving a choice and moral casuistry, and Roxana always chooses the path that is sinful and transgressive, lucrative and mobile. These choices lead her into a future to which the secondary voice of the narrative gives a sense of proleptic fatality. The plot's forward movement out of one place, situation, and novel into the next invents a kind of freedom as mobility. To be able to change disguise and move is to be free. This anthologized series of novels acquires a trajectory of moral decline, with Roxana's fall suggested at the end of the text. At the same time, the plausibility of both the moral sentiments voiced by Roxana the character and the moral interpolations of Roxana the narrator are vitiated by that which propels her life through an uncontrollable seriality: the compulsion to capitalize upon the income potential of her body; the will to go as far as she can, whatever the cost. Utterly absorbed by the adventure she is determined to live, Roxana advances in a hectic way that echoes the novel reader's compulsion to read on.

Such a summary might well lead one to question the interpretation of Defoe's text as a parodic or critical displacement of the novels of amorous intrigue. With *Roxana*, Defoe faithfully repeats the tendencies and formulas of much of Behn, Manley, and Haywood's fiction: the seriality of its action-centered plots, the foregrounding of the scheming ego of the protagonist(s), a turning of the social into masquerade, and finally, the gratification of fantasy, here involving not so much sex as the power and wealth accumulated through Roxana's success as a mistress. As with Haywood and Manley, serial form erodes ideological content: the author's moral judgments are put in question by the next installment of the narrative. In sum, Defoe so successfully embeds his narrative in the media culture of the novels of amorous intrigue that his critique of them may appear equivocal at best. This is of course a familiar aspect of Defoe. Later in this study, I will claim that Richardson and Fielding develop a fully self-conscious authorial response to media culture. Nonetheless, if one looks more closely at *Roxana*, and especially at what finally overtakes Roxana's effort to exercise full control of her own life, this text can be seen to offer a nuanced and compelling reading of the novels of amorous intrigue.

ROXANA'S TRANSGRESSIONS

Roxana transgresses the social order more completely than any libertine before LaClos and Sade. Like Behn's Silvia and Manley's Charlot, Roxana is initiated into her career as a mistress through an episode of seduction.

But the fall of Defoe's heroine is strikingly different from that of these precursors both by what is absent and by what is present. Unlike Silvia when she is seduced by Philander or Charlot when she is seduced by the duke, Roxana is not an isolated and naive virgin, suddenly confronted with the novelty of the intoxicating physical and psychological pleasures of sex, and persuaded by the discourse of love, clever contrivances of circumstances, or allures of an erotic present to follow the desire suddenly legible in her own heart. Instead of absorbing central character and reader in a narrative sequence that confers upon seduction a dreamlike sense of continuity and inevitability, Defoe inscribes seduction in rational dialogue. Thus the whole sequence in which the landlord seduces Roxana, including his first kindnesses, the generous supper, his first kiss, and his formal proposal of contractual settlements, unfolds in counterpoint with a series of clearheaded, ethical dialogues. In these debates, Amy urges the practical necessity of sexual compliance and the landlord argues the essential propriety of their affair, while Roxana insists that it would make her little better than a "whore." This dialogue among characters provides a reflective critique of the action, before and as it unfolds. Interspliced with this diegetic action, the secondary voice of the narrative echoes Roxana's warnings about the danger of the affair and gives the reader intimations of the fateful long-term consequences of this "fall." When Roxana finally succumbs to the landlord's campaign, her relenting is presented as an effect of his generous proposals and her "gratitude" for his help. Their first sex goes unnarrated. The moral interjections of Roxana, in both of her roles, as character and narrator, give this seduction a sense of weighty consequence and premeditation absent in the breathless present tense of Haywood's fiction, in which seduction moves forward with the desire-laden logic of an intense dream. In Behn, Manley, and Haywood, negative reflections tend to arrive too late to be of real use.

Roxana achieves her exteriority to the social order through one of the most notorious scenes in eighteenth-century fiction: the episode in which she strips her maid, Amy, and thrusts her into bed with her landlord "husband." Richetti has offered the most compelling reading of this scene: "the purpose of such a scene is to separate herself from those who have hitherto arranged her survival, to expose by her own arrangement the inadequacy of those who have arranged and defined the moral world she now lives in" (Richetti, *Defoe's Narratives*, 209). The landlord reminds Roxana that both he and she have been deserted by their respective spouses, argues his earnest love, and insists that their design for living is the practical equivalent of marriage. Amy promotes this living arrangement as more than a practical way to elude poverty. After the landlord's sumptuous supper, Amy is so "transported" with happiness that she rises from bed "and danc'd about the Room in her Shift" (32). A devil-may-care attitude gives a "wild" cast to the very syntax of her speech. Of the proposition that Amy have sex with the landlord on Roxana's behalf, she tells Roxana: "if he asks me, I won't deny him, not I; Hang me if I do" (39). Amy here adopts the libertine posture she will use to promote Roxana's subsequent adventures: that if opportunity invites and desire beckons, damn propriety, and just do it.

Roxana breaks out of this simulation of marriage by stripping Amy and thrusting her into bed with the landlord. The words with which this scene is narrated invoke the moral and social bonds that must be severed to enable Roxana's subsequent movement through her world:

> and at last, when [Amy saw] I was in earnest, she let me do what I wou'd; so I fairly stript her, and then I threw open the Bed, and thrust her in. (#1)
>
> I need say no more; this is enough to convince any body, that I did not think him my Husband, and that I had cast off all Principle, and all Modesty, and had effectually stifled Conscience. (#2)
>
> *Amy*, I dare say, began now to repent, and wou'd fain have got out of Bed again; but he said to her, Nay, *Amy*, you see your Mistress has put you to Bed, 'tis all her doing, you must blame her; so he held her fast, and the Wench being naked in the Bed with him, 'twas too late to look back, so she lay still, and let him do what he wou'd with her. (#3)
>
> Had I look'd upon myself as a Wife, you cannot suppose I would have been willing to have let my Husband lye with my Maid, much less, before my Face, for I stood-by all the while; but as I thought myself a Whore, I cannot say but that it was something design'd in my Thoughts, that my Maid should be a Whore too, and should not reproach me with it. (#4) [46–47]

This scene offers a rewriting of the most shocking feature of the novels of amorous intrigue: their direct representation of sex. The interplay of a shocking action (reported in paragraphs #1 and #3) and the ethical commentary of the narrator's secondary voice (reported in paragraphs #2 and #4), the counterpoint of Roxana's force and Amy's tentative resistance, produce a highly erotic scene. But the effect is utterly different from that produced by Behn, Manley, or Haywood. Instead of presenting sex as a spontaneous effect of desire, rendered in language shaped to draw the reader into an absorbed experience of its pleasures of arousal and climax, Defoe's narrative shows Roxana using sex to achieve an exteriority from the constraints of social values—indexed with the words "Principle," "Modesty," and "Conscience"—and of predetermined social roles—denoted with the words "Wife," "Husband," and "Maid." This scene is inscribed into a larger movement that makes sex subsidiary to Roxana's determination not to be defined by others. Richetti notes that Roxana's "pleasure, in effect, flows from that power and not from within the pleasurable acts themselves" (Richetti, *Defoe's Narratives*, 211). By instrumentalizing her body, her pleasure, and her experience, Roxana masters herself and others through a cool act of voyeurism: she does not join the two in bed, nor does she avert her eyes so as to leave them to their own pleasure; instead, she "stood-by all the while" the landlord does "what he wou'd" with Amy. Roxana's power comes from standing apart but nevertheless watching. It is this exteriority to the scene she contrives that is offered as evidence that Roxana lies outside any binding discourse of marriage.

This scene shows Roxana perfecting the most basic relation to her experience—what Richetti describes as her "ability to move through her narrative . . . and to remain outside it" (ibid.). It is this technique that will enable her life and memoir to have a serial structure. Roxana's exteriority to the social order is not just an effect of that secondary voice of the narrator, which provides commentary upon the present-tense action from a judgmental retrospective vantage point. Often, as in this passage, the utterly conventional ethics of this voice soften and recuperate the radicality of Roxana's position outside the social. Roxana's will to take her life beyond the confines of the present and into the next episode of her life explains what has been noted in this scene: her standing apart from the codes of social, moral Law (such as modesty) and the codes of romantic love and the itch of sexual pleasure. This compulsion to move on means that Roxana never mourns. After her move to France with the landlord jeweler, Roxana accepts with a chilling facility the death of the jeweler, the loss of her lover the prince, and the need to dispense with unwanted babies. Roxana's will to move on is not consistently explained by any character trait (such as her insecurity or her avarice) or justified by any goal (such as acquiring wealth, independence, or a higher social position). The seriality of Roxana's life is prior to the ideas that might be invoked to explain it. This is most spectacularly evident in her refusal to marry the Dutch merchant.

ROXANA'S FREEDOM

In refusing a proposal from the Dutch merchant, Roxana expresses her freedom from social convention in conceptual form. This third novel in the series is quite different from the previous two or the two that follow: there is little of the wonder of high life that is present in those other novels. Instead, Roxana strikes up a frank and honest friendship with the Dutch merchant who helps her escape from Paris with her wealth. Because of their equality and affection, and because both their spouses have apparently died, Roxana as narrator presents the action in such a way that the character Roxana is confronted with a fateful choice: either reform through a marriage that would take her toward respectability and the closure of her history, or hearken to the call of future adventures. Roxana's agent and alter ego Amy writes from London to promote the second option: "and now, Madam, . . . you have nothing to do but to come hither, and set up a Coach, and a good Equipage; and if Beauty and a good Fortune won't make you a Duchess, nothing will" (132). Within the admonitory autobiography that Roxana seeks to narrate, the central action of the "Dutch Merchant" novel is her refusal of his proposal of marriage, a choice that is defended in the debate at the novel's center. But a closer look at this debate shows that it is neither a genuine choice (Roxana never really considers marrying him) nor an authentic debate (Roxana disavows the very positions she articulates). Instead, Roxana's feminist arguments against marriage allow her to break through all conventional values invoked by the Dutch merchant, so that she is able to elude their constraints.

Here is the content of the debate between Roxana and the Dutch merchant in its antithetical purity: Roxana 1: Marriage gives all power and liberty to the man, divesting women of both (147–148); Dutch merchant 1: Because men do the work, and women enjoy the fruits, women "had the Name of Subjection, without the Thing . . ."(148); Roxana 2: As single, women are "masculine in [their] politick Capacity," and are therefore able to enjoy the pleasure of independence (148–149); Dutch merchant 2: Where there is sincere affection one can avoid all she says as to being "a Slave, a Servant, *and the like* . . . [for] where there was a mutual Love, there cou'd be no Bondage; but that there was but one Interest; one Aim; one Design; and all conspir'd to make both very happy" (149); Roxana 3: Once a woman gives her affection there is "one Interest; one Aim; one Design"—the man's; woman is to be but a passive creature, and if his welfare flounders, so does hers (149–150); Dutch merchant 3: With safe management such disaster can be avoided; and Roxana can guide their common "Ship" "Bottom" if she wishes (150); Roxana 4: Broadening her critique from the content of their particular contract to the way in which women are positioned by the social order in general, Roxana rejoins that individuals cannot so easily step outside of custom and the law: "It is not you, *says I*, that I suspect, but the Laws of Matrimony puts the Power into your Hands; bids you do it; commands you to command; and binds me, forsooth, to obey; you, that are now upon even Terms with me . . ." (151); Dutch merchant 4: "Marriage was decreed by Heaven" as a way to find felicity for both parties and transmit property to legitimate progeny. Roxana's feminist critique frees her from the commonsense assumptions about gender relations harbored by her Dutch admirer: "if we have sex, she will want to marry"; "if I let her keep her property, she will marry me"; and "surely if she gets pregnant she will want to marry me." In spite of sex, pregnancy, and iron-clad assurances about property, Roxana rejects his proposals, and chooses freedom.

In spite of the critical celebrity of Roxana's defense of her autonomy, the text of *Roxana* vitiates the feminist rationale for her refusal of the Dutch merchant in at least three ways. First, the occasion for this debate subverts its content. When the Dutch merchant surmises Roxana is loath to give up control of her money, he offers to relinquish any claim on her wealth. Roxana admits to the reader that this "putting my Money out of my Hand, was the Sum of the Matter, that made me refuse to marry." This fact being "too gross for me to acknowledge," she decides to "give a new Turn to it, and talk upon a kind of an elevated Strain" (147). The feminist critique of marriage follows as a kind of ruse to throw the Dutch merchant off the scent of her actual designs. Second, there is further evidence that Roxana does not accept her own feminist argument. Earlier in this same episode, the narrator's adjudication of the difference between a mistress and a wife has given a check to (the character) Roxana's quest for personal power. As a character, Roxana declares she would rather be a mistress than a wife, for while "a Wife is look'd upon, as but an Upper-Servant, a Mistress is a Sovereign . . ." As a rejoinder to this social satire upon marriage, Roxana as narrator immediately rejoins with the counterargument: while the mistress has no rights by law or social convention and must be seen in secret, and is dropped when the man reforms, the "Wife appears boldly and honorably with her Husband; lives at Home, and possesses his House, his Servants, his Equipages, and has a Right to them all, and to call them her own" (132). Lincoln Faller notes that "modern readers easily sympathize with Roxana's feminist declaration of independence, but, as it falls into a libertine tradition that was highly suspect, the original audience would likely not have been similarly inclined. One of the devil's general ruses according to Defoe, was 'to infuse notions of liberty into the minds of men; that it is hard they should be born into the world with inclinations, and then be forbidden to gratify them'" (Faller, "Toward a History," 226, citing Defoe, *Serious Reflections of Robinson Crusoe*, 281). Third, the future direction of the plot lends irony to the rationales for Roxana's refusal of marriage: Roxana marries this very same Dutch merchant years later. When it suits her changed purposes, Roxana casts off this specious, masklike functionality of her feminist critique of marriage.[8]

Roxana goes even further than the libertine heroines of the novels of amorous intrigue in refusing to make men, marriage, and sex the telos of a woman's life. She not only rejects a central social ethos of the novels of Behn and Haywood, usually affirmed through their virtuous heroines, that the fully reciprocated love of a man is the goal of both female desire and narrative plotting; in the third novel of this series, she also eludes the codes of courtship and marriage that prevail in the "woman's novels" of the 1710s and 1720s written by Jane Barker and Penelope Aubin (Backscheider, *Spectacular Politics*, 183–184). Roxana's refusal of marriage does more than refuse narrative closure for her life. Like the act of her putting Amy to bed with her landlord-husband, Roxana's refusal of marriage is based in, and helps to rationalize, the seriality of her life, in terms of its efficient, and profitable, movement from one adventure and "fortune" to another. Roxana keeps her life something ever about to be. Her self-proclaimed alibis and purposes—independence, wealth, and social position—are not consistently applied to either the living or the telling of her life. All are pulled into the ethos of seriality, motivated in advance by what might be called Roxana's ambition.

ROXANA'S AMBITION

The narrator presents Roxana's refusal of marriage as a decision to try her luck in further adventures: "I wou'd try my Fortune at *London*, come of it what wou'd" (161). In this sentence, "Fortune" means "luck" or "chance," and shows that Roxana has the tolerance for risk so essential to the new economic order Defoe promotes everywhere in his writing. Every time she moves from one social role and cultural location to another, Roxana moves investments—of her wealth, body, and energy—so as to maximize the return on "capital." But from the retrospective vantage point of the narrator, it is precisely Roxana's refusal of the Dutch merchant and her restless will to go on, "come of it what wou'd," that threaten her fortune in the second sense of "material wealth or financial conditions" (*American Heritage*

8. For an alternative way to read the incoherence of Roxana's feminism, see Laura Brown, *Ends of Empire*, 153–155. Brown shows how the characterization of Roxana's feminism as amazonlike, and her implication in murder, allow her to function as a scapegoat for the violence of the "masculine" economic acquisitiveness she practices.

Dictionary): she admits, "I might have settled myself out of the reach even of Disaster itself . . ."(158–159), and, "I threw away the only Opportunity I then had, to have effectually settl'd my Fortunes, and secur'd them for this World" (161). In this text, the word "fortune" often slides between "luck" and "wealth"; although these two senses of "fortune" are the primary ones engaged by the subtitle of *Roxana*—"the fortunate mistress"—the narrator also actively solicits its third major sense, for while seeking her "fortune," Roxana also pursues her "fate" or "destiny." In trying to interpret her perverse refusal of the Dutch merchant, an action which has come to appear fateful, the narrator speculates upon Roxana's motives, exhausts rational explanation, and has recourse to odd nonreasons and moral absolutes: "But my Measure of Wickedness was not yet full" (159). Finally, the narrator steps back from her own character and recuperates the story for the admonitory power of its negative example: "I am a Memorial to all that shall read my Story; a standing Monument of . . . how dangerously we act, when we follow the Dictates of an ambitious Mind" (161).

Ambitious for what? What does Roxana want? Nothing that comes to her, neither wealth, nor independence, nor fame, gratifies her ambition. Neither does her crowning success in becoming the king's mistress arrest her restless movement. Roxana's ambition is not an object but a vector: rather than "the object or goal," her ambition is an "eager or strong desire" (*American Heritage Dictionary*). To explore this ambition, we must ask not what Roxana wants, but *how* she wants. Roxana's desire is to be a "mistress." What precisely is entailed in being a mistress and how this role serves and incites Roxana's ambition are suggested in the scene that is the climax of Roxana's metamorphosis into the prince's mistress. In the scene of Roxana's investiture in her role as mistress, she allows her lover to play Pygmalion, while she submits to being the "idol" he adorns. Her changed dress signifies more than a changed social position: it denotes the assumption of a new self. The prince completes this change, and makes Roxana's image "perfect," by placing a diamond necklace around her neck. The prince's gift is bestowed in such a way as to make it the climax of Roxana's initiation as his mistress. By the mystery of its arrival, the pain it produces, and the magical transformation it effects, this necklace functions as an equivocal emblem of ambition:

> at last he leads me to the darkest Part of the Room, and standing behind me, bade me hold up my Head, when putting both his Hands round my Neck, as if he was spanning my Neck, to see how small it was, for it was long and small; he held my Neck so long, and so hard, in his Hand, that I complain'd he hurt me a little; what he did it for, I knew not, nor had I the

least Suspicion but that he was spanning my Neck; but when I said he hurt me, he seem'd to let go, and in half a Minute more, led me to a Peir-Glass, and behold, I saw my Neck clasp'd with a fine Necklace of Diamonds; whereas I felt no more what he was doing, than if he had really done nothing at-all, nor did I suspect it, in the least: If I had an Ounce of Blood in me, that did not fly up into my Face, Neck, and Breasts, it must be from some Interruption in the Vessels; I was all on fire with the Sight, and began to wonder what *it* was that was coming to me. [73, italics mine]

In this scene Roxana confronts more than the discipline of beauty—the pain or labor required to turn one's body into an icon of beauty for the gaze of others. Instead, she submits to a mysterious initiation by allowing herself to be led into "the darkest part of the room," to be held by her "long and small" neck so "long" and "hard" that it "hurt." These words give the prince's touch some of the character of strangulation. By submitting to a symbolic death as the "widow" of the jeweler, she is brought back to life as a woman of beauty. The magic spontaneity of this metamorphosis comes not only from the artful sleight of hand which conceals the prince's contrivance, but also from the way in which this gift returns Roxana to herself as an image that has an uncanny completeness: she tells the reader to "behold" the image that condenses a new Roxana and realizes her unconscious ambition. The shock of recognition makes her "all on fire with the Sight."

Roxana's blush signifies the pleasure she feels at this sudden gratification of her vanity: if she is not a princess, she is at least the bejeweled mistress of a prince. But this necklace is also a kind of halter of servitude, making her enslavement to her "Master" all too explicit. Her blush certifies an ambivalent mixture of pride and shame at a possession that at once enslaves and glorifies. To master her future she must accept this servitude. Roxana's necklace is made of diamonds because of the way in which they conduct white light yet refract it into every color, giving them an enigmatic transparency. They suggest all possible futures, while disclosing none. But what her ambition will entail remains obscure; she is in a state of wonder— amazement and doubt—as to "what it was" that is coming to her. The "it" of her ambition, that obscure object of her desire, is accessible through the affairs she undertakes and the duplicities she practices. Because it shifts content, "it" cannot finally be named. Roxana's ambition is traversed by a desire that harbors the negativity of this "it" within itself as its own condition of possibility and limit. This "it" is what Roxana will pursue, but, to her surprise, it also comes to pursue her.

The absoluteness of Roxana's ambition, as it comes to shape her life, throws her into a retroactive temporality. The future as the site for the realization of one's ambition determines the actions and choices of the present (for example, accepting the prince, saying "no" to the Dutch merchant, and dispensing with infants), and requires a fastidious erasure of the past (for example, evidence of an old husband, and her life as "Roxana"). Once she has passed into a new theater of life, Roxana finds her past can threaten her new performance. The multiplicity, variety, and profitability of her futures depend upon her mobility between performative spaces. This is why, as she acquires wealth, her movement to the next scene of adventure requires Whig financial instruments, which can turn jewels and silver plate into paper that accrues interest. When Roxana wants to cash in on her French earnings—as the "Wife" of the murdered jeweler and as the mistress to the prince—she turns to the Dutch merchant. But here, opposition takes the form of an old-style money changer, a Jewish jeweler who knows too much. The narrator's blatantly anti-Semitic depiction of this figure does not obscure the essential correctness of his accusation of Roxana: she is selling jewels she has allowed to be reported as lost to the thieves who murdered her jeweler "husband." The morbid melodrama of the narrator's account of the accusation of Roxana, and of her horrified response, suggests that the negativity of this raging Jew is being intensified by something within Roxana:

> the *Jew* held up his Hands, look'd at me with some Horrour, then talk'd *Dutch* again, and put himself into a thousand Shapes, twisting his Body, and wringing up his Face this Way, and that Way, in his Discourse; stamping with his Feet, and throwing abroad his Hands, as if he was not in a Rage only, but in a meer Fury; then he wou'd turn, and give a Look at me, like the Devil; I thought I never saw any thing so frightful in my Life. [113]

Speaking an unknown language, contorting his body into a "meer Fury," and giving her a look "like the Devil," this figure acquires its uncanny power from Roxana's own superego. Though the diegetic action will solve the problem of this unsettling representative of a rigid Old Testament Law—he is first tricked by the Dutch merchant and then mutilated by the French prince—he anticipates a much more compelling expression of the remorseless superego: Roxana's eldest daughter, Susan.

Where does Roxana come closest to realizing her ambition? Her memoir narrative gives pride of place to her dance in the habit of the Turkish princess, and critics have long viewed the scene as a crux for interpreting *Roxana* and its opportunistic central character.[9] There is no doubt that the

9. Critics find what they are looking for here—whereas, for example, Max Novak finds evidence in this scene of a provisional unity to the novel, Laura Brown

narrator presents Roxana's performances as the Turkish princess as the moment of her greatest power and freedom. Here, through a triumph of pure fictionality, her ambition achieves its most intoxicating gratification. Roxana realizes the fantasy of the fungibility of identity so central to the novels of amorous intrigue: the notion that you can be what you want by dressing that way. If Roxana is not queen for a day, she is at least a princess for a night or two. Within the rhetoric of the memoir narrative, these scenes also function as a kind of boast. "Here," Roxana seems to say, "I reached the apex of celebrity and social importance." However, this scene is also the one in which she is christened "Roxana" and receives the more problematic notoriety this novel exploits.

In these scenes, Roxana achieves mastery by fascinating the gaze of the powerful Other—here, the king. But how does she know this grand but disguised Other is out there in the audience, and confirming her centrality with his gaze? He never declares himself directly; his existence is a kind of act of faith, first for Roxana, and then for her reader. She is aware of his presence only indirectly—by the way his companions and messengers are "silent as Death" as to his identity (176); by his being "the only one with his Hat on" (180)—and, retroactively, by the liaison that results from her triumphant performances. Thus the centrality of this performance arises in part from the later unnarratable "Scene" for which it substitutes: the scene in which Roxana becomes the king's mistress. The Turkish dance precipitates that intimate sexual linkage with power and the Law, and it occurs just before the lacuna in the narrative that such a relationship mandates: "There is a Scene which came in here, which I must cover from humane Eyes or Ears; for three Years and about a Month, *Roxana* liv'd retir'd . . . with a Person, which Duty, and private Vows, obliges her not to reveal" (181). The third-person-singular usage of "Roxana" makes this sentence appear to be an editorial aside within the first-person memoir. It removes the protagonist beyond the reader's ken. Roxana's Turkish dance offers an enticing aestheticized sublimation of the action of that other "Scene," Roxana's affair with the king, the hidden place where the father suspends the Law while he enjoys, with an obscene absence of guilt, the woman who has seduced him. This other "place" might be the utopic space of popular fiction—the impossible place without prohibitions—but Roxana can't show it. The censoring

---

sees Roxana appropriating the "costume of an exotic and exploited other" in order to wear "the spoils of an expansionist culture" (Novak, "Some Notes Toward a History"; L. Brown, *Ends of Empire*, 147–148).

out of this "Scene" underlies the whole system of print and representation that enables the publication of this disguised story.

Is it the case that these scenes of apparently pure performativity and self-creation allow Roxana to achieve her ambition? No. For while we are told that Roxana's dance produced a voluptuous spectacle, the narrator does not offer the reader an enticing description of the dance. Instead, this dance is presented as a kind of ruse of the scheming ego. We as readers are taken behind the scenes, where we see that Roxana's orchestration of an illusion of erotic power is dependent on an orientalist masquerade: an ordinary English girl, by wearing the outfit of a Turkish princess and dancing a new Parisian "figure" to a French tune, appears as irresistibly exotic (Trumpener, "Rewriting Roxane"). While this dance is a tribute to Roxana's finesse and nerve, her own analysis of the rhetoric of her dance demystifies its erotic singularity.

Roxana's deft exploitation of this dance inscribes her in networks of repetition which finally prove uncontrollable. When she returns from being the king's mistress, the heroine finds that tongues have begun to wag, that many suspect she is a "meer *Roxana*" (182). Roxana now realizes that her "honor and virtue" and the renown of her independent fortune were necessary constituents of the allure of the spectacle of Roxana (182). While the king was wise enough to order only one repetition of the Turkish dance, Roxana, like a fading star, returns incessantly to her moment of glory. Even after her withdrawal from "the World," she cannot resist putting on the habit of the Turkish princess and showing it off to the Quaker and her Dutch husband (247–248). It is these nostalgic re-enactments of her triumph that propel the plot in a fateful direction. Roxana discovers that from the spectatorial side of her masquerade/performance an "other" self is watching, and she recognizes Roxana. It is her own daughter and the person named after her, Susan. Susan sees her mother—without recognizing her—for the first, and apparently only, time during her service in Roxana's household, while she performs this dance (206). Susan's memory of the costume—described with pride to the Quaker—becomes the detail that certifies the validity of Susan's claims on Roxana, and forecloses the efficacy of Roxana's masquerade.

ROXANA'S LAST MASK

Roxana's reformation pivots upon her attempt to go from being a reader to being a writer of novels. Where among cultural practices does one find the relation to life we find in the main character of *Roxana*? Roxana moves through an experience she remains outside of; she is transgressive yet pays no penalties; she progresses from success to success without feeling the gravitational tug of "reality"; she encounters boundless variety, and yet remains restlessly determined to find more. Roxana has the same relation to her life that a reader has to the "life" in a novel he or she reads. Like a print-media junkie, Roxana develops an ethos that facilitates the serialization of her life into a sequence of absorbing adventures. While she inhabits each of the novel-like episodes, her life takes on the autonomous, dream-like continuity of novels as they are experienced by an absorbed reader. At the end of each novel-like episode, Roxana moves on to new "fortunes" with the same ease and curiosity with which a reader passes from one novel to another. It is as if she can live her own life with the provisional indifference most appropriate to the way in which a reader consumes the lives of novelistic characters.

Roxana—unlike the heroines of Manley and Haywood—is not represented as a novel reader. Nonetheless, she simulates the life of a character from the novels of amorous intrigue by imitating the immunity of lives lived according to the imperatives of fantasy. The central illusion of this place of fiction is of the self's essential autonomy, of life as a free ride: one can have experiences which leave no traces and accrue no debts. This sense of steady, cost-free accumulation of experience is expressed within *Roxana* through the magical efficacy of capital accumulation. Roxana's financial advisor, Sir Robert Clayton, shows her how, if she returns part of interest earnings to principal, she can support herself handsomely and progress spontaneously toward ever greater wealth (167). By putting this method to work, Roxana becomes a woman of vast wealth.

But while Roxana's capital appreciates, her reputation becomes notorious. She begins to dread the moment of recognition when some stranger shouts, "D——— me, if that's not Roxana!" In order to secure a tranquil retirement, Roxana's reputation needs laundering. Her repentance is shadowed by the same critical skepticism that dogs Moll Flander's Newgate conversion: it seems to be motivated by a cost-benefit analysis. It is only after she has begun to grow old, and after she can no longer attract a monarch, that Roxana finds herself haunted with the unsettling question, "*What was I a Whore for now?*" (201–203) Roxana's reform program splices together the language of God-fearing seventeenth-century spiritual autobiography and twentieth-century public relations. As many critics have noted, her repentance is vitiated by her failure to develop within her "new" life either a new set of values (for example, honesty) or a new modus vivendi. Roxana's reformation is managed with the same sort of scheming and disguise, and the same adroit management of others through surrogates, that made her earlier successes possible. She tries to assume the honesty and honor of Quaker life by dressing and speaking as a Quaker, but there is a dangerous flaw to such a strategy: by going still further with disguise, Roxana confers upon truth, as a stripping away of disguise, a potentially disastrous force.

Roxana's written narrative originates within the fifth novel's attempt to retrieve her reputation. Only by constituting herself as one who initiates a sober reflection upon her past can she develop the secondary voice of the narrative. Roxana's memoir—by assembling a variety of lives and fortunes into one narrative series—requires the same kind of agile compositional skill exercised within this fifth novel of the narrative. In it, she takes her personal connections (with the prince and with the Dutch husband), the scattered remainders of her sex life (her children), and the vast "fortunes" (i.e., wealth) acquired during her adventures, and forges all of these into her life as the respectable, wealthy, and titled wife of the Dutch merchant. This re-formed, artfully com-posed life is the object of Roxana's last schemes, and motivates the writing of her memoir. But it has the essential character of a new disguise. On the title page, her claim to successful reformation is expressed through her last title, "the Countess de Wintselsheim." This narrative is Roxana's last mask.

Roxana: the Fortunate Mistress has the basic rhetoric of self-justification and exculpation. By balancing the first-person experience of the protagonist against the moralizing interpolations of the older and wiser courtesan, this memoir alibis the first with the moral saws of the latter. Throughout most of *Roxana* it is implied that the protagonist's last performance—as the reformed Roxana—makes her story a legitimate source of moral wisdom. By writing a narrative about her past, Roxana seeks to convert the "fortunes" (i.e., wealth) of each adventure into one Fortune (or destiny) which is "Fortunate" (i.e., lucky). The editor of the narrative, respecting that ambition, refuses to spoil the story by disclosing its final catastrophe and therefore effaces any sign of Roxana's disastrous final encounters with her daughter from the novel's title-page description of the whole narrative, from the first six novel-length segments of her history, and even from the moral defense of the whole text offered in the preface. The editor's deceit indulges Roxana's narrative disguises and sets up the surprise that greets the reader at the end of the novel.[10]

10. The long eighteenth-century title-page summary of plot so often used by Defoe has many functions: like the summary on the sleeve of a video rental or on

Only at the end of the fifth novel, after Roxana has successfully established her new life in Holland and apparently dispensed with the threat to her tranquillity posed by Susan, does the reader receive clear signs that something is profoundly amiss. A severe new tone inflects the narrative: Roxana feels guilty for mixing her *"ill-got Wealth, the Product . . . of a vile and vicious Life* of Whoredom and Adultery" with *"the honest well-gotten Estate of this innocent Gentleman"* (259); she finds "there was a secret Hell within, even all the while, when our Joy was at the highest" (260); reflections upon her own past "gnaw'd a Hole" "quite thro'" her "Heart" and "made bitter every Sweet, and mix'd my Sighs with every Smile" (264). These disquiets seem mysterious and somewhat uncalled-for, as they cut against the comic denouement of the romance with the Dutch husband and their titled positions at the end of a life of hurry and labor. Obscure forces prevent this text from being controlled by the compositional designs of the reformed Roxana. The effort to recast Roxana's life into a comic pattern was at best a wishful feint, at worst a disguise. Arriving at the "end" of her story, Roxana's profound disquiets suggest all has not been told: "I must now go back to another Scene, and join it to this End of my Story" (265). What complicates and confounds this movement toward closure, toward entitling her life as the "fortunate mistress," is the need to go back to events and facts which the narrative of the fifth novel has obscured. But rather than ending the story, this supplement only succeeds in reopening it.

ROXANA'S (SELF-)DIVISION

What is it that disrupts not only Roxana's life, but its telling in memoir form? What is it that terminates the hopeful, carefree movement toward the new that is built into the very nature of seriality? And finally, what is it that enables Defoe to break the fictional allure of the novels of amorous intrigue? The answer lies not with anything from outside the central character, but with something that erupts from within, splitting both Roxana and her compositional project asunder. To understand how this happens, it is necessary to go back to an as-yet-undiscussed feature of this text and join it to this analysis. Nothing is more characteristic of the novels of amorous intrigue than the way in which a scheming ego takes over the direction of the plot. Nothing is more important for Roxana's ability to do this than her use of

---

the back of a book, it offers a preview to the potential consumer, and thus should be understood as part of the discourse of advertising. As in the present epoch, unpleasant turns of the plot are often hidden from potential viewers.

surrogates. When she needs to dispose of children, recover property, investigate a husband, dispense some largesse, or end an affair, she has at her disposal Amy, who is always ready to busy herself for her mistress. Much of the critical literature on *Roxana* has found the relationship between Roxana and Amy to be one of the most striking features of the novel.

Over the many different contexts and episodes of *Roxana*, Amy is much more than the facilitator of Roxana's life of intrigue. Beyond being soul mates, surrogates, or alter egos, Roxana and Amy gradually become doubles. At different points in the narrative diegesis, it is easy to see Roxana and Amy as expressing different sides of one human character. As the deserted mother of starving children, Roxana is paralyzed by pathetic sentiment, but Amy is inventively active; during Roxana's wooing by the landlord, Amy plays the bawd while Roxana clings to respectability; when their ship is caught in a storm on the way to Rotterdam, Amy sees their peril as a judgment for past sins, while Roxana continues on her way after the ship's repair. As long as Amy suffers for and serves her mistress, her extreme loyalty can be interpreted within the coordinates of the servant/mistress relation. When they do things in parallel—have affairs, dress in finery, or grow wealthy—they evidence a mutual identification. But when Roxana strips Amy and puts her into bed with the landlord, we catch the first glimpse of a demonic potential to their relationship. There is also something compulsive, ruthless, and excessive in Roxana's determination to make Amy share the self-pollution Roxana herself feels. At the end of her story, Roxana as a narrator takes note of the antipathy between their two characters. While Roxana suffers the disquiets and persecutions of a bad conscience, Amy seems immune from troubling reflections: "for tho' *Amy* was the better Penitent before, when we had been in the Storm; *Amy* was just where she us'd to be, *now*, a wild, gay, loose Wretch, and not much the graver for her Age; for *Amy* was between forty and fifty by this time too" (265). As in the divergence between character and portrait in Wilde's *Portrait of Dorian Gray*, Amy maintains a vibrant sexuality and licentious youth, while her double, Roxana, bears the weight of sin and age.

What does this doubling of the central character accomplish? By dividing one character into different roles, Roxana expands the variety of her experience and the range of her possible fortunes. Doubling herself helps free Roxana from the limitation of having one particular body, history, or future. But doubling the central character blurs the moral responsibility of social exchange: it makes every social posture and emotional state seem arbitrary and reversible, and by loosening the force of social convention, it opens the plot to more options and enhanced mobility. When, in the

Supplement to the fifth novel, Amy relinquishes her role as indispensable surrogate, the Quaker assumes it in her place. But the narrative does not convey the sense that Roxana has corrupted the Quaker. Instead, "Roxana" has simply "expanded" to acquire a certain stock in the Quaker's respectability. In the last paragraphs of the text we learn that Roxana has to take Amy back into her life, even after Amy's unspeakable crime—the murder of Susan. Roxana can't really survive without her double.

In the final Supplement to *Roxana*, the double haunts the social with the possibility of radical evil. What kind of narrative supplement is "joined" to the fifth novel in order to complete its account? Viewed from Roxana's side, the final narrative is offered as a story of providential retribution: it describes the gradual steps by which Roxana and Amy are drawn into the unspeakable crime censored from the account of the same action in the previous novel: the murder of Roxana's daughter. But from Susan's vantage point, the narrative recounts a failed quest for a lost parent. In this way, it inverts the comic plot of countless romances, novels and dramas, and anticipates Romantic novels such as Godwin's *Caleb Williams* and Shelley's *Frankenstein*. What gives Susan's quest its disturbing power is the way it fuses together two antithetical postures. In nearly every scene in which Susan tenders her claims on Roxana, the narrative presents this quest in two very different ways. First, there is a plaintive sympathetic desire to be recognized by her true mother: "what have I done that you won't own me, and that you will not be call'd my Mother? . . . I can keep a Secret too, especially for my own Mother, sure . . ." (267). But there is also a demonic cast to Susan's investigation. Through a blend of brilliant surmises, lucky hunches, and resolute chase, Susan advances her search in spite of the admonitions and evasions of Roxana and her two agents, Amy and the Quaker. Thus in her very first interview with Amy, Susan's surmises are punctuated with an obsessive claim to an uncanny knowledge: Susan declares "I know. . . . I know . . . I know it all . . . I know it all well enough" (268). Susan's oddly powerful investigation into the hidden truth of Roxana's past means that decisive control of the plot shifts from Roxana's elaborate efforts at damage control to Susan's relentless pursuit of her mother.

Susan appears as the side of Roxana that her whole career has needed to suppress: the original unmasked self, carrying her own given name, "Susan." The rupture in Roxana's narrative progress appears to comes not from the social, but from the inside of her self, in the form of a demonic Other. Susan's address to Roxana takes the form of a demand that Roxana pay a symbolic debt. Viewed retroactively, Roxana's rejection of Susan (and the other younger children) was the condition of the possibility of Roxana's brilliant career. All these years, Susan has been paying the price for Roxana's freedom, pleasure, and good fortune(s). Now the debt must be paid. Susan will not accept an anonymous legacy; she won't be bought off with money, or with any object. Her demand is more primordial. She wants the one thing Roxana won't give: recognition of her as Roxana's daughter.

As the narrative supplement proceeds, it is evident that Susan, like Amy, cannot be seen simply as other than Roxana. As another side of the divided Roxana, Susan displays an uncannily increasing quantity of power and knowledge. Through a perverse intrapsychic economy, the more energy and deceiving wit Roxana, Amy, and the Quaker put into defending Roxana against Susan, the more knowledge and power Susan acquires (Backscheider, *Spectacular Politics*, 196). Susan assumes the position of a remorseless and punitive superego, an emanation of a Law that Roxana cannot elude, because it comes from within the self. This law gets its peculiar force from its form: it arrives as a truthful antithesis of the generic ground rules of the fictive narrative. In the novels of amorous intrigue, the intriguer's transgressions depend upon suspending any of the necessary weight of the self's social position, role, history, or relation to others. By using disguise, the ruse, and the lie, the protagonists fashion the social into a space of pleasure, with control going to the most cunning. As masters of these techniques, Roxana and Amy turn every element of the social into an instrument of their progress. Why, then, is Susan such a threat to Roxana? It is a threat because Susan's demand, if accepted, subverts all the modes of Roxana's control; that is, if she gives in to Susan's demand, she loses her control over her social identity (as a virtuous wife and worthy holder of a title, instead of the notorious "Roxana"), over her relationship to her surrogate and alter ego Amy (they fight over what to do about Susan), and even over the narrative of her past (which she exercises in this writing). But given that Susan claims she could keep a secret for her own mother, why does she appear as a traumatic antagonist to Roxana? Roxana claims that if she acknowledged Susan, she "must for-ever after have been this Girl's Vassal, *that is to say,* have let her into the Secret, and trusted to her keeping it too, or have been expos'd, and undone; *the very Thought fill'd me with Horror*" (280). Roxana feels horror at the loss of control to another, one with an utterly different agenda. Susan refuses to abstract the past, present, or future into a purely instrumental value. Thus the particular form of Susan's dangerous demand: she articulates her *self* as an end in itself. In wanting nothing from Roxana but recognition as her daughter,

Susan confronts her with the fundamental ethical relationship: the form of the face of the other as a self, articulated as a demand for human recognition as such.

As the one spectator at Roxana's Turkish-princess performance who was unseduced, as the one person who cannot be bought off, Susan becomes the single "stain" upon Roxana's life, and one with the power to disrupt its closure and mastery: suddenly and uncannily, an obscure kernel with the social symbolic returns the gaze (Žižek, *Enjoy Your Symptom!* 15). Susan, as the repressed part of the self, returns with her memory of costs and her bill for repayment: her demand for recognition. This return of an unincorporable self fragments the self and throws the parts into an antagonistic relation to one another. Within the struggle to survive an assault from its own superego, the ego is thrown into a vertiginous fury. For Roxana and her protecting servant, Amy, Susan is not a simple complication. Susan appears as "evil": Roxana claims, "she haunted me like an Evil Spirit" (310). Therefore she provokes evil measures to deal with her. Susan, as the only character with claims upon Roxana equal to Amy's, manages to split Roxana and Amy around the question of whether Amy should murder Susan. In the carefully spun conversations with which Amy seeks to put Susan off the scent, Susan's clever surmises acquire traumatic force. At the end of one of her intelligence reports about Susan, Amy rages, and Roxana is appalled: "I'll put an End to it, that I will; I can't bear it; I must murther her; I'll kill her B—, *and swears by her Maker, in the most serious Tone in the World;* and then repeated it over three or four times, walking to-and-again in the Room; I will, *in short*, I will kill her, if there was not another Wench in the World" (272). Swirling far beyond the ground rules for social exchange, Amy swears in words that can't be printed, thereby foreclosing the reader's access to the dialogue. In some sense a schizoid division of this novel's eponymous character has fissured the novelistic premise that different characters represent discrete social agents. Now characters like Roxana, Susan, Amy, and the Quaker are antagonistic avatars of a single split self, and the space for social and linguistic exchanges has imploded.[11]

---

11. The ending of *Roxana* has been a problem since the eighteenth century. Its anonymous 1745 continuation vitiates the power of Defoe's text by effacing the murder of Roxana's daughter and turning Susan from a double to just another character; by contrast, Godwin draws upon *Roxana* for the drama *Falkland,* which becomes the kernel for *Caleb Williams* (see Peterson, *Daniel Defoe,* bibliography). In *The Figure of Theater: Shaftesbury, Defoe, Adam Smith, and George Eliot,* David Marshall offers a somewhat different interpretation of *Roxana*'s ending, developing an analogy with psychoanalysis to index the oddity of what I am calling

ROXANA'S FAILURE

At text's end the failure of closure comes not as an ambitious choice but as a kind of short-circuit. Thus the text's last paragraph does not conclude, but instead marks its own failure to win an ending to the story or a resolution of its ethical meaning:

> Here, after some few Years of flourishing, and outwardly happy Circumstances, I fell into a dreadful Course of Calamities, and *Amy* also; the very Reverse of our former Good Days; the Blast of Heaven seem'd to follow the Injury done the poor Girl, by us both; and I was brought so low again, that my Repentance seem'd to be only the Consequence of my Misery, as my Misery was of my Crime. [329–330]

Why does *Roxana* fail to deliver any "sense of an ending"? Why does the novel fail to conclude? Rather than seeing this ending as a failure of authorial design or novelistic "structure," I am suggesting that the catastrophe that engulfs this narrative is a symptom of the crisis within early modern culture around licensing reading for entertainment. The rupture of the narrative in *Roxana* implicates three agents: the failure of Roxana as a character to secure her fortune (in both senses, of luck and wealth), the failure of Roxana as narrator to turn a retrospective narrative of her past crimes into a new species of moral wisdom; and, finally, the failure of Defoe to rewrite the novels of amorous intrigue in such a way that the improvement of the novel reader is assured. Another way to put this is that "Susan's Supplement" is a revelation of the bad repetition necessarily involved in any seemingly carefree seriality. Over the course of this uncontrollable series named "Roxana," the problem of true and false performance haunts Defoe's effort to write improving fiction in the guise of the novel—in other words, to do what Roxana attempts most spectacularly in her Turkish-princess dance: enter the space of popular entertainment and come away unscathed.

"Susan's Supplement": "Like the patient in the psychiatrist's office who says, five minutes before the end of the hour, 'by the way, there's something I haven't mentioned,'" (146) Marshall's discussion demonstrates how Defoe's recourse to first-person narrative reroutes the problem of truth and lie in narrative into the problem of false impersonation. Within the thematic that guides Marshall's reading, Susan appears as an embodiment of an audience that won't let Roxana escape from the condition of an essential theatricality (149). While Marshall's study gives theatricality the character of a global problematic of writing, representation, and culture, my study seeks to show how the early novelists translate the general problem of truth and error in performance into specific writing strategies for confronting the antinovel discourse.

The historical coordinates designated at the end of the title page—"Being the Person known by the name of Lady Roxana in the time of Charles II"—suggest that Roxana's world comes to her pre-formed by an earlier body of secret histories written by Behn and Manley. If the historical "Roxana" belongs to the time of Charles II, the textual character named "Roxana" indexes novels written with the loose morals and ludic intrigue associated with the Restoration. But if we understand the intertext of the novels of amorous intrigue as a code Roxana manipulates instrumentally, then she as a character, performing as a Turkish princess, and Roxana as the narrator describing that triumph, both occupy the position of Daniel Defoe, who rewrites the novels of amorous intrigue. This exteriority (to an earlier history, to an earlier body of novel writing) confers a certain ludic character on Roxana's gambit: can Roxana play the game she has learned from these texts, but elude their most constraining axioms? Can she, for example, grow rich as a female courtesan in the patriarchal system biased against women? And finally, can Defoe write a critically enlightened series of amorous novels in such a way as to elude their dubious ethical tendencies?

The exteriority to the social that proves so problematic to Roxana as a character also implicates Defoe. The separation this text contrives between Roxana the character—who goes from being a girl to being a naive and deluded wife to being a manipulative courtesan and shrewd investor—and Roxana the narrator—who shapes the narrative of the diegetic present according to the future toward which her life tends in order to claim access to a deeper moral wisdom—produces a book-length face-off between a desiring subject and an ethical one. This rift is at once temporal, epistemological, and ethical. For however vehement the ethical warnings of the narrator, the reader should have doubts about motive: does this narrative produce an honest confession that accepts the force of ethical law, or a cunning exculpatory "story" that evades that law? In such an imbroglio of character and narrator, the defense's case bleeds into the prosecution's indictment.

Roxana's intimate entanglement of transgression and the Law, pleasure and its foreclosure, puts into question Defoe's project to reform the novel of amorous intrigue. In the preface, the very last text, one surmises, that Defoe wrote after "Susan's Supplement," he suggests that the ultimate efficacy of novel writing becomes hostage to the response of that unruly and unpredictable interlocutor, the reader. There, Defoe admits that "Scenes of Crime can scarce be represented in such a Manner, but some may make a Criminal Use of them . . ."; asserts his authorial intent—"but when Vice is painted in its Low-priz'd Colours, 'tis not to make People in love with it, but to expose it . . ."; and concludes, "[therefore] if the Reader makes a wrong

Use of the Figures, the Wickedness is his own." Here in the preface, Defoe only hints at what "Susan's Supplement" will acknowledge: the existence of an incorrigible evil. Rather than assuming authorial responsibility for the effects of his text—as Richardson and Fielding attempt to do in the 1740s—Defoe packages his text with a warning to all consumers: This narrative contains criminal scenes which may be harmful . . . to the *wicked* reader. By washing his hands of some readers, Defoe evinces suspicions of the novel reader's dangerous autonomy and license. By reiterating this theme of the antinovel discourse, Defoe implicates his own reform project. But does *Roxana* reform the novel of amorous intrigue, or does it simply exploit its appeal? Does Defoe achieve a certain autonomy and exteriority to the print-market entertainment he attempts to rewrite? This question is similar to the question that has dogged Roxana: Can she develop an instrumental control of the adventures which enriched her, and pass through "repentance" to reform? The collapse of the narrative puts the projects of character, narrator, editor, and author into question, and suggests that the common answer to these questions is "no." The failure of *Roxana* throws the novel reader into ethical reflections that challenge the whole system of print entertainment, the whole mise-en-scène of the ego securing its ends within a masquerade of the social, the whole possibility of a carefree absorption of the reader in novel reading. By discrediting the pleasure of the reader's fantasy participation in the novel as a simulacrum of the social, *Roxana* overwhelms the implicit contract between novel reader and novel writer. It is perhaps appropriate that *Roxana* is the last novel Defoe would write.

5 The *Pamela* Media Event

An entire historical tradition (theological or rationalistic) aims at
dissolving the singular event into an ideal continuity—as a
teleological movement or a natural process. "Effective" history,
however, deals with events in terms of their most unique
characteristics, their most acute manifestations. An event,
consequently, is not a decision, a treaty, a reign, or a battle, but the
reversal of a relationship of forces, the usurpation of power, the
appropriating of a vocabulary turned against those who had once
used it, a feeble domination that poisons itself as it grows lax, the
entry of a masked "other."
—Foucault, "Nietzsche, Genealogy, History,"
in *Language, Counter-Memory, Practice*

If from a later historical vantage point it is clear that 1740 is when the novel
in Britain begins to be a cultural icon worth fighting to define, why does
this particular cultural struggle begin then and there? Although my
genealogical study of the rise of the novel thesis exposes what is arbitrary
about the retroactive interpretation of the rise of the novel, it fails to grasp
the obscure necessity of beginning the rise of the novel narrative with
Richardson and Fielding. It does not explain why the novels Richardson and
Fielding wrote in the 1740s are repeatedly designated, by historians of literary culture for 250 years, as the first real novels in England. How, one
might ask, did the programs for a "new species of writing" (Richardson) and
a "new province of writing" (Fielding) become the first drafts of the rise of
the novel thesis? If we are to recover some of what the rise of the novel narrative effaces—that which is unique and crucial about the event that triggered the novel's elevation in Britain—we must do more than earlier literary histories attempt, and more than my own study has attempted so far.
The alternative cultural history of the early novel offered in chapters 2–4
provides the context for understanding the generative power of what I am
calling the *Pamela* media event. Richardson's provocative solution to the
issue of how to license reading for entertainment, and the responses it
incites, help explain how, in the words of Habermas, "the mediocre *Pamela*
[became] the bestseller of the century" (43). To understand how the cultural
location and meaning of novel reading took a decisive turn with the publication of *Pamela* in November 1740, this chapter focuses on the *Pamela*

media event. By studying this event it will become clear how in this decade "the novel," as a contradictory and contested cultural monument, first appeared in Britain out of something more diffuse, inchoate and tangled— the vortex of novel reading.

If we are to grasp the anonymous publication of *Pamela* as the entrance of a masked "other" into the media-culture masquerade in 1740, we need to understand how one book triggers a "media event" with long-term consequences for novel reading in Britain. An event often acquires an enigmatic character from its decisive evanescence: because it appears to have determined the direction of later events, it compels attention; but because it leaves only traces (tracks, memories, or writing) that are partial—that is, both fragmentary and biased—it eludes comprehension and invites a rich elaboration. Chapter 1 comprised a genealogical study of the rise of the novel narrative that challenges just the sort of naturalizing continuity produced by the historiography Foucault decries. Over the course of the unfolding of the rise of the novel thesis, novels are given a plurality of purposes: they are said to improve morals, to catalyze national identity, to represent social or psychological reality, and to become part of "the great tradition." These prescriptions for the novel have the character of "fantasy," inasmuch as fantasy works with "memory" to restore the original essence of the novel; that is, they elaborate, in a progressive movement toward the present, an idealized cultural icon. Freud describes the complex undecidable interplay of fantasy and memory, fiction and reality in the (re-)constitution of a prior event (Warner, *Chance and the Text of Experience*, 47–55). Here I am suggesting an analogy between what motivates the compulsive return to the primal scenes in dreams and therapy—the unconscious memory of a personal trauma—and the compulsion of literary and cultural history to return to a scene which is partly memory and partly fantasy. When reading for entertainment within print-media culture is experienced as wounding trauma to humanistic reading practices, that trauma is overwritten by a romance of origins (of the novel), wherein it is told that Richardson and Fielding, as the true fathers of the novel in English, performed heroic exploits of aesthetic originality (Campbell, *Natural Masques*, 2–3; H. Brown, "Why the Story"). But fantasy does not have a "free hand" to work any way it might wish; in this instance, as in the primal scenes Freud theorizes, it works, I argue, upon the memory traces of an actual event, one that has a rigid, contingent character. In this particular case, that event is the *Pamela* media event, which is the focus of this and the next chapter.[1]

---

1. The interplay I here postulate between the memory of a real event and the retroactive work of fantasy distinguishes my approach from other approaches to

On December 13, 1740, Edward Cave, the editor of the *Gentleman's Magazine*, proclaims the success of *Pamela*: "[it was] judged in Town as great a sign of want of curiosity not to have read PAMELA, as not to have seen the French and Italian dancers" (Eaves and Kimpel, *Samuel Richardson*, 124). With these words, an important organ of the print media diagnoses a certain lack in the consumer of leisure entertainments: if you have not read *Pamela* you are without a "curiosity," a deficiency that only the reading of *Pamela* will repair. Because Cave was a friend of Richardson, there is an element of hype and contrived promotion at the beginning of the *Pamela* media event. But the extraordinary popularity of *Pamela* involves more than a transient shift in taste, a mere "vogue"; it is a media event that helps to inaugurate a shift in media practices. But what exactly *is* a media event? First, such an event is not precipitated by some prior historical event (such as a battle, a trial, or a coronation) which then becomes grist for representations in the media. Instead, it begins with a media production—in this case, the publication of *Pamela*. Second, the atavistic interest in the media event, as demonstrated by purchases and enthusiastic critical response, feeds upon itself, producing a sense that this media event has become an ambient, pervasive phenomenon which properly compels the attention and opinions of those with a modicum of "curiosity." Finally, this media event triggers repetitions and simulations, and becomes the focus of critical commentary and interpretation.

---

the where, when, and how of the novel's rise. If traditional accounts are too quick to commit themselves to re-membering particular acts of authorial creation (by, for example, Defoe and Richardson), then two recent revisions of that story, by Homer Brown (*Institutions of the English Novel*) and Clifford Siskin ("Eighteenth Century Periodicals and the Romantic Rise of the Novel"), exaggerate the autonomous authority and interpretative voluntarism of acts of retroactive fantasy. Elsewhere in this study I have sought to incorporate Brown's account of the crucial role in the constitution of the eighteenth-century novel played by Walter Scott's editing projects of the second decade of the nineteenth century. Siskin uses the increase in the reading and writing of novels in the last decade of the eighteenth century to argue not an eighteenth-century rise of the novel, but a Romantic one. For Siskin, the novel, as the comfortable form of writing we take it to be, depends upon a global shift from eighteenth-century anxieties about imitation (evident in my accounts of the antinovel discourse) to nineteenth-century accounts of the subject's development into an impossibly deep object of apprehension. Siskin underestimates the way in which Richardson previews a deep subjectivity that is given other articulations, in their later years, by Rousseau, Goethe, and the English Romantics; but both Brown and Siskin underestimate the decisive influence of the debate about novel reading effected by the novelistic productions of Richardson and Fielding in the 1740s. In this chapter I seek to demonstrate precisely what was decisive about the *Pamela* media event.

For a broad spectrum of twentieth-century cultural critics (from Adorno to Baudrillard), the media event, in the sense I am using it, has been seen as a calculated means for the culture industry to raise revenues, replace reality with fantasy, and take consumers from nature into a simulated post-modern world, where all is only representation. For scholars with more sympathy for the forms of popular consumption, the media event is nei-ther unreal nor cynically contrived. I suggest we consider the media event as a type of event rather than a simulation of one, and as such it should be interpreted on two registers: as a symptom of changes working within the avid consumers of the event, and as something that carries genuine effects into culture.[2]

What gives the *Pamela* media event its force and lasting effects? It is fueled by the struggle around licensing reading pleasure described in previous chapters—most notably by Behn's successful introduction of the novel of amorous intrigue onto the British print market, Manley and Haywood's formulation of fiction within an emerging media culture, and the scandal caused by novel reading for entertainment. The particular order of my con-sideration of novel writing and the cultural resistance to novels may have obscured the most striking feature of the interaction between novel reading and the antinovel discourse—a certain impasse that results from their increasingly symbiotic relationship. While the increased currency of novels within print-media culture intensifies the antinovel discourse, the novels of Manley and Haywood are not overwhelmed by that discourse; neither does the success of Manley and Haywood's novels prevail over the antinovel dis-course. Instead, Manley and Haywood exploit the antinovel discourse by incorporating it into the *New Atalantis* and *Love in Excess.* Conversely, when Defoe attempts in *Roxana* to short-circuit the allure of the novels of amorous intrigue, or when Aubin develops strategies to elevate and reform novel reading, they necessarily repeat elements of the novels they condemn. In other words, over the first decades of the century, novel and antinovel, novels and the antinovel discourse flourish alongside one another. But the *Pamela* media event breaks through this impasse and brings a decisive change to the culture strife around absorptive novel reading.

This consideration of the *Pamela* media event is spread over two chap-ters. This chapter first surveys three related elements of Richardson's

2. For a contrast between these two approaches to culture, expressed most recently in the work of Mark Crispin Miller and Andrew Ross, see my argument for giving both perspectives weight (Warner, "The Resistance to Popular Culture," 742 n.3). For a wide-ranging historical critique of the modern American marketing of the "pseudo event," see Boorstin, *Image.*

attempts to reform novel reading: his early promotion of the novels of Penelope Aubin as an alternative to the novels of amorous intrigue; his composition of *Pamela* as an allegory of the reformed novel reader; and his efforts to foreclose the misreadings of *Pamela* he anticipates, especially among those addicted to novel reading. This chapter then goes on to describe the diverse responses to *Pamela*: enthusiastic promotion and antagonistic critique, parodies, sequels, and debates about, for example, whether *Pamela* allows readers to see too much. It is these responses which make it the focus of a media event. Richardson responds to this evidence of the dangerous autonomy of readers by beginning to position himself as an author. Chapter 6 describes Fielding's complex critique of contemporary entertainment—from the spectacles of the theater of his day to the absorptive reading Richardson's *Pamela* invites. With his parody *Shamela*, and *Joseph Andrews*, his alternative to *Pamela*, Fielding offers a fundamentally different pathway for licensing entertainment.

The difficulty of controlling how readers read and use texts within the open system of media culture in the 1740s encourages Richardson and Fielding to develop the concept of the novel author as proprietor of the book. By the end of the decade the cultural practices referred to as "reading novels" had been remapped. The ethical program, mimetic coherence, and aesthetic ambition claimed by Richardson and Fielding for their novels were countersigned by many of their early readers, as well as by many early critics after 1750, such as Samuel Johnson in his *Rambler* no. 4 essay. This positive reception of their novels functioned as a contingent decision in favor of their novels and against the novels of Behn, Manley, and Haywood. The decision is "contingent" because it did not have to happen the way it did. Like the decision in a legal proceeding or sporting event, it establishes a hierarchical relation of one term or agent over another. Thus, in Foucault's words that appear as this chapter's epigraph, the *Pamela* media event wins "the reversal of a relationship of forces, the usurpation of power, the appropriating of a vocabulary turned against those who had once used it."

THE OPEN SYSTEM OF MEDIA CULTURE; OR, DEVISING ORIGINALS TO COPY

Terry Eagleton has usefully suggested that Richardson's novels "are not mere images of conflicts fought out on another terrain, representations of a history which happens elsewhere . . . but instruments which help to constitute social interests rather than lenses which reflect them" (4). Richardson's strategy for entering the market for novels, and for giving them the power to do things in culture, develops out of his understanding of the workings of media culture. The print market in which *Pamela* appears may best be described as an "open" system. By this I do not mean that it is random or chaotic, nor that it is free of constraints. But neither is it a self-regulating totality that sustains some essential character through the sort of homeostasis that is characteristic of, for example, many biological systems. The print market is a system of production and consumption in which no one can control or guarantee the meanings that sweep through its texts. It is open to seismic shifts and dislocations. Lacking centralized censorship or certification, the market is influenced by any who can get their writing printed. Here there are no commonly recognized standards, and remarkably few limits as to what can be said or written. During the eighteenth century, the libel of political writers and the pornography of Cleland and Sade demonstrate some of those limits by testing them. The very openness that allows the novels of Behn, Manley, and Haywood to proliferate within the print market is exploited by the reformers of the novel—such as Defoe, Aubin, Richardson, and Fielding—who wrote in their wake.[3]

In entering media culture, Richardson seems to have learned from, and emulated the strategies of, such precursors as Defoe, Aubin, and Hogarth, who sought to use modern fiction for ethical ends. Because the printing activity on this market is sustained by the profits it produces, success produces its own imperatives. The market orients reformers of the novel toward the novels of Behn, Manley, and Haywood, which offered the dominant prior instance of the sort of popularity and atavistic pleasure that reformers of the novel hoped to mobilize for different ends. If the popular success of novels by Behn, Manley, and Haywood had defined "the novel" as a racy, immoral story of love, Defoe, Aubin, Richardson, and Fielding rearticulate it to produce new effects on readers. The title, preface, and most obvious traits of a novel like *Roxana* make its proximity to the novels of amorous intrigue very explicit. In their prefaces too, Defoe and Aubin offer their novels as an improving alternative to less ethical entertainments. By contrast, the exchange between the novels of Richardson and Fielding in the 1740s and the novels of amorous intrigue they sought to supplant is obscure and vexed. Neither Richardson nor Fielding offers his writing as

---

3. The term "open system" is borrowed from computer terminology, where it designates software and hardware platforms that allow other vendors to develop compatible products without licensing that platform.

another narrative practice to be consumed *alongside* the novels of Behn, Manley, and Haywood—like different columns on a Chinese menu. Nor do either believe that the earlier, wayward novelistic writing can be subsumed dialectically into their own practice. Instead, by claiming to inaugurate an entirely new species of writing, Richardson asserts the fundamental difference of his project from that of his (notorious) antagonists—Behn, Manley, and Haywood—who continue to circulate in the market as threatening rivals.[4] If Behn's and Haywood's novels flourish, they will drain Richardson's project of its cultural efficacy. This antagonism is most difficult to define because it is an unstable nonrelation between two terms which Richardson has every interest in obscuring. It only becomes graspable from a later analytical perspective.

Against the practice of traditional literary history, which uses the principle of resemblance to designate the precursor texts and authors Richardson might have known and imitated, I find two broad ways in which Richardson rearticulates the print culture he inhabits.[5] First, through his antagonism to the novels of amorous intrigue, which he claims never to have read, but whose influence upon readers he decries, those novels enter his texts. This is less a conscious or unconscious influence than it is something akin to an influenza to which he seeks an antidote. Second, in shaping his intervention, Richardson repeats some of the strategies of those who preceded him in opposing absorptive novel reading, and who developed alternative narrative entertainments with which to improve readers. Like both Defoe and Hogarth, Richardson exploits the allure of the amorous intrigue he would restrain. Like Defoe, Richardson will use the naturalistic situations, ordinary speech, and ethical teleology of spiritual autobiography to establish the moral seriousness of his stories. Like Hogarth, Richardson rejects fashionable entertainments, which he sees as a treacherous model for imitation, yet weaves novelistic plotting into his own text. In Hogarth's *Progress Pieces*, from *The Harlot's Progress* through *Industry and Idleness*, plays, novels, and prints shape the action because Hogarth's characters imitate what they consume. Moll Hackabout,

4. Behn's novels are frequently reprinted in the first half of the eighteenth century. Mary Ann O'Donnell, for example, lists the following editions for *Love Letters*: 3rd ed., 1708; 4th ed., 1712; 5th ed., 1718; 6th ed., 1735; serialized in *Oxford Journal*, 1736; 7th ed., 1759; 8th ed., 1765. In 1725 Haywood publishes a four-volume octavo collection of her novels which is reprinted in 1742.

5. McKillop's discussion of *Pamela* in his 1936 book, *Richardson: Printer and Novelist*, is still the most subtle and thoroughgoing of the treatments of the many possible precursors of *Pamela*.

the protagonist of the *Harlot's Progress* (1732), begins her decline into the streets when she imitates the protagonists of novels by having an affair (plate 2), and accommodates herself to a life of crime by placing a print of the highwayman MacHeath next to her bed (plate 3). In the playful, amorous, erotic prints *Before* and *After* (1736), the heroine's succumbing to her admirer suggests that the influence of the volume of "Novels" and the poems of Rochester have prevailed over the other book on her nightstand, "The Practice of Piety." In his prints of the 1730s and 1740s, Hogarth sustains an ambiguity as to whether the many sorts of imitation he represents should be understood as prudential warnings to the unwary or as the intertexts through which readers of greater discrimination may savor the fate of entangled protagonists.[6]

Because Richardson follows Penelope Aubin (1685–1731) in using the positive example to reshape the novel into a vehicle for moral improvement, Aubin's novels function as Richardson's point of entrance into the media culture of novelistic entertainments. While Aubin's use of characters as moral examples appears to be indebted to seventeenth-century French heroic romance, her strategy for improving novels also arises from a consensus within the antinovel discourse. In worrying about the power of novels to induce imitation in their readers, Defoe, Hogarth, Aubin, and Richardson echo the paradox formulated by *The Whole Duty of Woman, Or, an infallible Guide to the Fair Sex* (1737). In the section "The Duty of Virgins" there are strictures against "the reading romances, which seems now to be thought the peculiar and only becoming Study of young Ladies . . . [because] it is to be feared they often leave ill Impressions behind them. Those amorous Passions, which it is their Design to paint to the utmost Life, are apt to insinuate themselves into their unwary Readers, and by an unhappy Inversion a Copy shall produce an Original." Like Defoe before her and Richardson after her, Aubin accepts the inevitability of reading to divert and amuse (see chapter 4). But to forestall the romances' "insinuating" of "amorous passions" into its readers, to prevent the "unhappy inversion" by which "a copy shall produce an original," Aubin produces exemplary

---

6. Hogarth shares many of the goals and practices of the early novelists such as Defoe, Aubin, Richardson, and Fielding: a shrewd analysis of his potential audience, the invention of new hybrid forms (like the *Progress Pieces*), and a sustained commitment to elevating the ethical and aesthetic register of the print-media culture. Ronald Paulson has demonstrated some of the two-way influences between Hogarth's projects and those of Richardson and Fielding (see Paulson, *Hogarth* [3 vols] and *Beautiful, Novel, and Strange*).

originals for her readers to copy. This use of the exemplary character differentiates her novels from Defoe's and affiliates them with *Pamela*. Both Aubin and Richardson aim to take the imitation-inducing powers ascribed to absorptive reading within the antinovel discourse and harness them to the cause of virtue.

After the double success in 1719 of Defoe's *Robinson Crusoe* and Haywood's *Love in Excess*, between 1721 and 1728 Penelope Aubin publishes seven novels which turn away from the brisk contemporaneity and explicit sexuality of the novels of amorous intrigue and return to the style and content of exalted virtue of the heroic romances of La Calprenède and de Scudéry (Richetti, *Popular Fiction*, 218–229). This return to romance lifts her characters out of the ego-centered plots of media culture and gives a nostalgic "retro" feel to her novels. Several motifs of her first novel, *The Life of Madam de Beaumount, a French Lady* (1721), suggest its indebtedness to heroic romance: the plot is replete with patiently endured trials and miraculous escapes told through a complex narrative scheme which features an anthology of embedded narratives. Belinda, the central heroine, has a magically radiant virtue that the hero, Mr. Luelling, need only see and hear in order to love. When a rival, the noble Mr. Hide, also falls in love with Belinda, and she refuses him, the speech Mr. Hide delivers at his "summer house" articulates one of the touchstones of romance—that one can die of love: "Madam, . . . fear nothing from me, Virtue and Honor are as dear to me as you; since you cannot be mine, I ask no more, but that you'll stay and see me die, and not detest my memory, since vice has no share in my soul" (68).

Three of the programmatic elements of Aubin's novels, when taken together, give them a distinctly English, bourgeois, Protestant cast. First, her narratives are guided by a particularly insistent doctrine of providential rewards, whereby "strange" and wonderful "accidents" guarantee final happiness to the virtuous. Second, she purifies her heroines of the sort of erotic desire so explicitly present in Behn, Manley, and Haywood. Finally, her novels make the heroine's literal physical virginity the indispensable criterion of virtue. When Belinda is rescued from her outlaw captives and returned home, her husband, Mr. Luelling, in an agony of suspense, asks the crucial question: "Alas! my Belinda, may I hope that I shall sleep again within those Arms? Has no vile ravisher usurped my right, and forced you to his hated Bed? . . . tho I believe your mind still pure, and that your soul loathed, and abhorred the damning thought; yet forgive me, if I tremble at the dreadful idea of so cursed an act, and long to know the truth" (128).

Belinda delivers her self-vindication with an indignation worthy of Clarissa.[7]

In 1739, the same year in which Richardson is writing the *Familiar Letters* and *Pamela*, Richardson writes the anonymous preface to a posthumous collection of Aubin's seven novels, *A Collection of Entertaining Histories and Novels*.[8] As a printer who had only written conduct books and who did not as yet consider himself a writer of stories, it seems entirely appropriate that Richardson would join his close associates in the book trade, Arthur Bettesworth, Thomas Longman, and Charles Rivington (one of the booksellers for *Pamela* and the *Familiar Letters*), by actively supporting this new collection (Zach, *English Studies*, 274; Eaves and Kimpel, *Samuel Richardson*, 43, 90). The preface that Richardson drafts does not only index those traits common to Aubin and Richardson—"purity of style and manners," providential punishments and rewards, and a mixing of diverting incident with improving "reflections"—it also modulates, as Zach notes, between being a critical introduction to the sort of novel Aubin has written and being a proleptic account of the novels Richardson would write.

7. In the stilted syntax and diction of Clarissa's high style she shows her debt to Aubin and the French heroic romance. Two of Aubin's projects of the 1720s suggest how her elevation of novel writing pivots upon finding moral examples for youth. The first of these is a preface written by Aubin to an expensive folio volume—a hybrid between a conduct book and an emblem book—entitled "*Moral Virtue Delineated*, in One Hundred and Three short Lectures, both in French and English, on the most important Points of Morality. Each Lecture exemplified with a Copper Plate, done by the Famous Monsieur Daret, Engraver to the late French King. The Design of the said Plates being taken from the celebrated Gallery of Zeno at Athens, Founder of the Stoic Philosophy. The Whole recommended for the Instruction of Youth, especially those of the Highest Quality." The second of these projects is a loose translation published by Aubin in 1727 of a set of novels by the French author Robert Challes entitled "*The Illustrious French Lovers; Being the True Histories of the Amours of several French Persons of Quality*. In which are contained a great number of excellent examples, and rare and uncommon accidents; showing the polite breeding and gallantry of the gentlemen and ladies of the French nation. Written originally in French, and translated into English by Mrs. P. Aubin."

8. In "Mrs. Aubin and Richardson's Earliest Literary Manifesto," Wolfgang Zach makes the case for attributing the anonymous preface to Richardson by noting the striking similarities both in style and content between it and Richardson's subsequent defenses of his novels. Zach also notes that Richardson is known to have written anonymous prefaces for booksellers, and that some of the publishers of the collection were close associates of Richardson. This preface offers important evidence of the close affiliation between Richardson and women writers Richetti calls "pious polemicists." Todd (*Sign of Angelica*) and Spencer (*Rise of the Woman Novelist*, 88) note this affiliation, as well as Zach's attribution.

The preface also evidences an antagonism to Aubin's rival female novelists—most especially Eliza Haywood—whom Richardson obliquely critiques but refuses to name. By their practice of "this species of writing," these unnamed novel writers have brought a "disreputation [*sic*] on the very name" "Novel." "Like the fallen angels, having lost their own innocence, [they] seem, as one would think by their writings, to make it their study to corrupt the minds of others, and render them as depraved, as miserable, and as lost as themselves." By casting the female novelists as "fallen angels," Richardson confers insidious satanic powers of influence upon them.

Richardson's antagonism toward the novels of amorous intrigue expresses itself in his decision to disassociate his own writing from the very term "novel"—despite delivering praise for Aubin's "good novel(s)" in his 1739 preface. Even so, the term "novel" is still used by the editor of the *Weekly Miscellany*, William Webster, to describe *Pamela* in the weeks before its publication; and it is later applied to *Pamela* and *Clarissa* by two sympathetic critical allies, William Warburton (in his preface to the second [1748] installment to *Clarissa* [first edition, volumes 3–4]) and Edward Young (in his 1761 *Conjectures*). Little wonder, then, that readers throughout the 1740s will assume, against Richardson's claim that it is an utterly "new species of writing," that *Pamela* is, after all, a type of novel. Perhaps nothing contributed more to triggering the *Pamela* media event than Richardson's provocative claim, submitted within the ongoing cultural strife around novel reading, that however much *Pamela* might resemble a novel, it is not one, and further, that reading it will promote (rather than corrupt) the virtue of the reader.

PAMELA: AN ALLEGORY OF NOVEL READING

Pamela recounts how a young girl imbued with prudential paternal warnings and innocent of novel reading nonetheless finds herself within a novel. When her young master indulges in novelistic assumptions about their common situation and pressures her to yield to his desires, she refuses to play the novelistic role of seduced victim. The heroine only escapes her captivity within the novel by deflecting the action through a new kind of writing—the letters with which she records her trials. By educating her antagonist, Mr. B., into being the right sort of reader of her narrative of their common situation, Pamela casts Mr. B. as a reformed novel reader. Through her subordination of Mr. B.'s novelistic scheming to her own ends, Pamela, like Richardson, becomes the author of a new species of morally elevated entertainment.

In order to prevent the insidious circulation of novels, Richardson must teach readers how to read. It is therefore appropriate that *Pamela* begins with parental alarm and an injunction to read vigilantly. Pamela's parents feel the peril of Mr. B.'s attentions to their daughter, as reported in the novel's first letter, and respond with a letter fraught with suspicion: "I hope the good 'Squire has no Design; but when he has given you so much Money, and speaks so kindly to you, and praises your coming on; and Oh! that fatal Word, that he would be kind to you, if you would do as *you should do*, almost kills us with Fears" (27). The hermeneutic of suspicion introduced here is directed not only at the squire's behavior and words, but also at her own: "you seem so full of Joy at his Goodness, so taken with his kind Expressions . . . we fear—you should be *too* grateful,—and reward him with that Jewel, your Virtue, which no Riches, nor Favour, nor any thing in this Life, can make up to you" (27). With these words Pamela receives the parental Law of her social identity: virginity is to be the sine qua non of her being their "dutiful daughter" (the words with which she signs her letters); otherwise, they suggest, she is dead to them. The letter ends with the practical "charge" that she "stand upon [her] Guard" and "if you find the least Attempt made upon your Virtue, be sure you leave every thing behind you, and come away to us" (28). These parental admonitions puncture Pamela's initial pleasure in her master's gifts and attention. Her response reports the change wrought in her: ". . . your Letter has fill'd me with much Trouble. For it has made my Heart, which was overflowing with Gratitude for my young Master's Goodness, suspicious and fearful" (28). Although Pamela's parents' reading lesson is cast within the severe terms of the prudential-guide tradition, the content of its warning is consistent with the injunction given her by Mr. B.'s blunt sister, Lady Davers: "[you are] a very pretty wench [so] . . . take care to keep the fellows at a distance" (29). The advice of both parties warns about that action—seduction of the beautiful and unwary—so common in the novels of amorous intrigue.

What is the effect of these warnings? Pamela's suspicions, once they take root, are like the conscious blush of modest virtue: they imply a knowledge of the immodest facts she hopes to ward off. Pamela's reading lesson is also ours: from here on, we as readers must read *through* Pamela, her language, and her avowals. We must wonder what Pamela knows and wants. Why is she so willing to stay after his first attacks in order to finish Mr. B.'s "waistcoat"? Why is she so angry at Mr. B.'s proposal of Parson Williams as a suitable match? (86, 129–134) These episodes invite readers to suspect that Pamela harbors an unconscious love for Mr. B. While intended to protect Pamela from the wrong sorts of novelistic desire and knowledge, her reading lesson vitiates the original innocence the story postulates for her.

Richardson's antagonism toward novels is expressed in the assumption, woven through the early pages of *Pamela*, that Pamela's sexual innocence and her innocence of novel reading are of a piece. However, Pamela is said to be "a great reader" (26, 37), and her behavior suggests that she has learned practical lessons from novelistic fictions: she learns of virtuous resistance in the story of Lucretia (40–42); of great men stooping below their rank in marriage (49); "that many a Man has been asham'd at a Repulse, that never would, had they succeeded" (50); and of the captain who escapes from his pursuers by throwing clothes in the water (149). In short, Pamela has absorbed a good deal of novelistic wisdom about gender strife and the way in which resistance increases desire.

Pamela's first-person narrative does not allow us to understand what provokes Mr. B.'s sudden attempts on the heroine (Roussel, *Conversation of the Sexes*, 73–75). One may speculate that the spark comes from the suspicions of himself he reads in Pamela's correspondence. Described by the editor as a "Gentleman of Pleasure and Intrigue" (89), Mr. B. is told of Pamela's "virtue" and "innocence," but develops his own suspicions about his servant. When his housekeeper, Mrs. Jervis, uses these words to describe Pamela, he speculates on her true nature and motives: "*Innocent!* again; and *virtuous*, I warrant! Well, Mrs. *Jervis*, you abound with your Epithets; but 'tis my Opinion, she is an artful young Baggage; and had I a young handsome Butler or Steward, she'd soon make her Market of one of them, if she thought it worth while to snap at him for a Husband" (39). Like the libertines in the novels of amorous intrigue, Mr. B. assumes that everyone maximizes advantage and pleasure at the expense of others. When he counters her resistance by saying "we shall make out between us, before we have done, a pretty story in romance" (42), there is more than jocular irony in this retort. These words offer a quite explicit statement of his intention to compose an action—her seduction—that will make Pamela a victim in a novel of his own design. Mr. B. even interprets Pamela's resistance to his advances through the prism of novelistic fiction. Thus, in his letter to Goodman Andrews, he attributes Pamela's sudden removal from Bedfordshire not to his plotting but to her novel reading: "the Girl's Head's turn'd by Romances . . . And she assumes such Airs . . . and believ'd every body had a Design upon her" (90).

With the summerhouse assault, Mr. B. attempts to take compositional control of the action. He deploys all the machinery used by the libertines in novels to bend the action to their will: forged letters, disguise, unprincipled servants, sudden nighttime assaults, the lure of love, and the promise of money. Following the rhythm of an agon, Mr. B.'s assaults and Pamela's resistance increase in intensity, from the initial Bedfordshire attacks, through the kiss Mr. B. wins from Pamela while she is disguised in her country dress, to the first bedroom assault, Pamela's abduction and captivity in Lincolnshire, the articles offering her the position as a "vile kept mistress," and Mr. B.'s second nighttime attack disguised as Nan. Pamela's resistance produces the melodramatic scenes that have their antecedents in the novels of amorous intrigue. Her tenacious refusals, grounded in her observance of her father's law against self-enjoyment, block narrative closure.

Pamela counters Mr. B.'s designs partly through recourse to the counterplots of the type used or threatened in novels of amorous intrigue: corresponding secretly with Chaplain Williams, attempting to escape but failing, and feigning suicide. But more crucially, she fights back also by developing an alternative interpretation and narrative; her being woven into the plot of Mr. B.'s novel is presented, through recourse to Biblical typology, as a form of captivity that tests faith and virtue (Burnham, "Between England and America"). She incorporates this narrative interpretation into the letter journal she keeps after her abduction. The very aspect of B's Lincolnshire estate bespeaks its protogothic peril to the heroine: "this handsome, large, old, and lonely Mansion, that looks made for Solitude and Mischief, as I thought, by its Appearance, with all its brown nodding horrors of lofty Elms and Pines about it . . ."(102). In this place, Pamela finds herself transported still deeper into the labyrinth of a novel of amorous intrigue. Thus she is carried from the civility of the motherly and practical Mrs. Jervis to the arbitrary brutality of the bawdy Jewkes; from community support to the isolation of captivity; from everyday reality to a sexualized fantasy; from the normal to the exaggerated; from outer to inner; from the social to the psychological. In Lincolnshire, things become eroticized, menacing, fanciful, and extreme.

Because Pamela is increasingly confused by herself and her world, the reliability of her narrative in Lincolnshire becomes compromised. In one episode, which describes her failure to take advantage of a fine opportunity for escape, Pamela's antagonists take the form of two bulls. Her narrative describes an odd metamorphosis:

> O how terrible every thing appears to me! I had got twice as far again, as I was before, out of the Back-door; and I looked, and saw the Bull, as I thought, between me and the Door; and another Bull coming towards me the other way: Well, thought I, here is double Witchcraft, to be sure! Here

is the Spirit of my Master in one Bull; and Mrs. *Jewkes's* in the other; and now I am gone, to be sure! O help! cry'd I, like a Fool, and run back to the Door, as swift as if I flew. When I had got the Door in my Hand, I ventur'd to look back, to see if these supposed Bulls were coming; and I saw they were only two poor Cows, a grazing in distant Places, that my Fears had made all this Rout about. [137]

When "two poor Cows" appear as bulls—emblems of erotic aggression—then Pamela's own fearful fantasy of sexual danger lends support to Mr. B.'s plot and takes her deeper into the novel she strives to escape.

How are Pamela and Mr. B. to escape the novel that programs the terms of their exchanges? After Mr. B. arrives in Lincolnshire, a perverse chiasmic pattern overtakes the relations between him and Pamela: every time Mr. B allows himself or Pamela allows herself to become vulnerable to the other, the other draws back. These nuanced but emotionally fraught exchanges, often celebrated within the critical tradition for their insight into the psychology of love, show not only that, in Pamela's words, "love borders so much upon hate" (59), but also that the social problem confronting the would-be lovers has a generic ground. How can Mr. B and Pamela break out of a compulsive repetition of the scenarios scripted by the novels of amorous intrigue, with their zero-sum game of the battle of the sexes, with every representation of their relationship under suspicion of being nothing more than a ploy motivated by self-interest? The staying power of the novelistic codes that structure their exchanges can be grasped by examining the impasse that develops following Mr. B.'s final physical assault on Pamela, when the young couple converse by the Lincolnshire pond and begin to modulate their relationship toward the mutuality of an equal love (184–186).

In this scene their different relation to a scenario of novelistic seduction makes each unwilling to trust the other. To schematize, Pamela's defensive posture—what one might call her vigilant modesty—leads her to suspect every favorable gesture as concealing dangerous new ruses; thus, Mr. B.'s expressions of love may conceal "criminal" desires and evidence an attempt to "melt" her with "kindness" (186). In a complementary fashion, the libertine autonomy and class independence that had justified Mr. B. in composing a novelistic plot to undo Pamela now becomes articulated as a jealous indignation that Pamela's counterplots led her to solicit the aid of Chaplain Williams (186). Wavering between asserting his authority as author of a novelistic scenario and collaborating with Pamela in another kind of plot, Mr. B. feels an increase in his passion for Pamela and an intensification of the enigma she has become to him. Her beautiful surfaces might, paradoxically, conceal dangerous tricks: "See, said he, and took the

Glass with one Hand, and turn'd me round with the other, What a Shape! what a Neck! what a Hand! and what Bloom in that lovely Face!—But who can describe the Tricks and Artifices, that lie lurking in her little, plotting, guileful Heart!" (162)

The solution to this impasse is not available from within the terms of the novels of amorous intrigue. From within that genre, Pamela's performances, and the tension between her claim to simplicity and her more ambiguously desiring behavior, continue to produce doubts about her both within the novel (in Lady Davers) and, as is made clear below, outside it (in Fielding, Haywood, and the anti-pamelists). The solution to the enigma that Pamela has become depends on her withdrawal from Mr. B.'s presence, and on his reading her letters. This displacement of attention entails a sublimation of Mr. B.'s archaic desire to possess her body into the pleasure of reading her letters; such a displacement can usher in the change that Nancy Armstrong places at the center of her influential reading of *Pamela*: Mr. B. learns to love Pamela not as an "object of desire" but for her "female sensibility" (Armstrong, *Desire and Domestic Fiction*, 117). The success of this sublimation and displacement of the object of desire depends upon the "realist effect" produced by the detouring of Pamela's correspondence away from its intended destination—her parents—and toward Mr. B. When read by him, Pamela's journal letter to her parents produces for him the "truth effect" of knowing what is inside the envelope, inside Pamela's clothes, and inside all the disguises of the social: the letter of the heart. But her letters can only deliver their message of authentic, rather than performed, virtue if they are overheard, or intercepted, on their way to the parental superego. It is this detouring of the letter/novel that enables a new kind of (non-)novel reading, whose purpose is not merely to entertain, but to repeat a self-evident virtue.

Within this reform of reading, Mr. B.'s absorptive pleasure depends upon his experiencing Pamela's journal as a kind of novel: "I long to see the Particulars of your Plot, and your Disappointment, where your Papers leave off. For you have so beautiful a manner, that it is partly that, and partly my Love for you, that has made me desirous of reading all you write . . ." (201). Mr. B.'s ethical reform does not pivot upon reading Pamela's writing—after all, he has been reading her letters secretly from the beginning. Nor does it merely depend upon a renunciation of his desire for her body in favor of an enlightened passion for her mind. Instead, Mr. B.'s reform pivots upon his turning away from the Hobbesean war of all against all implicit in the novels of amorous intrigue, and, instead, enthusiastically embracing Pamela's journal as a new type of fiction. Through his avid absorption in Pamela's narrative, and his countersigning of its truth and value, he represents the reformed novel reader outside the text who accepts *Pamela* as an elevated and improving antinovel. Because it teaches him to love her "with a purer Flame than ever I knew in my whole Life!" (228), her journal becomes his bedside "Entertainment" (254) and incites the curiosity of unreformed readers like Lady Davers (374). However, turning Pamela's letters into entertainment for Mr. B. and others also menaces their "truth effect." If this detoured correspondence became an established communication circuit, it would mean Pamela could no longer, as she warns in handing over a packet of letters, "write so free, nor with any Face, what must be for your Perusal" (208). To avoid the reality of virtue being contaminated by the rhetorically motivated performance of virtue written directly *for* Mr. B., Pamela must assume, or pretend to believe, that each packet of letters or journal entries she gives him is to be the last he will read.

PAMELA IN DISGUISE; OR, THE NOVEL OF AMOROUS INTRIGUE APPEARS BENEATH ITS OVERWRITING

Pamela's intertexts—the conduct-book guide tradition and the novel of amorous intrigue—lead in two utterly unacceptable directions for the action. The novels of amorous intrigue suggest the first bad result—that Pamela will be seduced into an affair with Mr. B. At the same time, the conduct book that Richardson interrupts writing in order to compose *Pamela*—the *Familiar Letters*—suggests a result that is no less unacceptable to successful narrative closure: that Pamela will see the threat of Mr. B.'s schemes and will return to her father's house.[9] Such a result would obey the literal injunction of letter 2 of *Pamela*, as well as the advice tendered by a father in letter 138 of the *Familiar Letters*, that is immediately followed in letter 139 with his dutiful daughter's announcement that she has "this day left the house" and is returning home as instructed (165). In order to achieve a rewriting both of novels of amorous intrigue and of conduct discourse, within the new hybrid text of *Pamela* narrative action must steer its characters between the Scylla of virtuous withdrawal and the Charybdis of compliant seduction.

9. According to Eaves and Kimpel, Richardson starts the *Familiar Letters* in September or October 1739, and interrupts them to write *Pamela* between November 10, 1739 and January 10, 1740 (Eaves and Kimpel, *Samuel Richardson*, 88–90). Presumably the preface to Aubin's *Collected Novels* dates from earlier in 1739 or even from 1738.

What takes Pamela and Mr. B. past the danger of an early short circuit of their story? Nothing within the text appears more crucial than the disguise scene, in which Pamela, the woman who claims not to have read novels, acts like a heroine from one by appearing incognito in her country dress. Here is the first episode of the novel in which Pamela becomes ambiguously complicit with the codes of love, disguise, and manipulation fundamental to the novels of amorous intrigue. Up to that scene, Pamela's story could have ended in virtuous withdrawal, but after that scene, in which Mr. B. wins a kiss from her, Mr. B.'s desire is triggered and he develops the Lincolnshire plot. But beyond its effect upon Mr. B., the scene offers a performance in excess of Pamela's intended meaning.

This disguise scene suggests how Richardson seeks to overwrite the novels of Behn, Manley, and Haywood. From the vantage point of his conscious project to elevate novel reading, such an overwriting means writing above and beyond them, toward higher cultural purposes. But overwriting the earlier novel involves a paradoxical double relation: the earlier novel becomes both an intertextual support and that which is to be superseded, that which is repeated as well as revised, invoked as it is effaced. Thus the elevation of novel reading is founded in an antagonistic, but never acknowledged, intertextual exchange with the earlier novel. This concept of overwriting offers the possibility of reading against the grain of earlier literary histories.

To interpret the unacknowledged exchanges working between a text like *Pamela* and the network of entertainments within which it circulates, it is necessary to reverse the procedures of the sort of literary history that goes back to earlier noncanonical texts to find the sources for canonical texts. Thus I am not reading the novels of Behn, Manley, and Haywood, or those of Penelope Aubin, Elizabeth Rowe, and Jane Barker, in hopes of finding the closest possible resemblance to the stories, characters, or ethos of Richardson's novel.[10] Such an assemblage of single sources, supposed to operate as influences upon the author of the privileged text, fails to develop a general profile of those antithetical novels circulating as media culture for readers before 1740. Nor will I be focusing on the intertextual networks of explicit allusion subservient to the conscious intentions of the author evident, for example, in Fielding's announcement on the title page of *Joseph Andrews* that the "history" is written in "the manner of Cervantes."

---

10. This kind of strategy is pursued most convincingly for Richardson's *Pamela* by McKillop (*Samuel Richardson*) and Doody (*Natural Passion*), in their chapters devoted to literary and cultural backgrounds of the novel.

To read the general cultural antagonism between Richardson and the novelists he hopes to displace, it is more fruitful to begin with the rather perverse question, "Where does one find a character who *could not be more different* from Pamela?" Although there are many plausible candidates, my choice is the erotically inventive central character of Eliza Haywood's *Fantomina; or, Love in a Maze* (1725). By reading a scene of Richardson's novel alongside one of Eliza Haywood's, an alternative can be developed to conventional studies of the "influence" of one text or writer upon the author of another. Richardson does not have to have read Haywood, and even less does he have to allude to her, in order to have his text receive the shaping force of the "influenza" of her popularity.

The following is a summary of Fantomina's story: Fascinated with the erotic freedom of prostitutes at the theater, Fantomina exchanges her upper-class dress for the garb of these ladies. When she is approached by the charming Beauplaisir, one who has long admired her but has always been in awe of her reputation, she decides to follow the dictates of her own passion, and indulges his solicitations. Through a gradually escalating series of half-steps she loses her virtue and finds herself entangled in a secret affair with him. When his desire for her begins to languish she contrives an original solution: by changing her dress, hair color, accent, and manner, she transforms herself into a series of erotic objects to engage Beauplaisir's fascination: Celia, the "rude" "country lass" who serves as the maid in his guest house in Bath; Mrs. Bloomer, the charming widow in distress, who begs his assistance on the road back to London from Bath, and finally, that upper-class enchantress called Incognita, who carries him through an erotic encounter in her London apartments, while staying masked and anonymous. This chain of Fantomina's performances is brought to an abrupt and punitive close with the sudden return of Fantomina's mother, and the discovery that the heroine is pregnant.

If, as I am suggesting, *Pamela* incorporates and displaces many of the narrative and thematic elements found in *Fantomina*, near the end of Pamela's tenure as a servant in Mr. B.'s Bedfordshire estate there is a scene that provides one of Richardson's strongest grafts to the novels of amorous intrigue. This disguise scene is at once similar to and the opposite of parallel scenes in Haywood's novel. In preparation for her return to her father's modest home, Pamela has "tricked" herself out in "homespun" country clothes. This metamorphosis from the silks she had been wearing is so striking that the housekeeper, Mrs. Jervis, doesn't recognize Pamela when she appears in her new outfit. Mrs. Jervis prevails upon Pamela to be introduced anonymously to Mr. B., who calculatedly (Pamela thinks) uses the chance to kiss her. Pamela narrates: "He came up to me, and took me by the Hand, and said, Whose pretty Maiden are you?—I dare say you are *Pamela*'s Sister, you are so like her. So neat, so clean, so pretty! . . . I would not be so free with your *Sister*, you may believe; but I must kiss *you*" (61). This provokes Pamela's emphatic assertion of her true identity. After her escape she is called back to receive Mr. B.'s accusation that she had changed her clothes by design, for, since he had recently resolved to give Pamela no more "notice," now "you must disguise yourself, to attract me." She offers this defense: "I have put on no Disguise. . . . I have been in Disguise indeed ever since my good Lady, your Mother, took me from my poor Parents" (62). After Pamela leaves the room, a servant overhears Mr. B. say, "By G———I will have her!"(64) As noted earlier, this disguise scene has decisive consequences: following it, Mr. B. becomes the active promoter of the novelistic coordinates of the action.[11]

Pamela redirects the resources for fantasy and pleasure working in such a novel as *Fantomina*. In both stories the heroine's disguise functions in the same way—it stimulates a male desire that is in danger of fading, and carries the narrative forward to a new phase. Both a transformation of life and a romantic plasticity of the self are initiated by the heroine's artistry in changing her dress. By putting this empowering fantasy into practice, Fantomina can control the desire that would control her: by appearing as a succession of beautiful women, she fulfills an impossible male demand for variety; by tricking the male gaze that would fix her, she cures that gaze of its tendency to rove; by taking control of the whole mise-en-scène of the courtship scenario, Fantomina directs the spectacle of courtship that would subject her. In all these ways, Fantomina achieves a temporary reprieve from the courtship system described by Backscheider as a discursive system that positions women as subject to judgment, always in danger of becoming grotesque, and threatened with the loss of love (Backscheider, *Spectacular Politics*, 140–145). But the critique of courtship in *Fantomina* encounters its limit when Fantomina's mother investigates her pregnancy and closes down the spaces for erotic play by imposing harsh measures—a secret lying-in, and retirement to a convent.

Earlier in this study, I noted the instrumental advantages that accrue to Silvia and Roxana as a result of their recourse to disguise. Most crucially, it enables them to move through the social as a masquerade, maximizing

---

11. Throughout this discussion, I am indebted to Tassie Gwilliam's argument that a recourse to disguise is a necessary element of *Pamela* and its reception. See Gwilliam, *Samuel Richardson's Fictions of Gender*, 31–36.

their pleasure and freedom, and temporarily eluding legal or moral constraints. Behn and Defoe also make metamorphosis effected through disguise fascinating in itself, a species of feminine magic. Today's women's magazines continue to underwrite the magic of the "makeover." By adding exercise, diet, and plastic surgery to the age-old resources of clothes and cosmetics, these magazines offer medico-scientific support to the notion that the most ordinary girl could be a Cinderella. In contrast to *Roxana* and *Fantomina*, in *Pamela*, Richardson incorporates an explicit critique of disguise. Thus, *Pamela* represents the heroine's makeover as a complex double movement: a descent in class signifies an elevation in virtue. However, from the moment Pamela tries on her outfit in her bedroom, her pleasure in her new appearance is presented in a risky and morally equivocal light: looking in "the Glass, as proud as any thing . . . I never lik'd myself so well in my Life" (60). Pamela's conduct-book self-assessment of her impending social decline ("O the Pleasure of descending with Ease, Innocence and Resignation!" [60]) is qualified by the way in which the scene echoes the narcissism of Eve looking in the pool in Milton's *Paradise Lost*, and of Belinda's "rites of pride" before her mirror in Pope's *Rape of the Lock*. Pamela's complicity in acquiescing to the masquerade staged by Mrs. Jervis—Pamela admits "it looks too free in me, and to him"—means she must submit to the kiss which she does not consciously seek. But what starts out as the naive frolicking of the teenage heroine, through the intensity of Mr. B.'s desire turns into the violence of his accusations. Instead of reading Pamela's change of clothes as a sign of virtuous resignation, Mr. B. reads it as evidence of her intriguing designs upon him. Pamela's defensive insistence that her new dress is her truest clothing, while her recent dress was a kind of disguise, does not ensure that her clothes can be read as reliable signs. Instead, her clothes and manner, just like her letter writing, appear as instruments for dressing across and between classes, and therefore carry an uncontrollable plurality of meanings.

How does Pamela find herself in the ethically risky position of masquerading as herself? In order for *Pamela* to function as an alternative to novels, Richardson seeks to produce the absorption ascribed to novels. To absorb his readers, Richardson has his heroine emulate the disguised heroines of the novels by performing her virtue before unreformed "readers" like her master. Pamela and Richardson, as composers of textual meaning, must therefore pull off the kind of performance of which Pamela's disguised appearance in her country dress offers more than an instance; her disguise in fact epitomizes the fundamental communicative posture of Richardson's text. In this scene, the novels of amorous intrigue take on a life of their own in the text of *Pamela*, suggesting that they have not been fully assimilated to the elevated novel, but instead are incorporated in such a way as to circulate like parasitical foreign bodies within *Pamela*. Richardson's "new species of writing" becomes their host.

A certain errancy of communication is programmed into the disguise scene the moment Pamela allows herself to be introduced by Mrs. Jervis to Mr. B. as someone other than herself. Pamela's performance, by manipulating her appearance, produces an effect of disguise, and stimulates questions about the deeper meaning of this arresting spectacle. Thus the tendentious surmises that Mr. B. directs at Pamela: "I was resolved never to honour your Unworthiness, said he, with so much Notice again; and so you must disguise yourself, to attract me, and yet pretend, like an Hypocrite as you are—" (62). By interpreting Pamela's dress as a contrived disguise, he plots her into his novel. But his response results from at least two general aspects of her aestheticized self-presentation. First, because of the way in which a performance seems to be furnished for the spectator's gaze, it mobilizes the sense of being personally addressed. Second, because of the way in which disguise foregrounds the difference between what someone appears to be and what they actually are, it stirs spectator curiosity to know the face behind the mask. This curiosity may issue in fascination, anger, or desire— and Pamela's disguise provokes all three in Mr. B. His responses suggest that a disguised performance incites a wish to understand why the performer has chosen this particular performance out of all that might have been performed, in order to fathom the truth supposed to subsist behind disguise.

In developing a justification for her performance, Pamela finds herself caught up in an uncontrollable interplay between a performance space of surface appearances which bear a plurality of possible meanings and an inner space for the articulation of intended meanings claimed to be both temporally and ethically prior to the spaces of reception. The "disguise scene" suggests the impossibility of securing that interior place of original intention—her self—as radically prior to, and unaffected by, the plural social contexts for performance. In both letter writing and performance, meaning cannot be controlled from the position of the performer or letter writer. The wavering of meaning does not merely result from the vagaries of human psychology or the plurality of interests that could be ascribed to a reader. Both of these could be seen as extrinsic to an original intended meaning. Richardson's letter-novel and performances are not put at risk of misreading by something that comes along *after* writing and publication. Rather, there is something in the very structure of both the system of early modern entertainment wherein the letter-novel *Pamela* is composed and circulates and the space that opens around Pamela's performance of her virtue that produces meanings that disrupt claims to an interior univocal meaning. In both letter writing and performance, a slippage necessarily will open between the initial mark or performance and its cultural articulation and social reception.

The detours of communications complicate that aspect of the disguise scene that offers the straightest line to the ethical conduct-book agenda of Richardson's novel—Pamela's presentation of self. When Pamela says, "O Sir, said I, I am *Pamela*, indeed I am: Indeed I am *Pamela, her own self!"* (61), the very repetition of the first-person pronoun, the double chiasmic assertion, the intensifiers "indeed, indeed," the emphasis and overemphasis of this circular enunciation of identity betray the difficulty of stabilizing identity. The precariousness of this incipient self, and the virtue ascribed to it, result from the fundamental features of the communication system within which both character and author function. Richardson's program for elevating novel reading is founded upon an instrumental subordination of envelope to letter, form to content, mask or surface to deep self. This program is committed to an idealization of the signified as the true meaning inside (that is, in the inmost recesses of the heart). Such a program depends upon a refusal to recognize that any communication that happens—whether "true" or "false," "deep" or "shallow," authorized or perverse, conscious or unconscious—is an effect of the whole communication system, with its series of differential relays. And because each relay modifies the sites and context of reading, it modifies the message sent along its network. There is no way to separate the initial mark, with its promise of identity and semantic closure, from its relation to something nonsemantic, the place(s) of its marking, as well as its relation to a series of other marks which can never be totalized or brought to a final destination.[12] For this reason

---

12. See Gasché, *Tain of the Mirror*, 217–223; in *The Post Card*, Jacques Derrida shows how the bipartite structure of the letter and envelope suggests what unsettles the communication ideal that the postal code attempts to institutionalize. Because of the numberless ways in which letters fail to arrive at their destination—from errors in address to the death of the addressee, from sloppy handwriting to the ineptitude of the carrier—any letter could end up in the "dead letter office." Because the possibility of errancy is built into the postal system, Derrida argues that this system exposes a necessary gap between an initial inscription of meaning and its final reading by the addressee. In composing an emission, the writer aspires to send the full meaning written into the letter to the addressee, so that it will be read properly, the way it was intended. But because its full meaning is never received as intended, because an excess of meanings crowd into every inscribed mark, because every re-location of a sign produces a certain minimal dis-location of meaning, the

there is no way to limit the plural and unexpected reserves of the media-culture system for producing and disseminating meaning. It is precisely because it is set in motion by someone who strives so hard to get his message to its proper destination that the *Pamela* media event is an especially rich matrix for reading the perversely plural effects of communication.

It should be apparent that the three distinct forms of communication I have been discussing share a common dynamic. In order to be read properly, Pamela's letters, her disguise, and Richardson's letter-novel all must risk being misread. Thus, only by being read by the skeptical eye of Mr. B. can Pamela's detoured correspondence produce its truth effect; to become the heroine of an antinovel, Pamela must represent her virtue as if in disguise; to write an alternative to novels, Richardson must write the story of virtue's reward so it reads like a novel. In sum, to change novel reading, *Pamela* must travel the discourse network and reading practices of the media culture of the early novel of amorous intrigue (of seriality, entertainment, and absorptive reading), but for this very reason, the letter-novel may receive a kind of textual interference from the novels of amorous intrigue and lose its way. If this happens, *Pamela*'s account of the rewards of virtue may be read with the same skepticism Mr. B. directs at the heroine in the disguise scene.[13]

---

ideal of communicative transparency is shadowed by opacity, ambiguity, and deviation. Derrida formulates these insights into a "postal principle" said to subtend all communication—namely, "the letter never arrives at its proper destination."

13. It will be useful to suggest how my reading of *Pamela* differs from Nancy Armstrong's. A short summary of Armstrong's thesis, put forward in *Desire and Domestic Fiction*, suggests why she does not view Richardson's novel as a site of dubious performance and ambiguous communication. For Armstrong, the invention of the "domestic woman" within the languages of the fiction and conduct books of the eighteenth century split the social world into masculine and feminine spheres of poetry and prose, politics and home, outside and inside, public and personal, state and family. This change focused desire and value so that the person's worth was internalized and psychologized. The invention of the modern subject gradually achieved cultural and social hegemony, and in so doing, occulted the political power that subject expressed. Armstrong places *Pamela* at the beginning of this momentous reconfiguration of subjectivity and politics. In the disguise scene, Armstrong finds that "Richardson creates a distinction between the Pamela Mr. B desires and the female who exists prior to becoming this object of desire" (116). "As it provides occasion for [Pamela] to resist Mr. B's attempts to possess her body, seduction becomes the means to dislocate female identity from the body and to define it as a metaphysical object" (116–117). The central turn of the plot—the displacement of Mr. B.'s desire from Pamela's body to her letters—defines her deep subjectivity as the locus of Mr. B.'s desire, while conferring upon a woman's writing the "power to reform the male of the dominant class" (120). I find two fundamental problems with this reading.

PROMOTING PAMELA

By interpreting *Pamela* as the first literary novel, twentieth-century critics downplay the significance of Richardson's consultation with his readers, the *Pamela* ad campaign, and Richardson's didacticism. These are the

---

First, Armstrong fails to see the way in which the performative underpinnings of Pamela's virtue, and of Mr. B.'s reform, put in question the resolution of the mind/body dualism. Armstrong's reading stays close to the unctuous terms Mr. B. uses to celebrate his reform. "Sir, said Mr. *Brooks, . . .* You have a most accomplished Lady, I do assure you, as well in her Behaviour and Wit, as in her Person, call her what you please." "Why, my dear Friend, . . . I must tell you, That her Person made me her Lover; but her Mind made her my Wife" (389–390). By accepting the terms of Mr. B.'s reform, Armstrong countersigns the opposition between body and mind that Pamela's own performance has put in play, and Armstrong underestimates the extent to which Mr. B.'s act of reading and acceptance of Pamela's performance is itself a kind of writing. In challenging Armstrong, Gwilliam has argued that the "presumably beneficial change, and Armstrong's depiction of it, depend on the same metaphors—the body as surface and the soul or metaphysical self as depths— . . . that are used elsewhere to posit a disfiguring fault in the female subject. In fact, the finding of value in 'inner' qualities does not transform existing ideologies of femininity as much as it reinscribes them" (17). Gwilliam suggests how the body in Richardson and elsewhere continues to circulate as divided and complex. Similarly, in "Novel Panic," James Turner has argued that *Pamela*, against its avowed program, provokes strenuous efforts (in criticism, opera, and painting) to visualize and embody Pamela's body. In short, by crediting the idea that this sort of novel invents a new kind of subjectivity, Armstrong's reading of *Pamela*, like other rise of the novel readings of the text, thereby also extends too much credit to the claims made by Mr. B. (and Richardson) for Pamela's interiority, for her virtue, and for the novelty of her novelistic narrative.

The second problem with this reading, deeply indebted as it is to Foucault's account of the working of the panopticon in *Discipline and Punish*, is that Armstrong argues that Pamela's domestic subjectivity evolves out of surveillance—both by others and by her own self—that becomes internalized in her writing, especially after her abduction to the Lincolnshire estate. Armstrong's grand narrative of the middle-class invention of the domestic woman orients every aspect of the novel toward the "big" and abstract question of power. An evaluative and analytical hierarchy at work in Armstrong's text abstracts and simplifies the operation of letters, performance, and desire so as to subordinate them to power, the political, and class struggle. This hierarchy justifies postulating a transparent instrumental relationship between text, author, and potential readers. The invention of the desirable domestic self—as a "metaphysical object" that appears to go beyond the political— becomes Pamela's fictive task, Richardson's authorial strategy, and their decisive contribution to the transformation of culture. This critical narrative has the effect of making the culture and its texts a homogenized and totalized space, a perfectly efficient medium of communication, where the idea of the domestic woman, once produced, circulates freely and without significant resistance. The effective transparency of communication claimed by Armstrong for *Pamela* corresponds much more to what Richardson dreamed for his novel than to what he in fact effected.

acts not of an author or novelist, but of a print-media worker attempting to intervene in media culture and change novel consumption practices. To do this, Richardson first has to gauge the response of ethically trusted readers; next, he has to persuade readers to take *Pamela* as something essentially different from the novels they knew; and finally, he has to persuade readers that reading *Pamela* is good for them. But in order to lure readers into this reformed reading, all of this has to be pulled off with a calculated indirection.

To reform novel reading, Richardson engages what Madeleine Kahn calls "narrative transvestism," hiding himself behind an alluring story of a sexually embattled fifteen-year-old girl. Because he has never claimed to be anything so exalted as an author, but instead has assumed the disguise of an anonymous editor, Richardson can recede from view and offer readers a narrative in the letters of another. The indirectness of Richardson's engagement of his reader is a correlative of the immediacy promised for Pamela's letters; the alluring beauties of the latter can screen the shy awkwardness of the former. Richardson is even coy about coming out as the writer of *Pamela* to his friend and literary advisor, Aaron Hill: a month after its publication and apparent success, Richardson sends a copy of the novel to Hill and his two daughters, and on December 17, 1740, Hill sends Richardson a letter of lavish praise: "Who could have dreamt, he should find, under the modest Disguise of a novel, all the soul of religion, good-breeding, discretion, good-nature, wit, fancy, . . . of the wonderful author of Pamela,— Pray, Who is he, Dear Sir? and where, and how, has he been able to hide, hitherto, such an encircling and all-mastering Spirit?" (Letter quoted in Eaves and Kimpel, *Samuel Richardson*, 119–120.) After the success of *Pamela* is evident, and after he has sent the anonymously published work to an esteemed friend, Richardson finds himself addressed as the disguised author of a book that appears in the "modest Disguise of a novel." Only then can he emerge from behind what he calls the "umbrage of editor" to offer a retroactive explanation for his project.

Hill's letter prods Richardson into his clearest statement of the circumstances surrounding the origins of *Pamela* (ibid., 119–121). He first describes how he received the kernel of a story twenty-five years earlier,

---

Because Armstrong's reading spatializes the temporality of Pamela's narrative, she cannot take account of the way in which Richardson's novel is like both Pamela's letters and her performances: all are communication acts that can misfire, or fail to arrive at their proper destination. For a fuller discussion of these issues, see Warner, "Social Power and the Eighteenth-Century Novel."

when a gentleman told him a story he had heard while traveling—the history of a "girl" who "engaged the attention of her lady's son, a young gentlemen of free principles, who, on her lady's death, attempted . . . to seduce her. That she had recourse to many innocent stratagems to escape the snares laid for her virtue . . . at last, her noble resistance, watchfulness, and excellent qualities, subdued him, and he thought fit to make her his wife" (Richardson, *Selected Letters*, 40). This is the "foundation in truth" referred to on the title page. Richardson then incorporated elements of that story as letters 138 and 139 of his *Familiar Letters*, the hybrid conduct book/writing manual he was then writing, "as cautions to young folks circumstanced as Pamela was." Finally, he began to enlarge the story because of its potential to reroute the reading practices of young people:

> I thought the story, if written in an easy and natural manner, suitably to the simplicity of it, might possibly introduce a new species of writing, that might possibly turn young people into a course of reading different from the pomp and parade of romance-writing, and dismissing the improbable and marvelous, with which novels generally abound, might tend to promote the cause of religion and virtue. I therefore gave way to enlargement: and so Pamela became as you see her.
> [Richardson, *Selected Letters*, 41 (Jan.–Feb. 1741)]

The terms used by Richardson to dismiss romances and novels—"pomp and parade," "improbable and marvelous"—are imprecise critical clichés. But they do suggest that producing a "new species of writing" to promote the cause of virtue pivots upon a shift in style—from decadent ornamentation to "an easy and natural manner," from aristocratic ostentation to "simplicity." Richardson will reform the novel by redressing it. The sartorial metaphor latent in this passage suggests the antagonistic proximity to novels Richardson's explicit statement denies. The experimental posture that Richardson assumes in introducing *Pamela* onto the print market in 1740 is expressed through reiterated use of the verb "might" to describe the positive effects sought in publishing *Pamela*: that he "might" introduce a new species of writing; that he "might" turn young people toward a new course of reading; and that he thereby "might" promote religion and virtue. Yet the success of this ambitious project is hostage to the effects it has on actual empirical acts of reception. If the project is to succeed, Richardson must win novel readers over to his own novel-substitute.

Because of its manifold similarity to the novels of amorous intrigue, the text of *Pamela* must ward off the sort of novelistic reading it might inadvertently court. In order to prevent his readers from doing to *Pamela* what Mr. B. does to its heroine—namely, read within the codes of the novels of amorous intrigue—Richardson not only represents the genesis of its own proper reader, the reformed Mr. B., he also enfolds as if in an envelope his text, in a title page, a preface, and two letters that function as a guide to reading. When anti-pamelists confer a hostile reading upon *Pamela* after its publication, Richardson insists upon the priority of his original message, and tries to describe these readings as having come along later and befallen his text with arbitrary violence. Richardson's deflection of these readings resembles Pamela's characterization of Mr. B.'s response to her country dress as being perversely opposed to an original guiding intention. However, what I am referring to as Richardson's own "reader's guide" suggests that these misreadings are not belated in their arrival, but were anticipated all along. Novelistic misreadings are programmed into *Pamela* from its inception. It is as if the disease of misreading *Pamela* is inscribed in the text, so as to stimulate within the empirical reader of the text antidotes against the general contagion of novelistic reading.

The reader's guide to *Pamela* was a source of embarrassment to Richardson's eighteenth-century allies and the focus of derision for the anti-pamelists; it is likely that it is simply skipped by most modern readers of *Pamela*. It is, however, of considerable interest for the way in which it anticipates a distinctly modern discourse of advertising, product promotion, and cultural improvement. Unlike many other early novelists (Haywood and Aubin, for example), Richardson does not use dedications to seek the "protection" of recognized cultural authorities, but instead accepts the rigorous independence the market imposes upon authors. However, although he eschews traditional rituals of authorial self-abasement, his prefatory materials leave themselves open to Fielding's mockery of them as transparent self-flattery (see chapter 6). Nonetheless, this reader's guide also demonstrates Richardson's shrewd grasp of the market system of media culture he is attempting to redirect.

Richardson develops a new kind of promotional discourse in order to transmit a text stripped of any pre-given generic identity from the (hidden) author to an anonymous general readership. In an effort to cut through the clutter of numberless alternative forms of reading entertainment and catch the interest of potential readers, the reader's guide offers a fleeting profile of the heroine and her story. But to anticipate and foreclose the misreadings *Pamela* may provoke in unwary readers, and to distinguish his product from competing entertainments, Richardson promises that his (non-) novel will improve the reader. In order to prepare readers to read in the right way, Richardson's reader's guide makes three broad claims about the text it introduces: it warranties its beneficial effect upon readers; it promotes the special efficacy of the letter form; and it stipulates a simple reader for *Pamela*. Each claim suggests the lines of resistance Richardson expects to encounter in rewiring media culture.

The first claim is about *Pamela*'s effect on readers: they are assured that this is not, and should not be read as, a type of novel. The onrush of media-culture entertainments of dubious moral value requires a filtering process.[14] The title page of *Pamela* performs the function of the modern ratings system used in film distribution: in advance of first audience encounter, it promises that something is absent from the text being purveyed. Just as the modern moviegoer is assured by the "G-rating" affixed to a film that there will be no nudity, violence, or four-letter words, so the title page of *Pamela* assures potential readers it "is intirely divested of all those Images, which, in too many Pieces calculated for amusement only, tend to *inflame* the Minds they should *instruct.*" This claim is supported by the two anonymous prefatory letters apparently written by Jean Baptiste de Freval, a French translator living in London, and the Reverend William Webster, vicar of Thundridge and Ware.[15] Freval mobilizes English nationalism in offering *Pamela* as an "Example of Purity to the Writers of a neighbouring Nation [i.e., France] . . . which has so long passed current among us in Pieces abounding with all the Levities of its volatile Inhabitants" (5). The second letter, apparently by Webster, lauds *Pamela*'s entrance into a "World, which is but too much, as well as too early debauched by pernicious *Novels*. I know nothing Entertaining of that Kind that one might venture to recommend

14. Richardson's "rating" of *Pamela* is an early step toward the modern ratings systems, seen at work in the passage through Congress in 1996 of a communications deregulation law that would require a "V-chip" be put in every television set sold in the future. This would enable parents to filter out programs containing high levels of violence. The networks are displeased with two aspects of this legislation: it requires a ratings system to determine which programming would be excluded by the V-chip, and it limits the potential audience and advertising revenues for shows screened out by the V-chip. However, one unintended effect of such a rating and screening system will be to offer legal and ethical cover for the development of still more violent shows for television. Ratings systems are an outgrowth of the impulse to screen out the increasingly powerful and pervasive systems of media culture.

15. The letter that Eaves and Kimpel attribute to Webster was first published in Webster's *Weekly Miscellany* on October 11, 1740, 26 days before *Pamela*'s publication. There it is attributed to an anonymous friend of Richardson, and is described as having been written in response to an advance reading of the manuscript. Although such scholars as William Sale (*Samuel Richardson*, 15) have discounted the possibility that Richardson himself might have written or heavily revised the letter before it appeared in Webster's magazine, this seems to me a distinct possibility.

to the Perusal (much less the Imitation) of the Youth of either Sex: All that I have hitherto read, tends only to corrupt their Principles, mislead their Judgments, and initiate them into Gallantry and loose Pleasures" (8). *Pamela* passes through the critical mediation of these testimonials to its reader.

Having asserted *Pamela*'s distance from novels, the reader's guide supports the reader's moral vigilance by offering coming attractions. The second letter offers a summary of *Pamela*, first by describing the entertainment the letter writer experienced by identifying with the heroine in her "Sufferings," "Schemes of Escape," "little Machinations and Contrivances," and so forth, and then by underwriting the morality in the piece by explaining how, over the course of her many trials, Pamela's virtue prevails. But how do these letters gain the authority to act as censors for the potential readers of this text? Since the authors of the title page, preface, and two letters are all anonymous, the acceptance of these prefatory judgments cannot be guaranteed by the reputation of a recognizable critic. Instead, the prefatory material persuades through other means. First, each element performs a testimonial: an anonymous reader has read the text and testifies to its virtuous properties and effects, addresses the editor of *Pamela* with pious wonder, and advocates its speedy publication with a tone of earnest enthusiasm. Second, each of these elements of the reader's guide appeals to the presumed responses of general readers. Thus, for example, the editor ends his preface by stating the following principle: *"he can Appeal from his own Passions (which have been uncommonly moved in perusing these engaging Scenes) to the Passions of Every one who shall read them with the least Attention"* (3). In considering the popularity of Manley and Haywood in earlier chapters, the concept of the general reader of media culture was developed as the open set of all who might respond to a book's solicitation of the most common passions (such as love, fear, and the pursuit of self-interest). But in his letter to Aaron Hill, Richardson can only generalize from his own response to "Every one" who reads these letters "with the least Attention" by making the "bold stroke" of assuming "the umbrage of the editor's character to screen myself behind" (Eaves and Kimpel, *Samuel Richardson,* 119–120). A third way in which the prefatory material persuades is through disguise, as, in the guise of editor, Richardson baldly asserts an objectivity he cannot legitimately claim: *"because an* Editor *may reasonably be supposed to judge with an Impartiality which is rarely to be met with in an* Author *towards his own Works"* (3). Publishing himself in disguise, apparently editing the letters he authors, Richardson's promotion of *Pamela* passes itself off as the enthusiasm of an indifferent reader.

The second major claim made by the reader's guide about *Pamela* is focused upon its letter form. Because this story is told in a series of familiar letters written by the virtuous and innocent protagonist to her parents, this text eludes the fanciful and shifty tendency of media culture. By casting his narrative as an edited collection of real letters, Richardson deflects the accusation of trivial fictionality, as well as the critical worry about repeating overworn generic conventions—what the writer of the first prefatory letter calls "the romantic Flights of unnatural Fancy" (4). At the same time, the reader's guide makes two claims for this narrative in letters: first, that they have their source in actual life (it has a "foundation in truth"); and second, that its technique of writing to the moment produces an illusion of immediacy that is exciting and vivid in comparison with retrospective narrative. The reader's guide claims that there are three reasons that the technique of "writing to the moment" evident in *Pamela* allows a more powerful mimesis of the mind of the writing subject: first, it depends on the moral character of the writer whose thoughts are reflected in her style of "Simplicity," "Propriety," and "Clearness"; second, the temporal proximity to events allows reality itself to use Pamela as its amanuensis ("the Letters being written under the immediate Impression of every Circumstance which occasioned them"); and finally, they are addressed to parents who may justifiably expect the most absolute openness—"those who had a Right to know the fair Writer's most secret Thoughts" (4). What Richardson will later call "writing to the moment" offers a technical rationale for claiming for his novels a transparency that is unprecedented in media culture. When they are later inserted into various aesthetic defenses of the novel as a form of literature, these two claims about the letter-novel—concerning its facticity and its immediacy—will be taken up by critics to bolster Richardson's claim to have invented a new kind of realism. In this way, *Pamela*'s letters are given a certain anti-generic, anti-aesthetic self-evidence. Of course, the "found document" topos was one of the most familiar devices of print culture.

"Familiar Letters" is the term that appears in large capital letters halfway down the title page of both of Richardson's sibling projects of the years 1740–1741: *Pamela* and the letter-writing guide. On the novel's title page, it appears after the novel's title, so as to designate the form that circulates between a "damsel" and her parents. In the letter-writing guide, it specifies the particular type of letter writing the text will teach its reader. In both cases, the "familiar letter" becomes the royal road to good conduct. Richardson's recourse to the letter form in *Pamela* evidences his effort to eschew the precariously public character of novels written for the general reader. The familiar letter, as a letter between familiars who know and trust each other, offers Richardson a tactical and nostalgic temporal regression in media: from the mechanical, automated, general address to a public linked through print, to the idiosyncratic, personally crafted one-to-one communication of a manuscript letter. Richardson's use of the familiar letter engages a rhetoric of radical sincerity—transparent communication from heart to heart, with nothing held in reserve, nothing disguised. By looping the reader into a familiar, intimate form of reading and writing, he offers a counterthrust to the masked and rhetorical use of language by the novels of amorous intrigue. Those novels cut themselves off from ordinary familiar ties so as to draw their readers into an erotic reading practice. Richardson hopes to counteract the insidious mimicry of print, its ability to imitate every form of writing and address. Ironically, however, far from ending mimicry, his letter-novels instead draw a space represented as domestic, familiar, and private into the public sphere of print.

Richardson's third claim is that the reader must read in a certain way. What he is saying to the reader is, "In order to grasp the innocence and virtue of Pamela, you the reader must become naïve and innocent in your reading." The reader's guide establishes a crucial reciprocity between Pamela's character as simple and virtuous and the reader's simple and virtuous reading. The prefatory letter apparently by William Webster mandates a trustful reading of a young girl who, unlike many modern teenagers, is ready to show her parents exactly what she experiences and feels: "She pours out all her Soul in [her letters] before her Parents without Disguise; so that one may judge of, nay, almost see, the inmost Recesses of her Mind" (7). This we must take on faith—that Pamela is abundantly generous in pouring out her soul; that what she pours out is utterly devoid of disguise; and that her stream of words takes us not part way, but all the way into the "inmost Recesses" of her mind. After narrating the happy consequence of Pamela's resistance to Mr. B, his reform, and their marriage, the writer of this prefatory letter defines what makes her moral victory so remarkable. His commentary clears Pamela of any of the dubious tendencies and mixed motives I have suggested in reading the disguise scene: "And all this without ever having entertain'd the least previous Design or Thought for that Purpose: No Art used to inflame him, no Coquetry practised to tempt or intice him, and no Prudery or Affectation to tamper with his Passions; but, on the contrary, artless and unpracticed in the Wiles of the World, all her Endeavors, and even all her Wishes, tended only to render herself as un-amiable as she could in his Eyes" (7). Here is an exaggeration characteristic of the reader's guide. Surely a good deal within the novel, from the country-dress scene to her strenuous self defense, evidences a wish to look amiable in Mr. B.'s eyes. But to heighten her virtuous renunciation of any "liberty and ambition," and to dispel the possibility that she simply doesn't care for Mr. B., this letter writer insists that Pamela does not feel unattracted to "his Person," but in fact "seems rather prepossess'd in his Favour, and admires his Excellencies." This letter articulates a familiar paradox: "The more she resisted, the more she charm'd; and the very Means she used to guard her Virtue, the more indanger'd it, by inflaming his Passions: Till . . . the Besieged not only obtain'd a glorious Victory over the Besieger, but took him Prisoner" (7). This passage brings us to the crux of a problem: the reader of *Pamela* and other novels, knowing the effect of Pamela's virtuous resistance—that it increases desire in Mr. B. and enables her to win him in marriage—is enjoined to read with the ignorance and innocence not in fact found in either *Pamela* or its eponymous heroine, but attributed to it and her by the reader's guide. Otherwise, the happy reward of virtue could be vitiated, retroactively.

In order to simplify reading, so that it supports the construction of an innocent and virtuous heroine and text, both Richardson and Pamela must refuse what might be called the eye and ear of social judgment—that performative dynamic resulting from the fact that it is others and not ourselves who judge the moral tendencies of our actions and writings. In order to screen out social judgment, both Richardson's reader's guide to *Pamela* and the reformed Mr. B. within the text engage in a promotion and praise that modulates into self-promotion and self-praise. They drown out others' voices not after they speak, but before. This discourages others from reading *Pamela* as a performance with a contestable variety of meanings. A counterperspective comes from the *Pamela* media event: it reinscribes *Pamela* within a contentious public sphere, where what a text means will be the negotiated outcome of sustained critical scrutiny by sophisticated adult readers.[16]

ANTI-*PAMELA*

Richardson's carefully orchestrated promotional campaign is striking for two reasons—for its success in anticipating the future misreadings of

---

16. In *Reading Clarissa*, I attribute the struggle of interpretations among readers of *Clarissa* to two different factors: the constitutive openness to interpretation of all texts (this is the Nietzschean, deconstructive horizon of that study), and the form and moral rhetoric of Richardson's practice. The latter included serial publication; an effacement of the author disguised as editor, who can try to control reader

Pamela, and for its failure to protect the novel from these misreadings. My reading demonstrates the many ways in which *Pamela* is engaged with the terms of the antinovel discourse. With *Pamela*, Richardson hopes to transcend the debased and compromised terrain of media-culture entertainments. When, on a date before January 6, 1741, Dr. Benjamin Slocock of St. Saviour's in Southwark weighs in to recommend *Pamela* from the pulpit, and some compare the "simplicity" of the novel to that of the Bible (Eaves and Kimpel, *Samuel Richardson*, 121), Richardson's project to reform reading receives unprecedented support. But by raising the stakes of *Pamela*'s popularity, such support also helps incite the anti-pamelist reaction. Three anonymous responses to *Pamela* are published between April and June 1741: Fielding's *Shamela*, *Pamela Censured*, and Haywood's *Anti-Pamela*. All three of these texts situate *Pamela* by using the terms of the debate about novel reading, and all three betray anxiety about the effects of absorption in novel reading. The extent of the *Pamela* media event—with the varying revisions, extensions, and adaptations of *Pamela*—is documented by McKillop, Sale, and Eaves and Kimpel, by Kreissman's *Pamela-Shamela*, and (most recently) by James Turner and Richard Gooding. A selected list of the books and performances published in the wake of the popularity of *Pamela* forms an appendix to this book. Here, however, I will attend to the *Pamela* media event as it becomes a point of convergence within the debate about novel reading and rearticulates the struggle around licensing entertainment.

Pamela Censured and *Shamela* target the reader's guide for its blatant self-promotion. The Censurer of *Pamela Censured: a Letter to the Editor* insists on addressing Richardson as a "half-editor half-author" (9) and reproaches him for his "vanity" (12) in publishing so many self-praises at the front of his own book. Fielding's rejoinder to the frontmatter in *Pamela* is more indirect. In place of the letters from Freval and Webster, *Shamela* has two brief letters. The first, entitled "The Editor to Himself," predicts extravagant success, and overwhelms the author's putative modesty with these words: "... out with [*Shamela*], without fear or favor, dedication and

---

response indirectly; the winning of reader identification by the author through the impersonation of characters (130–131); and subject matter such as love and sex that encourages reader identification (125–142). Most of these factors are also at work in the publication and reception of *Pamela*. In this study, I am suggesting another source of hermeneutic openness: what precedes Richardson's writing—the "discourse network" of media culture with its novels of amorous intrigue—also authorizes *Pamela*'s skeptical reading and rewriting by others.

all; believe me, it will go through many editions, be translated into all languages, read in all nations and ages, . . . "(275). It is signed "Sincerely your Well-wisher, YOURSELF." The second, slightly longer letter is signed "John Puff, Esq." Fielding's parodies of the reader's guide, while staying close to language found in Richardson's letters, capture the smug and vacuous expansiveness of modern advertisement. The blunt and lively brevity of Fielding's two letters invites us to see the prolixity of Richardson's promotional letters as an index of a somber self-inflation.

Fielding and "the Censurer" reject the claims with which the reader's guide to *Pamela* has sought to prescribe a certain way of reading it. They insist that a text cannot designate its own genre, or mandate the effects its reading will incite. Both Párson Oliver in *Shamela* and the Censurer of *Pamela Censured* treat *Pamela* like another novel on the market, and both deplore the effects it will have on susceptible young readers. The Censurer rejects the idea that *Pamela*'s concern with virtue is unheralded, pointing to the new translation of a French novel, *La Paysanne Parvenue* (a feminizing of Marivaux's *Le Paysan Parvenu*, by the Chevalier de Mouhy). The Censurer also refuses to give the narrative form of *Pamela*—as "a series of letters"—any special claims to truth. Thus he refutes the lofty claim that this "series of letters" comprises a "narrative" with its "foundation in truth and nature," claiming instead that *Pamela* is "but a romance formed in manner of a literary correspondence, founded on a tale which the author had heard, and modelled into its present shape" (7).

Fielding shows two ways in which the epistemological claims Richardson makes for his so-called collection of letters are undermined by what one might call the duplicitous plasticity of print media. Within *Shamela*, Fielding explains the publication of *Pamela* by having Mr. Booby commission Shamela's story (as the letter-novel "*Pamela*") to be written by a Parson who, as Shamela explains to her mother, "can make my husband, and me, and Parson Williams, to be all great people, for he can make black white, it seems" (303). Fielding then circulates the letter-novel within the correspondence between the *Pamela* enthusiast Parson Tickletext and the rational skeptic Parson Oliver. When the latter provides Parson Tickletext with the true story and actual correspondence of Shamela (as opposed to the fabricated correspondence of "*Pamela*"), the meaning of Pamela's letters is transformed. Fielding's subversive displacements of *Pamela* are possible because of a trait that is inherent in all writing, and that is still more in evidence when manuscript writing is abstracted into print—namely, that there is nothing within a text to distinguish a true narrative from its false simulation. This not only means that anyone who "buys" a narrative or its truth had best beware—it also means that there is nothing to stop critics at any time from doing what Fielding and Haywood and the Censurer do to *Pamela* in the spring of 1741: treat it as a novel.[17]

In chapters 3 and 4 I argued that the antinovel discourse is haunted by the specter of the erotically aroused (usually female) body, absorbed in novel reading. By writing *Pamela* in a protracted series of letters, almost all written from the point of view of the heroine, and depicting extreme states of anxiety, fear, and struggle, Richardson strives to induce hyperabsorption in his reader. In order to prevent his own reading from resembling novel reading, Richardson's reader's guide prescribes a virtuous and naïve reader for *Pamela*. Against this prescription, the anti-pamelists assert a broad range of possible readers, each assuming a different disposition toward the text. Some are described as young, absorbed, susceptible, and liable to imitative acting-out of the text. Others are described as safely past their "grand climacteric." Some are worldly, sophisticated readers able to comprehend double entendres and savor the pornographic tendency of certain scenes. All these readers, however, are in need of the wariness the anti-pamelists would teach.

By making the question of how *Pamela* is read an issue, the anti-pamelists inscribe the question of novel reading within a public-sphere exchange. I have noted how Fielding inserts a debate about the pleasures and dangers of reading *Pamela* within a correspondence between two mature, public-spirited parsons; in a similar vein, *Pamela Censured* is prefaced with a dedication to the Reverend Slocock, urging him to withdraw the encomium to *Pamela* he has offered from the pulpit. The pamphlet proper is written in the form of a public exhortation, addressed to the "Editor of *Pamela*," urging the editor to remove the offending passages of an otherwise laudable performance. After making censures on the prefatory materials and offering his own third-person summary of Pamela's story, the Censurer devotes the bulk of the pamphlet to citations of the "inflaming" passages of *Pamela*, interlaced with critical commentary deploring their effect on unwary readers. This narrative form seeks to shatter *Pamela*'s

17. For a full discussion of this debate within early print culture and the problem it produced for readers of stories claimed to be true because they are based upon found documents, see McKeon, *Origins of the English Novel*. In an essay on McKeon's book, I suggest an "ineluctable gap that opens beneath the quest for truth in narrative: once it has been transported from the place or time of its production, no text, whatever its aspirations to facticity and truth, can bear a mark in its own language that can truly verify its relation to something outside itself" (Warner, "Realist Literary History," 67).

power to absorb its reader; yet, in its public-spirited alarm, it also extends the erotic potential of reading *Pamela*.

In "Novel Panic: Picture and Performance in the Reception of Richardson's *Pamela*," James Turner shows how it comes about that in the *Pamela* wars, the stark oppositions of the antagonists bleed into one another. Those within Richardson's "discursive circle" use a language of reformed sensation that implies the very erotic imagination they strive to censor; the anti-pamelists reject the character of an inner Pamela so as to embrace a theory of reading that "pornographizes" those scenes "that for Pamela herself provoke terror rather than erotic reverie" (78). Turner argues that by moving inexorably toward visualizing Pamela's body, both pamelists and anti-pamelists assume the automatic responses of readers. At the same time, the general impulse to visualize the heroine takes *Pamela* into paintings and illustrations, stage productions and opera. Turner's subtle essay suggests that neither the promoters nor the antagonists of *Pamela* can so easily elude the tug of its absorptive and absorbing scenarios. This insight confirms what my reading above suggests: that in claiming that readers respond to *Pamela* as if it were a novel, the anti-pamelists imitate the terms and scenerios of *Pamela* and its prefatory material. Like Mr. B., every reader faces the critical problem of assessing Pamela's performance—for example, by discriminating a virtuous girl from a scheming girl who would "snap at a husband," and the text of *Pamela* from that of a mere novel. By staging the solution to this question around a morally polarized interplay between inner and outer, soul and body, spiritual sensibility and erotic arousal, *Pamela* gives the question of the body—that is, whether it is innocent or lubricious—allegorical force.

THE READER WHO SAW TOO MUCH: VISUALIZING PAMELA'S "ETC."

Turner concludes his article by attributing the emergence of the body within the *Pamela* media event to the general nature of fiction, asking rhetorically, "Can the process of reading fiction ever escape the endless circle of enclosing and displaying, divesting and investing, an imaginary body?" (92) But rather than making the visualization of the body a universal trait of fiction, I suggest that the insistence of this body within the *Pamela* media event has a specific historical reference. The body of that precocious reader Pamela, trapped within the anti-novel Richardson is trying to write, is a descendent of the body that Manley exposes to seduction in the Duke's library (in the *New Atalantis*) and the body that Haywood places at the side of a stream, reading alone but observed by her lover (in

Love in Excess). Within each novel, these bodies figure the contested body, that of the absorbed novel reader, outside the text (see chapters 3 and 4). Although Richardson seeks to remove his text and its readers from a bad novelistic absorption, his own hyperabsorptive strategies intensify the questions raised by the absorbed novel-reading body: From what do readers get pleasure? What do they see when they read? What are the ethical effects of this pleasure? Because reading may be surmised to be somewhat different in each reader, and because it leaves no traces, these questions become a nexus of interminable cultural strife.

We can get a grasp of how *Pamela* reconfigures these questions by following the critical exchanges around one passage of *Pamela*—the scene in which Pamela catches her dress in the door while fleeing from Mr. B., then falls down unconscious in a "fit" of "terror." In this early scene, Mr. B. is still very far from having learned to look for Pamela's truth within the folds of her letters. Instead, he is looking at the surface of her body. This passage condenses many of the pivotal elements of *Pamela*: Mr. B.'s compositional designs and sexual assault, Pamela's sturdy resistance, and a mise-en-scène of the visualization which *Pamela* obliges the reader to attempt, but which it also seeks to restrain.

> He by Force kissed my Neck and Lips; and said, Who ever blamed *Lucretia*, but the *Ravisher* only? and I am content to take all the Blame upon me; as I have already borne too great a Share for what I have deserv'd. May I, said I, *Lucretia* like, justify myself with my Death, if I am used barbarously? O my good Girl! said he, tauntingly, you are well read, I see; and we shall make out between us, before we have done, a pretty Story in Romance, I warrant ye!
>
> He then put his Hand in my Bosom, and the Indignation gave me double Strength, and I got loose from him, by a sudden Spring, and ran out of the Room; and the next Chamber being open, I made shift to get into it, and threw-to the Door, and the Key being on the Inside, it locked; but he follow'd me so close, he got hold of my Gown, and tore a Piece off, which hung without the Door.
>
> I just remember I got into the Room; for I knew nothing further of the Matter till afterwards; for I fell into a Fit with my Fright and Terror, and there I lay, till he, as I suppose, looking through the Keyhole, spy'd me lying all along upon the Floor, stretch'd out at my Length; and then he call'd Mrs. *Jervis* to me, who, by his Assistance, bursting open the Door, he went away, seeing me coming to myself; and bid her say nothing of the Matter, if she was wise.
>
> Poor Mrs. *Jervis* thought it was worse . . . [42]

This passage records a tear in the narrative. Within the continuous first-person narrative of what Pamela has seen or heard, she falls into a "fit" of "fright and terror." But despite the absence of the consciousness who narrates the events, the narrative goes on. To fill in the gap in her knowledge, Pamela allows herself to "suppose" that Mr. B. looks at her through the door that has locked by itself behind her as she flees. This voyeurism is an expression of both Mr. B.'s desire and his restraint. This scene's contentious conversation, and its literally rendered physical struggle around Pamela's body ("He then put his Hand in my Bosom") does not, after her fit, issue in Mr. B.'s rape of her. He does not simply force the door and have his way with her (as Lovelace eventually would with Clarissa). Instead, he calls Mrs. Jervis. And even later on, in Lincolnshire, when he has the bawdy Mrs. Jewkes to urge him on and Pamela is passed out naked in bed, he does not gratify his lust. There is, as many critics have pointed out, an important reticence about Mr. B.'s desire. He desires more than sex—that more-than-sex the plot will figure as reading Pamela's letter journal. So, through the tear in the narrative, we glimpse . . . a structure of looking: in an oddly suspended narrative tableau, Mr. B. accepts a position behind the door, and looks through the keyhole at the prone body of Pamela. That this scene is based upon nothing more than Pamela's surmise makes it a condensation point of her desire, too. Through this gap in the narrative of *Pamela*, the reader, like Mr. B., is surmised to be looking.

In the critical reception of *Pamela*, contending visualizations of the text articulate themselves around this passage. In *Pamela Censured* this scene is quoted at length and draws the strongest condemnation of Richardson. Here, the Censurer insists, Richardson is surely allowing the reader to see too much. The passage is introduced with a heavy irony: "And here the Author . . . contrives to give us an idea of Pamela's hidden beauties, and very decently to spread her upon the floor, for all who will peep through the door to surfeit on the sight" (28). After a full quotation of the text, the Censurer poses invidious questions, details what he supposes every reader of this scene must be able to see, and then surmises its effect upon different readers.

Was not the Squire very modest to withdraw? For she lay in such a pretty posture that Mrs. Jervis thought it was worse, and Mrs. Jervis was a woman of discernment; . . . The young lady by thus discovering a few latent charms, as the snowy complexion of her limbs, and the beautiful symmetry and proportion which a girl of about fifteen or sixteen must be supposed to show by tumbling backwards, after being put in a flurry by her lover, and agitated to a great degree, takes her smelling bottle, has her laces cut, and all the pretty little necessary things that the most luscious and warm description can paint, or the fondest imagination conceive. How artfully has the author introduced an image which no youth can read without emotion! The idea of peeping through a keyhole to see a fine woman extended on the floor, in a posture that must naturally excite passions of desire, may indeed be read by one in his grand climacteric without ever wishing to see one in the same situation, but the editor of *Pamela* directs himself to the youth of both sexes; therefore all the instruction they can possibly receive from this passage, is, first, to the young men that the more they endeavor to find out the hidden beauties of their mistresses, the more they must approve them; and for that Purpose all they have to do, is, to move them by some amorous dalliance to give them a transient view of the pleasure they are afterwards to reap from the beloved object. And secondly, to the young ladies that whatever beauties they discover to their lovers, provided they grant not the last favor, they only ensure their admirers the more; and by a glimpse of happiness captivate their suitor the better. [31–32]

How does the writer of *Pamela Censured* support the claim that this scene has "introduced an image which no youth can read without emotion"? *Pamela Censured* exposes the latent eroticism of Richardson's scene by translating it into the language and situations of the novels of amorous intrigue. Now Pamela's strenuous defense of her virtue is simply another episode in a sportive battle of the sexes. Pamela is a designing heroine who displays her charms as weapons during an erotic frolic while "put in a flurry by her lover" and "tumbling backward." What she discovers to the Censurer—"the snowy complexion of her limbs," and their "beautiful symmetry and proportion"—is cast in the trite descriptive terminology of love novels. The Censurer does not believe that putting the spectacle of the fallen Pamela before the eye of mature readers would lead to them to wish to experience such a sight for themselves. However, he reproves the editor of *Pamela* for opening such a scene before the "youth of both sexes." Here there's a reiteration of the central warning of the antinovel discourse: novels will incite a bad emulation by their readers. This scene, it is supposed, not only creates a lascivious desire for a "transient view" of "hidden beauties," it teaches young men and women to manipulate this viewing to their own advantage.[18]

18. In her very interesting reading of this passage from *Pamela Censured,* Tassie Gwilliam looks through the keyhole of the opening in *Pamela*'s narrative and locates the scandal of gender performativity. By her argument, Mr. B. is here more than a voyeur; he identifies with Pamela as a spectacle, making her (duplicitous) femininity a pathway to masculine self-knowledge. This act of identification acquires synecdochical force by the way it repeats the fundamental terms of Richardson's narrative transvestism: "The excitement generated by this scene

An analytic perspective can be developed on the censures of reader visualization in *Pamela* by taking account of how Jean Marie Goulemot places a visualization of the aroused body at the center of eighteenth-century pornography in his *Ces livres qu'on ne lit que d'une main* (*Those Books that One Can Only Read with One Hand*, but entitled in English translation *Forbidden Texts*). Goulemot reads Marivaux's *Le Paysan Parvenu* and Diderot's *Jacques La Fataliste* and develops the thesis that the pornographic novel orchestrates a scene with certain elements: the body ready for arousal; the gradual display of that body (often in fetishized parts); and the voyeur in the text (sometimes the agent of sexual attack, or often another person who is shocked or pleased with the sexual act—and participating somehow). Thus he argues that the "key element of the erotic novel" is "the making of pictures, organized in order to solicit the gaze, a call to the reader that he should take up the proper distance from the narrative in order to see, to admire, and to examine" (48–49). In contrast to the libertine novel, which develops the art of persuasion to overcome resistance, the erotic novel finds bodies ready for sex, resistance trivial, and obstacles easily overcome (50).

By applying Goulemot's template for pornography to the erotic texts covered in this study (from Behn to Richardson), it is clear how the Censurer's pamphlet intervenes to articulate a relation between *Pamela* and earlier novels. In *Love Letters*, the *New Atalantis*, and *Love in Excess*, there

---

comes from the representation of Pamela seeing herself as a man would see her through the keyhole, itself perhaps the fantasy of a man imagining himself as a woman being watched by a man" (41). Gwilliam's reading shows why the assertion of Pamela's inner nature or identity is menaced by the very system of disguise that is supposed, through a moment of unveiling, to discover the true body or self beneath. Both Gwilliam and Madeleine Kahn (the latter in *Narrative Transvestism*) interpret Richardson's recourse to writing as a woman as his attempt to make the mystery of ungraspable femininity a means of stabilizing his own (finally ungraspable) masculinity. But often in Gwilliam and Kahn the anxiety surrounding confusions of gender identity is supposed rather than demonstrated. I am struck by the ease with which writers from Behn through Fielding stage disguised reversals of gender. There is much to suggest that eighteenth-century writers, whether they were male or female, did not find gender boundaries as fixed or fraught as later critics have; nor do eighteenth-century writers ground personal identity in sexual practice as insistently as has been the case since Freud. This is one of the salient themes of Foucault's *History of Sexuality* (vol. 1). Jill Campbell, in her discussion of the theoretic work of Joan Scott and Judith Butler, offers useful cautions on the necessary anachronism of using gender as an analytical category for reading eighteenth-century texts (*Natural Masques*, 4–8). Here, I focus on gender identity as only one of several terms that is threatened with confusion by the practice of absorptive novel reading.

are elaborately staged scenes of sexual arousal that are clearly pornographic in the way they construct voyeuristic pleasure for an absorbed
reader. In the scenes of sexual attack in *Pamela* there are several elements
of the theatrical sex scenes found in Behn, Manley, and Haywood—sexual
aggression, a literal depiction of bodies, and a hectic intensification of the
narrative prose. However, in the place of the aroused erotic subject, the
body ready for sex, there is Pamela resisting her would-be seducer, and
pushed, through the violence of Mr. B.'s assault, into unconsciousness. For
Richardson, Pamela's "fit" of unconsciousness offers evidence of her virtuous resistance to the climactic novelistic sex scene Mr. B. would put her in.
But for the Censurer, Pamela's being "out cold" invites the reader to imitate Mr. B. in luxuriously gazing at Pamela's body, thereby implicating
Richardson in staging a pornographic scene to arouse the reader.

On May 28, 1741, slightly over a month after the publication of *Pamela
Censured,* John Kelly publishes his sequel to Richardson's novel, entitled
Pamela's Conduct in High Life. In the preface, Kelly responds to the Censurer on *Pamela*'s behalf, attempting to impose limits upon the Censurer's
pornographic elaboration of it. The supposed editor of Pamela's papers in
Kelly's sequel, one "B.W.," demonstrates that the perverse and lascivious
author of *Pamela Censured* has seen more "ideas" than the text contains.
Following the pattern of the pamphlet, B.W. quotes the same *Pamela* passage the Censurer has quoted, and asks rhetorically what there is in this
passage to "kindle desire" or allow us to suppose that Pamela fell into an
"indecent posture." B.W. goes on, "Well, but the warmth of imagination in
this virtuous Censurer supplies the rest," and accuses the Censurer of giving "an idea of Pamela's hidden beauties, and would have you imagine she
lies in the most immodest posture." Thus it is the Censurer, not the edi-
tor/author, who endeavors "to impress [upon] the minds of youth that read
his Defense of Modesty and Virtue, Images that may enflame."

> Is there any particular posture described? Oh, but the Censurer lays her in
> one which may enflame, you must imagine as lusciously as he does; if the
> Letter has not discovered enough, the pious Censurer lends a hand, and
> endeavors to surfeit your sight by lifting the covering which was left by
> the editor, and with the hand of a boisterous ravisher takes the
> opportunity of Pamela's being in a swoon to——But I am writing to a
> lady, and shall leave his gross ideas to such as delight to regale their
> sensuality on the most luscious and enflaming Images.
> [Kelly, *Pamela's Conduct in High Life,* xv]

Kelly's restoration of the veil of modesty torn from Pamela by this "bois-
terous ravisher" has a contradictory double edge. By contesting the textual

accuracy of the Censurer's visualization of the scene, Kelly attributes its prurient tendency to the Censurer. But Kelly's censoring interruption— "But I am writing to a lady"—reiterates a cliché of erotic discourse. By refusing to repeat the words with which the Censurer reports what may be supposed to be seen after Pamela's fall, Kelly produces an elision in his own text at the place of pornographic elaboration he refuses to cite. In other words, he marks the interdicted spot of the Censurer's text, and his own text, with an implicit "etc."—the eighteenth-century slang for women's genitals, which is used in this way by Fielding in *Shamela*.

Despite the contrast between the Censurer's exuberant and unseemly visualizations and Kelly's modest textual exactitude, both justify their revision of Pamela's narrative by defining a normative response for *Pamela*'s reader. This is the game that has been played around popular media culture ever since. However, there are factors outside the text of *Pamela* that prevent this tear from being mended by any definitive suturing. What fragments this text is the contested plurality of programs for reading unleashed by the *Pamela* media event. The intensity of the strife around this scene from *Pamela* is symptomatic of the negotiation of terms for a casting out of bad erotic writing, as pornography, and a concomitant elevation of novel reading. While *Pamela Censured* returns *Pamela* to the discursive terms and readerly expectations associated with the erotic novels of Behn, Manley, and Haywood, Kelly asserts the ethical restraint about visualization concomitant with Richardson's project.

In attempting to provide an "antidote" to what is called the "epidemical frenzy" of *Pamela*'s popularity, Fielding's *Shamela* forecloses precisely the sort of visualization by the reader that the Censurer elaborates and condemns. In spite of the blunt sexuality of the action, and its bawdy use of innuendo, *Shamela* eschews any visualization of sex. In its place, readers hear the worldly voice of the scheming Shamela. Instead of gratifying the curiosity of a reader who is absorbed and isolated, Fielding brings Pamela into a public discursive space where she can be exposed as a sham. The *Pamela* media event draws the eighteenth century's most prolific writer of novels—Eliza Haywood—back into novel writing after a hiatus of nearly a dozen years; on June 20, 1741, she publishes anonymously the *Anti-Pamela; or Feigned Innocence detected; in a SERIES of Syrena's Adventures*. In this text, Haywood ingeniously rewrites her own early novels of amorous intrigue so as to critique *Pamela*. Like Fielding's *Shamela*, the *Anti-Pamela* suggests that the latent sexuality of *Pamela* mandates that it be read as a novel; and like Fielding, Haywood shows that women as well as men may ensnare and seduce, and that modest femininity can be a canny performance. Haywood's "detection" of "feigned innocence" pivots upon exhausting seriality—of the compulsive sexual appetite that impels Syrena into a succession of intrigues; of the consumption of the novels of amorous intrigue Haywood herself had perfected; of the *Pamela* rip-offs to which she herself here contributes; and of the dubious entertainments that she describes experiencing in her own youth in a passage from volume 1 of the *Female Spectator*: "My Life, for some years, was a continued round of what I then called Pleasure, and my whole time engrossed by a hurry of promiscuous diversions" (2). This multifaceted critique of seriality prepares Haywood for the reform that enables her turn to domestic fiction in the 1750s.

In *Memoirs of a Woman of Pleasure* (1747), the first indigenous British pornography, John Cleland negotiates a distinct course through the issues activated by the *Pamela* media event. While he accepts the fundamental goal of pornography—to arouse the reader—his text, like Richardson's, carries its own improving agenda. In an introduction to a 1986 edition of Cleland's novel, Peter Sabor argues that the *Memoirs* develops an elaborately euphemistic language to render its erotic scenes in order to eschew the crude language of earlier French pornography found in, for example, the *School of Venus* (xvii–xviii). To provide a framework for the gallery of erotic scenes in the *Memoirs of a Woman of Pleasure*, Cleland plots Fanny through an action that offers an optimistic revision of Defoe's *Roxana* (1724) and Hogarth's *Harlot's Progress* (1732). When its success precipitates the arrest of Cleland and his publisher, Ralph Griffiths, Cleland (as if following the advice from *Pamela Censured* that Richardson refused) expurgates the explicitly sexual scenes, cutting the text by a third. Then the novel can circulate as the single-volume *Memoirs of Fanny Hill* (1750), within the market for improving novels (Sabor's introduction to Cleland, *Memoirs of a Woman of Pleasure*, ix–x). The consolidation of the morally improving novel after 1740 is reciprocally complicit with the condensation of the debased category for fiction called "pornography." In this way, the cultural terrain that the novels of Behn, Manley, and Haywood had worked—including idealistic love, licentious sex, and much in between—is subdivided between the elevated novel and pornography.[19]

19. I follow Goulemot in using the word "pornography," although the term is anachronistic (see introduction to Hunt, *Invention of Pornography*). Goulemot suggests 1650–1750 as being the period in France when censorship gave pornography a distinct generic identity (Goulemot, *Forbidden Texts*, 10–13). Although press regulation was more relaxed in Britain, toleration of pornography was not. In defending the expurgated edition of Cleland's *Memoirs*, its publisher Ralph Griffiths reviews it in these terms: "it does not appear to us that this performance . . . has

CATCHING YOUNG AND AIRY MINDS

Richardson's doctor, George Cheyne, advised Richardson on his own sequel to *Pamela*, urging him to "avoid fondling—and gallantry, tender expressions . . . especially in the sex (i.e. women)" (Richardson, *Selected Letters*, 46). But if Richardson is to elevate novel reading, he knows he must offer young readers attractive substitutes for the novels they now consume. In a reply to Cheyne, written on August 31, 1741, after the onslaught of the anti-pamelists, he offers his most precise statement of the risks and rewards of writing *Pamela* as a lively story with a fair share of amorous intrigue. His letter sketches the formula for his own elevation of novel reading. First, in what he represents, he must aim neither too high nor too low: "And the principal complaints against me by many, and not libertines neither, are, that I am too grave, too much of a methodist, and make Pamela too pious. . . . In my scheme I have generally taken human nature as it is; for it is to no purpose to suppose it angelic, or to endeavor to make it so" (ibid., 47). Second, his writing will engage the curiosity about sex that passionate young readers are determined to gratify: "There is a time of life, in which the passions will predominate; and ladies, any more than men, will not be kept in ignorance; and if we can properly mingle instruction with entertainment, so as to make the latter seemingly the view, while the former is really the end, I imagine it will be doing a great deal." However, an entertaining gratification of curiosity entails a degree of literal depiction that Richardson is aware may open his text to perverse debasement: "There is no writing on these subjects to please such a gentleman as that in the *Tatler*, who could find sex in a laced shoe, when there was none in the foot, that was to wear it." Then, Richardson mocks the sort of licentious reading—a perverse fascination for looking under skirts—all too evident in *Pamela Censured*. "And what would such a one have said to pass now through Covent-Garden, under twenty hoop-petticoats, hanging over his head at the habit shops?" (47) Just as perversion involves a deflection of the sexual act (Laplanche and Pontalis, *The Language of Psycho-Analysis*, 306), so Richardson sees it as being necessary to expose his text to perverse

anything in it more offensive to decency of sentiment and expression than our own novels and books of entertainment have: . . . The news-papers inform us, that the celebrated history of *Tom Jones* has been suppressed in France as an immoral work" (*Monthly Review*, March 1750, cited in Foxon, *Libertine Literature in England*, 57–58).

readers and risk a general deflection of his meaning, in order to reach his target audience. To reach young readers, who "will not be kept in ignorance," *Pamela* must risk allowing readers to see or hear too much. Thus, for example, some readers may hear double entendres where the author assures us none were intended. The author of *Pamela Censured*, for example, finds one passage particularly indecent:

> After some little tart repartees and sallies aiming at wit, the author seems to indulge his genius with all the rapture of lascivious ingenuity:
>
> I wish, said he, (I'm almost ashamed to write it, impudent Gentleman as he is!) I wish, I had thee as QUICK ANOTHER WAY, as thou art in thy repartees.—And he laughed, and I snatched my hands from him, and tripped away as fast I could . . . .
>
> Here virtue is encouraged with a vengeance and the most obscene idea expressed by a double entendre, which falls little short of the coarsest ribaldry; yet *Pamela* is designed to mend the Taste and manners of the Times, and instruct and encourage youth in virtue . . . [44]

The Censurer's rebuke to the editor of *Pamela* ignores the signs of Richardson's own unease with the freedom of Mr. B.'s words, evident in Pamela's modest parenthetically expressed shame about transcribing B's repartee: "(I'm almost ashamed to write it, impudent Gentleman as he is!)" Richardson was stung enough by this censure to remove this jest from his final edition of *Pamela* (Eaves and Kimpel, *Samuel Richardson,* 129). But surgery on this passage does not control other double meanings. The long defense of *Pamela* against its critics appended by Richardson to the prefatory material in the second edition (February 14, 1741), consisting mostly of excerpts of letters from Aaron Hill, responds to the letter of an anonymous critic of *Pamela's* double entendres with an appalled determination to ignore its criticism: "[this is] too dirty for the rest of his Letter. . . . In the occasions he is pleased to discover for jokes, I either find not, that he has any signification at all, or such vulgar, course-tasted allusions to loose low-life Idioms, that not to understand what he means, is both the cleanliest [*sic*], and prudentest [*sic*] way of confuting him" (16).

If Richardson can win readers willing "not to understand," or at least to *pretend* they don't understand, the licentious meanings that may proliferate within the text, then he can use scenes of kissing and erotic touching to promote moral improvement. Thus in reply to Cheyne's cautions, he writes, "To say, that these tender scenes (between Mr. B. and Pamela) should be supposed rather than described, is not answering my design, when the instruction lies in them, and when I would insinuate to my younger readers, that even their tenderest loves should be governed by motives of gratitude for laudable obligations; and I have been told I am in danger of leaving nature, and being too refined for practice on some of these occasions. But I hope not!" (49) By having Pamela use sex as the reward for a virtuous sentimental commerce, Richardson can "insinuate" an upward displacement in the amorous practice of his young readers. It is only, he argues, through the literal depiction of his scenes of love that he can provide substitute gratifications for the young reader, and so catch his prey:

> I am endeavoring to write a story, which shall catch young and airy minds, and when passions run high in them, to show how they may be directed to laudable meanings and purposes, in order to decry such novels and romances, as have a tendency to inflame and corrupt: and if I were to be too spiritual, I doubt I should catch none but grandmothers, for the granddaughters would put my girl indeed in better company, such as that of the graver writers, and there they would leave her; but would still pursue those stories, that pleased their imaginations without informing their judgments.

Richardson has a print-market professional's sure grasp of the ultimate power of the reader—to be bored by a book and put it aside; he knows, too, that the natural proclivities of readers are as different as the bodies of grandmothers and granddaughters; and he has designated his target audience—"young and airy minds." It is with these things in mind that Richardson plots his seduction of the reader. By introducing his "girl" *Pamela*/Pamela to his readers at the most opportune moment, "when passions run high in them," and by decrying novels so as to depreciate their value to readers, Richardson attempts to redirect the passions of his readers "to laudable meanings and purposes." This deflection of passions is at the center of his project to reform reading and license entertainment. The potential efficacy of such a project—applauded by the pamelists and rejected by the anti-pamelists—results from the same factor that renders it uncertain: the ultimate freedom of readers. Exercising a freedom conferred by the market, readers (may) choose their own improvement.[20]

20. Richardson's problems adjusting the moral rhetoric of his use of sex in his novels continue with *Clarissa*. One of his most proprietous correspondents, Lady Echlin, complains in a letter dated September 2, 1755, that "the best instruction you can give, blended with love intrigues, will never answer your good intention" (*Correspondence*, v. 5, 54). For a fuller discussion of the problem of shaping the experience of readers, see W. Warner, *Reading Clarissa*, 137ff.

How does the *Pamela* media event affect the cultural location of novels, and what sorts of critical practices can, after this media event, proliferate around them? The very ambition of Richardson's project to reshape novel reading raises the stakes around novel reading, and this, as I have shown, becomes a provocation to those who refuse his reforming "scheme." The success of *Pamela* as a "new species" of elevated novel reading, and the intensity of the counteroffensive of the anti-pamelists, not only precipitate a debate about what reading for pleasure should be; this debate also means that the contending readers of the *Pamela* media event, in order to support or deflate *Pamela*'s pretensions, start reading *Pamela* in ways that are important to the long-term institutionalization of novel reading. To state the case most schematically, it is at this point that English readers start engaging in the sort of sympathetic identification with and critical judgment of fictional characters that will lie at the center of novel reading from Richardson, Fielding, and Frances Burney through Jane Austen, George Eliot, and Henry James.

The following are some of the interrelated elements of this new practice of reading: *Pamela*'s readers "read through" the words and ideas of the novel's eponymous heroine in order to assess her character to discover whether Pamela is what the text's subtitle declares her to be—a personification of virtue—or its reverse, a mere sham. By conferring on a character in a novel some of the free-standing qualities of a real person, and insisting that judgments of literary character reflect as much light on those who judge as they do on the judged, both sides in the *Pamela* wars confer an unprecedented moral seriousness upon the evaluation of fictional characters. The strife around *Pamela* draws readers into particular practices of detailed reading: selecting what to read so as to emphasize one thing instead of another; being provoked by incomplete descriptions; filling out the picture to one's own taste; using one's imagination to read between the lines; discerning the supposedly "real" intention of the author; and, finally, distinguishing the "proper" from the "improper" in a text, in order to judge whether a text is "readable" or "unreadable." All these practices of reading may produce a more or less "qualified" reading, which in turn becomes an index of a reader's position in the social hierarchy. By identifying the lives of characters with their own lives and by indulging a sympathetic confusion of the imaginary and the real, readers relocate the distinction between fiction and reality from an opposition between the novel and the world to one within a new species of elevated novel. Habermas suggests that this kind of reading helps constitute a critical public sphere of private subjects (Habermas, *Structural Transformation*, 50).[21]

ANTI-THEATRICAL THEATER THAT ABSORBS

The *Pamela* media event evidences a mutation in the print-media culture in Britain. By embracing the basic thesis of the antinovel discourse—that novels can induce a dangerously automatic imitation in their readers—Richardson incorporates that imitative tendency into *Pamela*'s invitation to the reader to take its heroine as an example. In this way, he develops the claim that reading *Pamela* will make a reader virtuous. Such a claim is endorsed in 1751 when Johnson introduces Richardson to the readers of the *Rambler* as the writer who "has taught the passions to move at the command of virtue" (Johnson, *Rambler*, head note to Richardson's guest appearance in No. 97, Feb. 19, 1751). As I have shown, the anti-pamelists refute this claim by directing many themes of the antinovel discourse against *Pamela*. However, in order to marshal their arguments, the anti-pamelists follow Richardson in assuming that there is an opposition between good and bad reading, true and false imitation, fact and fiction; like him, they assume that these distinctions can be negotiated *within* an interpretation of an anonymously authored love story. In doing so, they implicitly concede a new ethical potential for novel reading.

By publishing the antinovel *Pamela*, Richardson had *not* intended to confer a new legitimacy on novels. When he interrupted his composition of a conduct book (the *Familiar Letters*) in order to write a novel in letters, Richardson thought he was inscribing novels within conduct discourse. This, we have seen, is the central theme of the reader's guide within which he wrapped his collection of Pamela's letters. Readers since the eighteenth

---

21. Of course, critical debates about character precede the *Pamela* media event. For example, after Lafayette's publication of *La Princess de Clèves* (1678), debates swirled around the princess's shocking disclosure to her husband of her love for the Duke de Nemours. However, the novels of Richardson in England and of Rousseau in France triggered a type of identification that gave debates about the true nature of a fictional character a new level of importance. In "Readers Respond to Rousseau," Robert Darnton describes the way in which Rousseau stimulates the desire in his readers to confess their inmost feelings of identification that the novels have triggered in them: "A young woman wrote that she could identify with Rousseau's characters, unlike those in all the other novels she had read, because they did not occupy a specific social station but rather represented a general way of thinking and feeling, one that everyone could apply to their own lives and thus become more virtuous" (247). For some of the formulations of this paragraph, I am indebted to a paper written in my seminar at SUNY Buffalo by Kim Sungho.

century have remarked, and sometimes complained, that the last third of *Pamela* deflects the narrative of the protagonist's adventures into a guide on how to conduct oneself as a virtuous wife. This withdrawal from novelistic action is entirely consistent with Richardson's design on his readers. *Pamela* was to have exhausted the desire to read any other novel. But instead of ending the popularity of novels, *Pamela* helped to enlarge the repertoire of novelistic entertainments. To understand this reversal of Richardson's intended effects, it is necessary to grasp how the market of media-culture entertainments expands to assimilate *Pamela*.

Paradoxically, the very features of the system of media culture that allow *Pamela* to become a publishing phenomenon also limit Richardson's control over a text that is no longer precisely "his." Above, I characterized print-media culture as an open system in which entertainment circulates on a market for culture that is non-hierarchical, that is swept by whim and fashion, and that sanctions whatever succeeds. Richardson's carefully guarded anonymity in publishing *Pamela* should be understood as the most powerful way to exploit the tendencies of this system. By suppressing his own authorial role, Richardson can act through his text, as if by remote control, to elevate novel reading (W. Warner, *Reading Clarissa*, chapter 5). As an anonymous text, belonging to no one, and written about nobody in particular (Gallagher, *Nobody's Story*), *Pamela* can exploit media culture as an open system, in which the general reader engages texts for diverse reasons.

In order to reform novel reading, *Pamela* must avoid the delusive absorption attributed to novels over the course of the eighteenth century, and to *Pamela* itself by critics such as Fielding and the author of *Pamela Censured*. Derived from the Old French *absorber* and Latin *absorbere* "to suck away," "to absorb" means, according to the *Oxford English Dictionary*, not only "to take (something) in through pores or interstices," but also "to occupy the full attention, interest, or time of." As a synonym of "monopolize, consume, engross, preoccupy," this second meaning shares with these verbs the idea of having "exclusive possession or control of." This notion of the totality of absorption is also active in physics, where it means "to retain (radiation or sound, for example) wholly, without reflection or transmission" (*Oxford English Dictionary*). It is the idea of the *completeness* of absorption of the reader in the text—where the ideas of the novel enter the reader's brain without dilution, deflection, or mediation—that provides the novel's potential for corruption. Within the antinovel discourse, a reader who consumes a novel can be absorbed by that novel. If, for example, he or she acts out the manners and action of the characters, there is an "unhappy inversion": that which the reader seeks to absorb absorbs the reader and that which is consumed consumes the consumer. Addictive reading of novels could then produce an epidemic of the sort of "emulous desire" of which Arabella, Charlotte Lennox's romance reader in *The Female Quixote*, must be cured (366). But the novel's absorptive power over the reader also gives the novel the potential to turn readers toward virtue.

The critical work of Michael Fried on French eighteenth-century painting and David Marshall on Shaftesbury, Defoe, and Rousseau suggests that Richardson's development of an elevated novel lies right at the center of the century's attempt to represent honest feeling honestly. What must be avoided at all costs—what Fried finds in the Rococo, Marshall locates in Shaftesbury's critique of the printed book's address to its reader, and Richardson decries in the novels and romances—is a coy and self-conscious theatricality that panders to the gaze of the beholder. To avoid this theatricality, *Pamela* deploys the three salient strategies Fried ascribes to absorptive painting. First, according to Fried, Chardin and Greuze imbue their paintings with an aura of innocence by depicting the simple souls of the bourgeois home in states of absorption: reading, drawing, building a card castle, and so on. Similarly, Richardson seeks to charm his reader with the innocence of everyday activity by representing Pamela absorbed in writing to her parents, arranging her bundles of clothes, or chatting with other servants. Second, in the moments of crisis when Pamela defends her body against assault, melodramatic scenes of "virtue in distress" have the dramatic unity, intensity, and intelligibility that Fried demonstrates to be central to Diderot's program for an antitheatrical "narrowing, heightening and abstracting" of the beholding itself (104). And third, by avoiding a theatrical self-conscious address to the reader, Richardson's letter-novels promote what Fried finds in these paintings: the "supreme fiction" of the beholder's absence. This fiction helps achieve a realist effect of immediacy and unselfconsciousness, precisely the qualities Diderot praised with such extravagance in his *Eloge à Richardson* (1762).

In a cogent revision and extension, David Marshall points out that this antitheatrical strategy requires another kind of theater. Marshall shows that in order to avoid the false theatricality of books, with the "coquetry of authors" in their direct "I-you" address to their reader, Shaftesbury devises new forms of textual theater. Marshall's formulation of this paradox offers a suggestive gloss on Richardson's strategy for curing the bad absorption and false theatricality of novels: "Paradoxically, writing must turn to theater through the dialogue or present itself in the guise of a private text in order to deny its position before its audience of readers . . . Theatricality— the intolerable position of appearing as a spectacle before spectators—calls for the instatement of theater: the protective play of masks and screens that would deny the view of the spectators it positions and poses for" (Marshall, *Figure of Theater*, 66–67). In *Pamela*, authentic self-presentation depends upon masks and screens to project a new persona. Anonymous publication allows Richardson to publish his narrative in the form of naive familiar letters by throwing his voice into the mouth of a young girl.

However, there are built-in liabilities in a strategy of theatrical indirection. When Pamela becomes famous, whether as an object of emulation or as a scandalously false model, her sheer notoriety makes it increasingly difficult to prevent her from becoming a spectacle before spectators. "Pamela" becomes the focal point of the theatrical effect produced by the media event that precipitates her celebrity. Acts of reference, citation, and co-optation confer an involuntary greatness upon this modest young servant. Then, when the anti-pamelists insist upon Pamela's performative ruses—her cunning seduction of the unwary Mr. B. within the narrative or the disingenuous motives of *Pamela's* real writer—there is no author there to protect her. The threat this poses to the proper reception of *Pamela* mandates Richardson's belated appearance as author.

RICHARDSON'S BELATED APPEARANCE AS AUTHOR

While the texts of the anti-pamelists disturb the progress of *Pamela* to its reader, a much greater threat to the novel comes from those on the print market who would honor her with that highest form of flattery—imitation in the form of a sequel. In a letter to his brother-in-law James Leake, Richardson gives an account of his struggle to protect *Pamela* by preventing the appearance of the first of these sequels, *Pamela's Conduct in High Life*, published by the bookseller Richard Chandler, and written by his "bookseller's hackney," John Kelly.[22] Richardson's struggle with Chandler and Kelly to shape the public life of Pamela highlights a crucial feature of media culture. Because of the abstract uniformity of the print medium, media-culture commodities do not come stamped with the unique character of an authored work. Instead, they betray a dangerous plasticity. Through a sequel, Richardson's story could be "ravished out of his hands" and continued by another; or his own sequel might be promiscuously merged with the writing of an uninvited collaborator (such as Kelly); or the copyright of a sequel could become the possession of a bookseller (such as Chandler) not of his own choosing. His own *Pamela* might, through the

22. *Selected Letters*, 42–45; this story is recounted in Sale, *Samuel Richardson* (26–29) and Eaves and Kimpel, *Samuel Richardson* (135–139).

"bookseller's interest and arts" be bound with the false and debased sequel. Finally, Richardson fears that there is no way to stop these debased imitations from multiplying indefinitely, with "still more and more volumes intended possible by them, so long as the town would receive them" (*Selected Letters*, 44). "Pamela" might acquire all of the monstrous staying power of the undead. In all these ways, *Pamela* may be given a new shape and meaning retroactively, through the afterlives given her by an irresponsible crowd of imitators.

The response of the "Highlife Men"—as Richardson terms Chandler, Kelly, and their partners—suggests that the media culture of which *Pamela* is a part is an unenclosed common, where all may graze at will. On this aggressively competitive terrain, property in a hit like *Pamela* appears transitory and provisional. Richardson had actually encouraged unauthorized sequels in two ways: through anonymous publication, and "through the heroine's promising future." As a seasoned print-media insider, Richardson should not have been surprised that others would contrive to continue a story he had begun. The lucrative advantages of serial publication had been demonstrated in the previous sixty years with the multiple installments of *Love Letters*, the *New Atalantis*, and *Love in Excess* (see chapters 2 and 3). When *Robinson Crusoe* was a runaway best-seller in 1719, Defoe followed with the *Farther Adventures of Robinson Crusoe* (1919) and the *Serious Reflections* (1720). The recent revivals of films and television series, such as *Star Trek* and *Star Wars*, suggest a law at work in media culture since the early modern period—one that assures not simply that proven hits spawn imitators, but that they will come back to life.

The "Highlife Men" justify their sequel by claiming the freedom of entrepreneurs to meet the desires of a consuming public. Thus Chandler accuses Richardson of being like "the dog in the manger [who] would neither eat [himself] nor let them eat." Selfish as a dog with a bone, Richardson would not only deny his professional colleagues a piece of the action, he would frustrate the understandable curiosity of an enthusiastic public. When Richardson hears that *Pamela's Conduct in High Life* is nearing publication, he includes a denunciation of it in his May 7, 1741 advertisement for the fourth edition of *Pamela*. This first appearance of Richardson as "author" comes as a belated reaction to protect *Pamela* from debasement; in it, "the author thinks it necessary to declare" that the sequel does not have his "consent," and reflects no knowledge of Pamela beyond what can be read in *Pamela*. Finally, he adds, he is "actually continuing the work himself" (Eaves and Kimpel, *Samuel Richardson*, 135).

Pamela has by now taken on a life of its own. Nothing can give Richardson proprietary control over the sequels to *Pamela*. Indeed, without centralized censorship and licensing, or the trademark and copyright protection that contemporary law now extends to characters such as Mickey Mouse, there is nothing that guarantees the right Richardson is here trying to claim: to "end his own work when and how he pleased." Every text is open to an "engrafting" that can tap into the body of the original in a fashion that Richardson declares "scandalous." Thus, in order to protect *Pamela*'s future, Richardson finds he has little choice but to enter the market to condemn *Pamela's Conduct in High Life* in several critical reviews (ibid., 137–138). But more crucially, he promises his own authentic sequel to meet the demand for a continuation of Pamela's story. Richardson is reluctant to continue, in part because he is harassed by other work, and also because "second parts are generally received with prejudice, and it was treating the public too much like a bookseller to pursue a success till they tired out the buyers" (Richardson, *Selected Letters*, 44). But he must override this principled posture toward the reading public when he sees from samples of *Pamela's Conduct in High Life* that "all my characters were likely to be debased, and my whole purpose inverted," that "all readers were not judges." So Richardson reverses course and publishes his own sequel: *Pamela in her Exalted Condition*.

Richardson can only defend this commodity adrift on the open market by presenting himself as its author. To foreclose adversarial readings and patent rip-offs, a responsible sponsoring subject who may speak for the work has to come forward. But how can Richardson assert his possession of an anonymous text without compromising the considerable advantages of anonymous publication? Authorial appropriation comes as a reappropriation of that which is asserted to be, after its errant and vagabond circulation, always already the author's own. Richardson's (re-)possession of *Pamela* takes different forms. After publishing *Pamela in her Exalted Condition*, as volumes 3 and 4 of *Pamela: Virtue Rewarded*, Richardson appends a note that asserts his authority on the grounds of his physical possession of documents: he warns readers against counterfeit versions of Pamela's story, insists that *Pamela* is not a "fiction" with "imaginary" "characters," and announces that all papers are "in one hand only," as the "assignment of Samuel Richardson, editor of 4 vols. of *Pamela: Virtue Rewarded*." When the leading Dublin bookseller, George Faulkner, corrupts one of Richardson's workers to get early access to the copy for *Pamela in her Exalted Condition*, Richardson takes steps to protect another kind of property in his work—its profits. (This is a rehearsal of his later, more fully conceptualized and sustained defense of *Sir Charles Grandison*, described in the conclusion.)

Pamela in her Exalted Condition exposes a central tension within Richardson's novelistic projects: he consistently manifests a primary ambivalence about providing entertainment to his readers. On the title page, he declares that *Pamela* was contrived to achieve a careful balance between cultivating "the Principles of VIRTUE and RELIGION . . . at the same time that it agreeably entertains, by a Variety of *curious* and *affecting* INCIDENTS." The first sentence of the Editor's Preface also emphasizes this double agenda—"to Divert and Entertain, and *at the same time* to Instruct, and Improve the Minds of the YOUTH of both Sexes" [italics mine]. In an act that may be motivated by the criticisms of *Pamela* that surface in the *Pamela* media event or that may reflect his own reticence about novel writing, Richardson abandons this delicate balancing act by purging his sequel of the conflict and suspense central to *Pamela*.

In these two further volumes of narrative centered on Pamela's exemplary conduct in high life, Richardson intentionally changes the ratio of entertainment and instruction. He works this change by cutting away all of the adventure and intrigue that had linked *Pamela* to the novels of amorous intrigue: "But I hate so much the French marvellous and all unnatural machinery, and have so often been disgusted with that sort of management, that I am contended to give up my profit, if I can but instruct. I am very sensible that there cannot, *naturally*, be the room for plots, stratagems and intrigue in the present volumes as in the first," he wrote to Stephen Duck (ibid., 53). Richardson's caricature of French fiction is used to justify his abandonment of the effort to "divert" his reader. His defense of writing a natural and probable account of Pamela's life as Mrs. B. anticipates nineteenth-century programs for "slice-of-life" realism. However, Richardson's attack on the sources of interest in his own fiction makes him a dour spoilsport at his own entertainment. He uses the very absence of incidents in his sequel to announce his shift in priorities to Dr. Cheyne: "you'll observe that instruction is my main end . . . For I always had it in view, I have the vanity to repeat, to make the story rather *useful* than *diverting;* and if I could perform it in such a manner as should entertain, it was all I aimed at. The cause of Virtue and Religion, was what I wished principally to serve" (54–55). Here, Richardson offers the rationale for the gesture he will repeat in the last volume of *Clarissa,* as well as in the program of *Sir Charles Grandison*—a vengeful return of the superego, expressed through the withering repetition of didacticism. Unleashing this didacticism, usually at the end of his novels, allows Richardson to attack the sources of enjoyment within his own fiction.

6   *Joseph Andrews*
as Performative Entertainment

> . . . there were Amusements fitted for Persons of all Ages and
> Degrees, from the Rattle to the discussing of a Point of Philosophy,
> and . . . Men discovered themselves in nothing more than in the
> Choice of their Amusements.
>
> —Fielding, *Joseph Andrews*

TOWARDS AN AESTHETIC OF NOVEL ENTERTAINMENT

It is the argument of this book that "entertainment" is the most precise
general term for what Richardson and Fielding are providing their readers
in the 1740s. To explore what might be at stake in Fielding's presentation
of his narrative as an entertainment, I will begin by addressing a more
general question: what, in the mid-eighteenth century, is meant by the term
"entertainment"? The English words "to entertain" and "entertainment"
derive from the old French *entretenir*, to maintain, from the Latin
intertenêre, literally "to hold among" or "hold between." Many of the early,
now-obsolete definitions listed in the *Oxford English Dictionary* reflect
early and current French usage: to keep in a certain state or condition; to
maintain in use or repair; to retain a person in one's service; to provide support or sustenance. Quite early in its independent English development, "to
entertain" comes to mean to receive a guest, to engage someone's attention,
to admit an opinion to consideration, or to maintain an idea in one's mind.
In addition, the word "entertainment" (and the obsolete substantive "entertain") is applied to activities that might pass between and hold together two
or more people: a "pleasure, amusement and merry making," a meal, or a
conversation.

This brief history suggests the complex of ideas that become condensed
around the idea of "entertainment" in the eighteenth century. As referring
to a relationship between a host and guest or (by the eighteenth century) a
performer and an audience, an "entertainment" assumes a sustaining social
exchange between the provider of the entertainment and the one who consumes it. If the entertainment is to succeed, several conditions must be met:
it must amuse and please; it must draw the consumer into voluntarily

"entertaining" its ideas; and it must "hold" or absorb the attention of those entertained. At the same time, since entertainment is often judged on the basis of its power to divert or amuse, "entertainment" implies a detour from ordinary reality. "Diversion" or "amusement" become synonyms for an "entertainment." In the entry under "entertainment" in Johnson's *Dictionary of the English Language*, it is described as "lower comedy," as opposed to higher forms such as tragedy or comedy proper. Thus Johnson cites Gay: "A great number of dramatic entertainments are not comedies, but five act farces." "Entertainment" confers relief from serious thoughts or concerns. While it seems safe to surmise that theater of various kinds would have been the dominant context for conceptualizing entertainment in the Restoration and the first half of the eighteenth century, the entertainment function is extended to the heroic romance *L'Astrée* in its 1657 translation and to novels by Behn, Manley, and Haywood, as well to works by the improvers of the novel (Defoe and Aubin). In the first half of the eighteenth century, reading has developed into one of the main avenues of leisure entertainment.

In *The Beautiful, Novel, and Strange*, Ronald Paulson proposes a new way to account for the aesthetic ambition evident in Fielding's novels. According to him, *Joseph Andrews* and *Tom Jones* fulfill an aesthetic program first outlined in Addison's *Spectator* essays, "On the Pleasures of the Imagination."[1] A look at Addison's first *Spectator* paper in this series suggests an aesthetic proper to media culture. Addison's *Spectator* essay no. 411 offers a critique of leisure activities while at the same time developing a rationale for entertainment as a vehicle for enlightenment. In a passage

---

1. The following is a summary of key features of Addison's "aesthetic" as Paulson analyzes it: (1) Addison's regime of aesthetic pleasure assumes the priority of sight over the other senses (No. 411). For the consumer of a scene or spectacle, sight allows a relation to an object that is at once engaged—objects hold or fascinate the gaze directed toward them—yet detached—by the abstracting power of sight's operation at a distance. Thus, Addison cultivates the disinterested spectator who "considers the world as a theater, and desires to form a right judgment of those who are the actors on it" (No. 10). (2) Addison develops the value of a third aesthetic register, which he calls "the new," the "uncommon," or the "strange," and which lies between the "beautiful" (the traditional object of art as developed, for example, by Shaftesbury) and the great or sublime (which would come to dominate aesthetics at the end of the eighteenth century, with Burke and Kant). The aesthetics of the "new" assumes the spectator's curiosity and a pursuit of knowledge which, while being empirical and practical, values variety over unity, and takes pleasure in surprise (Paulson, *Beautiful, Novel, and Strange*, 49). (3) Addison's privileging of the new and novel as accessible through a detached spectator is realized by the theatrical narratives devised by Hogarth and Fielding.

that has strong similarities to the antinovel discourse discussed in earlier chapters of this study, Addison worries about the deleterious effects of the leisure activities all too often pursued by citizens:

> There are, indeed, but very few who know how to be idle and innocent, or have a relish of any pleasures that are not criminal; every diversion they take is at the expense of some one virtue or another, and their very first step out of business is into vice or folly. A man should endeavor, therefore, to make the sphere of his innocent pleasures as wide as possible, that he may retire into them with safety, and find in them such a satisfaction as a wise man would not blush to take. Of this nature are those of the imagination, which do not require such a bent of thought as is necessary to our more serious employments, nor, at the same time, suffer the mind to sink into that negligence and remissness, which are apt to accompany our more sensual delights, but, like a gentle exercise to the faculties, awaken them from sloth and idleness, without putting them upon any labor or difficulty.

Lodged between gross "sensual delights," which endanger morals, and the pleasures of "understanding," which are "attended with too violent a labor of the brain," Addison conceptualizes a middle sphere of "innocent pleasures," involving the visualizing powers of eye and mind condensed in the word "imagination." Such a diversion could consist in a walk in the city or country, or time spent in idle reading. While Addison's program shares with high aesthetic programs (for example, that of Shaftesbury) a certain sublimation of consumption, Addison also insists upon the need to diversify the objects used to "awaken" the imagination of the spectator through novel arrangements of nature, painting, or print. In the discussion of the pleasures of the imagination, Addison conceptualizes the cultural location that would be occupied by print-media culture and the elevated novels of Richardson and Fielding. Addison not only succeeds in making his own reflections upon entertainment entertaining; in a fashion that Fielding would imitate in the essays in *Joseph Andrews* and *Tom Jones*, he also makes them perform the aesthetic of the new that they describe and promote.

Several factors make Addison's aesthetic of the new particularly useful to later writers of novels. Throughout his essays on the "pleasures of the imagination," Addison uses "entertain" in the sense of the mind's being caught or engaged by something in nature or art. Here the meaning of "to entertain" as "to occupy or hold the mind" is developing toward the sense of an "entertainment" as a structured representation that we consume for pleasure. But Addison's way of characterizing this pleasure—as something that an individual mind retires into itself to obtain—makes it uniquely fitted to the eighteenth-century practice of silent and solitary novel reading. Finally, in his *Spectator* essay no. 412, his analysis of the perceptual or psychological fascination of the new seems ready-made for a form of narrative—the novel—shaped to deliver what is strange and uncommon to a general reader:

> Every thing that is new or uncommon raises a pleasure in the imagination, because it fills the soul with an agreeable surprise, gratifies its curiosity, and gives it an idea of which it was not before possest [*sic*]. We are indeed so often conversant with one set of objects, and tired out with so many repeated shows of the same things, that whatever is new or uncommon contributes a little to vary human life, and to divert our minds, for a while, with the strangeness of appearance: it serves us for a kind of refreshment, and takes off from that satiety we are apt to complain of in our usual and ordinary entertainments.

Although Addison's examples of the "new and uncommon" are drawn here from nature—fields are never so "pleasant to look upon" "in the opening of the spring, when they are all new and fresh"—his conceptualizing of the new provides a conceptual rationale for the implicit aesthetic of media culture. Ordinary life with its sameness and repetition has been found to be boring; novels provide a refreshing antidote to this familiar modern "complaint." The market for printed entertainments will thrive by serving a newly conceptualized hunger for novelty. Those, like Richardson and Fielding, who decried novels accused them of pandering to novelty as an end in itself; instead, they seek to meet this need to "divert our minds" with a new, and improved and improving, kind of . . . novelty.

In the previous chapter I noted that Richardson seeks to balance instruction and entertainment in *Pamela*. In *Joseph Andrews*, Fielding's most decisive contribution to the *Pamela* media event, Fielding foregrounds the "entertainment function" of his prose fictions. In the preface to *Joseph Andrews*, for example, he seeks to clarify what sort of "entertainment" the reader is to expect (3), and in the first chapter of *Tom Jones*, the narrator develops an elaborate conceit, describing himself as a "Master of an Ordinary" providing a "Bill of Fare" to the public "for their Entertainment" (I: i). Through the persona and voice of the narrator, a figure for the author becomes an entertainer, functioning as a constant mediator between the reader and the fictive action of the novel. Less a reliable guide than an artful actor or puppeteer, Fielding develops a novelistic species of performative entertainment which concedes to the reader his or her essential freedom as a pleasurable responsibility.

FIELDING'S CRITIQUE OF ABSORPTIVE NOVEL READING

Fielding's responses to *Pamela* condense and re-articulate many of the perspectives I have traced in the earlier chapters of this study. He accepts the licentious liberty of readers and their fascination with the print-media culture of his day, at the same time that he endorses the basic coordinates of the antinovel discourse's critique of absorptive reading. However, he finds *Pamela* to be worse than the disease of novel reading it was meant to cure. By having the reform of the novelistic libertine Mr. B. result from reading Pamela's pathetic and involving letter narratives, Richardson promotes a new species of absorptive novel reading. In contrast, *Joseph Andrews* offers a cast of characters who have been readers, and who imitate that reading in their everyday lives. Joseph has imbibed the Christian ethics of his mentor, Parson Adams, the London fashions of opera and playhouse (I:v), and the enthusiastic chastity communicated through a reading of his sister Pamela's letters. Joseph's repetition of his sister's defense of her virtue—in spite of their gender differences—provides the book's initial joke at the expense of an overly literal imitative reading. Adams models an endearing but outdated classical and scriptural reading: it is canonical, reverential, repetitive, and overly literal. Along with these two central characters, there are other readers, such as the deluded and selfish novel reader Leonora, the skeptical freethinker Wilson, and so on. When tested by experience, all these variants of imitative reading are found wanting. Thus the textual education provided by the novel *Joseph Andrews* is finally ironic: it turns out there is no book that can teach virtue by modeling what it is; of course this reflects upon the reading *Joseph Andrews* invites from its readers.

Building upon the general address and entertainment function of media culture, Fielding's performative entertainment puts a middle term—the author/narrator—between the reader and the story told. By incorporating a reflection upon reading into his text, Fielding locates his novel in the new discursive space opened by the *Pamela* media event: a critical public-sphere debate about what reading is and should be. Instead of an example of proper reading, *Joseph Andrews* weaves an open matrix of variable reading practices: reading as pleasurable consumption, reading as dialogical conversation, reading as a performative entertainment. In his role as an antiauthoritarian entertainer, Fielding must be distinguished from the narrator's theatrical performance as "author"; Fielding does not function as a spiderlike God, but as a leader of the revels. By developing a distinct new form of English comic novel, written "in the manner of Cervantes," Fielding promotes his own mode of elevated reading, and thereby prepares for a subsequent institutionalization of "the" novel.

If we are to trace the effects of Fielding's opportunistic intervention within the media culture of his day, we face an obstacle not confronted with Behn, Haywood, Defoe, or Richardson. With Fielding, as with such writers as Shakespeare and Milton, the evident brilliance of his rhetorical mastery gives the impression that he is always in control of the meanings he disseminates. Fielding has won the enthusiastic admiration of critics from the eighteenth century to the present. These critics wish to imagine that he has distilled Pope's rhetorical finesse, Milton's mastery of the classics, and Defoe's story-telling genius into the "perfectly" plotted form of his novels. This critical perspective, according to which Fielding is the first self-consciously literary novel writer in Britain, has the effect of severing Fielding's links to the media culture within which he wrote. I would argue that it is only by conceiving the entertainments that Fielding constructs as opportunistic responses to the *Pamela* media event that we can come to terms with Fielding's distinct reconfiguration of eighteenth-century novelistic entertainment.

Ronald Paulson applauds Fielding's response to the dangers posed by absorptive reading. In the following passage, Fielding figures as a big-game hunter who uses various narrative techniques to rescue the reader from a dangerous species of reading:

> When *Pamela* came into Fielding's sights, he seems to have sensed—certainly before his contemporaries—the peculiar danger of Richardson's hold over his readers. The effect of *Pamela*'s particularity, piled-up minutiae, repetitions, and prolixity was to draw the reader as close as possible to the heroine's immediate experience and mind, in fact to suck the reader in and immerse him in her experience. . . . the reader becomes uncritical, a "friend" of the character, and having accepted Pamela's rationalizations as completely as he would his own, he emerges ready to modify his own conduct accordingly.
>
> [Paulson, *Satire and the Novel*, 101]

"Seeing *Pamela* as a moral chaos in which the reader was invited to wallow self-indulgently," Fielding, by Paulson's account, develops a normative commentator, an "arbiter of morals and manners," a "creator and/or historian, who sets before the reader an object that can be accepted as objectively true." In addition, Fielding becomes a manipulator who interrupts even in moments of high emotion (such as after Fanny's abduction). Finally, the narrator is an ironist who creates "the impression of neutrality and authority, as opposed to the disreputable, prejudiced, and limited vision of

Pamela." Fielding's narrative technique offers a more "generous and inclusive" view, which "holds the reader at some distance from the action," so that "the air of artifice is compensated for by the sanity of the exposition, the clarity and, in that sense, realism of the picture" (106–107).

Why does this difference about the effect of two types of novelistic narrative become so tendentiously polarized into sane, generous, and inclusive versus disreputable, prejudiced, and limited? Like Ian Watt, Paulson is here writing within a critical tradition that sees "realism" as the sine qua non of novelistic writing (see chapter 1). But Paulson is also writing against *The Rise of the Novel*, in which Watt's critical narrative makes Richardson the inventor of "formal realism," and thus the first real novelist in English, while Fielding is stuck in a belated and secondary position, offering comparatively superficial characters and a pallid "realism of assessment." Paulson is just one of many defenders of Fielding to argue that Watt's conceptual categories were rigged against Fielding. In order to break the spell of Watt's critical narrative upon absorbed mid-twentieth-century critical readers, Paulson makes a move that has a long history in the critical reception of Richardson and Fielding: he marks their difference as being analogous to that between a woman and a man (Campbell, *Natural Masques*, 3–4). Thus, in the passages quoted above, Fielding figures as the masterfully objective masculine author saving the reader from the "moral chaos" of wallowing "self-indulgently" in Richardson's implicitly feminine fiction. Then, by insisting that Fielding's fiction provides an "impression of neutrality and authority" that can "be accepted as objectively true," Paulson makes the case for wresting the prize Watt had awarded to Richardson— namely, realism's grasp of the real—and conferring it upon Fielding. In my own account of this debate, I am seeking to disentangle Paulson's useful insight about the pivotal importance of the issue of absorptive reading from debates about whether it is Fielding or Richardson who has first claim to having fathered "the" English novel. My own study suggests that Fielding's rewriting of *Pamela* is inscribed in a more general cultural struggle around the terms for licensing entertainment.[2]

In *Natural Masques*, Jill Campbell argues that Fielding's response to *Pamela* arises out of a critique of the effect of entertainment on culture that was already well advanced by 1740. Campbell shows how Fielding's plays

---

2. For a fuller discussion of the problematically retroactive use of "realism" in an account of the eighteenth-century novel, see chapter 1; for a discussion of the fruitful effects of even tendentiously staged critical accounts of the difference between Richardson and Fielding, see conclusion.

of the 1730s rotate around a familiar satiric critique: in modern entertain-ments, luxury, commodification, and foreign fashion menace native English identity and virtue. Xenophobic strife around entertainment becomes entangled with the struggle to prescribe proper gender roles. While some, like Richardson, promote a feminized domestic virtue as an alternative to corrupting foreign amusements, satires upon modern entertainments often target susceptible female consumers as leading the vogue for corrupt for-eign imports. Thus, for example, Italian opera is said not only to subordi-nate moral sense to fantastic spectacle, but also to draw female fans to take celebrity castrati (such as Farinelli) as a fetishized substitute for the "nat-ural" English phallus. Lured by the spectacles of a false masculinity, women wander from their proper roles of lover, wife, and mother (*Natural Masques*, 35–36). Like opera, novels are castigated as foreign imports that threaten to feminize England. These eighteenth-century episodes of gen-der trouble suggest "that male and female identity might be in some sense conventional, acquired, or historically determined" (ibid., 12).

By Campbell's account, *Joseph Andrews* is where Fielding begins to shape a positive "natural" alternative to the early-eighteenth-century entertainments that engage in a disguised play with gender identity, such as the masquerades (of Heidegger), the spectaculars (of John Rich), the Ital-ian opera, and the novels of amorous intrigue (such as those of Haywood). To Fielding, however, these entertainments don't just blur gender identity, they imperil any identity at all. Within a culture mediated by these enter-tainments, there is, in Campbell's words, "the threat of an exchange or collapse of [the interior and exterior selves] into each other that turns both personal feeling and public action into mere dramatic acting" (27). This perspective helps explain why Fielding responded so urgently to the problem posed by *Pamela's* presentation of its heroine as virtuous. Richardson's rendering of native English virtue not only echoes the spe-cious self-promotion of all market-based entertainments, it also touts as virtue what Fielding takes to be the most insidious form of "affectation": a performance where the actor doesn't know she is acting, where there is a heroine who sincerely believes her own (false) performance.

Campbell's study helps explain why the extraordinary popularity of *Pamela* appears to Fielding as the symptom of a "general social disorder" (Battestin, *Henry Fielding*, 303). His attack in *Shamela* is targeted less at the anonymous *Pamela* than at the response of its enthusiastic readers (Paulson, *Satire and the Novel*). In *Shamela*, the *Pamela* vogue is charac-terized as "an epidemical frenzy now raging in the town" (278): mysteri-ous and pervasive and spreading, its popularity suggests a collective delusion. How could reading a book cause an "epi-demic," becoming literally spread over the people (from the Greek *epi* and *demos*)? While the enthusiasm for *Pamela* rages, it can induce a mad frenzy of imitation. The bad book requires the sort of intervention brought to bear on smallpox through inoculation in the early eighteenth century: exposure of healthy readers to small doses of the disease so as to produce antibodies within them.[3] Just as Shamela imitates the self-interested amours she finds in "the third volume of the *Atalantis*" (295), so, in his summary indictment of *Pamela*, Parson Oliver surmises that readers might imitate the behavior in *Pamela*: "young gentlemen are here taught . . . to marry their mothers' chambermaids . . . all chambermaids are strictly enjoined to look out after their masters . . . etc." (305). Since ideas such as these could become toxic to readers, publishing Shamela's true letters is prescribed, by Parson Oliver, as "an antidote to this poison" (305).

Framed within a public-sphere exchange between two mature readers, what sort of antidote does *Shamela* administer to its reader? The bawdiness of Shamela's fictional story motivates Parson Oliver's indignation with the "many lascivious Images in *Pamela*, very improper to be laid before the youth of either sex" (305). In *Shamela*, Fielding sets out to counter *Pamela*'s power to absorb the reader into an illusionistic alternative world. Indebted to strategies of Menippean satire perfected by Swift (Paulson, *Satire and the Novel*, 103), *Shamela* is a complex and overdetermined text that does several things at the same time. First, as an anti-*Pamela*, it interrupts the prolix, dreamlike continuity of *Pamela* with brevity, humor, and a critical reflection upon reading. At the same time, Pamela's high moralizing style is shifted into a vulgar vernacular, and delicate sentiment is reduced to sex. Second, as a super-set of *Pamela*, *Shamela* offers a supplement to it—the small added part that completes but also reframes the logic of the whole. After reading this "dangerous supplement" (Derrida, *Of Grammatology*), we cannot help but suspect that Pamela's virtue is merely a calculated performance. Third, as a novel of amorous intrigue, *Shamela* exposes the novel within *Pamela*. Because *Shamela* is only fifty pages long and features relatively "flat" characters who use sex, disguise, and intrigue

3. "In 'Inoculation Against Smallpox' [1718], Lady Mary Wortley Montagu reports a workable method known in the East since ancient times. As wife of the English minister to Constantinople, Lady Mary describes inoculation parties she has witnessed at which a small wound is made in the arm, a few drops of smallpox pus inserted, and a walnut shell tied over the infected area, a procedure that produces a true case of smallpox but one so mild that 98 percent of those inoculated recover" (Trager, *People's Chronology*).

to shape the action, it offers a parody of the novels of amorous intrigue. But although *Shamela* pleases readers in some of the same ways that Haywood's novels do, and thereby exploits their popularity, it is also rigorously anti-absorptive and anti-pornographic. Thus *Shamela* exposes *Pamela* as a novel of amorous intrigue in the guise of a conduct book.[4] Finally, since *Shamela* displays some of the improving goals of the text it mocks, this travesty of *Pamela* imitates, however ironically or indirectly, a crucial thread of Richardson's project: while luring its readers into what appears to be a light entertainment, *Shamela* actually draws them into a more reflective and improving reading. In this way, it offers a first sketch toward the alternative elevated novel reading that *Joseph Andrews* would later provide.

MIXING CRITICISM INTO FICTION

Late in 1749 Richardson writes a letter to Lady Bradshaigh that couples a complaint about the taste of the town with an intemperate attack on Fielding:

> So long as the world will receive, Mr. Fielding will write. Have you ever seen a list of his performances? Nothing but a shorter life than I wish him, can hinder him from writing himself out of date. The *Pamela*, which he abused in his *Shamela*, taught him how to write to please, tho' his manners are so different. Before his *Joseph Andrews* (hints and names taken from that story, with a lewd and ungenerous engraftment) the poor man wrote without being read, except when his Pasquins, roused party attention and the legislature at the same time.
>
> [Richardson, *Selected Letters*, 133–34]

Richardson initiates his attack—interleaved with a thinly veiled death wish—by mobilizing tropes used to revile the unprincipled hack writer: Fielding will continue to write as long as "the world will receive," even though he writes himself to death, or out of favor. Whatever success Fielding enjoys comes from his copying the invention of others—in this case, that of Richardson himself. Not only did *Pamela* teach him "how to write to please," Fielding develops *Joseph Andrews* through a "lewd and ungenerous engraftment" upon Richardson's story. What remains unstated in Richardson's comments is the stubborn fact of Fielding's enormous popularity with readers. Lady Bradshaigh is not the only one of Richardson's

4. Fielding would offer a more sex-ploitative version of the novel in his anonymously published *The Female Husband: or, The Surprising History of Mrs. Mary, alias Mr. George Hamilton* (1746).

circle who urges Richardson to read *Tom Jones;* the daughters of Aaron Hill do so also, and in response to their positive recommendations Richardson complains to them of Fielding's "public and private" "principles," though he loves Fielding's "four worthy sisters" (ibid., 127; Eaves and Kimpel, *Samuel Richarson,* 297–298). Richardson was much less stung by Fielding's morality, or by that of his characters, than he was by the success of *Tom Jones.* The Richardson-Fielding rivalry that figures so prominently in literary histories of the early novel was, for the principal figures involved, less about literary fame than it was about shaping the contemporary terms for licensing entertainment. In Richardson's correspondence, ungenerous slams at Fielding's libertine principles are invariably coupled with a general lament about the baseness of readers' tastes, and about the unlikelihood that readers will be inclined, in the wake of the spectacular success of *Tom Jones,* to value and emulate such characters as Clarissa or Sir Charles Grandison.[5]

Richardson is only partly correct about the effect of *Pamela* on Fielding. Although *Pamela* may have taught Fielding something about how to write novels to please, it was not the first time he adjusted to market conditions and developed an ingenious compromise with the proclivities of his audience. *The Author's Farce* is Fielding's earliest assault on the uncritical absorption of spectators in modern entertainment, and it rehearses the tactics he will use in combating the "epidemical frenzy" of *Pamela*'s popularity. After the tepid reception of Fielding's first comedy, *Love in Several Masques,* Colley Cibber declines to produce his next comedies at the Drury Lane Theatre. Fielding responds by writing and producing a play that represents the forces that mediate the production and writing of plays. This production at the New Theatre in the Haymarket was entitled *The Author's Farce: and the Pleasures of the Town.* By following the efforts of the impecunious playwright Harry Luckless to get a serious play produced and published, the play offers a critical view of the contemporary entertainment industry. But what begins as a satire upon the cynical demands and unprincipled maneuvers of the various participants in the market— theatrical producers (Marplay Sr. and Jr.), booksellers (Bookweight), and

5. While Fielding's defenders, from Blanchard (*Fielding the Novelist*) to Battestin (*Henry Fielding*), seek to parry the charges against Fielding's sexual morality, Eaves and Kimpel acquit Richardson of ungenerous attacks upon his rival by conceding his "envy" of Fielding's success: "Envy is not now regarded as so amiable a feeling as lust, but it is no less natural and perhaps as widespread" (*Samuel Richardson,* 296). In this chapter I seek to demonstrate that the strife between Richardson and Fielding was more than personal.

scribblers (Blotpage)—modulates into something more. By producing his own puppet show and farce, entitled "the Pleasures of the Town," Luckless adopts the ironic advice of his friend Witmore: "But now, . . . when the the-aters are puppet-shows, and the comedians ballad-singers; when fools lead the town, . . . if thou must write, write nonsense, write operas, . . . be profane, be scurrilous, be immodest; if you would receive applause, desire to receive sentence at the Old Bailey" (Fielding, "The Author's Farce," 204). In this, the first of his "rehearsal plays," Fielding shows how the whole system of theater and book production subordinates wit and sense to showy spectacle (Battestin, *Henry Fielding*, 85).

Unlike Richardson, who attempts to build (and who keeps rebuilding) a defensive perimeter for his texts, *The Author's Farce* meets light entertainment more than half way. While Fielding's play adopts the general strategy of parodic incorporation used by Pope in the 1728 *Dunciad*, it is closer in mood to Gay's *Beggar's Opera*. *The Author's Farce* also modulates into a comic closure that seems extravagantly unearned, without offering the bleak glimpses at the working of power found in Gay's hit. The resulting theater moves the spectator into a twilight region between satire and spoof, between a self-reflection upon dramatic entertainment and a carefree repetition of the trivial entertainment it mocks. As with *The Beggar's Opera*, Fielding's play involves characters in the metamorphosis from shallow satiric butt to endearingly comic character. Thus, in spite of the satire directed at Mrs. Novel (Eliza Haywood), she acquires a pivotal role that implies the beguiling attractions of novel reading. At the end of *The Author's Farce*, farce melds into the framing play, suggesting the way in which entertainment media engulf their consumers, so neither the main characters (such as Harry Luckless and Harriet) nor we as the audience are left a secure position outside of the entertainments they and we consume.[6]

The Author's Farce suggests the conditions out of which Fielding responds to *Pamela*. Up against the whole system of media culture and the market imperatives that shape the flow of resources, the author is isolated and weak. Therefore, he or she must develop tactics for intervening upon the terrain of the other (see chapter 4). In 1741, the most influential "other" is *Pamela*. Accepting the adage "if you want to be read, write about

---

6. Battestin points out that Fielding may be indebted to his friend and associate James Ralph, who wrote essays, entitled "The Touch-Stone: or, Historical, Critical, Political, Philosophical, and Theological Essays on the reigning Diversions of the Town" (1728), that produced an effect of travesty and burlesque, in ironic praise of the entertainments of the town (Battestin, *Henry Fielding*, 81).

what others are reading," Fielding follows the short travesty *Shamela* with a much more intricate graft to *Pamela*, by telling the story of Pamela's brother in the ambitious two-volume work, *The History of the Adventures of Joseph Andrews, and of his Friend Mr. Abraham Adams* (1742). The critical tradition has recognized *Joseph Andrews* as Fielding's first serious attempt at prose fiction. But although he describes *Joseph Andrews* as a new "Species of writing" (10), Fielding knows he has no absolute authority to engender new genres of writing. Thus, in order to clear the ground for this new kind of novel, he interweaves a global critique of the prose entertainments of his day with a course in criticism that enables readers to become critics in their own right. It is only by creating a new kind of reader, through his own writing, that Fielding can hope to get *Joseph Andrews* read in the proper fashion.

Joseph Andrews shows how the system of modern media culture has turned all of its preordained roles—of, for example, bookseller, author, and reader—into factors of the market. Thus at the height of the novel's melodramatic crisis, when Fanny, "that beautiful and innocent virgin," "[falls] into the wicked hands of the captain" (echoing Pamela's abduction to Lincolnshire in a darker key), the narrator introduces an odd break in the action, in order for a poet and a player to debate the reasons for the decline of the theater. In their opening statements each blames the other parties to theatrical production for this decline. The poet declares that a playwright can hardly be expected to overcome "the Badness of the Actors," and to gratify "a Town, [which] like a peevish Child, knows not what it desires," "without the Expectation of Fame or Profit." The player rejoins that "modern Actors are as good at least as their Authors" (260). Then, in a pure reversal, poet and player take up each other's position, and politely exempt each other from the general condemnation of authors and players. The poet compares the player to Betterton, the greatest Shakespearean actor of the previous generation, and the player declares that there were "manly Strokes, ay whole Scenes, in your last Tragedy, which at least equal *Shakespear*" (261). This sample of the promotional hyperbole used to advance modern plays suggests the difficulty in developing dispassionate criticism upon a terrain rife with interested parties. In place of criticism there is personal invective: the poet roundly condemns most modern plays, while the player satirizes those who act in them. But in a final reversal of positions, poet and player argue over who was to blame for the failure of the poet's last play, in which this particular player played a part. Did the audience hiss the "passage" from the play, or the player's delivery of the lines in "speaking" them (263)? At the same time, the playwright blames the first night's audience—"the whole Town know I had Enemies, . . . a Party in the Pit and Upper-Gallery, would not suffer it to [succeed]." This audience, one may surmise, would blame either the playwright, the actors, or both. In an impasse all too familiar in modern debates about the decline of culture, this "facetious Dialogue" (267) suggests how everyone in the feedback loop of production and consumption can claim to be a middleman, powerless to influence the general direction or quality of culture.

In order to dramatize the radical transformations wrought by the modern market in print, Fielding develops Parson Adams as an embodiment of an earlier regime of reading and writing. As a learned and endearing denizen of the old culture of print, Adams has "published" in the most primitive sense of the word, through oral delivery to his parishioners. Adams' wisdom is the fruit of an intensive and reverential reading of scripture and the classics, such as his beloved edition of Aeschylus, which he has hand copied and bound into calf skin (148, 155). Adams assumes the classics have an intrinsic value that is not dependent upon their popularity. His practice with his beloved Aeschylus is the very opposite of the extensive modern reading that "consumes many texts, [and] passes nonchalantly from one text to the next" (Chartier, *Order of Books*, 17). When his Aeschylus is accidentally destroyed, Adams asks where he can buy another copy. As a practitioner of patient repeated readings, Adams "had never read any translation of the classics," even those as prestigious and popular as Pope's edition of the *Iliad* (196–197), and knows nothing of the government's *Daily Gazetteer* (183). In his reading, as in his dress, Adams eschews all that unfolds under the banner of modern fashion. Because Adams has digested his reading so completely, all that he has imbibed is ready at hand for tavern debates or extemporaneous homilies.

However, Adams' esteem for the classics gives him boundless confidence in the knowledge he has extracted from them. When a tradesman is vain about his understanding of the ways of men, which he has acquired through his travels, Adams rejoins by bragging of the numberless places he knows by reading books, "the only way of travelling by which any Knowledge is to be acquired" (182). While revealing a perilous dearth of practical knowledge in judging character, Adams shows a comic inflexibility in applying to everyday situations the maxims he has garnered from his reading. Thus, when Joseph has apparently lost Fanny to the Roasting Squire, Adams articulates so strict a version of the Christian resignation to misfortune that he falls short of this ideal when his son is apparently drowned (264–267; 309–310). In his literal application of the ideologies of the books he reveres, Adams repeats the liabilities of an overly reverential reading evident in the story of his novelistic prototype, Don Quixote.

However much Adams figures as a nostalgic touchstone of enduring human values, and however much his styles of literacy offer a foil to the new order of printed books, he too is educated in the full rigors of the print market he aspires to enter. The reader meets Adams while he is on a journey to London to enlarge his audience by selling his sermons to the book trade. The decisive blow to Adams' expectations comes from a bookseller whom he has met on the road. When Adams offers his sermons to him, the bookseller delivers this sentence: "Sermons are mere Drugs [defined in the *Oxford English Dictionary* as 'commodities no longer in demand']. The Trade is so vastly stocked with them, that really unless they come out with the Name of *Whitfield* or *Westley*, or some other such great Man . . . I had rather be excused" (79–80). When the bookseller contrasts unfavorably the popularity of sermons with that of plays, Adams reproaches him for making a comparison between that which is designed to do good and that which is not. The bookseller rejoins with an unsentimental statement of the laws of the market, and his own ethos for executing that law: "[F]or my part, the Copy that sells best, will be always the best Copy in my Opinion; I am no Enemy to Sermons but because they don't sell: for I would as soon print one of *Whitfield's*, as any Farce whatever" (80–81). This bookseller has disciplined himself into becoming a neutral, and therefore efficient, conductor of the judgment of that ultimate arbiter of what's "best," that is, the market.

How does Fielding contrive to get an appeal of this market-based judgment against the sermons Adams would impart to his would-be reader? First, Fielding writes in a mixed form of narrative that includes diverting characters and surprising adventures. However, although making this concession to popular taste, he also sets out to elevate his reader by including within his entertainment just the sort of improving sermons on charity (233–235) or resignation to loss, calculated "for the instruction and improvement of the reader" (264), that Adams himself might have published if a bookseller had accepted them. Finally, in order to defend the efficacy of this mixed form of entertainment, Fielding develops a critical discourse that will teach readers to comprehend and judge what he is doing in *Joseph Andrews*. Understanding the reader's radical freedom to read or not read, and thus the highly circumscribed nature of the narrator's own critical authority, Fielding cannot be an authoritative critic of his own text, except as a goad and provocation to the reader. Instead, the strains of criticism that the narrator mixes into the novel—the prefatory discussion of the history of narrative, the account of the value of biographical examples, the mediating role of the market, the "mysterious" uses of dividing his text into parts, and the interdependent relation between audience, poet, and player—all suggest that within *Joseph Andrews*, the Court of Criticism Fielding was to set up six years later in his *Jacobite's Journal* (no. 6 [January 9, 1748]) is actually already in session. In *Joseph Andrews*, the broader social stakes of licensing entertainment become explicit. By inscribing criticism into fiction, Fielding not only develops an account of the type of writing he is offering with *Joseph Andrews*, he also provokes readers into becoming critics in their own right.

EXEMPLARY LIVES IN *JOSEPH ANDREWS*

In the first sentences of *Joseph Andrews*, the narrator draws back from the broad satire of *Pamela* offered in *Shamela*. Instead, he offers what appears to be a straight defense of exemplary "Lives in general," through the automatic effect of examples on specific readers: "It is a trite but true Observation, that Examples work more forcibly on the Mind than Precepts: And if this be just in what is odious and blameable, it is more strongly so in what is amiable and praise-worthy. Here Emulation most effectually operates upon us, and inspires our Imitation in an irresistible manner. A good Man therefore is a standing Lesson to all his Acquaintance, and of far greater use in that narrow Circle than a good Book" (17).

The automatic, imitation-inducing effect of novels is the dread of the antinovel discourse but the engine for Richardson's elevation of novel reading. Here, Fielding apparently embraces the effort to place positive examples—such as Joseph, Adams, and Fanny—before his reader. This has been an axiom of Fielding criticism. But there are subtle hints of countercurrents to this project. This passage begins its praise of examples with the words, "It is a trite but true Observation"; and if a "good Man" is of "far greater use" "to all his Acquaintance" than a "good Book," then why bother writing books like this one? Is it only to reach a wider circle of influence? When the narrator describes books that spread "amiable Pictures" to readers who do not know the "Originals," a certain implausibility clings to his condescending descriptions. Jack the Giant Killer, Guy of Warwick, and other chapbook heroes hardly seem calculated to accomplish *Pamela's* program of "sow[ing] the Seeds of Virtue in Youth . . . [so] Delight is mixed with instruction, and the reader is almost as much improved as entertained" (18). Finally, the narrator's discussion of the modern histories of

Colley Cibber and Pamela is much too gentle and appreciative to be anything but ironic. This veiled irony opens an ambiguity as to what Fielding's narrator is offering with this history. But the narrator's reticence about criticizing *Pamela* is essential if Fielding is to retrace his steps backward from the comprehensive indictment mustered in *Shamela* and use *Pamela* as an intertextual support for *Joseph Andrews*.

To secure a graft to *Pamela*, Fielding's own history is then offered, in a passage of finely balanced equivocation, as an instance of the positive moral effects of reading *Pamela*: "The authentic History with which I now present the public, is an Instance of the great Good that Book is likely to do, and of the Prevalence of Example which I have just observed: since it will appear that it was by keeping the excellent Pattern of his Sister's Virtues before his Eyes, that Mr. *Joseph Andrews* was chiefly enabled to preserve his Purity in the midst of such great Temptations" (19–20).

The narrator presents his story as the case history of the response of a reader of *Pamela*. But notice the qualifiers with which the narrator hedges around the claim that the brother's emulous desire to imitate his sister's "Pattern" of "Virtue" enables him to "preserve his Purity": *Pamela* is only "likely" to do "great Good"; and it only "appears" that Pamela's example allows Joseph to preserve his purity. When we get to the story proper, we find much more than Pamela's example protecting him from "temptations," and the temptations don't appear nearly so "great" as this passage claims. The reading that follows shows that this introductory defense of exemplary lives is provisionally asserted not to offer an alternative object of emulation, but instead to overthrow the whole attempt to induce imitation through good examples. The action of *Joseph Andrews* suggests that examples fail, and thus reading the behavior of others no less than reading modern entertainment needs to become critical and reflective rather than emulous or automatic. Because of the ways in which Fielding's narrative of Joseph's history exceed the life of a reader who would imitate Pamela's account of her virtue, this history displaces the genre of the exemplary life and develops an alternative to its educational project. According to Fielding's perspective, the greatest "good" *Pamela* will do is to provoke the writing of its replacement and sibling text: *Joseph Andrews*.

In order for readers to become suspicious of the examples offered by Richardson, Cibber, and others, Fielding's text seeks to develop a critically aware reader. To promote the practice of the critical faculty, Fielding incorporates into *Joseph Andrews* several different kinds of "lives" to augment and reflect back upon the narrator's "life" of his principal characters. Thus by reading the lives of Leonora, Mr. Wilson, and Betty the chambermaid, the reader can become a critically aware reader of Fielding's "authentic" history of Joseph Andrews and Parson Adams. In introducing the history of Leonora, the female narrator tells her stagecoach audience she "only wished their Entertainment might make amends for the Company's Attention" (102). This is the economic exchange that subtends all entertainment: in return for the pleasure it might bring, the audience makes the expenditure of energy needed to pay attention. The banter and groans during this narrative offer glimpses of the positive identification and critical antagonism storytelling provokes. When the story is interrupted by a stop for food, Adams is disappointed, for his "Ears were the most hungry Part about him . . . being . . . of an insatiable Curiosity"; however, he does not wish success "to a Lady of so inconstant a Disposition" (118). Thus he becomes a model for the proper consumption of entertainment on the market.

Leonora's life is told in explicit imitation of the novels of amorous intrigue. Fielding labels the chapter in which the story begins with the title "The History of Leonora, or the Unfortunate Jilt." It seems to allude to such novels as Behn's *Fair Jilt* (1688) and *The Unfortunate Happy Lady* (1698), and Haywood's *City Jilt* (1726). Here, Fielding both imitates and deviates from the manner of Cervantes, who incorporates into a tavern scene in *Don Quixote* a communal reading of the manuscript of a novel of amorous intrigue entitled "the novel of the impertinent curiosity." Cervantes' novel-within-a-novel recounts the bizarre complications that develop when a jealous husband (Anselmo) convinces his best friend (Lothario) to test the virtue of his wife (Camilla). Featuring the baroque plotting and ingenious counterplotting for which Spanish novellas were famous, and which Behn incorporates into *Love Letters*, Cervantes' novella has the qualities of an antithetical "set piece," embedded within a novel (*Don Quixote*) of a radically different tone, style, and ethos. By contrast, Fielding effaces the alterity of the interpolated narrative by having one of the ladies in the stagecoach offer an oral account of an "unfortunate" "woman." Although this anonymous narrator tells her story in a mannered "romantic" account (Hunter, *Occasional Form*, 158), the moral of the story is fully compatible with the dominant narrative of *Joseph Andrews*.

Leonora, Horatio, and Bellarmine are characters whose ideas of undying love, elaborate formal address, vanity in fashion, and proclivity for intrigue derive from the novels they have obviously consumed. While the "History of Leonora" suggests that there is something fundamentally self-centered about those who imbibe these fictions and seek to apply them to their own lives with an air of grandiloquence, the human qualities of decency (in Horatio), selfish vanity (in Leonora, her aunt, and Bellarmine), and miserliness (in Leonora's father) are all their own, and merely receive their forms of expression from the novels they have read. Leonora's scheming with her aunt to shift her affections from Horatio to Bellarmine is fully compatible with the scheming of Shamela and Syrena Tricksey (in *Anti-Pamela*) with their mothers to catch the best match. The barbs at the novels of amorous intrigue are narrowly directed at Horatio's elaborate conceit in proposing to Leonora, at the extravagance of the letters the young lovers exchange, and at the romantic fustian of Bellarmine's address. These styles of speech and writing help support unnatural emotions and unwise actions.

In addition to the interpolated, semi-autonomous stories of Leonora and Wilson, Fielding also offers his readers a more journalistic analytic species of biography. When Betty the chambermaid is caught with Mr. Tow-wouse by Mrs. Tow-wouse in a posture "it is not necessary at present to take any farther Notice of" (88), the narrator goes through a flashback and analysis of the character of one who responds very differently than Pamela does to the sexual importunities of her master, Mr. B. By describing the many temptations that come to those who are pretty and must "endure the ticklish Situation of a Chamber-maid at an Inn" (86), by recounting Betty's several sexual indiscretions in a tone of worldly banter, and by reporting the frequent attentions she had withstood from her master, Mr. Tow-wouse, the narrator contextualizes Betty's lapse. After this review, the narrative moves into the present to describe the "extraordinary Liking" she had recently contracted for Joseph, and his firm rejection, upon this very day, of her favors (87). Then the narrator recounts the unlucky coincidence that brings Betty to her master's bedroom just moments after being spurned by the Joseph: "In this Perturbation of Spirit, it accidentally occurred to her Memory, that her Master's Bed was not made, she therefore went directly to his Room; where he *happened at that time* to be engaged at his Bureau" (88, italics mine). When Tow-wouse renews his attentions, "the vanquished Fair-One, whose Passions were already raised, and which were not so whimsically capricious that one Man only could lay them, though perhaps, she would have rather preferred that one: The vanquished Fair-One quietly submitted, I say, to her Master's Will . . ." (88). In a defense of Betty that is finally casuistical, convergent factors are piled into parallel clauses so as to build a chain of circumstances that appears irresistible.

"The History of Betty the Chambermaid" offers yet one more rewriting of Pamela's story. Betty's essentially good nature—before Adams arrives, she is the only one in the Tow-wouse establishment who helps Joseph in his weakened condition—separates her from Shamela or Leonora or Haywood's Syrena. Betty's "history" invites the reader to imagine some-thing the heuristic moral polarities of Richardson's novel discourage: that there are persons in the world like Betty whose morals are neither rigor-ously chaste nor licentiously depraved. Betty is a prototype for the "mixed characters," such as Tom Jones and Mrs. Waters, for which Fielding will offer a systematic defense in his next novel (*Tom Jones*, X:i). By offering the reader various examples of not-so-exemplary lives, Fielding attempts to instill a critically informed sense of the relation between the moral content of a biography and the form or style with which it is told. Thus Fielding develops his counsel to the unwary, overly enthusiastic readers of *Pamela*: before one accepts an account of another's character, and before one takes that life as an example to imitate, one had better be alert to the way in which it is told.

INIMITABLE CHARACTERS

In choosing to write *Joseph Andrews* "in the manner of the Cervantes," Fielding was doing more than following his personal taste or his artistic muse—he was exploiting a proven winner on the British print market. Jerome Beasley demonstrates that *Don Quixote* was a work "whose fame exceeded that of any other single work, domestic or foreign," with at least ten English translations between 1700 and 1740, and eight more in the 1740s (10). *Don Quixote* was not only an aesthetically sophisticated model for prose narrative (with preface, divisions, and elaborate plot structure), it also cleaved to the purpose of entertaining the reader, and offered an acute critique of the dangers of absorptive reading. In all these ways, Cervantes' classic offered a model for writing an alternative to Richardson's naïve and inadvertent vehicle for entertainment.

Cervantes seems to be the first early modern novelist to offer a nuanced account of absorptive reading. The eponymous hero, spurning all other ordi-nary activities and calculations of value, has given himself over to an obses-sional reading of romances: "[Don Quixote] addicted himself to the read-ing of books of chivalry, which he perused with such rapture and application, that he not only forgot the pleasures of the chace, but also utterly neglected the management of his estate . . . [and he] sold many good acres of Terra Firma, to purchase books of knight-errantry . . ." (Cervantes, *Adventures of Don Quixote*, 28). By selling firm land to buy errant books, Don Quixote feeds his habit. Addictive reading subordinates all other activities to itself: "So eager and entangled was our Hidalgo in this kind of history, that he would often read from morning to night, and from night to morning again, without interruption" (ibid., 29). Teased by books that conclude "with the promise to finish that interminable adventure" in the next volume of the series, Don Quixote "was more than once inclined to seize the quill, with a view of performing what was left undone" (ibid.). The difficulty of breaking out of the seriality of reading results from the way in which the absorbed reader wills his own subjection to the text that "entangles." The reader's identification with the hero in the text is so complete that he seeks to become that hero: "he was seized with the strangest whim that ever entered the brain of a madman. This was no other, than a full persuasion, that it was highly expedient and necessary, not only for his own honor, but also for the good of the public, that he should profess knight-errantry, and rise through the world in arms, to seek adventures, and conform in all points to the practice of those itinerant heroes, whose exploits he had read" (30). A literal mimicry, which wishes to conform "in all points" to what is read, completes the text by an act or performance that elides the distinction between reading and writing, consumption and re-production.

In spite of the satire at the expense of absorptive reading in *Don Quixote*, there is at least one way in which the reader of Cervantes' novel must be like its hero. By beginning his text with an address to the "idle reader" (ibid., 22), Cervantes summons a reader who is not constrained to read through any religious, political, or pedagogical imperatives, but who instead reads during an "idle" moment, for entertainment. In both Cervantes and Fielding, novels are part of "free reading"; in both, the readers solicited are critical and independent, rather than mindlessly absorbed by the characters put before them.

Joseph and Parson Adams are not shaped to be taken by readers as exemplary objects of identification. In fact, in two divergent ways, they are antiexemplary. Presented to the reader as a real character, Adams is exceptional, one of kind, stamped out to look and feel distinct. As an original, he is inimitable. This kind of character (in both senses of that word) has a literary genealogy: Don Quixote, Sir Roger de Coverly (of the *Spectator*), and Parson Abraham Adams are three vigorous, independent, middle-aged males who are whimsical in their conduct and well-stocked with ticks and repeatable traits. Not merely indifferent to the praise or blame of others, they are almost unaware of what others think of them. Intent upon doing things in their own distinct fashion, they elude modern systems for regularizing character—bureaucracy, psychology, and public opinion. Incapable of indirection or disguise, they have a boyish innocence and an endearing honesty that is menaced by modern culture. In all these ways, they function as touchstones of authenticity and offer an alternative to the unconscious mimicry and ductile characterlessness of the modern citizen. This hyper-readable character becomes a stock feature of certain types of novelistic entertainment (from Uncle Toby of *Tristram Shandy* and Lismahago of *Humphrey Clinker* to the many characters in Dickens' novels). If Parson Adams is finally too simple and too readable to incite any reader's emulous desire, Joseph is inimitable for another reason. At the beginning of the novel, Joseph is not fully formed and, as many critics have noted, he only acquires a certain character gradually, over the course of the novel, through his adventures (Hunter, *Occasional Form*, 113).

TRICKING THE READER

In "The Education of the Reader in Fielding's *Joseph Andrews*," Raymond Stephanson argues that "Fielding's active narrative concern with the education of the reader is indeed new in the history of fiction" (257). Stephanson demonstrates the many ways in which Fielding subjects readers to education, not merely by foregrounding their responses, but by tricking them into the uncomfortable recognition that their own responses often echo the satirized weaknesses of the characters. He also shows how Fielding's project—of making readers self-conscious about the act of reading and distrustful of their own powers and tendencies—becomes more overt and explicit in *Tom Jones*. While I agree with central elements of this account, I take issue with the grounding assumption of this analysis, an assumption common to a broad range of Fielding criticism: that Fielding hovers over his text and its fictive and actual readers, knows what these readers must be taught, and so shapes his plot to expose them to their own incapacities. Instead, I take Fielding to understand that each reader must assume his or her role as an unguided critic of both the story and his or her own practice of reading, and he writes *Joseph Andrews* in order to promote this shift of authority from author to reader. His critical conception of this kind of fiction and the concepts of author and reader it entails reach their fullest articulation in the essays of *Tom Jones*.

I can begin to suggest the unconventionality of this educational program by tracing how Fielding's narrator presents Joseph's first life test. Following Joseph's removal with his family to London is the first detailed episode of *Joseph Andrews*: Lady Booby's attempted seduction of Joseph. These are the most discussed chapters of a much-discussed book. By offering an explicit parody and gender reversal of Pamela's situation, this episode seems to call out for the critics' exegetical activity. These scenes, which Joseph, like Pamela, describes in letters, test Joseph's capacities as an interpreter. At the end of this arch of the action, when Joseph is dismissed from Lady Booby's service and begins his journey from London, the narrator develops the analogy between reading books and reading characters, and warns us that neither is so easy to see through as may first appear: "It is an observation sometimes made, that to indicate our Idea of a simple Fellow, we say, *He is easily to be seen through*: Nor do I believe it a more improper Denotation of a simple Book. Instead of applying this to any particular Performance, we chuse rather to remark the contrary in this History, where the Scene opens itself by small degrees, and he is a sagacious Reader who can see two Chapters before him" (48).

This passage introduces the narrative surprise—that upon leaving Lady Booby's service, Joseph goes not to his parents or his sister Pamela (to whom he had written to inquire about jobs for him), but instead to the neighborhood of Sir Thomas's country seat, so as to see his true love, Fanny. With this revelation, the narrator makes good on the claim that neither his book nor its central character is so "easily to be seen through" as at first appeared. In fact, the reader may feel tricked.

If one then rereads the earlier chapters with this information in mind, the issue of reading characters and texts becomes vexed and complex in a fashion that not only cuts against the practice of *Pamela*, but puts in question the notion that any reader of *Joseph Andrews*, whatever his or her acuity, can learn to read through appearances.[7] Thus each of the four successive phases of the trial of Joseph's virtue gives us only fragments toward a disclosure of his motives and character. The following is a reconstruction of what the reader may surmise about Joseph at each point in the action:

1. When Lady Booby uses innuendo and touching to turn Joseph on, Joseph's response is confused and ambiguous. He appears not to comprehend the signs of her seduction. The reader may surmise that this is the only way he can recall his mistress Lady Booby to the propriety she should observe without making her meanings explicit and embarrassing her with an open rejection. In her anger, Lady Booby reads through his obtuseness: "your pretended Innocence cannot impose on me" (30).

2. In Joseph's account in a letter to Pamela, he narrates the episode so we see that he correctly interpreted Lady Booby's signs of amorous interest: "she ordered me to sit down by her Bed-side, when she was naked in Bed; and she held my Hand, and talked exactly as a Lady does to her Sweetheart in a Stage-Play, which I have seen in *Covent-Garden*, while she wanted him to be no better than he should be" (31). This cogent reading of

7. For a useful summary of the tendency of Fielding critics to emphasize the epistemological problem of reading character, see Campbell, *Natural Masques*, 120–122.

Lady Booby suggests that, within the communication circuit of the familiar letter, Joseph can recount Lady Booby's desire for him, his own refusal, and his supposition that he may be dismissed. However, at the same time, Joseph omits to mention his love for Fanny, declaring that if dismissed he will return to Lady Booby's country seat, "if it be only to see Parson Adams, who is the best man in the world" (32).

3. After the erotic attack upon Joseph by Mrs. Slipslop and the debates about firing Joseph conducted between mistress and chambermaid, Joseph is compelled to appear before Lady Booby for her final assault. When she is scandalized by Joseph's invocation of his "virtue," Joseph counters by wondering why "my Virtue must be subservient to [your] Pleasures" (41). When Lady Booby releases Joseph from scruples by appealing to conventional societal indulgence on the issue of male chastity, Joseph grounds his exceptionalism in his reading of Pamela's letters: "[but] that Boy is the Brother of *Pamela*, and would be ashamed, that the Chastity of his Family, which is preserved in her, should be stained in him. If there are such Men as your Ladyship mentions, I am sorry for it, and I wish they had an Opportunity of reading over those Letters, which my Father hath sent me of my Sister *Pamela's*, nor do I doubt but such an Example would amend them" (41). Pushed into responding by Lady Booby's sexual harassment, Joseph's words become an advertisement for *Pamela* and its program for imitative reading of exemplary characters. In the narrator's aside, Joseph is protected from any doubts the reader may have begun to harbor about his "Understanding" of the "Drift of his Mistress": "and indeed that he did not discern it sooner, the Reader will be pleased to apply to an Unwillingness in him to discover what he must condemn in her as a Fault" (46). Apparently a loyal servant and good fellow, Joseph is predisposed to think the best of even Lady Booby. Or so our narrator tells us.

4. Lady Booby's dismissal of him does not bring Joseph's character into the open. In his second letter to Pamela, Joseph hides his true motive. He misinterprets the reasons for his successful resistance of Lady Booby's importunities by attributing it to the education given him by Parson Adams and the example of Pamela: "Indeed, it is owing entirely to his excellent Sermons and Advice, together with your Letters, that I have been able to resist a Temptation, which he says no Man complies with, but he repents in this World, or is damned for it in the next" (46). Entirely? Joseph adds an enticing ambiguity when he writes: "I am glad she turned me out of the Chamber as she did: for I had once almost forgotten every word Parson *Adams* had ever said to me. . . . but, I hope I shall copy your Example, and that of *Joseph*, my Name's-sake; and maintain my Virtue against all Temptations" (46–47).

Critics have noted that the different value culture ascribes to male and female chastity makes Pamela's male sibling's claim to virtue oddly inappropriate. Joseph's zealous promotion of Pamela's letters means that Joseph appears (only for this short interval of the action) as a particularly automatic and witless imitator of his sister's example. At this Shamela-esque moment of *Joseph Andrews*, a Richardsonian moralism sweeps into Joseph's language. Perhaps most crucially, the more natural reason for Joseph Andrew's resistance to Lady Booby—his love for Fanny—is withheld by Joseph and/or the narrator. This lag in the disclosure of the most emotionally satisfying reason for Joseph's resistance to seduction is either (a) known to him but hidden from Lady Booby and his sister (but such a possibility cuts against the frankness Joseph displays through the rest of the novel), or (b) hidden from Joseph himself as an unconscious and therefore involuntary disguise. However, we are not given any indications of Joseph's duplicity or his overcoming of any deep psychic resistance to acknowledging his love for Fanny. Upon turning the page to chapter XI, which is entitled "Of several new matters not expected," we find the narrator indulging in a certain mock solemnity in telling us why Joseph does not direct his journey toward either his parents or his sister: "Be it known then, that in the same Parish where [Lady Booby's country] Seat stood, there lived a young Girl . . ."(48). We therefore need to develop an alternative account of how and why Joseph's best motive for resisting Lady Booby is hidden from both Joseph and the reader by the narrator.

The reader of these scenes has every reason to feel tricked. Joseph's response cannot be understood through his explanations—by his affiliation with Pamela or his enthusiastic endorsement of her letters—yet his accounts of motive are apparently allowed to stand by the narrator. The narrator's insistence upon the opacity of both Joseph's character and his own book means that Joseph's exchange with Lady Booby is initially presented as an apparently complex referent, only to gradually metamorphose into a conscious performance by the narrator. In *Pamela*, Richardson strives to correlate Pamela's speech to her master with her letters to her parents so that together they deliver a truthful account of virtue; instead, as we have seen, he produces a text that involuntarily lapses into disguise. In *Joseph Andrews*, although the characters appear more readable and superficial, they are in fact mediated in their appearance to us by the interposition of a designing author/narrator who subverts efforts at full disclosure. The narrator's premeditated disguise of the main character (Joseph) frees this character from the charge of deceit, but also means that the text eschews the attempt—so evident in *Pamela*—to produce a relationship between referent and representation that has the character of verisimilitude. Instead, *Joseph Andrews* presents itself as a consciously contrived performance.

In *Joseph Andrews* the narrator often declares the narrative to be incomplete. This incompleteness is sometimes the result of the narrator's solicitude for the reader's entertainment. At one point in the action it is reported that Adams, Joseph, and Fanny "had a great deal of innocent Chat, pretty enough; but as possibly, it would not be very entertaining to the Reader, we shall hasten to the Morning" (159–160). At other times, the narrator describes the limits of his own knowledge in rather coy terms— for example, in not describing what Fanny and Joseph might have been doing while Adams was visiting the hog farmer Minister Trulliber: "They were so far from thinking his Absence long, as he had feared they would, that they never once miss'd or thought of him. Indeed, I have been often assured by both, that they spent these Hours in a most delightful Conversation: but as I never could prevail on either to relate it, so I cannot communicate it to the Reader" (168). Here the curiosity of the reader is piqued not only by the sexual associations of the eighteenth-century word "conversation," but also by the narrator's curiosity, which he "never could prevail" on Fanny or Joseph to satisfy. Alternatively, the active reader may suspect that the narrator intentionally withholds from us what Fanny and Joseph were doing during Adams' breakfast with Trulliber. Here Fielding reminds us that novels do not provide a seamless, complete account of an alternative reality, and shouldn't be imagined to do so. Novels solicit an alternative world necessarily fragmented by a narrative that is necessarily partial.

The essay "Of Division in Authors" that begins Book II of *Joseph Andrews* suggests other ways in which Fielding subverts the expectation that there is a documentary relation between narrative and what is being narrated. Reveling in his own power, Fielding's narrator celebrates the "mystery" of division as part of the "Science of *Authoring*" (90). Deflecting the suspicion that division into books and chapters is simply a vain way to "swell our Works to a much larger Bulk" (89), and appealing to the precedents of Homer, Virgil, and Milton, Fielding's narrator defends his systems of division as preferable to the financially cynical attempt to increase the profitability of a work by "publishing by Numbers, an Art now brought to such Perfection, that even Dictionaries are divided and exhibited piece-meal to the Public" (91). Fielding clearly sees his practice of "division," which rather closely follows the example of *Don Quixote*, as superior to the relatively shapeless flow of novels (like those of Defoe and

Richardson) that use the letter, journal, or memoir as their narrative vehicles. However, he resists making the claims that critics have made for his divisions ever since: he does not claim that his book and chapter divisions imply an expressive mimesis of the object of narration, or some truth about that object. Nor does Fielding claim for the resultant "form" of his novel a conscious aesthetic shaping (which, for example, Henry James argues for his own novels in his prefaces to the New York edition of his work). Instead, the narrator, in a characteristic turn toward the reader, treats his division into books and chapters as a device to introduce a two-way communication between author and reader. First, division into books enables the periodic introduction of critical essays on novel writing (such as this one on division). Second, chapter divisions are useful in keeping the readers' places should they, "after half an Hour's Absence," "forget where they left off" (90). Finally, the author recognizes and sanctions the readers' freedom by offering chapter titles which, "like inscriptions over the gates of inns . . . [inform] the reader what entertainment he is to expect," so readers can pass over a chapter "without any injury to the whole" (90). Division becomes one more way for Fielding to slow down readers. He compares chapter divisions to the traveler's taking "Refreshment" at "Stages, where, in long Journeys, the Traveler stays some time to repose himself, and consider of what he hath seen in the Parts he hath already past through" (89–90). In this way, Fielding promotes acts of reflection that will militate against the headlong rush to consume absorptive narratives. Later, in the twentieth century, critics of film worried about its power to enthrall spectators in hurried acts of consumption that render self-reflection impossible (Benjamin, *Illuminations*, 238).

Although the narrator poses as the reader's taskmaster, the educational project he advances with so much ostentation is in fact spurious, always exceeded by the confusions the novel involves its readers in. Since its action is inimitable and its characters are not exemplary models of behavior, the readers of *Joseph Andrews* are thrown back upon their own resources and insights. Readers are, however, given a very useful species of negative knowledge—that one cannot master the direction of one's life with virtue or discernment—and certain highly ironic negative lessons, like not trusting one's teacher, including the narrator of this text. Like the good teacher Nietzsche describes in "Schopenhauer as Educator," Fielding's narrator knows that most of what readers will learn will be something they are ready to learn, because they already half know it, so the text Fielding writes can only function as a catalyst that induces a certain re-cognition.

A STAGED WORLD IN (DEEP) DISGUISE

The contested reception of *Pamela*, with its competitive efforts to take control of the textual body of a hit, gives the terrain of media culture some of the visual coherence of a proscenium stage, with its entrances and exits, flops and hits, public celebrity, and contrived efforts behind the scenes by anonymous authors. Those who engage this debate find themselves negotiating the terms according to which a performance will be believed. The battle between "pamelists" and "anti-pamelists" involves two senses of the word "performance": whether Pamela's defense of her virtue is an action or an act, and whether *Pamela* should be taken as an action to emulate or a mere performance. If *Pamela* succeeds in absorbing its readers by successfully suppressing the difference between the author behind the scenes and the onstage writer Pamela, then *Shamela* is contrived to arrest spectator identification by removing the partition between onstage spectacle and offstage contrivance. If, in writing *Shamela*, Fielding attempts to close down the antitheatrical performance called *Pamela*, then *Joseph Andrews* is Fielding's attempt to develop an alternative "act" in the theater of media culture.

In *Joseph Andrews*, Fielding accepts the pervasive inevitability of theater and sets out to cure the naive absorption of *Pamela*'s reader by intensifying the theatricality of writing. This strategy helps justify the compositional choices I have discussed in the previous sections of this chapter. By foregrounding the roles of author and reader, producer and spectator as they complicate and interpenetrate the mimetic space of narrative diegesis, by asserting the necessary incompleteness and arbitrary division of the narrative, and by making his characters oddly exceptional and therefore anti-exemplary, Fielding gives *Joseph Andrews* some of the features of a staged performance. Rather than encouraging the unmediated reader identification sought by *Pamela* or the ironic distance achieved by satire, "lives"—like those of Leonora or Betty the chambermaid or Joseph or Parson Adams—are positioned as separate "texts" where they can be subject to critical inspection by the reader. Characters no longer resemble freestanding beings, but instead appear as effects of narrative rhetoric and authorial manipulation. Fielding gives his novelistic entertainment some of the "staged" "provisionality of social forms" described by Paulson (*Beautiful, Novel, and Strange*, 59), and these are evident in the transactions within the novel.

Since the eighteenth century, the opponents and partisans of consistent illusionistic styles of novelistic mimesis have praised and damned Fielding's novel for being theatrical. Thus, for example, authorial stagecraft puts the central characters Joseph and Fanny into a deep disguise, where their identity is unknown not only to readers, but even to themselves. However, the generic codes of romance solicited by *Joseph Andrews* encourage the expectation of a final unveiling of characters. Many critics accept the genial but wily narrator as a figure for the author who, making himself present to the gaze of the spectator, will be the ultimate performer of this text. Thus, in *The Art of the Novel*, Henry James praises this narrator as having enough "amplitude of reflection" (68) to make up for a lack on that score in Fielding's characters, and I have already noted that Ronald Paulson puts his critical faith in this figure. However, it is the thesis of my reading of *Joseph Andrews* that Fielding, in spite of encouraging reader faith in the narrator, finally frustrates it. The narrator is not the responsible father-originator of the text, but a trickster illusionist who withdraws from the text; "he" can't be fixed or located. We end up with a performance without a performer, a "great creation" without a creator, a device for instruction and entertainment without an identifiable instructor or entertainer. Through this absence, Fielding exploits the new formations of reading that the *Pamela* media event helped to precipitate: he enfranchises the reader as the ultimately responsible agent in the consumption of entertainment.

Here a cautionary word is called for. In a recent collection entitled *Performativity and Performance*, the editors Andrew Parker and Eve Sedgwick warn that although a fruitful convergence in contemporary philosophy and theater studies has made the term "performative" common and pivotal to both disciplines, the word hardly could be said to mean the same thing in both. Indeed, eighteenth-century studies suggests that the terms "performance" and "theatrical" are open to expansive application. Fielding's careful development of the critical and didactic resources of the concept of theatricality in his own journalistic and novelistic writing begins with an astute awareness of culture's expansion of the usage of the trope of theater to interpret social life: "Stage and Scene are by common Use grown as familiar to us, when we speak of Life in general, as when we confine ourselves to dramatic Performances" (*Tom Jones*, VII: i, 323). Fielding's development in *Joseph Andrews* of what he calls (in an essay from *Tom Jones*) the "comparison between the world and the stage" does not imply that drama is the pivotal source for Fielding's novels. "Theatricality," like "realism," has a plurality of different practices and critical determinations; thus, to say that Fielding has recourse to a certain theatrical foregrounding of the narrator to interrupt the absorption he detects in *Pamela* does not mean that drama becomes the privileged critical coordinate for his fiction.[8] In fact, the distinct style of the narrator who recounts the action of *Joseph Andrews*, and who occasionally interrupts the action to write essays, is perfected in "The Champion," a decade after Fielding had established himself as a playwright. So Fielding's recourse to an explicitly theatrical mode of address to the reader allows him to link the traditional purposes of theater—providing entertainment—with the didactic resources of a time-honored metaphor of social life as a theater.

In chapter 1 of Book VII of *Tom Jones*, entitled "A Comparison between the World and the Stage," Fielding rewrites the classical topos of "the world as a stage" as developed by Epictetus. Since any judgment will pivot upon the excellence of the performance rather than upon the greatness of the role, Epictetus emphasizes the moral imperative of every person to perform well the life role given him by the poet (i.e., God). In Fielding's revision, it is not God who judges the performance; rather, it is Fielding's readers, as spectators of the world, who assume this role and are coached by Fielding to be suspicious: it is wisest to look at "the larger Part of Mankind in the Light of Actors, as personating Characters no more their own, and to which, in Fact, they have no better Title, than the Player hath to be in Earnest thought the King or Emperor whom he represents" (I: i, 324). In "An Essay on the Knowledge of the Characters of Men," published in the *Miscellanies* only fourteen months after *Joseph Andrews*, Fielding elaborates this account of a social reality invaded by theater, and therefore treacherous to the unsuspecting: "Thus while the crafty and designing part of mankind, consulting only their own separate advantage, endeavor to maintain one constant imposition on the others, the whole world becomes a vast masquerade, where the greatest part appear disguised under false vizors and habits; a very few only showing their own faces, who become, by so doing, the astonishment and ridicule of all the rest" (155). This passage suggests the didactic potential of his use of the world-as-stage trope in his essays and novels. If the world is like a stage (where hypocrisy dupes the unsuspecting), and if readers could learn to apprehend the principles of theatrical

8. The sources of the distinct style of narrative fiction Fielding began to write with *Joseph Andrews* are various. Critics have laid emphasis upon journalism (Davis, *Factual Fictions*), satire (Paulson, *Satire and the Novel*), epic (Bender, *Imagining the Penitentiary*, 146), romance (Miller, *Tom Jones and the Romance Tradition*), irony (Levine, *Henry Fielding and the Dry Mock*), the anti-romance *Don Quixote* (Bakhtin, *Dialogic Imagination*), drama (Campbell, *Natural Masques*), and a blend of several of these (see works by Paulson, Bender, Hunter, and Campbell).

entertainment, then they could protect themselves from being abused by cunning. While "An Essay on the Knowledge of the Characters of Men" offers itself as a practical guide, *Joseph Andrews* features a host of dissembling characters who test the reading skills of Joseph and Adams, as well as those of readers outside the text. But at the end of the essay, Fielding concedes that while an artful hypocrisy knows how to play on the vanity and self-love of others, there is no sure defense against duplicity. The narrator of the novels offers himself as one "admitted behind the scenes of this great theater of nature" in order to teach the difficulty of knowing character: by putting his characters in deep disguise, by misguiding rather than guiding the reader, the narrator would stagger self-confidence and slow down the reader's interpretation.

In my reading of *Pamela* (see chapter 5), I showed how the text uses the disguised performance and the detoured letter as strategies to get meaning to its proper destination. I noted that a certain wavering and displacement of meaning gets built into the letter and into Pamela's country dress: every mark implies its re-marking in the space of reception toward which it is written but which it cannot control. If the reader's guide to *Pamela* attempts to refuse the insight that all behavior has a performative structure, then Fielding's theatrical framing of his texts offers a way to let performativity and the social into his text and acknowledge the crucial power and freedom of the reader. Fielding's strategic recourse to the world-as-stage trope—wherein every performance is inflected by the spectator it entertains, every writing is broached by the reading it invites—does not bring him any more control over his readers than Richardson had achieved with *Pamela*. Instead, through a theatrical representation of the reception of the work, Fielding produces a mise-en-scène of what befalls Pamela's inscription of herself (and Richardson's inscription of her) as virtue. To the extent that Richardson promotes a radical mimicry—Pamela's virtue and truthfulness provides a model for what readers could imitate in their lives—Richardson's text must suppress the performative dimensions, the disguise and detoured communication that enable his own fiction. These are precisely the terms that Fielding brings to the fore in *Joseph Andrews* through the metaphor of the world as a stage. By weaving theatricality into the rhythms and semiotic systems of *Joseph Andrews*, the novel will be viewed as one views the "stage" of a theater: not as "the same" but instead "like" (and thus always at a distance from) the (actual) world.

By aligning novelistic narrative with theater, Fielding can welcome the way his novel effects a dissemination rather than an insemination of meaning. Instead of the one-to-one familiar correspondence Richardson had envisioned for *Pamela*, with the ideal of the reader's normative response (for example, sympathy for the suffering heroine), Fielding offers another paradigm for communication—something closer to a "broadcast model," where there is one sender text, but there are many diverse sites and modalities of reception. Thus, in *Tom Jones*, when Tom takes Partridge to a production of *Hamlet* with Mrs. Miller, Partridge becomes fearfully absorbed in the illusion of the ghost on the stage, while Tom and Mrs. Miller exhibit the critical sophistication of practiced theatergoers (XVI: v). Also in *Tom Jones*, Fielding demonstrates his narrative's dispersal of meaning by imagining the diverse responses of his readers to Black George's theft of Tom's £500. The narrator schematizes reception through the four different seating areas of the theater (the upper and lower galleries, the pit, and the boxes), and the sorts of critical response the occupants of each might be supposed to have (vociferation, demand for punishment, indifference, and so on). However, with a printed text, the dispersal of both the time and the space of the performance venue means that reception is still more diffuse and various, such that the author cannot control the reception he will nonetheless seek to influence. While the hyperabsorption of the reader is one of the aims of Richardson's text, the failure of that project, even among the most assiduous and loyal of his correspondents, suggests that absorption is never complete. Fielding's development of a fiction presented as theatrical in its modes of reception assumes the incompleteness of absorption in a reader who is always potentially distracted. By incorporating the dispersal of effect familiar from theatrical productions into his account of novel reading, Fielding offers a paradigm of communication that takes account of the freedom of the reader and the limits upon the authorial control of reading. This freedom, and these limits, have taken on special urgency in the print market during the reception of *Pamela*.

PERFORMING AUTHORSHIP

How is Fielding's reader, who has been schooled to be suspicious of the world as a stage, to negotiate the most theatrical aspect of *Joseph Andrews*—the narrator's act? For the enthusiasts of Fielding's writing, nothing has promoted his authority over his own texts more than the narrator's performance of the role of the "author." In this role—an apparently unmediated presentation of the author to the reader—the narrator strikes a series of different postures, all of them explicitly authorial. First, he poses as the masterful originator of a text, which though called a history and aspiring to represent truth, does so in the form of a fiction invented by the author (Davis, *Factual Fictions*, 200). In both *Joseph Andrews* and *Tom Jones* this narrator plays the role of a lawgiver who declares himself entitled to prescribe the terms of the reader's reception of his text. Thus if the author writes what is both possible and probable, and suits a character's action to his or her personality, yet also surprises the reader with what is "wonderful," the author is "then intitled to some Faith from his Reader, who is indeed guilty of critical Infidelity if he disbelieves him" (*Tom Jones*, VIII: i, 407). Finally, this "author" within the text claims to be a critic with an objectivity sufficient to define the proper critical coordinates for reading his text. He differentiates his narrative, on the one hand, from the tendentious representations of historians, and on the other, from the fanciful inventions of the novelists—"[those] Authors of immense Romances, or the modern Novel and *Atalantis* Writers; who without any Assistance from Nature or History, record Persons who never were, or will be, and Facts which never did nor possibly can happen: Whose Heroes are of their own Creation, and their Brains the Chaos whence all their Materials are collected" (*Joseph Andrews*, 187). Then, in defining his own practice, this author writes words that have launched a thousand critical discussions of *Joseph Andrews* and Fielding. These words are more than a statement of the neoclassical assumptions that underwrite his practices of representation in *Joseph Andrews*. Cast into carefully structured antithetical clauses, proffering general propositions and informal questions, mixing high and low forms of address, at once analytical and conversational, polemical and charming, Fielding's language projects an "author" few readers have been able to resist: "I describe not Men, but Manners; not an Individual, but a Species. Perhaps it will be answered, Are not the Characters then taken from Life? To which I answer in the Affirmative; nay, I believe I might aver, that I have writ little more than I have seen. The Lawyer is not only alive, but hath been so these 4000 Years, and I hope G——— will indulge his Life as many yet to come" (189).

A critic outside the text may agree or disagree with this "author's" claim: that *Joseph Andrews* pulls off a representation of a general human nature that is utterly different in kind from, and superior to, the productions of those authors such as Behn, Manley, and Haywood who form "originals from the confused heap of matter in their own brains" (188). But few would disagree that this passage offers a rhetorically skilled enactment of the synthesizing power of the author. This "author" within the text is the hero of numberless critical interpretations of Fielding developed since the laudatory pamphlet written by Francis Coventry in 1751 (Beasley, *Novels of the 1740s*, 39). In order to challenge the authority of this "author," we need to consider how he appears before us.

While most explicitly foregrounded in the essay that begins Book III of *Joseph Andrews*, the figure of the narrator as author periodically appears within the narrative proper to perform a set piece for the reader. Thus, to cite one celebrated example, when Joseph, between his two interviews with Lady Booby, draws the amorous attentions of Mrs. Slipslop, the culminating moment of the latter's attack is described in the high epic style of two Homeric similes:

> As when a hungry Tygress, who long had traversed the Woods in a fruitless search, sees within the Reach of her Claws a Lamb, she prepares to leap on her Prey; or as a voracious Pike, of immense Size, surveys through the liquid Element a Roach or Gudgeon which cannot escape her Jaws, opens them wide to swallow the little Fish: so did Mrs. *Slipslop* prepare to lay her violent amorous Hands on the poor *Joseph*, when luckily her Mistress's Bell rung, and delivered the intended Martyr from her Clutches. [33–34]

Here the excess of these two similes may express an old maid's sexual appetite and a young footman's danger. But its tongue-in-cheek exaggeration of Mrs. Slipslop's amorous violence and Joseph's near martyrdom foregrounds the author's self-consciously assumed role as the reader's entertainer. In fact, this seems to be one of those "Burlesque Imitations" promised by the author in the preface, intended for the "Entertainment" of the "Classical Reader" (4). Such a passage requires the reader to desist from reading for the plot and instead savor a bravura performance.

A measured parallelism of syntax suggests the rhetorical control of the author, whose voice is at once genial and urbane, ironic and arch. Through his performance as author, the narrator shows that he's got "attitude" and chutzpah. The narrator as "author" becomes a center which apparently stabilizes the meaning of the novel. Battestin's readings promote this "author" within the text as the ultimate performer of the narrative. But in spite of the considerable allure of this figure, there are fundamental problems with extending too much faith and authority to him. As I noted above in discussing the narrative presentation of Joseph's resistance to Lady Booby, the narrator allows the reader to be misguided; he coyly withholds while he presents; he keeps his characters in deep disguise; and he seems to enjoy teasing the reader with the specter of untoward disasters. Above all, the narrator's claim to authorial control seems to be a way in which to claim an authority over the action that he cannot finally make stand. Fielding (the historical writer behind the scenes) tempts the reader to accept the simulacrum of the author as an absolute authority, while at the same time he refuses to underwrite this figure's authority.

Fielding's play upon the authority of the author is understandable given the anarchic rivalry of print narratives within early media culture. Authorship and novel writing had not, by the early 1740s, achieved the sort of assured institutional stability they achieved later in the century (see conclusion). Fielding's performance as "author" displays the fusion of form and idea into a particular style which was, in this period, becoming a sine qua non of the legal claim to ownership of the text one had written. At the same time, the brash bluster of that performance—the need to earn the status of authorship by performing it—suggests that the claim to be an author could only be secured with a bluff.

Despite the doubts that shadow Fielding's claim to full authorial control, critics and scholars keep finding new ways to underwrite these claims. Thus, nothing could seem farther from Martin Battestin's account of the moral basis of Fielding's art than John Bender's casting of Fielding as one of the pivotal players in imagining modern systems of penitentiary surveillance, yet both critics assume Fielding's authorial mastery. However, while Battestin restores the figure of the Christian moral author to visibility as the "basis" of his art, Bender argues that Fielding's special contribution to the novel comes from the way in which the author as judge fades into two structures shaped for transparent observation of the subject: free indirect discourse and the penitentiary. By critically examining Bender's argument, I can suggest an alternative way to interpret Fielding's development of the performative dimensions of authorship. Bender follows the evolution of a narrator he characterizes as essentially "juridical," from the "good magistrate" who intervenes to restore order in *Jonathan Wild*, to the voluble, beneficent narrators of *Joseph Andrews* and *Tom Jones*, to the less obtrusive narrator of Fielding's last novel, *Amelia*, to the reform projects of his later years (such as *An Enquiry Into the Cause of the Late Increase of Robbers* [1750–1751]). In his reading of *Amelia*, Bender interprets Dr. Harrison, the energetic, lively, sententious divine who manipulates the main characters to bring about their improvement, as a vestige of a satiric and moral sensibility that belongs to an early part of the century. Dr. Harrison is, by Bender's account, a figure on his way to becoming the reforming judge and utopian reformer that Fielding himself became in his last years. By reading retroactively from reform projects that seek to imagine more effective control of a violent urbanizing population, and by describing how Fielding anticipates the construction of the panopticon—

Foucault's metonym of a disciplinary society of humans subject to power and knowledge—Bender imbues Fielding with so much authorial power that he appears sinister.

Rather than seeing Fielding's novels as producing a theatrical foregrounding of the author, Bender argues that Fielding helps achieve the author's insidious disappearance. Bender's history of the development of the idea of "transparency" allows us to grasp the arbitrariness of the conventions of novelistic narrative and reformist thought in the late eighteenth century. Through these discursive alignments of power and knowledge, one is invited to accept the premise that in both Fielding's texts and the penitentiary, "both author and beholder are absent from a representation, the objects of which are rendered as if their externals were entirely visible and their internality fully accessible" (Bender, *Imagining the Penitentiary*, 201). Although this representational convention creates the illusion of translucent immediacy, an apparent absence of mediation, it is in fact the effect of forms of architecture and a certain style of narrative, "free indirect discourse." The omniscience of the warden or guard in the panopticon is never actually realized; instead, in a fashion analogous to the novel's structure, the panopticon's architecture seeks an authority commensurate with the idea of omniscience, by forcing the inmate to imagine the possibility of an all-seeing inspector (ibid., 198). However, I would add that the transparency of object to subject in the social spheres of the novel and penitentiary is an impossible theoretical ideal of those who seek an indefinite extension of knowledge and power.[9]

Bender's reading of Fielding consistently reduces the plurality of Fielding's strategies for marshaling narrative authority in *Joseph Andrews, Tom Jones,* and *Amelia*. Bender also underestimates the ambivalence with which Fielding invests the father figures in his text. In a pattern I identified in chapters 2–4 of this study, the eclipse of the monarchy and the founding of a more democratic, market-based media culture lead to profoundly ambivalent representations of fathers and mothers in the early novels: from the lascivious fathers of *Love Letters*, the *New Atalantis*, and *Love in Excess* to the dangerously punitive mothers of *Fantomina* and *Roxana;*

9. For a fuller development of my critique of Bender, see W. Warner, "Social Power and the Novel." In a new introduction to *Tom Jones*, Bender softens the disciplinary teleology of *Imagining the Penitentiary* by linking Fielding's style of narration with the negotiation of a rational public consensus within the public sphere. In this way, Bender argues that Fielding's novels incite the existence of a reader who is ready for public-sphere exchange. (See also MacArthur's article on Beaumarchais' *Marriage of Figaro*.) However, Bender continues to downplay what I am emphasizing here: the pleasure-producing effects of entertainment.

from the ineffectual father of *Pamela* to the failed example (and non-mentor), Parson Adams. While building upon the assumption that guides Bender's reading of *Amelia*—that there is a significant affiliation between Fielding's narrators and the father figures within the narrative—I would suggest that Bender's reading misconstrues the function of the variously characterized agents of authority in Fielding's texts—Parson Adams and the Roasting Squire, Allworthy and Squire Western, and Dr. Harrison—as well as the succession of narrators and "authors" to whom Fielding gives a more or less clearly defined personality. Humanized and personified, authority is not made to inhere in a diffuse representational system. It takes the form of an agent and maker who intercedes between subject and object, between knower and known. These figures of authority—as both narrators and characters—purvey humor and violence, philosophy and practical jokes, bungled efforts at explanation, and the many moral answers that never fully serve. The narrators use the resources of Renaissance rhetoric to display a verbal wit and ethical invention that the action invariably opens to correction. Because Fielding aims to make his novel an entertainment as well as an improving test of moral wisdom, the narrator does not just tell and present. As I have noted, he is also habitually misleading the reader by withholding information—about, for example, the paternity of Joseph Andrews and Tom Jones, or the switch of disguise that allows the reader as well as Amelia's husband, Booth, to be fooled into thinking Amelia has compromised her fidelity to him by going to a masquerade. In these ways, the narrator produces effects of opacity and mystery within the reader's movement toward understanding.

This perspective helps explain why so much of Fielding's fiction lacks the transparency Bender finds emerging through its profusion of artful mediations—why, in short, Fielding's novels are so *un*-transparent. The failed figures of the father in Fielding's novels suggest the limits to Fielding's own narrative authority. Just as Fielding's narrators perform the role of the author with compromising exaggeration, so too the fathers within the Fielding novel offer theatrical performances of paternity which put its authority in question. There is ample evidence within Fielding's novels that there is something amiss with paternal authority—in fact, with any authority that poses as absolute.[10] Adams' failure to mentor, educate, or set an example, his lack of perspicuity about those he meets, and his famous

---

10. In a valuable essay, "*Tom Jones*: The 'Bastard' of History," Homer Brown has developed the parallelism between the bastard hero in *Tom Jones* and Fielding's political activism during the '45 revolt against Stuart absolutism.

absent-mindedness all promote the unguided wandering of the characters over the course of the middle two books of *Joseph Andrews*. Rather than being a lawgiver or guide, Adams is more like the hapless leader of a field trip who is constantly losing his charges. Although Adams is favorably contrasted within the novel to the aggressive masculinity of the Roasting Squire, whom Fielding no doubt intends us to dislike (Campbell, *Natural Masques*, 102–104), the direction of Fielding's own narrative plays tricks upon the reader not unlike those with which the Roasting Squire persecutes Adams. Both squire and parson are sources of narrative disorder indispensable to the characters' adventures and to our entertainment.

In contrast with the social reformers who will, in a later day, diffuse authority through huge modern bureaucracies, Fielding's fiction circulates father figures who are attractive precisely because of the openness with which they wield authority. Whether exhibiting traits of a dour oedipal father (Allworthy and Dr. Harrison) or portraying the obscene father of the primal horde (the Roasting Squire and Squire Western), whether a champion of Christian stoicism (Parson Adams) or of a moral psychology based on sympathy (Dr. Harrison), these figures become the instigators of narrative action. Thus, for example, Parson Adams' naive blunders allow him to serve as a whimsical but disruptive descendant of the master of the revels in a saturnalia. Like all Fielding's flawed father figures, Adams does not embody the Law he sometimes tries to speak; instead, he mediates the tension between authority and pleasure. In tandem with the narrator, these figures draw the boundaries—at once social and ethical—within which pleasure is authorized and entertainment sponsored. Within this fictional space, piety can be mocked, the times can be condemned, hypocrisy can be exposed, and a comic society of the good can be constructed. Although the fiction is full of surprising incidents, the consequences never seem to be disastrous. Within these narratives, the moral agent, together with the male protagonist and his beloved (Adams, Joseph, and Fanny; Allworthy, Tom, and Sophia; Harrison, Booth, and Amelia) can, by being heroically sensible—at once feeling and thoughtful—produce a new standard of humanness. The narrator, as teller of the story, kindly guarantees the complicity of Providence in this design. Or so it seems.

FIELDING'S NEW [A]VENUE FOR ENTERTAINMENT

In *Joseph Andrews*, Fielding develops a new venue and avenue—and an alternative place and pathway—for novelistic entertainment. Throughout this chapter I have described the features of *Joseph Andrews*, *Shamela*, and

The Author's Farce that interrupt the absorption of the reader. Featuring false examples (such as Leonora) and admirable but exceptional, and therefore inimitable, characters (such as Parson Adams), *Joseph Andrews* overthrows the educational program of the exemplary life. The theatrical feints of the narrative discourage the expectation that *Joseph Andrews* can be read as a realistically rendered alternative world. Instead, the text is offered to the reader as a self-consciously produced performance that foregrounds the narrator as "author," without extending full authority to this figure. *Joseph Andrews* implements these (and other) strategies to provoke its reader into becoming a self-conscious consumer not just of *Joseph Andrews*, but of the whole spectrum of media-culture entertainments Fielding seeks to replace or supplement. But what are the chief positive features of the novelistic entertainment that issue from this critical encounter?

The literary history and critical writings of Mikhail Bakhtin offer the most precise way in which to characterize the fiction that results from Fielding's writing "in the manner of Cervantes" to counter the "epidemical frenzy" of *Pamela's* popularity. Although a comprehensive Bakhtinian reading of Fielding's first novel lies beyond the scope of this study, if Bakhtinian concepts are used to return to some of the motifs of *Joseph Andrews* already discussed, it is possible to see why Bakhtin positions Fielding as one of the inventors of the modern comic novel (Bakhtin, *Dialogic Imagination*, 301). Offering a compelling alternative to *Pamela* involves Fielding in affiliating his writing with a tradition of print entertainment—one which included, in particular, Cervantes and Rabelais—that had devised a whole repertoire of formal techniques for countering what Fielding found in Richardson's text: the impulse to purify and idealize. Most crucial among these techniques is the incorporation within the boundaries of the comic novel of a diversity of genres, derived from the social world, which Bakhtin calls heteroglossia—"another's speech in another's language" (ibid., 324). The speech of the characters of *Joseph Andrews* offers metonymic fragments of distinct "socio-ideological systems" (ibid., 412; 403–404). Thus, in the dialogue between the bookseller and Parson Adams about printing the parson's sermons, Adams is a naive representative of an earlier literate culture, functioning as a "fool" who exposes the "lie" of the bookseller's smug modern discourse of the market. Within Fielding's fiction, the linguistic traits of Mrs. Slipslop's overly ambitious diction, of Pamela's stiff propriety, and of the novelistic rhythms of Leonora's intrigue are all subject to parodic stylization (ibid., 311). The resulting "hybridization"—the erasing of boundaries between the speech of characters and narrators (ibid., 320)—assumes, indeed requires, an active reader. Thus, in the first pages of *Joseph Andrews*, Fielding's reader is obliged to negotiate a broad spectrum of different types of writing and speech: the narrator's critical introduction, the narrator-historian's account of Joey's early life, Adams' catechizing of Joseph, Joseph's two interviews with Lady Booby and his encounter with Mrs. Slipslop (with its climactic Homeric similes), Joseph's two letters to Pamela, a "satire on love," and so on. Even when Fielding's narrator seems to be speaking directly to the reader as the "author," Fielding allows the "speech of everyday" to enter and complicate a narrative that comes from no one (Miller, *Essays on Fielding's Miscellanies*, 162).

Fielding's hybridizing of the novel offers a powerful challenge to Richardson's program to purify the novel of amorous intrigue by incorporating it into an allegory of virtue. By denaturalizing any one language for rendering truth (Bakhtin, *Dialogic Imagination*, 367), Fielding's comic novel participates in an enlightenment desacralization of myth that cannot become consolidated into any new generic form. Caught up in the process of "novelization" it epitomizes, *Joseph Andrews* articulates a dialogic—and often antagonistic—relation with an untotalizable variety of genres, speech, and writing. Several ideas follow from this thesis. While Bakhtin develops the concepts of dialogism and heteroglossia from a study of Menippean satire written in the epoch of classical manuscript culture, all the aspects of his account acquire greater force with the development of a market-based print culture. The increased availability of printed texts to readers in the early modern period increases the scope and variety of speech genres actively influencing culture. When language and discourse are materialized as print, a greater profusion and variety of writing and speech becomes available to writers such as Fielding for incorporation into their printed texts. Bakhtin's concept of the comic novel suggests that Fielding's recourse to the use of epic form (evident in *Joseph Andrews* but most explicit in *Tom Jones*) is less a way to unify his fiction than it is a way to offer a capacious, encyclopedic form for the largest possible incorporation of social heteroglossia. The "comic epic in prose" enlarges the container of differences rather than reconciling them to one design. In this use of epic, Fielding anticipates Joyce's *Ulysses* (W. Warner, "Play of Fictions").

The comic novel that results from these dialogical exchanges resists stable interpretation. Bakhtin's dialogism, because it has the whole social and linguistic order as its horizon for present and future exchanges, assumes that the discourse of the novel never reaches temporal or semantic closure. Necessarily interminable, the dialogism of the comic novel cannot be construed as a communication system. Fielding does not situate the text as a dialogue—for example, between reader and "author"—for a successful transfer of information or ideas; nor is it (in contrast to a Platonic dialogue or a session of the court) a way in which to make a final adjudication of truth or justice; and thus, it cannot be the cleverly encoded conduct book disguised as entertainment that Richardson thought he was writing, and that critics such as Battestin try to make of *Joseph Andrews*. (Battestin's *Moral Basis of Fielding's Art* is finally Richardsonian.) Instead, Fielding's novel turns dialogue toward conversation, where it becomes a species of entertainment.

In "An Essay on Conversation" (1743), Fielding describes the basic ethos that informs his conversational novel: good conversation consists in "the art of pleasing" (127). All the rules recommended by the essay for the conduct of conversation are contrived to avoid embarrassment, awkwardness, and coercion and, instead, to promote pleasure and happiness to all the parties to conversation—regardless of differences of sex, rank, or fortune. Conversation is understood to be one of the great ends of life, a source of enjoyment as well as improvement. Above all, it is a cultural space that accommodates variety in the exchange of words, moods, and conviviality. Although reading one of Fielding's novels can never be the same as social conversation, Bender, in his introduction to a new Oxford edition of *Tom Jones*, suggests that *Joseph Andrews* "was Fielding's first novel to attempt the narrative stance combining detachment . . . and a good natured conversational alliance with the reader" (xiv). Nevertheless, this alliance has a wishful hortatory cast. Bakhtin's probing analysis of the irreducible difference within heteroglossia suggests that conversation seldom brings two parties to one position; instead, as in many of the conversations recounted in *Joseph Andrews*, conversation ("speaking together") can always lapse into controversy ("speaking against"). Since conversation is never assured of arriving at a destination in truth or goodness, it is perhaps sufficient for it to entertain those compelled by the rhythm of its exchanges. In this way, conversation becomes a species of entertainment.[11]

---

11. I have been influenced in my use of Bakhtin by Paul de Man's suggestive essay upon Bakhtin, "Dialogue and Dialogism" (de Man, *Resistance to Theory*). DeMan suggests the ambiguity within Bakhtin about the nature of dialogism—it can be interpreted either as a term that could allow us to fix the relation between fact and fiction, world and novel, or as a term that is fundamentally intralinguistic, and that indexes a more fundamental "otherness" or alterity (ibid., 110–112). De Man advocates reading Bakhtin in terms of the latter possibility, one that would arrest a movement from dialogism to dialogue of an interpersonal sort.

The underlying interminability of Fielding's conversational novels—their refusal to bring closure to the conversations conducted at cross purposes and so often interrupted—can be attributed to the way in which the ideas within speech are constantly being subverted, confused, or exceeded by the body that speaks. In his studies of Rabelais and the carnivalesque, Bakhtin calls attention to what one might call the critical potential within novelistic narrative of the body as topos and agent. In my reading of the *Pamela* media event, I have noted how the anti-pamelists critique Richardson's presentation of Pamela's body. They argue that the very effort to sublimate the female body involves a veiling and withdrawal of the body that incites a pornographic gaze (see chapter 5). In both *Shamela* and Haywood's *Anti-Pamela* the heroine's body and her ungovernable desires overthrow the plots motivated by self-interest. In drawing upon the tradition Bakhtin elucidates, Fielding develops a body-centered and body-valuing fiction. Thus, against the restrained idealization in heroic romance, against the insinuating pornographic fragmentation of Pamela's body and its alluring censorship of sight, Fielding offers lush formal portraits of his hero, Joseph ("He was of the highest Degree of middle Stature. His Limbs . . ." [38]), and his heroine, Fanny (". . . in the nineteenth Year of her Age; she was tall and delicately shaped; . . ." [152]). Presented as beautiful and worthy of the reader's desire, their beauty and health make them emblems of good nature. Campbell has argued that instead of reifying the clichés of gender difference, Fielding transcodes the gender of Joseph's body so as to draw upon the feminine traits of Milton's Eve (Campbell, *Natural Masques*, 79–82). Because its plot is structured as a physically strenuous journey, with the hardships of hunger, poverty, and physical encounters with adversaries, *Joseph Andrews* is constantly reminding its readers of the tenacious centrality of the body. In scenes of comic relief, familiar from picaresque fiction, and usually centered upon the hapless Parson Adams, bodies become besmeared with blood or shit, or are stripped bare, so they are exposed to the bemused gaze of others. In Fielding's witty rewriting of the nighttime rendezvous that figures so prominently in the novels of Behn, Manley, and Haywood, the rake Beau Didapper tries to sneak into Fanny's bed and accidentally ends up in close commerce with Mrs. Slipslop, but when Parson Adams responds to the ensuing screams, Adams mistakes Beau Didapper for a "young Woman in danger of ravishing," because of his "extremely soft" skin (*Joseph Andrews*, IV: xiv, 332). These "Night-Adventures" reroute the tragic misadventures of the second book of Haywood's *Love in Excess* II through the comic confusions of Chaucer's *Reeve's Tale*.

As Fielding's characters have physical bodies ready for distress or enjoyment, so the reader, too, is understood to have a body, and to consume Fielding's books as though they were food. Understanding the pleasure that theatergoers receive from viewing the performing bodies at a play, Fielding attracts his reader to a richly articulated textual body, with a preface, "books," and chapters, all ornamented with a full complement of rhetorical figures and lively characters. Accepting the commonplace that the physical and mental health of bodies will depend upon what they take in, Fielding claims in his preface to offer his reader a healthy comic body for incorporation into the reader's own body. Through their consumption of this entertainment, Fielding hopes to induce a "Mirth and Laughter" in his readers that will promote their "Good-Humour and Benevolence" and be a better "Physic" for them "after they have been sweeten'd for two or three Hours with Entertainments of this kind, than when soured by a Tragedy or a grave Lecture" (ibid., 5).

By inciting the reader to be skeptical and critical, by involving the reader in a "conversation" that is interminable and open-ended, Fielding enfranchises the reader to become a writer. Addressing readers who are presumed to be various (as the "Classical Reader" (ibid., 4), the "sagacious Reader" (ibid., 36), and so on), Fielding acknowledges a reader's liberty that neither text nor author can master. In order to negotiate Fielding's text, reading must evolve into a kind of writing. Nothing is a greater incentive to the reader's counterwriting of the text than the discovery that the author has duped him or her. Beginning with the example of the early metamorphosis of Joseph from "Pamela's brother" to Fanny's lover, I have noted how the novel teases the reader with its unpredictability. In Fielding's novels, incidents usually come from beyond the horizon of ordinary expectations. Novelistic action is not the work of the performing and speaking "author," so very much on display in the narrative; rather, it is the work of a hidden author functioning as a trickster or illusionist. In "The Champion" no. 69 (April 22, 1740), Fielding makes the spectacular entertainments of John Rich (1682–1761) the hinge of his satire on the "Grand" political "Pantomimes played on the stage of life" (Williams, *Criticism of Henry Fielding*). However, his description of the predicament of the "Spectator" of "one of Mr. Rich's entertainments" corresponds very closely to the predicament of the readers of *Joseph Andrews*:

> we see things only in the light in which that truly ingenious and learned entertainmatic [*sic*] author is pleased to exhibit them, without perceiving the several strings, wires, clock-work, etc. which conduct the machine; and thus we are diverted with the sights of serpents, dragons, and armies,

whereas indeed those objects are no other than pieces of stuffed cloth, painted wood, and hobby-horses, as such of his particular friends as are admitted behind the scenes, without any danger of interrupting his movements, very well know.

[Fielding, "The Champion" no. 69, 37]

If Joseph's metamorphosis from "Pamela's brother" to the lover of Fanny involves some of the same cunning this essay ascribes to Rich's special effects, then the cascade of coincidences that produces a happy ending for *Joseph Andrews* involves the author behind the scenes in an equally spectacular set of manipulations.

The heterosexual marriage plot of *Joseph Andrews* is one that Fielding, following rather than departing from Richardson, shares with Classical New Comedy, heroic romance, and some of the novels of amorous intrigue. In the comic instances of these generic subtypes, there is an orchestration of the love and marriage of a young man and woman so that their union expresses the desires and values of their society. Like *Pamela* and numberless other early modern texts from *Paradise Lost* to *The Magic Flute*, *Joseph Andrews* offers a test of virtue under the conditions of the eclipse of parental authority. Fielding's novel combines elements of the "novel of trial," in which a preformed character is tested according to a preexistent ideal, and the more modern novel of development, in which experiences precipitate a growth and change in the protagonist (Bakhtin, *Dialogic Imagination*, 392–393). Joseph and Fanny come together only by overcoming a host of obstacles, from the lust of Lady Booby to that of the Roasting Squire; from those who would let Joseph die on the road to those who would ruin Fanny; and including also the agonizing delays imposed by Adams. In Fielding's treatment of the marriage plot, there is an intertextual exchange with the novels of amorous intrigue: *Joseph Andrews* replaces the schemes of the intriguing ego, exemplified by Leonora and Beau Didapper, where "love" is something artificial and base, with an amorous discourse between Fanny and Joseph which, by being impulsive, chaste, and physical, is coded as "natural." However, unlike the elaborate conversations that Richardson's novel features, the amorous conversation between Fanny and Joseph is withdrawn from view: the reader never hears the words of their love.

Not all of Joseph's virtue, valor, and charity, not all of Adams's help, nor all of Fanny's valiant resistance, are enough to get Joseph safely married to Fanny, in order that "The Happiness of this Couple [could become] a perpetual Fountain of Pleasure to their fond Parents" (*Joseph Andrews*, IV: xvi, 344). The young lovers require an "assist" from the contrivances of the hidden author. But instead of giving their story's ending an aura of plausibility and probability—instead, as in *Pamela*, of making the ending seem to follow logically from the character of the characters and the flow of the action—Fielding laces the plot with coincidence. When Adams and Joseph and Fanny have failed to raise the money necessary to release them from an inn, a mysterious pedlar comes to the rescue and the narrator tells us: "when the most exquisite Cunning fails, Chance often hits the Mark, and that by Means the least expected" (ibid., II: 15, 170). That same "Chance" "hits the Mark" when Adams and Fanny are falsely arrested and Squire Booby happens to be present and recognizes and vouches for Adams (ibid., II: 11, 149); when John the servant saves Fanny from the disaster of her abduction by Mr. Peter Pounce (ibid., III: 12); when Squire Booby arrives in time to save Joseph and Fanny from the legal machinations of Lady Booby and her lawyer; and finally, when Fanny escapes rape by the servant of Beau Didapper only because "the Deity who presides over chaste Love sent her *Joseph* to her Assistance" (ibid., IV: 7, 304). But as if to push implausibility still further, the pedlar who happened to be around to provide money in Book II, chapter 15 returns in Book IV, chapter 12 to disclose the secret of the gypsy exchange that had, many years earlier, put Joseph in the place of Fanny in Mrs. Andrews' cradle. When the truth of this story is confirmed by Mrs. Andrews, and the Pedlar announces that Joseph's true father lives "about forty Miles" from the Andrews' house, the narrative saves Joseph the trouble of search or journey: "But Fortune, which seldom doth good or ill, or makes Men happy or miserable by halves, resolved to spare him this Labour" (ibid., IV: 16, 338).

Why the semiotic blatantness of these contingencies? Not motivated in some natural way, they become evidence of the whimsical operations of an author behind the scenes, the traces of the author's kindly pressure upon the action. In Aubin's *Life of Madam Beaumount*, a similar cascade of coincidences, recognitions, and reunions ends the novel; there, however, the action is read as an analogue of the workings of Christian Providence. But Fielding quite explicitly rejects this idea of Providence, and the aesthetic doctrine of rewards and punishments for good and evil which is derived from it. Thus, as *Tom Jones* wends its way toward its own ingenious and surprising conclusion, the narrator prepares the reader for the worst: "There are a Set of Religious, or rather Moral Writers, who teach that Virtue is the certain Road to Happiness, and Vice to Misery in this World. A very wholsome and comfortable Doctrine, and to which we have but one Objection, namely, That it is not true" (*Tom Jones*, XV: i, 783).

Rather than see the hidden author as an avatar of a providential God, it is more precise to see him as a kind of good fairy who guarantees the favorable direction of the fable, even while he scares the reader with the possibility that Fanny and Joseph are sister and brother. The happy ending Fielding wants for his reader is the effect of his own arbitrary control of his text, and it confers upon this text the contrived and artificial character he had ascribed to Rich's theatrical productions. The cascade of coincidences that ends the novel strains the mimetic claims for the text, and aligns the happy ending with the magical reconciliations of romance. However, as a gratuitous gift from the author to the reader, a sleight of hand that receives no rationale except from the collective wish that may be assumed to be shared by both author and reader, the happy ending assures that the story will be an enjoyable entertainment. Such is the rationale offered for the implausible ending of more than one Hollywood film entertainment.[12]

12. See, for example, the debate around the happy endings appended to Hitchcock's *Suspicion* (1941) and to Scott's *Blade Runner* (1982). Like Hitchcock's films, Fielding's novels have developed a way to straddle the boundary between entertainment and art.

Conclusion
The Freedom of Readers

"Thou, Lovelace, hast been long the *entertainer;* I the *entertained.*"
—Belford to Lovelace, *Clarissa*

The account of the literary history of the novel's rise I offer in chapter 1 assumes that the novel's institution is, by the late twentieth century, an accomplished fact. Within this initial horizon of my study, the novel appears as a self-evident object studied by scholars and students within discourses (such as literary criticism and literary history), through certain practices (such as teaching, specialization, cataloguing, survey courses, and contemporary experimental writing), and within specific social institutions (such as the publishing "house," the bookstore, the English department, and the MLA). From these settings, the novel appears fully *instituted.* By doing a genealogy of accounts of the novel's rise, I have sought to describe the arbitrary critical articulations necessary to constitute the novel as a form of literature: if a prose narrative improves its reader, represents the nation, and is realistic, critics may claim literary status for it as a novel. With this genealogy, I hoped to defamiliarize the novel, and release it for the more radical historical inquiry begun in chapter 2. In the body of this book, I have sought to open another scene behind the standard accounts of the novel's rise: within early modern print culture a challenge is posed to the enlightenment educational project by reading novels for entertainment, and there, strife opens between those who write novels of amorous intrigue for a general reader and those who would elevate novel reading. Having described in considerable detail the ways in which Defoe, Richardson, and Fielding seek to absorb and overwrite the novels of Behn, Manley, and Haywood, I have brought my story to the point where the institution of the novel can be confronted *not* as an accomplished fact, but as an ambitious project, *not* as that which is instituted, but as a dynamic transformative process of "instituting . . . founding, creating, and breaking with an old order and creating a new one" (Lourau quoted by Weber, *Institution and Interpretation,* xv).

This second, active sense of "institution" designates those contingent articulations that precede the presumption of integrity and continuity ascribed to "the" novel after its institutionalization (Lynch and Warner, *Cultural Institutions of the Novel*). The potent little "the" in the phrase "the novel" indexes its arrival as an abstract substantive. But literary historians agree that at the start of the eighteenth century, there is no coherent consensus about what "the" novel might be. Instead, readers and writers assume the promiscuous plurality of novels and romances to be enjoyed or spurned. This book has suggested the active discursive work that brings about the idea of the novel's presumed integrity. An active instituting of "the" novel can be glimpsed in the critical activity of pamelists and anti-pamelists in *Pamela's* publication. Fielding's antagonistic rejoinder to Richardson in *Shamela*, together with his writing of *Joseph Andrews* and *Tom Jones*, develops the grounds for an alternative instituting of prose entertainment. But the institution of "the" novel as a literary type depends upon a complex tautological relay: a literary work must have a legitimate author, and the author is one who produces authentic literary works. But the legitimacy of the author and the authenticity of the work are secured by literary criticism. Literary criticism contributes a dense formal analysis of the work so as to imply the existence, beyond the horizon of the work, of the writer of original genius—the author; literary history and biography demonstrate how an author subdues historical determinants and contexts to the work (Weber, *Institution and Interpretation*, xv–xvi). Through this interdependent discursive apparatus, both history and media become focused into something more refined and singular; the author and the work become what Mark Rose has called the "twin suns of a binary star [defining] the center of the modern literary system" (Rose, *Authors and Owners*, 91).

The modern literary system begins to take shape in the second half of the eighteenth century, when new practices of reviewing and criticism are developed to teach readers to discriminate between good and bad novels, proper and improper reading practices (Donaghue, *Fame Machine*; Siskin, "Eighteenth Century Periodicals"). As I have shown in chapter 1, these critical projects offer a rejoinder to the new wave of antinovel discourse that is incited in the second half of the eighteenth century by the success of the circulating libraries. However, the selection of one strain of fiction, and the elevation of its cultural address, is not simply a story of cultural consolidation and social hegemony. The expansion of reading for entertainment, as driven by economically enfranchised readers, and as evidenced by the vogue for the circulating library, offers resistance to the full institutionalization of "the" novel as a literary type. It is able to do so because no act of criticism succeeds in separating novels from media culture. Out of the amorphous matrix of media culture come new forms of "formula fiction," such as the gothic novel, which render their respectable double, the novel, an opaque and ambivalent cultural object. In concluding, I will suggest systematic reasons for the incompleteness of the novel's institution and sketch some of the ongoing effects of the gravitational influence of media culture upon novel reading and writing.

THE CRITICAL ARTICULATION OF NOVEL WRITING WITH AUTHORSHIP

The power of the market comes from the way in which circulation spreads print over culture. This has the effect of making novel writers mere factors of the market. Within the eighteenth-century book trade, the first copyright law, the Queen Anne Law of 1710, secures precious little power for writers. Most writers remain subordinate to the bookseller and lodged within the belly of early media culture. Often entirely hidden from view, and frequently working upon a legally risky political terrain, the author functions as a hack writer. When the popular success of novels brings writers into view, it most often makes them objects of scandal. Thus, the notoriety and celebrity won by the writers of the novels of amorous intrigue makes them liable to what we might call (referring to our own epoch's most famous female rock icon) the "Madonna effect": "Behn," "Manley," and "Haywood" become merged with the texts they write, and are most visible as the projected effect of their own novels. I have noted, in chapters 4 and 5, how Defoe and Richardson rewrite reading by providing substitutes for the novels of amorous intrigue. However, although they imbue media culture entertainments with new ethical designs, they do not make a full public claim to be "authors." In 1740, authorship is still construed in the neoclassical terms as modeled by Milton, Dryden, and Pope.

How is a novel writer, one tethered to all the systems of media culture, to separate him- or herself from the system of production and consumption that supports this writing? The novelist faces a particularly severe version of the general problem faced by all eighteenth-century writers. How can that which is designed to circulate among many ever belong to one? An impressive body of new scholarship on the emergence of authorship offers a way to rethink the difference between the writer of media culture and the literary author.[1] If a book is composed of physical elements (such as paper,

1. I am most indebted to Peter Stallybrass and Allon White, and to Mark Rose, Martha Woodmansee, and Catherine Gallagher.

ink, leather, string, and glue), if it is provided by the bookseller and sold to the book buyer, if it is made up of words and language that belonged to everyone (and therefore no one) and carries ideas that by their very nature pass from one mind to another mind, then what within the book could be said to *belong* to the author? An answer to this question was essential to the development of a social and legal consensus upon the authorial property right, a consensus which was, in turn, indispensable for providing a secure basis for a trade in books. Within Martha Woodmansee's historical narrative, *The Author, Art and the Market*, Fichte solves this problem in an ingenious fashion: the physical book carries two kinds of content—the "ideas it presents" and the "*form* of these ideas, the way in which, the combination in which, the phrasing and wording in which they are presented" (51). Both the physical book and the ideas it transmits pass to the reader. But the particular *form* within which the ideas are vested, the unique style of thought and language, are as unique and distinct to the author as his or her face (ibid., 50–52; Rose, *Authors and Owners*, 125). Thus the book purchased by the reader harbors a reserve—the form or style of the work—that remains the distinct property of the author. The conceptual terms of Fichte's solution are cast in very similar terms to Saussure's concept of the sign. If the semiotic implications of Fichte's analysis are mapped out, the ideational content of the book can be seen to be divided between form (or signifer) and conceptual idea (or signified); but this peculiar work's unity of form and content becomes a new signifier (as style) that denotes a new signified (the author). Now the style of the work signifies the originating author in his or her uniqueness: an "author" suddenly rises above the flux and reflux of his or her print-media support. It will be the role of criticism to certify the success of the work's signifying of its author as unique, to distinguish between works that are original and those that are not. The new mid-century insistence that only original invention qualifies for the honorific of "authorship" helps open the way for the novel writer to become an author.

The *Pamela* media event demonstrates the ethical potential of novel reading, as well as the dangerously unruly license of readers. The concept of the author, as the autonomous creator of the book, enables writers to imagine that they can stand apart and oversee the reading of the books they have written. I have noted the ways in which, after *Pamela*, Richardson and Fielding seek to articulate their own narrative entertainments with authorship. Here (for the first time in Britain), authorship, which already had a rich history in drama and poetry, is articulated with novel writing. But Richardson and Fielding follow distinctly different paths in moving the novel toward authorship. Within *Pamela* and *Clarissa*, characters such as Pamela, Clarissa, and Belford model morally responsible authorship as truth telling, as rhetorical restraint in using language, and as a part of the consistent pursuit of an ethical life. In the movement from *Pamela* to *Clarissa*, Richardson "fixes" the epistemological problem exposed by the criticisms of *Pamela*, in which, since readers get almost all their information directly from Pamela, even the most sympathetic reader must concede the possibility that Pamela is engaged in a sham performance. In an effort to enhance the authority and credibility of Clarissa's letter narratives, *Clarissa*, unlike *Pamela*, is composed of two parallel correspondences. The first consists of Clarissa's letters to her best friend, Anna Howe, from whose response she draws sympathetic criticism and useful reality checks. The other correspondence is that between Lovelace and his fellow rake Belford, which embed adversarial accounts of Clarissa within libertine interpretation, but confirm the veracity of her narrative of their common situation. Although Richardson continues to write epistolary novels that efface the direct role of a narrator or author, he seeks to step forward and assert himself as author, as the ultimate authority, in the last instance, concerning the meaning and proper effect of his novels.

In discussing the *Pamela* media event, I noted the way in which the momentum of criticism and rejoinder draws Richardson and Fielding into an increasingly explicit practice of novelistic authorship. Gradually the novel author names himself. While neither is named on the title pages of *Pamela* and *Joseph Andrews*, on the title page to the first edition of Fielding's second novel one reads "By Henry Fielding, Esq." under "*The History of Tom Jones, A Foundling*. In Six Volumes." While Richardson cleaves to a token anonymity as "Editor of *Pamela*" (in *Clarissa*) and as "Editor of *Pamela* and *Clarissa*" (in *Sir Charles Grandison*), he continues the practice begun with *Pamela in Her Exalted Condition* in indirectly inscribing himself as author with the words, "Printed for S. Richardson." When readers question Clarissa's and Richardson's authorial authority by petitioning for a "fortunate ending" to the story (W. Warner, *Reading Clarissa*, 143–218), Richardson lengthens the postscript to the final volume (Richardson, *Clarissa*, IV: 552; Sale, *Samuel Richardson*, 48–50, 56). In this defense of the ending of the "preceding history," "the author" appeals to critical laws for tragedy as defined by Aristotle and explicated by Addison and Rapin (Richardson, *Clarissa*, IV: 554–55).

In the movement from *Joseph Andrews* to *Tom Jones*, Fielding gives heightened centrality to his role as author. By severing his link with explicit intertexts (evident in *Pamela* and *Don Quixote*), he implicitly asserts his autonomy as an original inventor; his use of epic form tends less toward mock-epic jeux d'esprit (though these exist) than toward providing an encyclopedic frame for a much more ambitious representational tableau of the English nation; finally, instead of offering Joseph or Parson Adams as strikingly virtuous alternatives to Richardson's exemplary characters, Fielding promotes mixed characters as more true to life and useful to the reader. Although the introductory essays to the eighteen books of *Tom Jones* develop a much more comprehensive rationale for Fielding's new species of novelistic entertainment, the "author" who develops this critical argument in conversation with the reader becomes more playfully devious and ironic. In *Tom Jones*, the author appears more theatrical and less straightforward than the author-narrator of *Joseph Andrews*, and less sure than ever of the efficacy of attempts to prescribe the principles for modern entertainment. Thus, the insight suggested by the puppet show within *Tom Jones*—namely, that since people read so as to suit their desires, even the most "grave and solemn Entertainment" may incite misbehavior—implicates Fielding's own efforts to elevate entertainment (XII: v, 638).

The appearance of novels of the scope and ambition of *Clarissa* and *Tom Jones* required more than the initiative of two writers and the fact that one of them was a printer of considerable means. If eighteenth-century novelistic authorship after 1740 received its economic impetus from the commercial potential demonstrated by *Pamela*, then the development of that potential depended, to a remarkable degree, upon the active labor of one bookseller, Andrew Millar. One of a group of influential Scotsmen in the London book trade, Millar was celebrated by Richardson as "a fair, honest, open man, and one who loves to deal generously by authors" (Battestin, *Tom Jones*, I: xlii). In the two decades after *Pamela*, he was the bookseller-publisher, either alone or in concert with others, for *Joseph Andrews*, *Clarissa*, *Tom Jones*, *Amelia*, *Sir Charles Grandison*, Charlotte Lennox's *Female Quixote*, and the 1755 Tobias Smollett translation of Cervantes' *Adventures of Don Quixote*. By publishing the *Works of Henry Fielding* (1762) in four lavish quarto volumes, with an "essay on the life and genius of the author" by Arthur Murphy, Millar monumentalizes Fielding in a format worthy of a "major" author.[2] Further, by leading legal battles to

---

2. The possibly fictional anecdote of Fielding's shock at the nearly £200 Millar offered him for the copyright to *Joseph Andrews* and several short works, as well as Johnson's remark that Millar "raised the price of literature" (Battestin, *Joseph Andrews*, xxvii–xxviii), confirm Millar's pivotal role in elevating the cultural position of the novel.

secure copyrights against infringement by those without legal right to copy in *Millar v. Kinkaid* and *Millar v. Taylor* (Rose, *Authors and Owners*, 68), and by providing new levels of financial support for novel writers, Millar served as the authors' indispensable mediator with the market.[3]

In his last years, Richardson collaborated in a critical discourse designed to give an extravagant extension to the authority of the author. He encouraged his friend of many years, the poet Edward Young, to theorize the "originality" of the author, in a text that passed between Young and Richardson several times. The resulting text, *Conjectures on Original Composition in a Letter to the Author of Sir Charles Grandison*, is printed by Richardson, addressed to him, and compliments him as a signal instance of the sort of originality Young advocates. *Conjectures* characterizes the author as one who has mysterious powers of originality. It develops an extended critique of the more modest Renaissance concept of the author who accepts the prior authority of the tradition whose authors and genres he only presumes to imitate. Devaluing the poetry of allusion practiced by Alexander Pope, the *Conjectures* also implicitly criticizes Fielding's use of foreign and ancient literary models. By contrast, it enhances the claims for heralding as a genius the author who uses powers impenetrable to others to create something

---

3. However, if a bookseller can sustain an author, he can also rip him off. Richardson's battle with the leading Irish bookseller, George Faulkner, over control of the copyright to *Sir Charles Grandison* suggests how precarious the author's position on the market could be. When Faulkner corrupts two of Richardson's workmen to get proof copies of Richardson's last novel and succeeds in publishing an early edition of Richardson's novel in Dublin, Richardson responds, on September 14, 1753, with a pamphlet entitled, *The Case of Samuel Richardson, of London, Printer; on the Invasion of his property in the History of Charles Grandison, Before Publication, By Certain Booksellers in Dublin*. This pamphlet aligns an author's property in his text with the sentimental heroine's property in her body. Just as the Irish booksellers contest Richardson's control of his literary property in the name of Irish economic independence, so too, as I have shown, did many early readers of *Pamela* contest the heroine's representation of her story. Richardson's texts habitually fantasize the author's decisive authority over readers, but his actual experience with historical readers suggests not only the strict limits on an author's control of how texts circulate and what they mean, but also that an author's authority (concerning the heroine's virtue and the author's property) depends in some crucial fashion on exposing the heroine's body to rape and the author's property to theft. To claim authorship in Richardson's texts seems to entail exposing the author's text (that is, the heroine's virtue and the author's property) to invasive forms of repetition: the libertine's rewriting of the heroine's story; the Irish pirates' retelling of Richardson's efforts to retain his property as a tale of English exploitation. To be an author, one must expose the "original copy" to a copying that may put in question the integrity of the original. In such a communication circuit, the relationship of the subject who reads to the textual meaning is never assured.

original, vital, and new. While it can be read as a puff for the sort of unstudied "natural" authorship Young and Richardson claimed to practice, the *Conjectures* also offers a glimpse of the heroic role imagined for authors in the next century.

One passage in the *Conjectures* suggests the pivotal role Young and Richardson envision for the author in shaping reading practices. (I quote from a nineteenth-century edition of Young's works because the gloss of the editor, James Nichols, on this passage allows this edition to serve as a palimpsest for tracing the institutionalizing of the novel.) First, Young characterizes the "divine" ambition that must animate the greatest author; next, he compliments Richardson for performing an exorcism of the early novel; finally, Nichols adds a footnote which offers a rhapsody upon the novel, suggesting the many cultural functions it can claim after it has "arrived" as an elevated form of "national literature." While Young's tribute to Richardson as a heroic author reflects his memory of an antagonism to novels of amorous intrigue still considered pernicious in the late 1750s, the panegyric to the novel assumes the reader's consent to the triumph of "the" novel:

> And for man not to grasp at all which is laudable within his reach, is a dishonor to human nature, and a disobedience to the Divine; for as Heaven does nothing in vain, its gift of talents implies an injunction of their use. A friend of mine has obeyed that injunction: he has relied on himself; and with a genius, as well moral as original, (to speak in bold terms,) has cast out evil spirits; has made a convert to virtue of a species of composition, once most its foe; as the first Christian emperors expelled demons, and dedicated their temples to the living God.*
>
> * This fine and well-merited compliment to the author of "Sir Charles Grandison" and "Pamela," comes with peculiar grace from his old friend and admirer. This "species of composition," of which Richardson had "made a convert to virtue," has, since his time, risen to a high rank in the scale of our national literature, and eclipsed all the glories of the ancient epic. For many years, persons of great genius, and profound students of the human heart, have chosen this novel mode for the discussion of the most interesting topics connected with domestic life, social relations, and political institutions. In classical and attractive language these new moral epics have exhibited much useful truth and sound morality, the contemplation of which has enlightened the philosopher, and charmed the Christian.—Edit. (1854)
>
> [Young, *The Complete Works*]

The suppression of the pagan gods by the first Christian emperors was lauded in the eighteenth century as an early instance of the enlightenment triumph over superstition. Young's "bold" analogy does more than compliment

Richardson on the use of his talents. His analogy suggests that Richardson, by casting out the evil "demons" who had made the novel the "foe" of virtue, "dedicate[s]" the novel as a kind of temple of culture, imbued with the "original" moral "genius"—not so much of the "living God," but of the author. As a vehicle not for profane entertainment but in which to hold the spirit of the author, the novel leaves behind the undiscriminating reader and ascends to those various uplifting uses itemized by the nineteenth-century editor Nichols in his note: "discussion of the most interesting topics." However, Fielding's much less reverential deployment of the author as trickster-illusionist refuses this orthodox piety surrounding his performative entertainments, and concedes the autonomy of readers of media culture.

With his *Rambler* no. 4 essay of 1750, Samuel Johnson, the major critic of the British eighteenth century, gives criticism a crucial role in the institution of the novel as an elevated cultural form. The implications of the inscription of Johnson's critical program within elevated fiction become visible in Charlotte Lennox's first novel, *The Female Quixote* (1752). Instead of the beautiful young heroine Arabella being saved from a dangerous rake by the hero, she is "saved" from the dangers of her romance reading by a critic.[4] In other words, criticism rescues this quixotic reader from the "emulous desire" incited by absorptive reading of romances. Lennox's Englishing of Cervantes rewrites Fielding's *Joseph Andrews* in such a way as to develop a more plausible mimicry of fiction than that provided by Joseph's imitation of Pamela. By gendering the novel reader female, Lennox incorporates the fantasm of the woman novel reader into her narrative. Like Richardson and Fielding, Lennox elevates novel reading by linking an ethically motivated narrative to an antagonistic critique of debased novel reading. In the novel's climactic penultimate chapter, the "doctor" (widely read as a figure of Dr. Johnson) condemns the implausible fabrications of the heroic romance and promotes the wise uses of fiction. Then he quotes Johnson's commendation of Richardson's novels (from Johnson's note to *Rambler* no. 97, February 19, 1751) in the following commentary: "Truth is not always injured by fiction. An admirable writer of our own time, has found the way to convey the most solid instructions, the noblest sentiments, and the most exalted piety in the pleasing dress of a

---

4. The doctor's stern lecture to Arabella about the dangers of her romance reading is a particularly vivid instance of what Martha Woodmansee has described as the effort to "police" reading. In *The Author, Art and the Market*, Woodmansee argues that Young's *Conjectures* played a crucial role in German aesthetics, in which it provided a rationale for conceiving of authorship as an organic process that tethers the text to its single author (53–54).

novel, and to use the words of the greatest genius in the present age, 'has taught the passions to move at the command of virtue'" (377). This programmatic statement of the value of Richardson's fiction, fully compatible with the case made in Johnson's *Rambler* no. 4 essay, puts the emphasis not on the opposition between fiction and fact, but on the instruction and sentiment that enable novels to develop a positive relationship between fiction and an affective, moral truth.[5]

Lennox's *Female Quixote* explicitly thematizes the effects of the *Pamela* media event—namely, a new textualizing of the opposition between fiction and reality so that what becomes central is not the presence or absence of

5. See Catherine Gallagher's *Nobody's Story* for a compelling reading of the logic of the doctor's cure of Arabella: in order to teach her to read romances as fiction, the doctor uses a "suppositional logic" compatible with fiction (185–195). Although my understanding of Lennox is here indebted to Gallagher, I do not agree with a central feature of her thesis. Gallagher inserts Lennox into a succession of women writers, thereby suggesting that the women authors, by having an especially compelling commerce with stories of nobody, and by developing the sympathetic identification readers could have with fictional nobodies, play a decisive role in inventing the concept of fiction. By locating the modern invention of fiction in one group of eighteenth-century texts, Gallagher's thesis has strong resonance with the rise of the novel thesis I have criticized throughout this study. Gallagher argues that, unlike Manley's disguised fictions about "Somebodies" who are identifiable by consulting the Key, the plenitude of detail in Lennox's *Female Quixote* suggests that "the particulars of the novel character have no extra-textual existence" (174). For me, the issue is not whether Lennox or Richardson or Fielding is most responsible for the shift Gallagher convincingly documents—namely, the rearticulation of the uses of fiction in the middle of the eighteenth century in Britain. Once the uses of verisimilitude within fiction have been grasped, all three writers show a keen sense of the need to blend truth and fiction in their narratives. Thus, for example, when William Warburton's preface to the second installment of *Clarissa* is too open about its fictionality, Richardson complains that such explicitness spoils "that kind of Historical Faith which Fiction itself is generally read with, though we know it to be Fiction" (Richardson, *Selected Letters*, 85 [April 19, 1748]). None of these eighteenth-century novelists invents the concept or practice of fiction. The following texts provide examples of the sophistication of pre-eighteenth-century concepts of fiction: the quotation from Bacon on fiction that Dunlop offers near the beginning of his *History of Fiction* (see chapter 1); and the manifesto for fiction addressed "To the Reader" by "J.D." as an introduction to Honoré d'Urfé's heroic romance *L'Astrée* (French version, 1607–1627, English translation, 1657) and echoed in later discussions of the pleasures of fiction in Madame de Scudéry's *Clelia* (French version, 1654–1661; English translation, 1678 [Folger Collective, 2–5]). Thus, the new currency of fiction in Britain in the mid-eighteenth century was less an invention than a rediscovery. On the issue of the invention of the fictional premises of the eighteenth-century British novel, I agree with Margaret Doody, who, in her review of Gallagher in the *Times Literary Supplement*, asserted that the story of the rise or invention of "fiction" cannot be told without including earlier writers, non-British writers, and male writers.

extratextual reference. Now, the modern reader must negotiate different and competing novels, such as the new novels of Richardson or Fielding versus the French heroic romances that fascinate Lennox's heroine, Arabella. In addition, there is a new concern with *how* one reads; whether one reads with the wrong or right kind of absorption or self-consciousness will determine whether the practices of reading are delusive or truthful. Arabella's literal faith in the referent behind the text authorizes the dangerous acting out that had been the target of the antinovel discourse. Lennox's choice of the French heroic romances as her text's comic butt is, as Reeve and others pointed out, false to the reading practices of the mid-eighteenth century. However, this choice serves two distinct purposes. First, it asserts the equivalence of romances and novels of amorous intrigue I have demonstrated in the criticism of Richardson, Fielding, and Johnson. By substituting romances for the novels of amorous intrigue, with the latter's corrupting erotic appeal, Lennox elides the novel of amorous intrigue's potentially embarrassing similarities to the elevated novel. Second, by aligning Arabella with an idealistic, immaculately virtuous practice of love, these intertexts give her an endearing country-bred innocence and make her reform imaginable.

THE INCOMPLETE INSTITUTION OF "THE" NOVEL

Each dislocation of the novel involves its relocation. By becoming articulated with the cultural prestige of authorship, and by becoming the object and occasion for criticism, *selected* novels become more than a vehicle of leisure entertainment—they come to be valued as a literary genre, objectified as "the" novel. In the process, the rest of that promiscuous and unclassified mass of romances and novels are cast into limbo as "non-novels." In order to secure the distinction between "the" novel and these others, criticism acquires a gatekeeping function through a number of developments during the sixty years following the *Pamela* media event: the emergence of journals that review novels (*Monthly Review*, 1749– and *Critical Review*, 1756–); the publication of literary histories of the novel, such as Reeve's *Progress of Romance* (1785) and Dunlop's *History of Fiction* (1814); the collection of novels into anthologies such as those of Griffith (1777), Barbauld (1810), and Scott (1821–1824); and the inclusion of novels in pedagogical projects, from those of Clara Reeve directed at young girls to those of Scottish university professors such as Adam Smith and Hugh Blair (Ballaster, *Seductive Forms*, 201–204; Court, *Institutionalizing English Literature*, 17–38; Siskin, "Eighteenth Century Periodicals"). After the passage of two centuries, the novel has today become an object defined by an

elaborate discursive system: within the confines of the English depart-
ments of colleges and universities, specialists teach courses and devise their
syllabi at a considerable remove from the din of media culture and its
modes of supporting the publication of novels. Of course, this book itself
offers an interweaving of contemporary academic discourses for defining
novels. However, in spite of over two hundred years of efforts to confer a
fixed identity on "the" novel and guide its reading, there are significant
forces that limit the institution of the novel.

The writers I have discussed, from Behn to Fielding, develop forms of
mass entertainment that have one feature of a broadcasting method of
communication: they write to all who will "listen" by reading. The happi-
est denizens of media culture are those writers and booksellers who are
flexible and opportunistic. Thus, in shaping formula fiction, Haywood
exhibits a blithe disregard for the high critical demand for creative originality. But because the repetitions built into formula fiction are grounded
in the obstinate demands of readers for more of the entertainment they
have already enjoyed, and because writers and publishers abandon the
forms of the formula at their own peril, formula fiction resists reform. If
formula fiction demonstrates staying power which resists projects of elevation, it is because the reader, whose demand the whole apparatus of
media culture is shaped to gratify, also resists improvement.

For the producers of media culture, as well as its hopeful reformers, no
matter whether their aim is entertainment or education, the reader becomes
an elusive but crucial enigma. When readers became buyers, every producer
had to come to terms with the reader's essential autonomy. The reader's
resistance to various projects of education and cultural improvement can
always be expressed by a simple but powerful expedient: getting bored (Baudrillard, *In the Shadow*). Boredom triggers the restless quest for some new
variety of entertainment, which, of course, for reasons of economy in production and the inertia of audience taste, may turn out to be a repackaging
of an old formulaic one. This implies the thesis argued by many cultural
theorists—that activity within media culture is not restricted to authors and
publishers, but also inheres in the acts of consumption that reward certain
cultural products with a purchase, and eschew others. No one who teaches
novels in the university classes of the late twentieth century needs to be
told how the autonomy of readers limits the institution of the novel: when
confronted by a long or difficult assignment, even students who know how
to read often choose not to (Siskin, "Eighteenth Century Periodicals").

In the late eighteenth century, the terrain I have dubbed media culture
became the ground for most cultural production. Media culture, as the
mutual imbrication of media shaped to entertain and the cultural practices

of consumption and production that proliferate around them, does not exist in some region apart from "higher" culture—quite the contrary, in fact; since its formulation, the elevated novel has been a subset of media culture. The plasticity of media culture allowed the writers of the elevated novel to engage in an opportunistic morphing of previous cultural texts—the novels of amorous intrigue. But this process works both ways. The forces working within media culture do not stop after the novel's institution; they continue to operate by deforming elevated novels in order to augment formula fiction. Thus, in 1936, Margaret Mitchell would use one of the most literary of novels—Tolstoy's *War and Peace* (1864–1869)—as a plot template for the most popular of novels, *Gone With the Wind*. Within the flows of media culture, the novel's objective character wavers: "the" novel turns out to be an ambivalent, unstable, non-identical object open to disguise, transformation, and resignification. It is an opaque and ambivalent object, carrying within itself the potential to be marked or remarked, in such a way as to resist arriving at a completed form or acquiring any stable social function. However much authors or critics labor to make it a definable literary type, the novel cannot be fixed as literary because it sustains its status as a form of entertainment and continues to feel the deforming tug of media culture. For all these reasons, the incomplete institutionalization of novels is less a contingent eventuality than a systematic necessity.

The scandalous power to move readers that is attributed to novels engenders the imperative to center novels. In this book I have argued that the novel comes to be centered through reference to a series of subjects (in the philosophical sense of a *cogito*): first the character, then the author, then the critic, and finally, and most questionably, the reader. However, each of these subjects proves, in turn, to be quite elusive. Thus, for example, during the course of the *Pamela* media event, Pamela's character does not anchor meaning but becomes the focus for dispute. Claims based in the authority of the author occasion suspicion and provoke more writing, together with new, competing claims to authorship. Critics step forward to assert the superiority of their judgment, seeking to mediate between the author's work and the reader's reading. But in spite of diverse attempts to fix the meaning and effect of novels by centering them through character, author, or critic, or through some global concept defined by critic or author (such as the nation or reality), the reader is positioned to be the final arbiter of the novel's circulation. Within the debates that swirl around novel reading, the reader emerges as the subject in the last instance. However, reading remains oddly resistant to shaping. It is not just that readers are variously motivated, or that the purposes of reading are mobile and shifting. The heterogeneity of reading practices is underwritten by the dynamism of media culture. It proves impossible to separate the reader from his or her reading; nor can one characterize the "novel" as a cultural agent apart from its (purported) effect upon this protean reader.[6]

The incomplete institutionalization of the novel can be understood within the terms developed in my readings of *Pamela* and *Joseph Andrews*. Richardson's compositional ruse depends upon the truth effect of the detoured correspondence I explicated in my reading of *Pamela*: in the place where one expects an amorous intrigue, one reads the story of virtue rewarded. This model of communication works splendidly on Mr. B. within the text, and it is supposed to be prescriptive for the ordinary reader. However, the *Pamela* media event demonstrates the unruly autonomy of readers. In my reading of *Joseph Andrews*, I have suggested the many ways in which Fielding does more than meet the reader's taste half-way; he accepts the reader as the final arbiter of textual meaning, as the ultimate writer of the novel he or she reads. Fielding offers a critique of modern media culture, and of the reading practices it promotes, without pretending (as Richardson hoped) to operate at a virtuous remove from its reach. The tactics of both Richardson and Fielding imply the continued allure to readers of the novels of amorous intrigue, as well as the freedom of readers to read what they want for entertainment. That Richardson reins in this liberty, while Fielding sanctions it, does not alter the fact of this consensus about the essential freedom of readers. At the same time that both writers attempt to initiate a certain definition and consolidation of "the" novel, their texts point toward an unrecuperable outside—the site of the reader who consumes the text. *Pamela* and *Joseph Andrews*, and later novels written to appeal to the taste for elevated novel reading these novels piqued, do not resolve the debate about novel reading, but instead open new rounds of dispute concerning the novel and its effects upon readers. Rather than clos-

6. The continued freedom of readers helps explain why the cultural elevation of selected novels does not result in an achieved cultural "hegemony," enabling authors and critics to lead novel-reading practices in a new, enlightened direction. The concept of hegemony assumes the transparency of a project of cultural improvement presided over by a controlling and self-conscious Author. This, as I have shown, has been an assumption of the critics and literary historians who celebrate Richardson and Fielding as reform-minded fathers of the novel. It is only within the rise of the novel narratives that these two writers' relocation of novel reading can be made to appear comprehensive and inevitable, rather than leading to a contingent closing-off of some pathways, while others are opened and pursued. Here, I am revising my own position (see W. Warner, "The Elevation of the Novel in England"); I am now convinced by the critique of hegemony theory offered by Laclau (*New Reflections*, 27–29).

ing down the space for licentious novel reading, their writing expands its precincts.

THE FUTURES OF NOVELS . . . .

During the same years in which the institution of the novel is moving forward, at least one writer resists the elevated novels of Richardson and Fielding, by finding them boring. This is the message that may be divined from Horace Walpole's rationales for his composition of the first gothic novel. In the anonymous preface to the first edition of *The Castle of Otranto* (1764), Walpole distances himself from the higher claims made for the elevated novel by admitting that this "work" "can only be laid before the public at present as a matter of entertainment" (17). Although he is somewhat tentative in defending the introduction of the miraculous into the narrative, he rejoins: "allow the possibility of the facts, and all the actors comport themselves as persons would do in their situation. There is no bombast, no similes, flowers, digressions, or unnecessary descriptions." What is it that leads Walpole to deviate so far from the more rational, ordinary reality to which Richardson and Fielding refer in their novels? After the spectacular success of *The Castle of Otranto*, Walpole drops the guise of anonymity in the preface to the second edition, in which he "explain[s] the grounds on which he composed" a "blend" of romance and novel that would overcome the limits of the modern novel (21): Since in the ancient romance "all was imagination and improbability," and in the modern novel "nature is always intended to be, and sometimes has been, copied with success," Walpole, as the "author," "thought it possible to reconcile the two kinds. Desirous of leaving the powers of fancy at liberty to expatiate through the boundless realms of invention, and thence creating more interesting situations, he wished to conduct the moral agents in his drama according to the rules of probability; in short to make them think, speak, and act, as it might be supposed mere men and women would do in extraordinary positions" (21).

In his first and second prefaces, Walpole suggests that readers have become bored with the realistic modern novel, and hanker after the magic of old romance. By mixing the romance with the novel, he offers an implicit endorsement of a mindless but entertaining practice of absorptive reading that requires a willing suspension of disbelief. Walpole's experimental invention of gothic narrative works so well that the gothic novel becomes the most popular formula fiction of the later eighteenth century. As he predicts, the "new route he had struck out" does in fact "pave a road" for men and women of "brighter talents" such as Ann Radcliffe, Matthew Lewis, and

Mary Shelley. When the vogue for the gothic becomes a prevailing taste, these "frantic novels" draw William Wordsworth's reforming impulse in his preface to the second edition of the Lyrical Ballads (Woodmansee, Author, Art and the Market, 114). This episode in generic mutation offers a model for the invention of later novelistic types. From the eighteenth century forward, formula fiction of varying sorts—from gothic novels to detective fiction, from science fiction to Harlequin romances—haunts the legitimate novel as its double, challenging its claim to be the only fiction worth reading, and deferring, interminably, the consolidation of "the" novel's institution (Glazener, "Romances for 'Big and Little Boys' ").

If Horace Walpole is the type of the cultured eighteenth-century gentleman dilettante, then Henry James is the type of the cultured nineteenth-century professional novelist. In spite of their differences, both work to inflect the prevailing modes of novel reading of their epoch. After a career replete with success and failure on the market for novelistic entertainments, James selects and edits his works into the New York edition. In the preface to each volume, James makes his case for detaching the novel from a media culture of popular entertainments, so as to define the novel as a form of "art" (James, Art of the Novel). Writing novels and criticism in symbiotic relation to one another throughout his career, James developed the terms that would be used by Percy Lubbock, F. R. Leavis, R. P. Blackmur, and others to incorporate selected novels into the "Great Tradition" of the Western canon taught in schools and universities throughout most of the twentieth century. However, James' intervention in the novel's ongoing institution reflects a keen grasp of the arbitrary articulations that made the novel, at any particular historical juncture, what it appears to be. Thus, in "The Future of the Novel" (written in 1900), he resists the arbitrary limitations of an earlier institutionalization of the British novel, and describes how that novel requires the "great omission" of adult sexuality. The essay is a short, witty, disgruntled look at the possibilities for future novel writing. James finds nothing more decisive for the future of "fictive energy" than "our long and most respectable tradition of making it defer supremely, in the treatment, say, of a delicate case, to the inexperience of the young" (James, "Future of the Novel," 38). This deferral leads to what he calls "an immense omission in our fiction" evident in the novels of Dickens and Scott, in which the absence of "the love making" seems so indispensable to what is there. James remarks how this omission has weighed increasingly heavily upon the possibilities of the novel with the passage of time, until "the simple themselves may finally turn against our simplifications." He imagines the young reproaching the novelists for taking "our education off of the hands of our parents and pastors," but having left "whole categories of manners, whole corpuscular classes and provinces, museums of character and condition, unvisited." This essay offers a vivid rejoinder to the assumption consolidated over the course of the debate about the effects of novel reading: that belief in the moral imperatives of the elevated novel leaves novelists "more royalist than the king," and "more childish than the children" (ibid., 40).

In order to imagine a new future for the novel, James's polemic suggests that one must break with the presumption that was produced in the eighteenth century and that was so useful for nineteenth-century novelists such as Scott and Dickens: that novels must be addressed to the youthful reader of both sexes, so as to nurture the innocence of readers. "The Future of the Novel" reflects the fact that James' novels—from *Daisy Miller* to *Portrait of a Lady*—pivot upon illicit amorous intrigue more familiar in nineteenth-century Continental fiction, but nevertheless found, as I have shown, in the earliest English novels—the novels of amorous intrigue written by Behn, Manley, and Haywood. James' essay prepares the way for a deepening of amorous intrigue in the late trilogy of *The Ambassador*, *Wings of the Dove*, and *The Golden Bowl*. James was joined in this cause in rather different ways by Thomas Hardy and D. H. Lawrence, and his engagement with this polemic heralds a preoccupation with sex in the "serious" novels of the twentieth century.

• • • • •

Because the institution of "the" novel is incomplete, it is ongoing; and because the early modern novels I have studied will be incorporated into future cultural projects we cannot yet specify, the reserves they carry are as yet undisclosed. For these reasons, they exceed the literary and cultural histories that seek to assess their value. Since the rise of the author, the rise of the critic, and the rise of literary studies are co-extensive with one another, and since all contribute to the elevation of novel reading, it is difficult to distinguish symptoms and causes. But I would like to hazard a thesis. It is often thought that popular fiction develops as a middle- or low-brow reaction to a pre-existent high culture. My study of the history of the early novel in Britain suggests the reverse. The very concept of the novel as a high literary form results from unease with the absorptive reading of the "low" amorous novel developed within early print-media culture. "The" novel, as a literary form with claims to modern cultural capital, was produced as a stay against early modern novel-reading practices which, by their atavistic power, threatened to short-circuit the enlightenment educational project. The alternative cultural history of the early novel in Britain

I have elaborated in this study suggests how a more general tendency of culture—the strife between "high" and "low" culture, the improving and the distracting, with the effort to sanction the first and inhibit the second—may have developed characteristic modern forms in the eighteenth century. Richardson and Fielding's contingent decision over the novels of amorous intrigue in the 1740s is transmitted through the literary histories written in the wake of that decision. Although this "decision" unfairly elides the subtlety and aesthetic ambition of Behn's *Love Letters* and the cultural significance of Haywood's formula fiction, Richardson and Fielding's splicing of the archive of an earlier literary culture into media-culture entertainments proved most productive. Even from the vantage point of the late twentieth century, *Clarissa* and *Tom Jones* appear to be among the most ambitious, innovative, and influential novels in the long history of novel writing. However, texts designated classics worthy of reading and of emulation by aspiring authors cannot stand apart from media culture. Instead, they make themselves available for imitation, adaptation, and popularization. The exchange between the restless and unruly quest for entertainment and the more sublimated and disciplined aims of literary culture proves to be both necessary and interminable. In the contact zone between literary and media culture, critics resist what readers cannot (W. Warner, "Resistance to Popular Culture").

In the late twentieth century, the struggle around licensing entertainment does not have the exteriority of forces opposed to one another that is characteristic of warfare between nations. Therefore, we are engaged less in "culture wars" than in strife within culture aimed at reconciling our own contradictory impulses. This struggle continues to produce responses like those used to tame and reform early media culture with the elevated novel: the celebration of authorship, literary criticism, and literary history, and the promotion of educational projects to teach the difference between legitimate culture and media culture. Many tendencies in our own cultural moment can be seen as efforts to mediate this strife, including the general anxiety about the eclipse of cultural literacy; the "Canon Wars"; the vogue for a cultural studies that can incorporate into the purview of the university new types of cultural production (such as film, television, photography, video, and new digital media); and efforts to use ethical or political criteria to censor representations of sex, violence, and hatred deemed dangerous to society. There is a sense in which modern culture may *be* the interminable struggle around where and how to draw the boundary line between good and bad reading and writing.

Appendix

Note: The story of the unprecedented response to *Pamela* has been frequently told—by, among others, Sale and McKillop, Kreissman (*Pamela-Shamela*), and James Turner in his recent *Representations* article on the *Pamela* vogue. While my study only gives detailed attention to selected texts of this media event, the phenomenon is much larger. It includes the following as major interventions, which, for the sake of reference, I have given in the order of publication.

Titles and Dates of the Key Texts of the *Pamela* Media Event:

November 6, 1740: Richardson's *Pamela* (first edition)
January 6, 1741: Before this date, Dr. Benjamin Slocock recommends
    Pamela from pulpit of St. Saviour's
February 14, 1741: Richardson's *Pamela* (second edition): including
    "Introduction," with "Letters to the Editor" and "Verses" [Aaron Hill]
March 12, 1741: Richardson's *Pamela* (third edition)
April 2, 1741: Fielding's *Shamela* (first edition)
April 25, 1741: *Pamela Censured*
May 5, 1741: Richardson's *Pamela* (fourth edition)
May 7, 1741: Richardson advertises against Kelly's sequel
May 28, 1741: Volume 1 of Kelly's *Pamela's Conduct in High Life*
June 16, 1741: Haywood's *Anti-Pamela* (first edition)
September 12, 1741: Volume 2 of Kelly's *Pamela's Conduct in High Life*
September 22, 1741: Richardson's *Pamela* (fifth edition)
November 3, 1741: Fielding's *Shamela* (second edition)
November 9, 1741: *Pamela: A Comedy* performed at Goodman's Fields;
    (published November 17)

November 23, 1741: Charles Povey's *Virgin in Eden*

December 7, 1741: Richardson's sequel to *Pamela*: *Pamela in her Exalted Condition*, published as volumes 3 and 4 of regular and deluxe octavo editions; the latter has engravings by Hayman

February 22, 1742: Fielding's *Joseph Andrews* (first edition: 1,500 copies)

May 31, 1742: Fielding's *Joseph Andrews* (second edition: 2,000 copies)

September 21, 1742: *Pamela in High Life* continues where volume 1 of Kelly left off

1742: *The Virtuous Orphan: or, the Life of Marianne.* Anonymous translation of Marivaux, "improved in its moral sensibility"

March 28, 1743: Fielding's *Joseph Andrews* (third edition: 3,000 copies)

Works Cited

Adorno, Theodor W., and Max Horkheimer. *Dialectic of Enlightenment*. Translated by John Cumming. New York: Continuum, 1982.

American Heritage Dictionary of the English Language. 3d ed. Boston: Houghton Mifflin, 1992.

Anderson, Benedict. *Imagined Communities: Reflections on the Origins and Spread of Nationalism*. London: Verso, 1983.

Armstrong, Nancy. *Desire and Domestic Fiction: A Political History of the Novel*. New York: Oxford University Press, 1987.

Aubin, Penelope. *The Life of Madam de Beaumount, a French Lady*. London: E. Bell, 1721. Reprint. New York: Garland Publications, 1973.

Backscheider, Paula. *Daniel Defoe: Ambition and Innovation*. Lexington: University Press of Kentucky, 1986.

———. *Spectacular Politics: Theatrical Power and Mass Culture in Early Modern England*. Baltimore, Md.: Johns Hopkins University Press, 1993.

Baker, Ernest. *The History of the English Novel*. 10 volumes. New York: Barnes and Noble, 1924–1939.

Bakhtin, Mikhail. *The Dialogic Imagination: Four Essays*. Edited by Michael Holquist. Translated by Caryl Emerson and Michael Holquist. Austin: University of Texas Press, 1981.

———. *Problems in Dostoevsky's Poetics*. Edited and translated by Caryl Emerson. Minneapolis: University of Minnesota Press, 1984.

Ballaster, Ros. *Seductive Forms: Women's Amatory Fiction from 1684 to 1740*. New York: Oxford University Press, 1992.

Bartolomeo, Joseph F. *A New Species of Criticism: Eighteenth-Century Discourse on the Novel*. Newark, Del.: University of Delaware Press, 1994.

Battestin, Martin C. *The Moral Basis of Fielding's Art: A Study of Joseph Andrews*. Middletown, Conn.: Wesleyan University Press, 1959.

Battestin, Martin C., with Ruth Battestin. *Henry Fielding: A Life*. London: Routledge, 1989.

Baudrillard, Jean. *In the Shadow of the Silent Majorities . . . or the End of the Social, and other essays.* New York: Semiotext(e), 1983.

Beasley, Jerry C. *Novels of the 1740s.* Athens: University of Georgia Press, 1982.

Behn, Aphra. *Love Letters Between a Nobleman and His Sister.* Vol. 2 of *The Works of Aphra Behn.* Edited by Janet Todd. Columbus: Ohio State University Press, 1993.

———. *The Fair Jilt and Other Stories.* Vol. 3 of *The Works of Aphra Behn.* Edited by Janet Todd. Columbus: Ohio State University Press, 1995.

Bender, John. *Imagining the Penitentiary: Fiction and the Architecture of Mind.* Chicago: University of Chicago Press, 1987.

———. Introduction to *Tom Jones.* Edited with Simon Stern. Oxford: Oxford University Press, 1996.

Benjamin, Walter. *Illuminations.* Edited by Hannah Arendt. New York: Schocken, 1969.

———. *The Origin of German Tragic Drama.* London: Verso, 1977.

Blanchard, Frederic T. *Fielding the Novelist: A Study in Historical Criticism.* New Haven, Conn.: Yale University Press, 1927.

Book of Common Prayer. New York: Church Pension Fund, 1945.

Boorstin, Daniel J. *The Image, or What Happened to the American Dream.* New York: Atheneum, 1962.

Bordwell, David, Janet Staiger, and Kristin Thompson. *The Classical Hollywood Cinema: Film Style and Mode of Production to 1960.* New York: Columbia University Press, 1985.

Boswell, James. *Life of Johnson.* London: Oxford University Press, 1904.

Bowers, Toni O'Shaughnessy. "Sex, Lies and Invisibility: Amatory Fiction from the Restoration to Mid-Century." In *The Columbia History of the British Novel,* edited by John J. Richetti, 50–72. New York: Columbia University Press, 1994.

Brennan, Timothy. "The National Longing for Form." In *Nation and Narration,* edited by Homi K. Bhabha, pp. 44–70. London: Routledge, 1990.

Brown, Homer Obed. "*Tom Jones*: The 'Bastard' of History." *Boundary* 2 7 (1979): 201–233.

———. "Of the Title to Things Real: Conflicting Stories." *ELH* 55, no. 4 (1988): 917–954.

———. "Why the Story of the Origin of the (English) Novel is an American Romance (If Not the Great American Novel)." In *Cultural Institutions of the Novel,* edited by Deidre Lynch and William B. Warner, pp. 11–43. Durham, N.C.: Duke University Press, 1996.

———. *The Institutions of the English Novel: From Defoe to Scott.* Philadelphia: University of Pennsylvania Press, 1997.

Brown, Laura. *Ends of Empire: Women and Ideology in Early Eighteenth-Century English Literature.* Ithaca, N.Y.: Cornell University Press, 1993.

Buchholtz, Curtis W. *National Parkways Guide to Yosemite National Park.* Casper, Wyo.: Worldwide Research and Publishing Co., 1989.

Burnham, Michelle. "Between England and America: Captivity, Sympathy, and the Sentimental Novel." In *Cultural Institutions of the Novel*, edited by Deidre Lynch and William B. Warner, pp. 47–72. Durham, N.C.: Duke University Press, 1996.

Butler, Judith. *Bodies that Matter: On the Discursive Limits of "Sex"*. New York: Routledge, 1993.

Campbell, Jill. *Natural Masques: Gender and Identity in Fielding's Plays and Novels*. Stanford, Calif.: Stanford University Press, 1995.

Canfield, J. Douglas. *Word as Bond in English Literature from the Middle Ages to the Restoration*. Philadelphia: University of Pennsylvania Press, 1989.

Castle, Terry. "'Amy, Who Knew My Disease': Psychosexual Pattern in Defoe's 'Roxana'." *ELH* 46, no.1 (1979): 81–96.

———. *Masquerade and Civilization: The Carnivalesque in Eighteenth-Century English Culture and Fiction*. Stanford: Stanford University Press, 1986.

Cervantes, Miguel de. *The Adventures of Don Quixote de la Mancha*. Translated by Tobias Smollett. London: Andrew Millar, 1755. Reprint, with introduction by Carlos Fuentes. New York: Farrar, Straus and Giroux, 1986.

Chartier, Roger. *The Order of Books: Readers, Authors, and Libraries in Europe between the Fourteenth and Eighteenth Centuries*. Translated by Lydia G. Cochrane. Stanford, Calif.: Stanford University Press, 1994.

Cleland, John. *Memoirs of a Woman of Pleasure*. Edited by Peter Sabor. Oxford: Oxford University Press, 1986.

Coleridge, Samuel Taylor. *The Complete Works of Samuel Taylor Coleridge*. Edited by Prof. Shedd. New York: Harper, 1854. Vol. 6: 521.

Copjec, Joan. *Read My Desire: Lacan against the Historicists*. Cambridge, Mass.: MIT Press, 1994.

Court, Franklin E. *Institutionalizing English Literature: The Culture and Politics of Literary Study, 1750–1900*. Stanford, Calif.: Stanford University Press, 1992.

Couturier, Maurice. *Textual Communication: A Print-based Theory of the Novel*. London: Routledge, 1991.

Coventry, Francis. "An Essay on the New Species of Writing Founded by Mr. Fielding." London: W. Owen, 1751. Augustan Reprint Society No. 95. Los Angeles: University of California, 1962.

Czitrom, Daniel J. *Media and the American Mind*. Chapel Hill: University of North Carolina Press, 1982.

Darnton, Robert. "Readers Respond to Rousseau: The Fabrication of Romantic Sensibility." In *The Great Cat Massacre and Other Episodes in French Cultural History*, by Robert Darnton, 215–256. New York: Random House, 1984.

Davidson, Cathy N. *Revolution and the Word: The Rise of the Novel in America*. New York: Oxford University Press, 1986.

Davis, Lennard. *Factual Fictions: The Origins of the English Novel*. New York: Columbia University Press, 1983.

DeBord, Guy. *The Society of the Spectacle.* Translated by Donald Nicholson-Smith. New York: Zone Books, 1995.

de Callières, François. *On the Manner of Negotiating with Princes.* Translation of *De la maniere de negocier avec les souverains* (1716). Boston: Houghton Mifflin, 1919.

De Certeau, Michel. *Practice of Everyday Life.* Translated by Steven F. Rendall. Berkeley: University of California Press, 1984.

Defoe, Daniel. *Roxana: The Fortunate Mistress.* Edited by Jane Jack. London: Oxford University Press, 1964.

————. *Robinson Crusoe.* Edited by J. Donald Crowley. Oxford: Oxford University Press, 1972.

DeJean, Joan. *Tender Geographies: Women and the Origins of the Novel in France.* New York: Columbia University Press, 1991.

de Man, Paul. *The Resistance to Theory.* Foreword by Wlad Godzich. Minneapolis: University of Minnesota Press, 1986.

Derrida, Jacques. *Of Grammatology.* Translated by Gayatri Spivak. Baltimore, Md.: Johns Hopkins University Press, 1976.

————. *The Post Card: From Socrates to Freud and Beyond.* Translated by Alan Bass. Chicago: University of Chicago Press, 1987.

Donoghue, Frank. *The Fame Machine: Book Reviewing and Eighteenth Century Literary Careers.* Stanford, Calif.: Stanford University Press, 1996.

Doody, Margaret Anne. *A Natural Passion: A Study of the Novels of Samuel Richardson.* London: Oxford University Press, 1974.

————. Review of Catherine Gallagher's *Nobody's Story. Times Literary Supplement* (London), 30 June 1995, 8.

————. *The True Story of the Novel.* New Brunswick, N.J.: Rutgers University Press, 1996.

Doody, Margaret Anne, and Peter Sabor. *Samuel Richardson: Tercentenary Essays.* Cambridge: Cambridge University Press, 1989.

Duffy, Maureen. Introduction to *Love Letters Between a Nobleman and His Sister,* by Aphra Behn. London: Virago, 1987.

Dunlop, John Colin. *The History of Fiction.* 3 vols. London: Longman, Hurst, Rees, Orme, and Brown, 1814.

Eagleton, Terry. *The Rape of Clarissa: Writing, Sexuality and Class Struggle in Samuel Richardson.* Minneapolis: University of Minnesota Press, 1982.

Eaves, T. C. Duncan, and Ben D Kimpel. *Samuel Richardson: A Biography.* Oxford University Press, 1971.

Faller, Lincoln. *Crime and Defoe: A New Kind of Writing.* Cambridge: Cambridge University Press, 1993.

Feather, John. *A History of British Publishing.* London: Routledge, 1988.

Fielding, Henry. *Amelia.* Edited by A. R. Humphreys. London: Dent, 1962.

————. "The Author's Farce." In *The Complete Works of Henry Fielding, Esq.,* vol. 1. Edited by William Ernest Henley. London: Frank Cass, 1967.

————. "The Champion." In *The Complete Works of Henry Fielding, Esq.,* vol. 2. Edited by William Ernest Henley. London: Frank Cass, 1967.

———. *Joseph Andrews.* Edited by Martin C. Battestin. Middletown, Conn.: Wesleyan University Press, 1967.

———. *Miscellanies.* Vol. 1. Edited by Henry Knight Miller. Oxford: Oxford University Press, 1972.

———. *The History of Tom Jones, A Foundling.* Introduction and commentary by Martin C. Battestin. Text edited by Fredson Bowers. Oxford: Oxford University Press, 1974.

———. *Shamela.* Edited by Homer Goldberg. New York: W. W. Norton, 1987.

———. *Shamela.* In *Joseph Andrews with Shamela and Related Writings.* Edited by Homer Goldberg. New York: W. W. Norton, 1987.

———. *The Correspondence of Henry and Sarah Fielding.* Edited by Martin C. Battestin and Clive T. Probyn. Oxford: Oxford University Press, 1993

Flint, Kate. *The Woman Reader: 1837–1914.* Oxford: Clarendon Press, 1993.

Folger Collective on Early Women Critics, ed. *Women Critics: 1660–1820: An Anthology.* Bloomington: Indiana University Press, 1995.

Foucault, Michel. *The History of Sexuality. Volume 1: An Introduction.* Translated by Robert Hurley. New York: Random House, 1978.

———. *Language, Counter-memory, Practice.* Edited by Donald F. Bouchard. Ithaca, N.Y.: Cornell University Press, 1997.

Foxon, David. *Libertine Literature in England, 1660–1745.* Hyde Park, N.Y.: University Books, 1965.

Freud, Sigmund. *Totem and Taboo.* Edited and translated by James Strachey. New York: W. W. Norton, 1913.

———. "On Narcissism." Edited and translated by James Strachey. New York: W. W. Norton, 1914.

———. *Beyond the Pleasure Principle.* Edited and translated by James Strachey. New York: W. W. Norton, 1920.

———. *Civilization and Its Discontents.* Edited and translated by James Strachey. New York: W. W. Norton, 1930.

Fried, Michael. *Absorption and Theatricality: Painting and Beholder in the Age of Diderot.* Chicago: University of Chicago Press, 1980.

Frow, John. *Marxism and Literary History.* Cambridge, Mass.: Harvard University Press, 1986.

Frye, Northrop. *A Natural Perspective: The Development of Shakespearean Comedy and Romance.* New York: Columbia University Press, 1965.

Gallagher, Catherine. *Nobody's Story: The Vanishing Acts of Women Writers in the Marketplace, 1670–1820.* Berkeley: University of California Press, 1994.

Gardiner, Judith Kegan. "The First English Novel: Aphra Behn's *Love Letters,* The Canon, and Women's Taste." *Tulsa Studies in Women's Literature* 8, no. 2 (Fall 1989): 201–222.

Garnham, Nicholas. "The Media and the Public Sphere." In *Habermas and the Public Sphere,* edited by Craig Calhoun, pp. 359–376. Cambridge, Mass.: MIT Press, 1992.

Gasché, Rodolphe. *The Tain of the Mirror.* Cambridge, Mass.: Harvard University Press, 1986.

Glazener, Nancy. "Romance for 'Big and Little Boys': The U.S. Romantic Revival of the 1890s and James's *The Turn of the Screw.*" 1996. In *Cultural Institutions of the Novel*, edited by Deidre Lynch and William B. Warner, 369–398. Durham, N.C.: Duke University Press, 1996.

Gooding, Richard. "*Pamela, Shamela,* and the Politics of the *Pamela* Vogue." *Eighteenth-Century Fiction* 7, no. 2 (January 1995): 109–130.

Goulemot, Jean-Marie. *Forbidden Texts: Erotic Literature and its Readers in Eighteenth Century France.* Philadelphia: University of Pennsylvania Press, 1994.

Guillory, John. *Cultural Capital: The Problem of Literary Canon Formation.* Chicago: University of Chicago Press, 1993.

Gwilliam, Tassie. *Samuel Richardson's Fictions of Gender.* Stanford, Calif.: Stanford University Press, 1993.

Habermas, Jurgen. *The Structural Transformation of the Public Sphere.* Translated by Thomas Burger. Cambridge, Mass.: MIT Press, 1989.

Haywood, Eliza. *Love in Excess; or the Fatal Enquiry, A Novel.* London: W. Chetwood, 1719. British Museum copy.

———. *Fantomina; or, Love in a Maze.* London: D. Browne and S. Chapman, 1725.

———. *The Female Spectator.* 4 vols. London: 1745.

Hazlitt, William. *Lectures on the Comic Writer.* London: John Templeman, 1841.

Hemmings, F. W. J. *The Age of Realism.* Harmondsworth, Middlesex: Penguin, 1971.

Huizinga, Johan. *Homo Ludens: A Study of the Play Element in Culture.* Boston: Beacon, 1950.

Hulme, Peter. *Colonial Encounters: Europe and the Native Caribbean, 1492–1797.* London: Methuen, 1986.

Hunt, Lynn, ed. Introduction to *The Invention of Pornography: Obscenity and the Origins of Modernity, 1500–1800.* New York: Zone Books, 1993.

Hunter, J. Paul. *Occasional Form: Henry Fielding and the Chains of Circumstance.* Baltimore, Md.: Johns Hopkins University Press, 1975.

———. *Before Novels: The Cultural Contexts of Eighteenth Century English Fiction.* New York: W. W. Norton, 1990.

Hutner, Heidi, ed. *Rereading Aphra Behn: History, Theory, and Criticism.* Charlottesville: University Press of Virginia, 1993.

Inglis, Fred. *Media Theory: An Introduction.* Basil Blackwell: Oxford, 1990.

James, Henry. *The Novels and Tales of Henry James.* "The New York Edition." New York: Charles Scribner's Sons, 1907–1917.

———. *The Art of the Novel.* Introduction by Richard P. Blackmur. New York: Charles Scribner's Sons, 1934.

———. "The Future of the Novel." Edited by Leon Edel. New York: Vintage, 1956.

Jameson, Fredric. *The Political Unconscious: Narrative as a Socially Symbolic Act.* Ithaca, N.Y.: Cornell University Press, 1981.

———. "Pleasure: A Political Issue." In *Formations of Pleasure*, pp. 1–14. Routledge & Kegan Paul, 1983.

Johnson, Samuel. *A Dictionary of the English Language.* London: J. Johnson, 1799.

——— . *Essays from the Rambler, Adventurer, and Idler.* Edited by W. J. Bate. New Haven, Conn.: Yale University Press, 1968.

Kahn, Madeleine. *Narrative Transvestism: Rhetoric and Gender in the Eighteenth-Century English Novel.* Ithaca, N.Y.: Cornell University Press, 1991.

Kaufer, David S., and Kathleen M. Carley. *Communication at a Distance: The Influence of Print on Sociocultural Change.* Hillsdale, N.J.: Lawrence Erlbaum Associates, 1993.

Kellner, Douglas. *Media Culture: Cultural Studies, Identity and Politics Between the Modern and the Postmodern.* London: Routledge, 1995.

Kelly, John. *Pamela's Conduct in High Life.* London: Chandler, 1741.

Kernan, Alvin. *Samuel Johnson and the Impact of Print.* Princeton, N.J.: Princeton University Press, 1987.

Kreissman, Bernard. *Pamela-Shamela: A Study of the Criticisms, Burlesques, Parodies, and Adaptations of Richardson's "Pamela."* Lincoln: University of Nebraska Press, 1960.

Lacan, Jacques. *The Seminar of Jacques Lacan. Book VII: "The Ethics of Psychoanalysis" (1959–1960).* Edited by Jacques-Alain Miller. New York: W. W. Norton, 1992.

Laclau, Ernesto. *New Reflections on the Revolution of Our Times.* New York: Verso, 1990.

Laclau, Ernesto, and Chantal Mouffe. *Hegemony and Socialist Strategy.* New York: Verso, 1985.

Laplanche, J., and J.-B. Pontalis. *The Language of Psycho-Analysis.* Translated by Donald Nicholson-Smith. New York: W. W. Norton, 1973.

Laugero, Greg. "Infrastuctures of Enlightenment: Road-making, the Public Sphere, and the Emergence of Literature." *Eighteenth Century Studies* 29, no. 1 (fall 1995): 44–68.

Lennox, Charlotte. *The Female Quixote; or, the Adventures of Arabella.* Edited by Margaret Dalziel. London: Oxford University Press, 1970.

Levine, George R. *Henry Fielding and the Dry Mock: A Study of the Techniques of Irony in His Early Works.* Hague: Mouton & Co, 1967.

Lynch, Deidre. *The Economy of Character.* Chicago: University of Chicago Press, 1998.

Lynch, Deidre, and William B. Warner, eds. *Cultural Institutions of the Novel.* Durham, N.C.: Duke University Press, 1996.

MacArthur, Elizabeth J. "Embodying the Public Sphere: Censorship and the Reading Subject in Beaumarchais's *Mariage de Figaro.*" *Representations* 61 (winter 1998): 57–77.

MacDermott, Kathy. "Literature and the Grub Street Myth." In *Popular Fictions: Essays in Literature and History.* Edited by Peter Humm, Paul Stigant, and Peter Widdowson, 16–28. London: Methuen, 1986.

Mack, Maynard. *Alexander Pope: A Life.* New Haven, Conn.: Yale University Press in association with W. W. Norton, New York, 1985.

Manley, Delariviere. *The New Atalantis.* Edited by Rosalind Ballaster. Harmondsworth, Middlesex: Penguin, 1991.

Markley, Robert. "'Be impudent, be saucy, forward, bold, touzing, and lewd': The Politics of Masculine Sexuality and Feminine Desire in Behn's Tory Comedies." In *Cultural Readings of Restoration and Eighteenth-Century English Theater,* edited by J. Douglas Canfield and Deborah C. Payne, 114–140. Athens, Ga.: University of Georgia Press, 1995.

Marshall, David. *The Figure of Theater: Shaftesbury, Defoe, Adam Smith, and George Eliot.* New York: Columbia University Press, 1986.

———. *The Surprising Effects of Sympathy: Marivaux, Diderot, Rousseau, and Mary Shelley.* Chicago: University of Chicago Press, 1988.

Martin, Henri-Jean. *The History and Power of Writing.* Translated by Lydia G. Cochrane. Chicago: University of Chicago Press, 1994.

Maza, Sara. *Private Lives and Public Affairs: The Causes Célèbres of Prerevolutionary France.* Berkeley: University of California Press, 1993.

McKeon, Michael. *The Origins of the English Novel, 1600–1740.* Baltimore, Md.: Johns Hopkins University Press, 1987.

McKillop, Alan Dugald. *Samuel Richardson: Printer and Novelist.* Chapel Hill: University of North Carolina Press, 1936.

———. *The Early Masters of English Fiction.* Lawrence: University of Kansas Press, 1956.

McLuhan, Marshall. *The Gutenberg Galaxy: The Making of Typographic Man.* Toronto: University of Toronto Press, 1962.

Miller, Henry Knight. *Essays on Fielding's Miscellanies.* Princeton, N.J.: Princeton University Press, 1961.

———. *Henry Fielding's Tom Jones and the Romance Tradition.* English Literary Studies monograph no. 6. British Columbia: University of Victoria Press, 1976.

Milton, John. "Areopagitica." In *Complete Prose of John Milton,* vol. 2. New Haven, Conn.: Yale University Press, 1959.

Misch, Charles C. *Restoration Prose Fiction 1666–1700.* Lincoln: University of Nebraska Press, 1970.

Modleski, Tania. *Loving with a Vengeance.* New York: Methuen, 1984.

Mukerji, Chandra, and Michael Schudson. *Rethinking Popular Culture: Contemporary Perspectives in Cultural Studies.* Berkeley: University of California Press, 1991.

Mullan, John. *Sentiment and Sociability: The Language of Feeling in the Eighteenth Century.* Oxford: Clarendon Press, 1988.

Nietzsche, Frederick. *Genealogy of Morals.* In *The Basic Writings of Frederick Nietzsche,* edited and translated by Walter Kaufmann, 437–599. New York: Random House, 1968.

———. "Schopenhauer as Educator." In *Untimely Meditations.* Translated by R. J. Hollingdale, 125–194. New York: Cambridge University Press, 1983.

Novak, Maximillian E. "Some Notes Toward a History of Fictional Forms: From Aphra Behn to Daniel Defoe." *Novel: A Forum on Fiction* 6, no. 2 (Winter 1973): 120–133.

O'Donnell, Mary Ann. *Aphra Behn: An Annotated Bibliography of Primary and Secondary Sources.* New York: Garland, 1986.

Onions, C. T., ed. *Oxford Dictionary of English Etymology.* Oxford: Clarendon Press, 1966.

Ovid. *Metamorphoses.* Translated by Rolfe Humphries. Bloomington: Indiana University Press, 1955.

Oxford English Dictionary. Oxford: Oxford University Press, 1971.

Pamela Censured: in a Letter to the Editor. London: J. Roberts: 1741.

Parker, Andrew, and Eve Kosofsky Sedgwick, eds. *Performativity and Performance.* New York: Routledge, 1995.

Paulson, Ronald. *Satire and the Novel in Eighteenth-Century England.* New Haven, Conn.: Yale University Press, 1967.

———. *Popular and Polite Art in the Age of Hogarth and Fielding.* Notre Dame, Ind.: University of Notre Dame Press, 1979.

———. *Hogarth.* 3 vols. New Brunswick, N.J.: Rutgers University Press, 1991–1993.

———. *The Beautiful, Novel, and Strange.* Baltimore, Md.: Johns Hopkins University Press, 1996.

Perkins, David. *Is Literary History Possible?* Baltimore, Md.: Johns Hopkins University Press, 1992.

Peterson, Spiro. *Daniel Defoe: A Reference Guide, 1731–1924.* Boston: G. K. Hall, 1987.

Plato. *The Collected Dialogues of Plato.* Edited by Edith Hamilton and Huntington Cairns. New York: Pantheon Books, 1961.

Pollak, Ellen. "Beyond Incest: Gender and the Politics of Transgression in Aphra Behn's *Love Letters Between a Nobleman and His Sister.*" In *Rereading Aphra Behn: History, Theory, and Criticism,* edited by Heidi Hutner. Charlottesville: University Press of Virginia, 1993.

Pope, Alexander. *The Dunciad.* Edited by James Sutherland. New Haven, Conn.: Yale University Press, 1943.

———. *Selected Prose of Alexander Pope.* Edited by Paul Hammond. Cambridge: Cambridge University Press, 1987.

Porter, Roy. *English Society in the Eighteenth Century.* London: Penguin, 1990.

Radway, Janice A. *Reading the Romance: Women, Patriarchy, and Popular Literature.* Chapel Hill: University of North Carolina Press, 1984.

———. "The Book of the Month Club and the General Reader: The Uses of 'Serious' Fiction." In *Reading in America,* edited by Cathy N. Davidson, 259–284. Baltimore, Md.: Johns Hopkins University Press, 1989.

Raleigh, Sir Walter. *The English Novel: A Short Sketch of Its History from the Earliest Times to the Appearance of "Waverley."* London: John Murray, 1894.

Reeve, Clara. *The Progress of Romance.* Colchester: W. Keymer, 1785. Facsimile edition. New York: Facsimile Text Society, 1930, with bibliographical note by Esther McGill.

Richardson, Samuel. *The Case of Samuel Richardson, of London, Printer; on the Invasion of his property in the History of Charles Grandison, Before Publication, By Certain Booksellers in Dublin.* London, 1753.

————. *Clarissa, or, the History of a Young Lady*. London: Everyman's Library, 1932.

————. *Selected Letters of Samuel Richardson*. Edited by John Carroll. Oxford: Clarendon Press, 1964.

————. *The Correspondence of Samuel Richardson*. Ed. Letitia Barbauld. 6 vols. London: R. Phillips, 1804. Reprint. New York: AMS Press, 1966.

————. *Pamela*. Edited by T. C. Duncan Eaves and Ben D. Kimpel. Boston: Houghton Mifflin, 1971.

————. *Pamela in Her Exalted Condition*. Introduction by M. Kinkead-Weekes. London: Everyman's Library, 1974.

————. *Familiar Letters on Important Occasions*. First published 1741. Reprint, with introduction by Brian W. Downs. New York: Dodd, Mead and Co., 1928.

Richetti, John J. *Defoe's Narratives: Situations and Structures*. Oxford: Oxford University Press, 1975.

————. *Popular Fiction Before Richardson. Narrative Patterns: 1700–1739*. Oxford: Oxford University Press, 1992.

————. ed. *The Columbia History of the British Novel*. New York: Columbia University Press, 1994.

Rose, Mark. *Authors and Owners: The Invention of Copyright*. Cambridge, Mass.: Harvard University Press, 1993.

Ross, Andrew. *No Respect: Intellectuals and Popular Culture*. New York: Routledge, 1989.

Rousseau, Jean-Jacques. *Oeuvres Complètes: Les Confessions et Autres Textes Autobiographiques*. Edited by Bernard Gagnebin and Marcel Raymond. Paris: Gallimard, 1959.

Roussel, Roy. *The Conversation of the Sexes: Seduction and Equality in Selected Seventeenth- and Eighteenth-Century Texts*. New York: Oxford University Press, 1986.

Runge, Laura L. "Gendered Strategies in the Criticism of Early Fiction." *Eighteenth Century Studies* 28, no. 4 (1995): 363–378.

Saintsbury, George. *The English Novel*. London: J. M. Dent, 1913.

Sale, William Merritt, Jr. *Samuel Richardson: A Bibliographical Record of His Literary Career with Historical Notes*. New Haven, Conn.: Yale University Press, 1936.

Salzman, Paul. *English Prose Fiction, 1558–1700: A Critical History*. Oxford: Clarendon Press, 1985.

Schofield, Mary Anne, ed. *Masquerade Novels of Eliza Haywood*. Delmar, NY: Scholars' Facsimiles and Reprints, 1986.

Schofield, Mary Anne, and Cecilia Macheski. *Fetter'd or Free? British Women Novelists, 1670–1815*. Athens, Ohio: Ohio University Press, 1986.

Scott, Walter. *The Lives of the Novelists*. Edited by George Saintsbury. London: J. M. Dent, 1928.

Shaftesbury, First Earl of. *Characteristics of Men, Manners, Opinions, Times, etc.* 2 vols. Edited by John M. Robertson. Indianapolis, Ind.: Bobbs-Merrill, 1964.

Shiach, Morag. *Discourse on Popular Culture: Class, Gender and History in Cultural Analysis, 1730 to the Present*. Stanford, Calif.: Stanford University Press, 1989.

Siskin, Clifford. "Eighteenth Century Periodicals and the Romantic Rise of the Novel." *Studies in the Novel* 26 (1994): 26–42.

————. "Novelism." In *Cultural Institutions of the Novel*, edited by Deidre Lynch and William B. Warner, 422–440. Durham, N.C.: Duke University Press, 1996.

Smith, Gregory, ed. *The Spectator*. London: J. M. Dent, 1956.

Spacks, Patricia Meyer. *Desire and Truth: Functions of Plot in Eighteenth-Century English Novels*. Chicago: University of Chicago Press, 1990.

Spencer, Jane. *The Rise of the Woman Novelist: From Aphra Behn to Jane Austen*. Oxford: Basil Blackwell, 1986.

Spufford, Margaret. *Small Books and Pleasant Histories: Popular Fiction and Its Readership in Seventeenth-Century England*. London: Methuen, 1982.

Stallybrass, Peter, and White, Allon. *The Politics and Poetics of Transgression*. Ithaca, N.Y.: Cornell University Press, 1986.

Steele, Richard. *The Tatler*. London: J. Parsons, 1794.

Stephanson, Raymond. "The Education of the Reader in Fielding's *Joseph Andrews*." *Philological Quarterly* 61, no. 3 (Summer 1982): 243–258.

Straub, Kristina. "Frances Burney and the Rise of the Woman Novelist." In *The Columbia History of the British Novel*, edited by John J. Richetti, pp. 199–219. New York: Columbia University Press, 1994.

Taine, Hippolyte A. *History of English Literature. Complete in One Volume*. New York: John Wurtele Lovell, 1879.

Todd, Janet. *The Sign of Angelica: Women, Writing, and Fiction, 1660–1800*. New York: Columbia University Press, 1989.

Tompkins, J. M. S. *The Popular Novel in England, 1770–1800*. Lincoln: University of Nebraska Press, 1961.

Trager, James. *The People's Chronology*. New York: Henry Holt, 1995–1996.

Trumpener, Katie. "Rewriting Roxane: Orientalism and Intertextuality in Montesquieu's *Lettres Persanes* and Defoe's *The Fortunate Mistress*." *Stanford French Review* 11, no. 2 (Summer 1987): 177–191.

Turner, Cheryl. *Living by the Pen: Women Writers in the Eighteenth Century*. London: Routledge, 1992.

Turner, James. "Novel Panic: Picture and Performance in the Reception of *Pamela*." *Representations* 48 (Fall 1994): 70–96.

Walpole, Horace. *The Castle of Otranto*. In *Three Gothic Novels*, edited by E. F. Bleiler. New York: Dover, 1966.

Warner, Michael. *Letters of the Republic: Publication and the Public Sphere in Eighteenth Century America*. Cambridge, Mass.: Harvard University Press, 1990.

Warner, William B. "The Play of Fictions and Succession of Styles in Ulysses." *James Joyce Quarterly* 15 (Fall 1977): 18–35.

————. *Reading Clarissa: The Struggles of Interpretation*. New Haven, Conn.: Yale University Press, 1979.

————. *Chance and the Text of Experience: Freud, Nietzsche, and Shakespeare's Hamlet.* Ithaca, N.Y.: Cornell University Press, 1986.

————. "Realist Literary History: McKeon's New Origins of the Novel." *Diacritics* 19, no. 1 (1989): 62–81.

————. "The Resistance to Popular Culture." *American Literary History* 2, no. 4 (1990): 726–742.

————. "The Social Ethos of the Novel: McKeon's Not So Social Allegory of the Novel's Origins." *Criticism* 32, no. 2 (1990): 241–253.

————. "Taking Dialectic with a Grain of Salt: A Reply to McKeon." *Diacritics* 20, no. 1 (1990): 104–107.

————. "Social Power and the Eighteenth-Century Novel: Foucault and Transparent Literary History." *Eighteenth Century Fiction* 3, no. 3 (1991): 185–203.

————. "The Elevation of the Novel in England: Hegemony and Literary History." *ELH* 59 (1992): 577–596.

————. "Spectacular Action: Rambo and the Popular Pleasures of Pain." In *Cultural Studies*, edited by Lawrence Grossberg, Cary Nelson, and Paula A. Treichler. New York: Routledge, 1992.

Watt, Ian. *The Rise of the Novel: Studies in Defoe, Richardson and Fielding.* Berkeley: University of California Press, 1957.

Weber, Samuel. *Institution and Interpretation.* Minneapolis: University of Minnesota Press, 1987.

————. "Genealogy of Modernity: History, Myth and Allegory in Benjamin's *Origin of the German Mourning Play.*" *MLN* 106, no. 1 (April 1991), 465–500.

Wehrs, Donald R. "*Eros*, Ethics, Identity: Royalist Feminism and the Politics of Desire in Aphra Behn's *Love Letters.*" *Studies in English Literature* 32, no. 3 (1992): 461–478.

Whole Duty of Woman, The; or, an infallible guide to the fair sex. London: T. Read, 1737.

Williams, Ioan. *The Criticism of Henry Fielding.* New York: Barnes & Noble, 1970.

————. *Novel and Romance, 1700–1800; a Documentary Record.* New York: Barnes & Noble, 1970.

————. *The Idea of the Novel in Europe, 1600–1800.* London: Macmillan, 1979.

Woodmansee, Martha. *The Author, Art and the Market.* New York: Columbia University Press, 1994.

Yolton, John W., ed. *The Blackwell Companion to the Enlightenment.* Oxford: Basil Blackwell, 1991.

Young, Edward. *The Complete Works, Poetry and Prose, of the Rev. Edward Young.* Edited by James Nichols. London: William Tegg, 1854.

Zach, Wolfgang. "Mrs. Aubin and Richardson's Earliest Literary Manifesto." *English Studies: A Journal of English Language and Literature* 62 (1981): 271–285.

Zimbardo, Rose. "Aphra Behn: A Dramatist in Search of the Novel." In *Curtain Calls: British and American Women and the Theater, 1680–1820*, edited by Mary Anne Schofield and Cecelia Macheski (Athens: Ohio University Press, 1991), 371–382.

Zimmerman, Everett. *Defoe and the Novel*. Berkeley: University of California Press, 1975.

Žižek, Slavoj. *Enjoy Your Symptom! Jacques Lacan in Hollywood and Out*. New York: Routledge, 1992.

Index

Compositor:	Braun-Brumfield, Inc.
Text:	10/13 Aldus
Display:	Aldus
Printer and Binder:	Braun-Brumfield, Inc.